THE LAST DISSENTER

THE LAST DISSENTER

H. N. Brailsford and His World

F. M. LEVENTHAL

CLARENDON PRESS · OXFORD
1985

Oxford University Press, Walton Street, Oxford OX2 6DP
London New York Toronto
Delhi Bombay Calcutta Madras Karachi
Kuala Lumpur Singapore Hong Kong Tokyo
Nairobi Dar es Salaam Cape Town
Melbourne Auckland
and associated companies in
Beirut Berlin Ibadan Mexico City Nicosia

Oxford is a trade mark of Oxford University Press

Published in the United States
by Oxford University Press, New York

© F. M. Leventhal 1985

All rights reserved. No part of this publication may be reproduced,
stored in a retrieval system, or transmitted, in any form or by any means,
electronic, mechanical, photocopying, recording, or otherwise, without
the prior permission of Oxford University Press

British Library Cataloguing in Publication Data
Leventhal, F. M.
The last dissenter : H. N. Brailsford and his world.
1. Brailsford, Henry Noel 2. Journalists—
Great Britain—Biography
I. Title
070'.92'4 PN5123.B5/
ISBN 0-19-820055-2

Library of Congress Cataloging in Publication Data
Leventhal, F. M. 1938–
The last dissenter.
Bibliography: p.
Includes index.
1. Brailsford, Henry Noel, 1873–1958. 2. Journalists
—Great Britain—Biography. 3. Journalism, Socialist—
Great Britain—History—20th century. I. Title.
PN5123.B56L49 1985 070'.92'4 [B] 84-20688
ISBN 0-19-820055-2

Set by DMB (Typesetting), Oxford
Printed and bound in Great Britain
by Billing & Sons Limited, Worcester.

For Jean

Acknowledgements

The following people and institutions have very kindly granted me permission to quote from unpublished material of which they hold the copyright: Transport and General Workers Union (Bevin papers); Syndics of the Fitzwilliam Museum (Blunt papers); Mrs Evamaria Brailsford (H. N. Brailsford papers); The British Library of Political and Economic Science (Dalton papers); The Provost and Scholars of King's College, Cambridge (Keynes papers); Clare Leighton; Mrs Sheila Lochhead and the Public Record Office (MacDonald papers).

Preface

This book is a study of Brailsford's times, but it is a product of my own. I first encountered his name in the late 1960s, nearly a decade after his death, when in response to the turmoil over the Vietnam war, I had decided to offer an undergraduate seminar on dissent in wartime. A. J. P. Taylor's *The Trouble Makers* drew my attention to Brailsford as a prominent opponent of British imperialism, the First World War, and the Versailles settlement. Attracted by his writings, I soon found myself impelled towards biographical research in an attempt to reconstruct a life about which so little seems to have been known. In the course of what became a more protracted enterprise than I had anticipated, I have acquired innumerable personal debts. Certainly this work would have been impossible if not for the co-operation and support of his family and friends, too many of whom have not survived to read it. I hope they would recognize the portrait that has emerged. I am deeply grateful to the three women closest to Brailsford in the latter half of his life: Mabel Richmond Brailsford, Clare Leighton, and Evamaria Brailsford. Each of them gave freely of her time, answered questions candidly, and furnished information essential to this book.

It is also a pleasure to acknowledge my gratitude to many of Brailsford's friends, colleagues, and acquaintances, who shared memories of him with me: Austen Albu, Luther Allen, Evelyn Anderson, Lord Archibald, Robin Page Arnot, G. E. Aylmer, H. L. Beales, Carl F. Brand, Julius Braunthal, Lord Brockway, Richard Church, Irene Clephane, Dame Margaret Cole, Dame Kathleen Courtney, Peter F. Drucker, R. Palme Dutt, Sydney Elliott, Leonard Elmhirst, Michael Foot, Heinrich Fraenkel, Reg Groves, Frank Hardie, Fritz Jahoda, Willie James, Alvin Johnson, Lord Elwyn-Jones, Christopher leFleming, Norman MacKenzie, Kingsley Martin, Sir Francis Meynell, Lord and Lady Mitchison, David Mitrany, Lady Plummer, Joe Pole, Sir Victor Pritchett, Robert Weaver, Sybil Wingate, Dorothy Woodman, and Leonard Woolf.

In a different category I would like to thank those who gave me access to Brailsford correspondence or directed me to important materials, among them Robert O. Anthony, Bruce Aubry, David Ayerst, Janet Carleton, Lady Hermione Cobbold, Arthur P. Dudden, H. N. Fieldhouse, Livia Gollancz, Alfred F. Havighurst, William H. Honan, Keith Hutchison, Elizabeth Longford, John H. MacCallum Scott, David Marquand, Keith Robbins, C. H. Rolph, Andrew

Rosen, John Saville, Toni Stolper, Jo Vellacott, and Sir Duncan Wilson. My task was facilitated by archivists and librarians in the United Kingdom, the United States, Germany, the Netherlands, and Canada. I wish that there were sufficient space to thank them individually for their unfailing helpfulness.

My research was assisted by grants from the Harvard Graduate Society, Boston University, the National Endowment for the Humanities, the American Philosophical Society, and the American Council of Learned Societies. I am particularly obliged to two institutions which provided facilities for writing at critical junctures: the Institute for Advanced Studies in the Humanities of the University of Edinburgh and Keynes College of the University of Kent at Canterbury. At Boston University I have received encouragement from many colleagues, especially Sidney Burrell, Dietrich Orlow, and Nancy Roelker.

Portions of this book originally appeared, in a somewhat different form, in the *Journal of Contemporary History*, vol. 9 (January 1974) and in *Essays in Labour History 1918-1939*, edited by Asa Briggs and John Saville (1977). I am grateful to the editors for permission to republish this material. I have also borrowed from the essay I contributed to *Edwardian Radicalism 1900-1914*, edited by A. J. A. Morris (1974).

At various times this manuscript has been read, in whole or in part, by Peter Clarke, R. J. Crampton, Andrew Griffin, Brian Harrison, Leslie Hume, Stephen Koss, Norman MacKenzie, and Peter Stansky. I have benefited enormously from their scholarly criticism and suggestions for improvement.

My greatest debt, as always, is to my wife Jean, who has been closely involved with this project from its inception. She shared in every aspect of the research, patiently listened to my views on Brailsford during all the years of our marriage, and cast her discerning eye over every page. Without her unwavering faith in the book and its author, this work would probably never have been completed. Its dedication to her cannot adequately express my appreciation. I hope that when my son David is old enough to read this book, it will make him proud of the middle name he bears.

Contents

	Abbreviations	x
	Introduction	1
I.	'Twixt Son and Father (1873-1890)	5
II.	Young Hegelian (1890-1897)	14
III.	Comrade-in-Arms (1897-1899)	29
IV.	The Streets of Adventure (1899-1909)	43
V.	Conciliation Committee (1909-1913)	67
VI.	A Dissenting Foreign Policy (1906-1914)	92
VII.	Glimpses of a Marriage (1898-1919)	114
VIII.	The Pen Against the Sword (1914-1918)	123
IX.	The Flawed Peace (1918-1922)	147
X.	The New Leader (1922-1926)	172
XI.	Candide Returns to Earth (1926-1932)	204
XII.	In the Nightmare of the Dark (1933-1938)	228
XIII.	'It's a Long Road to Victory' (1939-1946)	263
XIV.	Ripeness is All (1945-1958)	289
XV.	The Ideal Republic	303
	Sources	312
	Index	321

Abbreviations

ACIQ	Advisory Committee on International Questions
AP	Clifford Allen (Lord Allen of Hurtwood) Papers
BP	Wilfrid Scawen Blunt Papers
BOP	Hermann Bräuning-Oktavio Papers
CLC	Clare Leighton Correspondence
FP	Millicent Garrett Fawcett Papers
GMP	Gilbert Murray Papers
HNBP	Miscellaneous papers in Brailsford family possession
ILP	Independent Labour Party
IMRO	Internal Macedonian Revolutionary Organization
KMP	Kingsley Martin Papers
LP	Victor, Second Earl of Lytton Papers
MGC	*Manchester Guardian* Collection
MSP	Alexander MacCallum Scott Papers
NAC	ILP National Administrative Council
NBP	Noel Buxton Papers
ND	Diary of Henry W. Nevinson
NEC	Labour Party National Executive Committee
NUWSS	National Union of Women's Suffrage Societies
UDC	Union of Democratic Control
WSPU	Women's Social and Political Union
Broom	*The Broom of the War-God*
League	*A League of Nations*
Levellers	*The Levellers and the English Revolution*
Olives	*Olives of Endless Age*
SGC	*Shelley, Godwin and Their Circle* (2nd ed.)
WSG	*The War of Steel and Gold*

Introduction

For nearly sixty years Henry Noel Brailsford wrote about politics and world affairs. Few, if any, journalists of this century were as prolific or as durable as this cultivated, well-travelled English commentator, whose thousands of articles and score of books won esteem on three continents. From his early years on the *Manchester Guardian* and the *Nation*, to his brief, but illustrious editorship of the *New Leader*, to his authoritative editorials and columns in the *New Statesman, Reynolds*, and the *New Republic*, he gained a reputation as a perceptive interpreter of the political scene, whose left-wing orientation never obscured his vision. Kingsley Martin, his employer for nearly two decades, called Brailsford 'the finest British journalist of his time'.[1] Michael Foot, readily acknowledging an intellectual debt, described him as 'the most eloquent and incisive Socialist journalist of the age'.[2] Such tributes, singular, but not unique, testify to his stature rather than his influence. Brailsford was ruefully aware that the fate of the journalist was to see the distillation of a lifetime's experience consigned to the dustbin with the week's trash. To assert his influence, to claim that he helped to shape the thinking of two generations in England, in the United States, in Central Europe, and in India, poses a dilemma: so great an impact, presupposed by his admirers, can neither be confirmed nor refuted. During his long career hundreds of thousands of people read his comments at one time or another and may have based their opinions about the Balkans or the Versailles treaty or Indian nationalism on them, but his articles were only one of many competing sources of information. All that can be stated conclusively is that he was widely read and respected, but his posthumous neglect underscores the evanescence of journalistic reputations. Almost as soon as his articles ceased to appear in print, his name was forgotten, and his books, generally written in response to particular political events, retained only historic interest for the next generation.

Brailsford had emerged from the tradition of the Victorian man of letters to become a successful practitioner of mass journalism, capable of informing a large popular audience without betraying the moral tone and liberal ideals inherited from his early mentors, C. P. Scott and H. W. Massingham. The link between high-minded Victorian values and popular culture made Brailsford virtually unique, his career spanning

[1] *Encounter*, Vol. XIV, No. 2 (Feb. 1965), p. 85.
[2] Michael Foot, *Aneurin Bevan: A Biography, Vol. I: 1897-1945* (London, 1962), p. 102.

the the vast transformations that engulfed the mass media in this century. As an articulator of socialist values in the press, his only peer was Robert Blatchford, the redoubtable founder of the *Clarion* and author of *Merrie England*. In some ways his reputation more closely paralleled that of the American journalist Walter Lippmann, although Brailsford's career showed far greater consistency and less craving for power. Like Lippmann, he hoped to influence policy-makers and the public, yet Brailsford always saw himself as a dissenter. He was bred in the Nonconformist religious tradition and, despite his rebellion against that upbringing, its style was ingrained in him. His moral fervour, his capacity for indignation, the certainty of his convictions, were an inheritance from his Methodist background. But he attached himself to a much broader dissenting tradition—that of political radicals whose roots went back to the seventeenth-century Levellers. His intellectual ancestors were men like Walwyn and Voltaire and Shelley and Marx, rebels against political orthodoxy in the name of humanity. Brailsford's particular concern was with imperialism and foreign affairs; his belief in the need for conciliation and world government, in disarmament and an equitable sharing of natural resources, set him in opposition to every government in power in England during his lifetime. He eagerly sought the role of 'trouble maker', to adopt the terminology of A. J. P. Taylor, who accorded Brailsford an important place in his survey of dissent in foreign policy.[3] Fulminating against expansionism, appealing for reason and generosity in international relations, he fought lonely and fruitless battles. But unlike Lippmann, who exulted in the corridors of power, he preferred to be a gadfly, a perpetual irritant to Foreign Office mandarins from Sir Edward Grey to Anthony Eden.

Brailsford's importance lies not merely in his position at the crossroads of modern journalism. His writings encompass the entire range of left-wing preoccupations from the Boer War to the Suez campaign in 1956. By examining his work, one can trace the developing interest of English socialists in the world outside, away from the parochial concern with the work-force and the market-place. While castigating British leaders, he also sought to educate his readers about foreign affairs in order that they might exercise their democratic rights in a more enlightened fashion. No writer devoted himself as assiduously to explaining the intricacies of Balkan politics, to denouncing the folly of a punitive peace settlement or appealing for the appeasement of Germany in the 1920s, to championing the cause of socialist unity and internationalism. Prepared to shift his position as circumstances changed, he refused to violate the dictates of conscience or betray his passion for freedom.

[3] A. J. P. Taylor, *The Trouble Makers* (Bloomington, 1958) pp. 122-4, 175-8, 185-7.

Among the millions of words he wrote with such facility there are few about himself, aside from the occasional reminiscence. Martin and other friends who delighted in his anecdotes urged him to write his memoirs. One can only regret that he left only scattered recollections of the famous people he had known—statesmen like Lloyd George, Pilsudski, and Venizelos, prominent socialists like Jaurès, Trotsky, and Bernstein, or Indian leaders like Gokhale, Gandhi, and Nehru. But an obsessive reticence prevented him from risking autobiography. He intimated to several friends that memories of his father and first wife remained too painful for him to divulge personal details in print— and often even in conversation. Beyond these scars, which he carried through his life, was an extraordinary shyness, a private self which welcomed the distancing anonymity of journalism. His only literary effort at self-exposure was an autobiographical novel written at the age of twenty-three.

Almost from childhood he began to assume that he must be unpopular, that, unloved, he must struggle on alone. Estranged from his family for much of his adult life, he found it difficult to make or confide in friends. His sister, to whom he became reconciled later in life, wrote after he died,

I used to think he hated his fellow men & most of his fellow women, unless he was in love with them which frequently happened. My own friends used to ask me, 'Why does your brother dislike you so much?'[4]

Many associates found him enigmatic, and the images conveyed by those who recalled him after his death are full of contradictions. Several acquaintances found him remote, irascible, and easily wounded, while others spoke of his humility, warmth, and kindliness. Some noted his generosity, his controlled passion, his concern for inconsequential people. Courteous, especially towards women, he was modest to a fault and never self-seeking. Perhaps because he was too shy to communicate easily in person, he expressed his affection through small gestures of benevolence. Once discovering that a friend had lost his livelihood, Brailsford, then seventy-five and surviving on a meagre pension, wrote to him,

I've just had a windfall—a payment of royalties that I was not expecting. May I have the privilege of a friend and send you the enclosed cheque? It won't go far, I fear, in these days. Do let me know if I can do anything further.[5]

Visiting him a few days before his death, Martin wished that there were some way of letting the world know 'how brave and great-hearted

[4] Mabel R. Brailsford to Kingsley Martin, 13 June 1966, KMP.
[5] HNB to Julius Braunthal, 31 Aug. 1949, Braunthal Papers.

his life had been, and how much love and disinterested work he had achieved in return for so little recognition'.[6]

Yet the personal unhappiness is not entirely separable from the public activity and literary achievement. Having lost his belief in internal salvation, he sought to externalize his drives, to expiate the loss of religious faith through social activity. Like other sons of Nonconformist clergymen who abandoned Christianity—Martin, William Mellor, and Evan Durbin, to name a few—he was drawn to socialism with an almost missionary zeal, a substitute faith for the one so painfully discarded. In Brailsford's case that break with religion created a breach with his family that was never entirely healed. Norman MacKenzie, who came to know Brailsford in the 1940s, believed that he was seeking to recreate a family in the community at large, loving the world because he had no one else to love.[7] Some of his identification with the downtrodden, with exiles and refugees, stemmed from feelings of kinship with the rootless and the rejected.

I have not attempted either a psychological profile or a complete biographical study. There is too much about Brailsford that neither I nor those closest to him ever knew. I have instead examined his writings and political activity in the context of the times and of his own circumstances. The biographical framework illuminates his public role, but his publications must be regarded as a response to the world in which he lived rather than as an expression of inner torment. It should become apparent that I consider Brailsford a courageous and regrettably undervalued writer, but this book is in no sense an essay in hagiography. Brailsford's private life was full of unhappiness, much of his own making, and his career was occasionally marred by misfortune and misuse of his ample talent. He was sometimes mistaken about political events and impervious to the implications of the course he advocated. Yet none of this detracts from the nobility of his vision or his selfless pursuit of a humane society, freed from the shadow of war and the scourge of poverty. It was because his idealistic hopes remained untarnished that he could not acquiesce to political expediency; it was this defiant refusal to compromise that made him the last dissenter.

[6] Kingsley Martin, *Editor* (London, 1968), p. 135.
[7] Interview, Norman MacKenzie.

I
'Twixt Son and Father (1873-1890)

Throughout his life Henry Noel Brailsford felt a strong affinity for seventeenth-century English Radicals, especially for the Levellers striving to create a commonwealth based on religious toleration and political democracy. This was more than simply an ideological identification, for he could trace his own roots to sturdy Puritan stock, to yeomen and artisans who had defied and helped to overthrow Charles I. Family accounts suggest that shortly before the Civil War began a Henry Brailsford, living in the family village of Brailsford in Derbyshire, had his house burned to the ground on orders from the Crown for refusing to pay his taxes. One maternal ancestor, a Chester blacksmith named Pooley, shod the horses of Roundhead soldiers besieging Chester in 1645 and received retribution in 1660, when the local churchwardens, eager to reaffirm their allegiance to the Stuarts, refused to permit his burial in consecrated ground.

Apart from the existence of Joseph Brailsford, a minor eighteenth-century composer, little is known about the family until 1841 when Edward John Brailsford was born in Dudley, the only son of an architect who died while Edward was still a baby. The young widow returned to her parents' farm in County Wicklow, where much of Edward's childhood passed under the supervision of his Wesleyan grandmother. The fatherless boy was much indulged by his Irish relatives, extolled for his cleverness, and called upon to recite for family audiences. His grandmother, at some financial sacrifice, paid his tuition at St Stephen's School in Dublin, which he attended until he was apprenticed to a linen draper at the age of fifteen. His career in trade proved a false start: within a year he encountered a missionary who not only galvanized his Methodism, but instilled in him a conviction that he was summoned to preach the gospel. Although accustomed to a Wesleyan regimen Edward had none the less to experience personal conversion before his motivation became sufficiently compelling to change the pattern of his life.

Introduced at revival meetings by his mentor, the zealous convert found opportunities to preach and, despite his youth and lack of theological training, was put in charge of a chapel near Edinburgh. Methodist missionaries had long complained of Scottish obduracy, but not even unreceptive audiences could dampen Brailsford's ardour, and in 1861 he was formally accepted for the ministry, enrolling in Didsbury

College, the leading seminary for aspiring Methodist clergy. One of an entering class of eighteen, he embarked on the prescribed two-year course under the tutelage of Dr Thomas Hannah, who sought to impart to his students assurance of 'the supremacy and sole authority of the Scriptures in all matters of revealed Theology'.[1] Ordained in 1863, Edward Brailsford received his first appointment at Carnarvon, followed a year later by an assignment at Seacombe. During a fifty-three year career as a Circuit Minister, he was customarily transferred every three years, chiefly within Scotland and the north of England. It was during a one-year appointment at the Pitt Street Chapel in Liverpool that he met Clara Pooley, daughter of a Methodist ironmonger in nearby Liscard.

Brailsford's future father-in-law was a remarkable figure, an exemplar of Victorian self-help ideals. Imprisoned for debt as a young man, during which time his first wife and child died, Henry Pooley set himself up in business when he emerged from prison and married the daughter of a Dublin Methodist, who bore him twelve children. An enlightened employer, Pooley achieved success as the inventor of the railway turntable and spent most of his career supervising its installation and maintenance in various parts of the country. Business interests took him to London every week, but he would return in time to conduct his class meeting and teach Sunday School. His six sons laboured under few restraints, since their father was not home frequently enough to impose them and, in any event, lavished whatever attention could be spared from the turntables and his spiritual obligations on his six daughters. Clara Pooley, born in 1843, grew up a spirited girl, accomplished as a choir singer and organist. Her lively disposition and strict upbringing attracted Edward Brailsford, who married her in 1867, just as he was about to take up a three-year appointment in Bolton.

Their marriage was not without friction at the outset. Edward had never really known his own father and, as the surviving male in the family, was idolized by his mother and grandmother. He expected his wife to cater to him as his female relatives had always done, although he was rarely disposed to consider their feelings. For the first six of these years they had no children, a situation which appears to have suited Edward despite his intention of raising a family. There was nothing to deflect Clara from devoting herself to her husband, fending off the retinue of women who clung to him after chapel services, and sharing the popular Victorian pastime of long hikes in the country. Never concerned with money, he would spend freely upon himself,

---

[1] W. Bardsley Brash and Charles J. Wright, eds., *Didsbury College Centenary 1842-1942* (London, 1942), p. 49.

without regard for whether his wife was suitably dressed. Years later his daughter could recall her indignation as a child when her father bought himself two new suits. She reproached him with the fact that neither she nor her mother had had a new coat in years. He confessed that in satisfying his own needs he had inadvertently overlooked their needs, an excuse that lacked credibility when he, as the only golfer in the family, purchased a set of expensive clubs for Clara.

Did he deceive himself into imagining that his godly vocation gave him licence to neglect his family in favour of professional duties? Perhaps it was merely vanity, gratified more readily by the adoration of the faithful than by the affection of those he took for granted. While his wife and children occasionally bridled under his indifference, his followers lauded him as 'the Poet of Methodism', and the Conference acknowledged him as an effective officer in 'the holy warfare 'gainst His foes and ours'. He was rewarded with the chairmanship successively of the Scotland, Newcastle-on-Tyne, Cornwall, Lincoln, and Exeter districts. A revealing, if somewhat effusive, obituary identified his gifts as an orator:

He possessed uncommon powers of thought and language, and was complete master of a most felicitous style. When he preached or gave an address his whole being was swept with waves of feeling, and became tremulous with his message. Words took fire, and thoughts clad themselves in music.[2]

Brailsford's hymns and published writings suggest something of the tone of his sermons, few of which survive. They appear to combine an intense love of nature and of defenceless animals—which his son inherited—with a more typical Methodist abhorrence of wordly sin and corruption. Thus a hymn for children begins with the verse,

> All things which live below the sky,
>   Or move within the sea,
> Are creatures of the Lord most high
>   And brothers unto me.[3]

Conventional sentiments, perhaps, but they imply a gentleness that contrasts with his portrayal of the wages of sin:

> Far and wide around us,
>   See on every hand,
> Through the mighty city,
>   Satan's strongholds stand:
> Selfish greed and grinding
>   Lust, and drink, and hate—

---

[2] Minutes of [Wesleyan Methodist] Conference, 1922, pp. 111-12.
[3] Hymn 852, *Methodist Hymn-Book* (1933).

> These his chains which bind men
> With their iron weight.⁴

He also published several cautionary tales about the consequences of drink, the second of which, *Fairy Fingers*, appearing in 1889, bore the dedication, 'To my son, Henry Noel, born on Christmas Day and to all boys and girls who, like him, have never tasted alcohol.'⁵ These depict, in realistic, if sentimentalized fashion, village scences in which calamity leads a man to drink, to suspicion of crimes, and to regeneration through a young girl's innocent love. The accident of being born on 25 December seemed to carry additional burdens, Christmas being celebrated in the Brailsford household with 'peculiar solemnity'. In recalling his childhood, Edward Brailsford's son observed that he

> grew up feeling a certain envy of people whose birthday is not Xmas. My parents used to impress upon me the solemn responsibility which I incurred by being born on Xmas day. I had a bitter sense of revolt, for I felt (though ignorant of all details) that I was not consciously to blame.⁶

His sermon of 1893 entitled 'The Early Evangelist Newly Equipped' urged fellow clergymen to change with the times, but not to abandon 'the primitive passion for winning souls'. Speaking as Chairman of the Edinburgh district, he argued that Methodism must extend itself beyond the main cities of Scotland; he saw opportunity for evangelizing in mining and industrial areas and recommended that young and unmarried men go forth and conquer the untried regions.⁷

Even so cursory a glimpse indicates some of the themes which pervade Edward Brailsford's work. Teetotalism, the efficacy of prayer, a belief in the redemption of the soul—all these were the stock-in-trade of the Methodist preacher, and, in fact, little distinguishes him from his fellow ministers beyond a certain literary facility and liberal political sympathies. None the less by 1873, when he took up an appointment at Dewsbury—a part of the Leeds district including Mirfield and Normanton—he was beginning to make his mark in the Wesleyan community. Although the West Riding villages, populated by miners, spinners, weavers, and farm labourers, were receptive to missionaries, Brailsford found their bleakness oppressive. A minister in one of his stories remarks despairingly,

> The fields have a scorched, lonely look about them. They make me sad. But I suppose it's always so in mining districts. You can always tell when men

---

⁴ Hymn 957, *Methodist Hymn-Book* (1904).
⁵ Edward J. Brailsford, *Fairy Fingers; or, 'A Little Child Shall Lead Them'* (Glasgow, 1889).
⁶ HNB to H. Bräuning-Oktavio, 20 Dec. 1917, BOP.
⁷ Edward J. Brailsford, *The Early Evangelist Newly Equipped: A Sermon Preached Before the Edinburgh and Aberdeen District Synod, May 1893*.

value more what's underground than what's on top . . . if all the school-masters in Yorkshire were to strike, and empty their ink-bottles into the streams, they couldn't be blacker than they are.[8]

It was in Mirfield, on Christmas Day 1873, that Clara gave birth to their first child, a son whom they named Henry Noel for his Pooley grandfather. Two years later, while they were still in Mirfield, a daughter, Mabel, was born.

The arrival of children after six years of marriage threatened to disrupt the comfortable pattern to which Edward had grown accustomed. He was jealous of demands on his wife's attention, never having had to brook any rivalry before or after his marriage, and insisted that Clara continue to devote herself chiefly to him. Nor was he likely to change his egotistical ways simply because he had become a father. Harry—as he was then called—and Mabel, raised almost entirely by servants, saw him rarely except for prayers and for spanking when they misbehaved. Having been spoiled in his own childhood, Edward resolved to rescue his children from the pernicious effects of parental indulgence, even to the point of withholding praise for their accomplishments.

Deprived of his mother's attention and subjected to his father's stern regimen, Harry relied on his sister for companionship, and she responded devotedly. Since the family moved frequently—six times between 1873 and 1891—it was difficult for them to make friends, and the constant shifts of scene reinforced Harry's innate shyness. As the children of a minister, they were expected to comport themselves in exemplary fashion, not mingling too freely with the offspring of miners and weavers. As Methodists, they were also set apart from the more socially elevated local inhabitants. In London—an appointment brought the Brailsfords to Kensington from 1879 to 1881—they were regarded as Northerners; in Scotland as alien English. Nor were there relatives nearby to provide additional playmates. Edward's elderly grandmother lived with them for a time, but she was later remembered for the large, heavy Bible, which Mabel carried around for her.

Unlike his diffident sister, Harry proved intractable from the outset. He was dismissed as backward for failing to learn his alphabet at school in London, although he began to show progress when his mother took to teaching him. The problem was poor vision rather than lack of intelligence; despite recommended eye tests, Edward refused at first to permit his son to wear spectacles. In 1881 the Brailsfords moved to Scotland, their home for the next thirteen years. Harry's education was thus essentially a Scottish one, beginning with a dame school in Edinburgh. Its pedagogic methods were primitive: children received a

---

[8] Edward J. Brailsford, *'Only a Woman's Hair': A Tale of Yorkshire Life* (London, 1873), p. 15.

'palmie', i.e. a slap on the palm, if they did not know the answer when called upon to recite. Although Mabel accepted such punishments fatalistically, Harry, outraged by the injustice of it all, rebelled by refusing to learn. He was prone to fits of temper, during one of which he decapitated all of his sister's dolls, and retreated into solitary pursuits, mainly reading history and Sir Walter Scott. From the nursery window they had a view of Arthur's Seat, and at night, when the children would stare out at the rock towering over the city, their nurse would warn them, 'If you look long enough, the end of the world will come tonight!'[9]

But Scotland offered more than exciting vistas to explore: at its best, Scottish education had many advantages. Its private schools were socially more heterogeneous than their English counterparts; children of ministers might mix easily with those of professional and tradesmen's families. Less classical in curriculum, they were more rigorous intellectually, providing solid grounding for the Scottish universities. Nor were they as preoccupied with games or with inculcating social graces as schools south of the border. After his disastrous initiation at the local dame school, Harry was enrolled at George Watson's College in October 1883. Founded as a hospital in 1724, Watson's had become a day school in the 1870s and by this time it had about 1,500 pupils between five and sixteen. In the Junior Department boys from eight to twelve were taught English, grammar, geography, history, writing, and arithmetic. Latin was begun at ten, French at eleven, and science was beginning to surface as a respectable subject.[10] It was at Watson's, where he encountered a sympathetic teacher, that Harry began to flourish academically.

Once again, however, his education was interrupted, this time by a family move to Greenock in 1884 and to Blairgowrie in the following year. The latter assignment testified to Edward's growing reputation, for at Blairgowrie, a small Perthshire farming village, his task was to establish a Wesleyan congregation where none had existed. Within three years he had a following large enough to enable him to erect a chapel in an open space along the River Ericht. Harry encountered village characters such as the local postman, who taught him to appreciate Shelley. Since the local school was inadequate, he was sent to the High School of Dundee, some twenty miles away, where he boarded during term with a local minister.

His separation from his family coincided with the beginning of a conscious rebellion against his father, a battle in which he sought to free

[9] Interview, Mabel R. Brailsford.
[10] Hector L. Waugh, ed., *George Watson's College: History and Record, 1724-1970* (Edinburgh, 1970), p. 59.

not only himself, but also his sister from paternal control. In part this struggle involved a rejection of Methodism and the moralistic terror instilled in him from his earliest days. He always remembered—but at what age did it happen?—that once as a child when his mother had caressed him affectionately he had got an erection. Seeing the response her gesture had triggered, Clara had knelt down and prayed to God to forgive her for causing this evil and to keep Harry from sin. Certainly it was difficult for most Victorian children to avoid some feelings of guilt about sexual longings. How much more was this the case among the children of Methodist ministers? Whether or not Harry comprehended the atmosphere of sexual repression, he clearly reacted against 'a childhood spent in a Perthshire manse, where only a forbidding bookcase of religious works in gloomy bindings was open on the sabbath day'.[11] What made matters worse was his recognition that Edward did not always practise what he preached. Harry was astonished to discover one Sunday when his father had withdrawn to his study for meditation, that he was, in fact, relaxing on a chaise reading a novel. Trivial though the incident may have been, it confirmed his feelings of hostility towards his father, his sense that behind the façade of godliness was a fallible, even hypocritical, individual.[12] Few fathers are perceived as heroes by adolescent sons, but what was significant in Harry's situation was that the personal rejection implied a repudiation of his father's public role as well. Thus he struck not only at paternal authority, but at the religious strictures his father had imposed. Methodism came increasingly to appear as a fraud perpetrated on benighted worshippers, lulled into self-delusion by Edward's theatrics. With retrospective benevolence, Harry could later look back on a 'chapel which I attended as a boy and the minister who preached in it'. The reference, obviously to his father, goes on to recall the minister's favourite hymn, which began:

> Nothing has the saint to fear
> Though earth should be destroyed
> He can laugh at danger near
> And smile above the void.

'The whole chapel,' he continued, 'rose and sang it with a swing and a will. One heard the flames crackling, and the saint . . . warmed his fingers at the blaze.'[13]

---

[11] *Daily News*, 25 Jan. 1908. Reprinted in revised form in *Adventures in Prose*, p. 48.
[12] As Erik Erikson has observed, 'One of the deepest conflicts in life is the hate for a parent who served as the model and executor of the superego, but who (in some form) was found trying to get away with the very transgression which the child can no longer tolerate in himself.' *Childhood and Society* (Harmondsworth, 1965), p. 249.
[13] *New Leader*, 9 Feb. 1923.

If the years at Dundee brought relief from parental restraints, they also heightened Harry's feelings of isolation. Coming to a school where he knew no one, lonely and insecure, he assumed guises that would conceal his fear and win the esteem of his contemporaries. Intellectually precocious, he tried to impress others by his audacity. He let it be known that he had had his Shelley period at the age of five (at which time he was, in fact, defiantly refusing to learn his alphabet!), and an early essay entitled 'Is there a God?' created a minor scandal.[14] None the less, his academic performance was outstanding: during his first year he emerged first in his section in both Latin and English, and throughout his years at the school he figured prominently in the prize lists.[15] Dundee offered a traditional curriculum, emphasizing English, Latin, Greek, and ancient history. There were mixed classes, with pupils drawn from all social levels.[16] It was the lack of rigid distinctions that Brailsford recalled fondly years later:

We knew nothing of 'tone' or 'good form', or of that morality of caste and obedience which in England masters and elder boys impose upon the plastic minds of the young. . . . The playground was our kingdom. . . . Sometimes we played football, sometimes we rehearsed Bannockburn or Flodden Fell. Sometimes, in our later years, we argued hotly and eagerly about Atheism or Socialism, and the creation of the world. We were of all classes and origins. Farmers' sons, and sailors' sons, rubbed shoulders with the children of the manse, and the progeny of our dignified Lord Provost. The janitor's boy . . . moved among us as happily as the headmaster's son and the heirs of retired Colonels and Anglo-Indian officials. It was a world in which even eccentricity could thrive, and individuality command respect.[17]

In his five years at Dundee High School he began to develop as a classicist. He won the Dux Prize in English as the outstanding student in his class and the offer of bursaries at both Glasgow and Edinburgh. He chose the former, as yet unaware that his family would shortly follow him there.

Relations between father and son were becoming increasingly strained. Harry's irreverence irritated his father, who, both proud and jealous of his son's accomplishments, was determined to retain authority over him. Harry, reluctant to attend chapel services even to gratify his father, made no effort to conceal his religious indifference. Moreover, a tug of war was developing over Mabel, once her brother's closest ally. While he had been away at school, she had become even

---

[14] Alexander MacCallum Scott, MS 'Book of Characters' [1928], MSP.
[15] I am grateful to Mr E. M. Stewart, Rector of the High School of Dundee, for this information.
[16] *Dundee High School Magazine: Centenary Number 1834-1934.*
[17] *Adventures in Prose*, pp. 132-3. Originally published in *Daily News*, 18 Dec. 1907.

more timorous, incapable of resisting her father's tyranny. Recognizing her intellectual gifts—she was in due course to become an accomplished writer—Harry felt a mission to liberate her, which he believed possible only if she were to leave home. He had long since conceded defeat in regard to Clara's subservience, but Mabel was to be spared a comparable fate. Yet Mabel was herself torn by conflicting loyalties. While she yearned for the sort of education her brother had enjoyed, her mother was beginning to show signs of the inherited Pooley deafness, requiring attention that Edward could not provide. Her sense of duty coupled with an emotional timidity prevented her from asserting her own independence, and she began to assume the role for which she seemed destined, that of companion to her mother.

If Edward had lost control over his son's mind and, one might add, his soul, he insisted on dominating him in other ways. Harry might pursue the academic career that his father had missed, but only on his father's terms. The boy should be shielded from corrupting influences, protected from the worldly distractions of undergraduate life. Edward ordered a brown broadcloth suit for him, with a high Eton collar, knickerbocker trousers, and a tam-o'-shanter, an outfit which might still have been *de rigueur* in places for a schoolboy, but was hardly the uniform of the university student in the 1890s. In addition, he insisted that his sixteen-year-old son abstain from shaving on the grounds that he had pledged him from birth as a Nazarite—or was this simply the bizarre interpretation that Harry offered to others for his father's conduct? It revealed a perverse streak, since Edward himself invariably dressed fashionably. It was as though he wanted his son to appear peculiar, perhaps as a punishment for straying from the faith. What seems equally inexplicable is why Harry acquiesced, however briefly. He may have felt unable to flaunt his father's wishes in this respect as he had intellectually. Short and unattractive, he pretended to despise public esteem, although in reality he longed to conform, to be accepted.

Dressed unconventionally, unshaven, but not quite bearded, he began to attend classes at Glasgow University. His odd appearance evoked ridicule from his classmates and boys in the street. After several weeks his courage failed him, and he could no longer feign indifference. Eccentricity of dress heightened his feelings of isolation, and he decided to break his promise to his father. He shaved and dressed as his contempories did, but the inflicted wound, the indignity of his first weeks at the university, would not heal. He could not forgive his father for the humiliation to which he had been subjected, for making him appear in the eyes of the world the misfit he secretly feared he had become.

II
Young Hegelian (1890–1897)

In 1890 Glasgow University still retained many of the features that set higher education in Scotland apart from its English counterpart. Despite criticism of its much vaunted 'democratic intellectualism',[1] it offered an alternative to the exclusive recruitment and narrow specialization that characterized Oxford and Cambridge. Until 1892, when legislation was enacted to make Scottish universities conform to English standards, the policy of unrestricted admission produced a student body of remarkable diversity in social background, scholastic attainment, and age. The ordinary course leading to the Master of Arts degree extended over four sessions and consisted of seven compulsory subjects: Latin (or Humanity, as it was then called), Greek, mathematics, logic, moral philosophy, natural philosophy (i.e. physics), and English literature. Catholic in breadth, it permitted little choice, although there was some flexibility in regard to the depth of exposure. The regulations stipulated that a student must attend classes in Humanity, Greek, and mathematics for at least two sessions and in the other prescribed subjects for at least one, after which they would be certified by the respective departments for the degree. In subjects such as Latin, Greek, and mathematics an unusually proficient student might proceed immediately to the advanced classes and even complete his course in three sessions instead of the customary four.

If the uniform curriculum was geared to general cultural elevation rather than to the training of an élite, it did not sacrifice intellectual rigour. Scottish university education insisted on a thorough grounding in the classics and in mathematics, but its unique feature was the primacy accorded to philosophy. Even in the study of the classics, more attention was paid to an aesthetic appreciation of the values of ancient civilization than to grammatical analysis. In contrast to the English pattern most of the instruction was carried on by professors in lectures, attendance at which was compulsory for the degree. The content of these lectures, not independent reading under the direction of a tutor,

---

[1] G. E. Davie, *The Democratic Intellect: Scotland and Her Universities in the Nineteenth Century* (Edinburgh, 1961), p. 105. This description is based on the relevant sections of Davie, the *Glasgow University Calendar*, and on information furnished by the University Registrar's Office. Bursary lists, giving candidates' rankings at the time Brailsford matriculated, appeared in the *Glasgow Herald*, 5 Nov. 1890.

constituted the substance of the course on which the student was later examined.

To supplement their official salaries, professors personally collected a three guinea fee at the start of the session from each of those enrolled. Classes were large—often several hundred students—and each bench would have its censor who took attendance and reported the names of absentees. Lectures, beginning with a prayer and lasting for an hour, would be delivered daily throughout the session. These were follwed by one or more additional hours during which the professor would subject individual students to Socratic questioning or the public reading of excerpts from their essays. Even though they were denied the English privilege of non-attendance at lectures, Scottish undergradutes showed no inclination to suffer tedium silently. They customarily sang while awaiting the professor's arrival, and, despite a high degree of tolerance for lectures read at dictation speed, they would 'rough' boring speakers by noisily stamping their boots.

Twenty years earlier Glasgow University had moved from the High Street to new buildings designed by Gilbert Scott at Gilmorehill, but the architectural exuberance of the Gothic spires masked a distinct lack of facilities. The university, consisting chiefly of lecture halls and laboratories, provided little in the way of social accommodation. Its students, drawn largely from the environs of Glasgow, commuted from their homes—Gilbert Murray had a pupil who walked seven miles to class[2]—or lived in 'digs' scattered around the city. The range of extracurricular activities was limited, and several of the undergraduate societies were of recent origin: the Philosophical Society was founded in 1887, the *Magazine* in 1889, and the Union not until 1890.

What gave Glasgow its lustre was the reputation of its faculty which extended far beyond Scottish confines. Much the most eminent was William Thomson, Lord Kelvin, the celebrated physicist who repeatedly declined the Cavendish chair at Cambridge and who was soon to become a founding member of the Order of Merit. While Kelvin retained the professorship of natural philosophy for more than fifty years, many of his more distinguished colleagues pursued a different professional route. Glasgow was where they might establish their reputations—or enhance growing ones—but they showed a propensity to leave when prestigious offers came their way. Sir Richard Jebb, who had held the chair in Greek, accepted an invitation to Cambridge, recommending as his successor the twenty-three-year-old Murray, himself later to be appointed Regius Professor of Greek at Oxford. Edward Caird, Professor of Moral Philosophy from 1866 to 1894, came to Glasgow from

[2] Gilbert Murray, *An Unfinished Autobiography*, Jean Smith and Arnold Toynbee, eds. (London, 1960), p. 131.

Balliol and returned to replace Jowett as Master. A. C. Bradley, Professor of English Literature from 1889 to 1900, was also lured back to Oxford as Professor of Poetry. Yet Caird's long tenure and Murray's dedication to his teaching hardly suggest that these scholars perceived Glasgow as an academic backwater.

Not quite seventeen when the 1890-1 Winter Session began, Brailsford was subject to the entrance examination requirement. He elected to take the preliminary examinations in Latin and Greek, success in which would not merely qualify him for the advanced level, but would render him eligible to graduate in three years. His high scores in the tests, which consisted mainly of translation of passages into and from English, earned him an eighth place in the bursary competition as well as admission to the Senior Class in both Greek and Humanity. His preparation in mathematics, though less outstanding, was sufficient to enable him to enrol in the second year of Upper Junior class on advanced algebra and trigonometry.

One can scarcely imagine the terror which must have gripped him as he entered Murray's Greek class at eight o'clock on the first morning of term. Still sporting his strange attire and whiskers, shy and embarrassed about his ludicrous appearance, he found himself in the company of students most of whom were several years his elder. To them he seemed an enigmatic figure, his reticence at odds with his intellect. Murray, an exacting teacher who examined the class orally on assigned reading every day, had a talent for making even the shyest feel at ease, and Brailsford's ability was quickly noticed. Then in his second year at Glasgow and younger than some of his own students, the Australian-born, Oxford-trained scholar had begun to exert a powerful influence. In addition to exercising his matchless gift for translation on the prescribed texts for that session—two works of Demosthenes, one of Aristophanes, and part of the *Odyssey*—he attempted to convey a spiritual affinity for the Hellenic world in his lectures. His intention was to transform the teaching of his subject, moving beyond textual criticism to explore the values of classical civilization and stressing the ancient Greeks' 'active, positive, purposeful approach to existence'.[3]

Always accessible to the young, Murray imported an element of Oxford tutorial style to Glasgow, taking infinite pains with his better students and guiding their work outside formal class hours. It was his personality as much as pedagogic technique that won admirers. He was receptive to student confidences, never hesitating to offer candid advice. Reputedly sympathetic to socialism and an outspoken advocate of women's rights, he despised the stereotype of the cloistered academic

---

[3] C. M. Bowra, *Memories* (London, 1966), p. 228.

and tried instead 'to combine an enthusiasm for poetry and Greek scholarship with an almost equal enthusiasm for radical politics and social reform'.

Brailsford, promptly recognized as a 'very brilliant student',[4] began to receive coveted invitations from Murray and his aristocratic wife and to bask in their hospitality. Although only seven years separated them in age, Murray quickly assumed the role of father figure to his pupil. Having lost his own father at the age of seven, he could appreciate Brailsford's loneliness, a loneliness sharpened by guilt for having cut himself off from his family. Murray had strayed from Roman Catholicism at the age of eleven and could sympathize with youthful rebellion, offering the encouragement which Brailsford had ceased to find at home. If Edward's virtues were obscured—at least in his son's eyes—by tyrannical behaviour, Murray seemed by contrast a paragon of integrity, his principles and conduct always in harmony. Grateful for such solicitude, Brailsford resolved to prove that Murray's expectations were justified. His performance in the Senior Class in Greek was impressive for a first year student: he finished in sixth place in the prize list.

In the meantime family relations had reached the point of open conflict. His son's academic laurels mattered less to Edward than his apostasy, increasingly blatant after the family moved to Glasgow in 1891. Once having defied strictures on dress and shaving, it was easier to shed any pretence of religious belief as well. A return to his parents' home proved brief, the daily contact intensifying the friction between father and son. The university had not merely opened horizons to him: it had liberated him from the constraints of his upbringing and brought him into contact with others for whom religion had lost its meaning. While he shared little in undergraduate camaraderie, the stimulation of his classes and Murray's protective influence eased his isolation. Still plagued by self-doubt, he found solace in the cello and submerged himself in his studies.

Glasgow undergraduates had the option of doing additional work during summer vacations, and in order to prepare for a preliminary examination in logic in November 1891 Brailsford spent the interlude between his first and second years reading Descartes. His interest in philosophy was kindled, and he emerged from the examination with one of the two Junior prizes. In the 1891-2 session Brailsford attended the course on logic, the initial stage of the prescribed philosophy programme. John Veitch's class was the last bastion of the Scottish Common Sense school at Glasgow, where traditional philosophy had succumbed to Hegelian Idealism. His course was an amalgam of subjects, including not only logic, but rhetoric, metaphysics, and psychology. Regular

---

[4] Murray, *Autobiography*, p. 97.

essays were required, and prizes for excellence were judged by the classes themselves. At the end of the session his peers in the Junior division voted Brailsford first in the class.

Although only in his second year, he was qualified to enrol in the most advanced courses in Humanity and Greek, the Upper Senior or Private Class intended for honours candidates. The calibre of Brailsford's performance continued to impress his professor, and their relationship ripened. It was to Murray that he confided his indecision about a career, his quandary over the conflicting claims of classics and philosophy. They corresponded during the summer of 1892, when the eighteen-year-old undergraduate was 'spending a week upon Kant in order to see how I like him':

> I ran through the *Critique of Pure Reason* roughly first and am now working through it carefully, writing an analysis of it and comparing Hutchison Stirling's commentary. While not exactly fascinated or absorbed, I am still thoroughly interested. I have read a good deal in Logic already and always took pleasure in it. However what you say is very fatally true and I am afraid it is not in Philosophy in its most abstract shape that my interest lies, but in Ethics, Psychology, Comparative Religion and History philosophically treated. . . .
>
> I shall be careful never to close all avenues of escape. I may be disappointed even in my modest ambition to become a mediocre metaphysician, then I should merely be in the position of working at classics after Philosophy instead of before it as universal tradition seems to require. . . .[5]

It is less the brashness cloaked in modesty that one notices in the letter than the precocity, the sense of vocation. Painfully conscious of his awkwardness, to which he attributed his unpopularity, Brailsford never doubted his superior intellect. If Murray tried to temper his protégé's new enthusiasm, it was because he was reluctant to lose a potentially outstanding classical scholar whom he had begun to coach for the Blackstone competition in Greek, its name taken from the medieval chair in which candidates sat during the oral examination. Brailsford fulfilled his promise by winning the Cowan Gold Medal in November 1892, the pinnacle of achievement for the undergraduate classicist.

While pondering his future, he was obliged to decide among several options regarding immediate academic goals. He could have received the ordinary MA degree at the end of that session or attempted an honours degree in four years, but instead he chose an even more demanding course. According to new regulations imposed in 1892 honours students might take a minimum of five subjects rather than the seven

---

[5] HNB to Gilbert Murray, 21 June 1892, GMP, 124, fols. 1-2. The reference is to James Hutchison Stirling, *Text-book to Kant: The Critique of Pure Reason* (Edinburgh, 1881).

formerly prescribed. By eliminating natural philosophy Brailsford could devote his third year to the English literature course and examinations in Latin and Greek. He would then be able to spend a final year doing honours work in Mental Philosophy. Although this accelerated programme might cost him an almost certain First Class Honours in classics, it would enable him to do justice to his philosophical aspirations.

A. C. Bradley's English course on *Macbeth*, Addison's essays, and Romantic poetry was more than a diversion from more serious tasks. A voracious reader of English—and Scottish—classics since childhood, Brailsford had a flair for literary criticism and fancied himself something of a stylist, as his first, overwrought contributions to the *Glasgow University Magazine* would soon reveal. His efforts earned him first place in his class, a distinction confirmed by the award of the Buchanan Prize. But it was moral philosophy that consumed most of his attention that year.

Caird's reputation had been one of the factors prompting his choice of Glasgow over Edinburgh when leaving Dundee High School. Although nearly thirty years had elapsed since the Professor of Moral Philosophy first launched Anglo-German Idealism in Glasgow, his magnetism had scarcely diminished by the 1890s. Challenging the orthodox Scottish appeal to common sense as a verifying principle in philosophy and the disdain for ideological extremism, Caird had espoused the 'Germanising monism'[6] identified with T. H. Green and his Oxford circle. While disavowing originality in his metaphysics, he saw himself as an interpreter, applying Hegelian abstractions to the elucidation of ethical, theological, and political questions. If Idealism now seems less palatable than the moderate scepticism it aimed to supplant, generations of Glasgow students revered Caird as 'a revealer of new regions of thought'.[7] That his spiritual conception of the universe lacked clarity was obvious, but he imparted to his audience the certainty that mankind was moving forward and that morality would ultimately prevail. He summoned them to a life of commitment to some higher destiny in which their subjective natures would be united with an objective reality. Caird did more than teach the history of philosophy: he was a prophet seeking converts to a creed whose articles he expounded daily in the classroom. For Brailsford Idealism filled a void left by his break with Methodism, replacing the discarded creed of his father with the conviction that salvation must be sought in the present world by developing man's capacities as a social being. Hegelianism,

---

[6] Davie, p. 328.
[7] Henry Jones and John Henry Muirhead, *The Life and Philosophy of Edward Caird* (Glasgow, 1921), p. 58.

as interpreted by Caird and Green, lost its conservative, authoritarian trappings and was transmuted into a philosophy of progress.

Once he had completed his comprehensive examinations in Latin and Greek in October 1893—fifteen hours of translation and literary analysis which earned him Second Class Honours—Brailsford was able to settle down to a final year devoted entirely to the study of philosophy. He continued to excel, securing a first prize in moral philosophy and a second prize in logic for an essay on the methods of Kant and Hegel. Having attained a certain academic notoriety, he began to emerge from his shell, no longer the introvert he had been in his first years. He participated more readily in undergraduate activities, was elected Secretary of the Philosophical Society, and contributed several poems to the *Glasgow University Magazine*.

His earliest published works are disappointing. Experimenting with different styles, he tried several adaptations from Victor Hugo and a translation of a Heine poem into Scots dialect. His poems, like the stories published in the *Magazine* during the next few years, affect world-weariness. Pretentious and riddled with conceits, they none the less represent a phase in his literary apprenticeship, the first tentative steps of the future craftsman. Brailsford's writing emerges more characteristically in two papers delivered to undergraduate audiences in February 1894. The first, read at a meeting of the Philomathic Society, examined the psychological and ethical implications of *Measure for Measure*. Using both this play and *Troilus and Cressida*, he delivered what the *Magazine* reported as 'a most acute and brilliant analysis of the characteristics and ideal of the pagan renascence of Queen Elizabeth's time'. He also addressed the Philosophical Society on 'Poetry and Philosophy' and informed the audience that poetry was the most typical manifestation of the impulse towards differentiation in human consciousness.[8]

If Second Class Honours in Greek and Latin were less than dazzling for so promising a classicist, the achievement of double honours was a singular feat at Glasgow. The examinations in moral philosophy and logic, each lasting six hours, consisted of seven essays covering a wide range of topics with emphasis on Kant and Hegel. So brilliant were his papers that he obtained not merely First Class Honours in both subjects, but also the Thomas Logan Medal and Prize awarded annually to the most distinguished Arts graduate. English birth disqualified him from competing for the Snell Exhibition for study at Balliol, but his examination essays were successfully entered in the competition for the George A. Clark Bursary in Mental Philosophy, a four year fellowship at Glasgow University carrying an annual stipend of £180.

[8] *Glasgow University Magazine*, VI, No. 12 (21 Feb. 1894).

When Brailsford received his Master of Arts degree in November 1894, he had every expectation of pursuing an academic career. He had proved himself the outstanding scholar of a student generation which included a number of able young men—John Buchan, the novelist, Robert Horne, a future Chancellor of the Exchequer, and Archibald Charteris, later a professor of international law. The bursary imposed few constraints, although he was expected to assist in undergraduate instruction and to deliver a series of lectures at the conclusion of his term. Clark scholars were encouraged to avail themselves of educational opportunities at other universities as a way of broadening their experience. Intending to recuperate from the relentless pace of the previous months, Brailsford decided to remain for a time in Glasgow, more congenial now that his parents had moved to Newcastle. He was belatedly discovering a niche for himself in the community, acquiring new friends such as the Bone brothers, Muirhead, then a struggling young artist, and James, future London editor of the *Manchester Guardian*, and participating more actively in Glasgow's cultural life. He enrolled in Bradley's Honours Class in English literature and was elected President of the Philosophical Society.

By January 1895 Brailsford was ready to follow Caird's suggestion that he spend some time at Oxford as an unattached student, free from degree obligations. During two terms in residence Harold Joachim of Balliol supervised his Plato readings, W. H. Fairbrother of Lincoln gave him an abbreviated honours tutorial in ancient philosophy, and J. Cook Wilson, Wykeham Professor of Logic, agreed to teach him. His aptitude made a strong impression on his Oxford teachers: Wilson claimed that he had 'seldom had a more interesting pupil', and Fairbrother told him that 'I always felt that I received from you as much as (I hope) you gained from me'.[9] Oxford, however, failed to live up to his expectations. 'I have often got more from a single lecture in Glasgow,' he informed Murray, 'than from all the courses which I attended at Oxford.'[10]

When his term at Oxford ended in June, Brailsford left for the University of Berlin, where he attended summer lectures on the history of philosophy by Carl Stumpf, Friedrich Paulsen, and Georg Simmel. This first trip to Germany was a kind of intellectual pilgrimage for the young Hegelian, confirming an infatuation with German culture, as well as improving his facility with the language. Although the visit lasted only two months, the uncritical reverence that it inspired coloured his subsequent image of Germany. His sister Mabel had already been in Berlin for several months with a party of school friends when Brailsford arrived, and he tried in the weeks together to revive the

[9] Testimonial letters, Dec. 1896, HNBP.
[10] HNB to Gilbert Murray, 25 Mar. 1895, GMP, 124, fols. 3-6.

intimacy of childhood. Mabel had been an occasional student in German literature at Queen Margaret's College two years earlier, and he now sought to persuade her to continue her studies in Germany for an indefinite period in the hope that a spell away from paternal domination might strengthen her longing for independence. Her return home after only six months disappointed him, shattering his illusion that by emancipating her he might secure an ally in the family conflict. Her rejection of his lead left him more wretched than before, defiantly irreconcilable, yet haunted by feelings of disloyalty.

Despite his sense of estrangement, Brailsford was loath to cut himself off completely. At the end of his German trip he returned to England to spend a few weeks with his parents in Alnmouth. Here in August 1895 he and his father were attacked by a gang of drunken miners. Brailsford's injuries prevented his sitting a scholarship examination, although by the beginning of September he had recovered sufficiently to enable him to return to the university, where he was about to take up an appointment as Assistant to the Professor of Logic, Robert Adamson. No doubt highly recommended by the new Master of Balliol, Brailsford was an obvious choice for the post. Although Adamson had abandoned Hegelianism, he was still closer to Caird's intellectual position than his predecessor Veitch had been. Under his influence the teaching of logic at Glasgow was restructured, its antiquated concern with rhetoric giving way to a greater emphasis on contemporary philosophy and psychology. Brailsford was responsible for teaching women students as well as for marking essays in the men's course.

Among the new friends he made after returning to Glasgow in 1895 was Alexander MacCallum Scott, then still an undergraduate. The son of a poor widow, Scott was active in both the Union and the *Magazine* and was politically ambitious. His student diaries provide the most vivid portrait of Brailsford at this time, illuminating a side of his character that prize lists and academic testimonials cannot disclose. Like many friends throughout his life, Scott found him to be a 'puzzling, and indeed baffling, figure'. He stood in awe of the 'intellect like a corrosive acid', the capacity to assimilate the contents of an abstruse book while others were grappling with the first chapter, the facility for writing essays. In addition to the formidable intellect, he recognized in Brailsford a 'strongly artistic and emotional temperament', which seemed to vacillate between consciousness of intellectual superiority and 'abject self-abasement'. It was, Scott remarked, 'as if he had a wardrobe of masks and fancy dress' and could assume the personality that he chose for himself at a particular moment—'the studious scholar, the poet and artist, the philosopher, the man of action'. It was clear that these disguises were a kind of protective armour designed to conceal an 'intense and morbid self-consciousness'. Always yearning to be something that he was not, Brailsford regarded himself as 'a shivering stranger in a hostile world'. He was tormented by a conviction that he was different from other people and constantly struggled to efface that difference.

Although his shyness and prickly manner repelled many contemporaries, he became less inhibited in Scott's company, and the two spent long evenings discussing Meredith or Stevenson or the Glasgow school of painting. They subjected their own characters and those of their friends to close scrutiny and analysed their ambitions in Hegelian terms. Scott introduced Brailsford to a side of student life he had never experienced—the rough and tumble of the Union billiard room and the 'smoking concerts'. Outwardly contemptuous of the hearty athletes and politicians, Brailsford envied their informal camaraderie. On one occasion when Scott brought him to the Union,

> he entered with a swagger that was obviously self-conscious and artificial. He would affect the blunt directness and the intolerant self-assertion which he believed to be characteristic of the habitues of the Secretary's Room. He flavoured his conversation with one or two explosive 'Damn yous!' carefully directed. He made great play with his fierce manner of stuffing his tobacco into his pipe. His aim was to assume the pose of the natural, simple, uncomplex, and bluntly direct. But the pretence of unconsciousness would not have deceived an infant. The others stared at him as at a surprising phenomenon, and the more they stared the more nervously self-conscious he became.[11]

After several years of living virtually as a recluse, brooding over his books and music, the attraction of new interests proved unsettling. Growing doubts about the scholarly life, endlessly probed in discussions with friends, affected his studies. He had arrived at an intellectual crossroads, but even his Hegelian training had not pointed to a resolution of the dilemma. It was not that philosophical study precluded political involvement or even that a Hegelian perspective inhibited progressive thinking. Caird and Adamson were both identified in a Ruskinian way with the political left, and Murray demonstrated the possibility of reconciling scholarship with a social conscience. None the less for the first time Brailsford admitted to himself the attraction of the world of practical affairs, and it called into question the depth of his commitment to an academic career. If, as Hegel implied, man could realize his potential only by self-renunciation, then surely social activism must be preferable to the contemplative life. In arguing with more politically-conscious students, such as Scott and Tom Jones, his own values began to crystallize, the vague Liberalism of his upbringing taking on a more radical—and even socialist—tinge.

[11] Alexander MacCallum Scott, MS 'Book of Characters', MSP.

While in Newcastle during the 1895 General Election he heard Keir Hardie address a meeting on behalf of Labour. Repudiating the candidate's suggestion that his supporters accept rides to the poll in Liberal or Tory carriages, the ILP leader rebuked those who would degrade themselves by concealing their views for the sake of convenience. Brailsford was stirred by the 'moral genius' of a man who 'cared more for the self-respect of his class than for any of the calculations of daily politics'.[12] After Hardie's speech to the Dialectic Society in February 1896, a handful of enthusiasts, led by Murray's assistant, Ronald Burrows, called a meeting to launch the university's first socialist group, an ILP branch. Little seems to have come of it, although its Honorary President was the Professor of Greek himself, but several weeks later the same band of young socialists established a Glasgow University Fabian Society. Its seventeen members received recognition from the Fabian Executive Committee in April, elected officers, and proceeded to recruit members, chiefly among postgraduate students. Burrows was its first President, Jones the Secretary, and Brailsford one of the committee. Among the other founders were Norman Leys, MacCallum Scott, and Jane Malloch.[13]

Whether or not such extra-curricular activities affected Brailsford's classroom performance adversely, Adamson soon concluded that his assistant had mistaken his vocation. Complaints had reached him about unintelligible teaching, and he felt obliged to recommend that the appointment be terminated after one year. Murray attempted to intercede, but Adamson convinced him that the decision was irrevocable. If his dismissal was not wholly unforeseen, it was deeply wounding to Brailsford's self-esteem, and he made no effort to conceal his anger at Adamson's peremptory conduct.[14]

By virtue of his Clark Fellowship he was permitted to conduct tutorials on the history of philosophy for members of the advanced class in logic and metaphysics during the 1896-7 session, but this was to be his last teaching experience. In the wake of his own misgivings about a scholarly career, the loss of his assistantship precipitated a kind of 'identity crisis'. His disappointment over the reversal in his academic fortunes made him no less determined to realize himself in a Hegelian sense and to prove his worth to his father. Although keenly aware of how 'we torment ourselves with the lie about our own capacities',[15] he applied in December 1896 for a position as Assistant Lecturer in Logic

[12] *New Leader*, 28 Sept. 1923, 24 Sept. 1926.
[13] Fabian Society Executive Committee Minutes, Jan. 1895-Feb. 1897, Fabian Society Collection; *Magazine*, VIII, No. 16 (26 Feb. 1896), No. 18 (11 Mar. 1896); *Glasgow University Calendar, 1896-7*, pp. 587-8.
[14] Mary Agnes Hamilton, *Remembering My Good Friends* (London, 1944), p. 147.
[15] *Magazine*, IX, No. 7 (16 Dec. 1896).

and Philosophy at the University College in Aberystwyth. Glowing recommendations from Murray, who described him as 'full of intellectual life and force', and from Caird, who regarded him as 'one of the most distinguished students of his time', failed to secure him the appointment.[16] While contemplating alternative possibilities, Brailsford continually mulled over the idea of a career in journalism during soul-searching conversations with Scott. Several sketches published in the *Magazine* reveal his introspective mood in these months, his preoccupations with the pretences and illusions which surround human actions. In the guise of fiction he probed his own background with insight:

My case was somewhat different. The parental arm was unfatigued; the birch elastic that fell upon me. I am an eldest son; one of a sad race. I have known the bitterness of him who must disown the lies of his own blood, and hide his properest child among the bulrushes. I learned to sit mute and correct in the broad light of the sun, truth written on my forehead, and probity in my gait. . . . A long course of oppression had bred in me a plethora of slow humours, and here I am, a professional sophist, who can lie only about the Absolute. I am convinced that it is from the well-whipped eldest sons of the middle classes that all our clerics and philosophers must spring.[17]

Just as an academic career had once represented a victory for enlightenment against obscurantist religion, so its abandonment might be rationalized as a further step towards self-liberation. The university had fulfilled its purpose in equipping him intellectually to contend with the burden of his past; he had now to try to fend for himself in the outside world.

Although certain that Brailsford was not suited to be an academic philosopher, Adamson was concerned about his assistant's future. When his old Manchester friend C. P. Scott made one of his periodic inquiries about young prospects for the *Guardian* staff, Adamson suggested him as 'an excellent scholar' with 'a turn for writing and of the kind that would be useful to you. He is very quick and bright and a mass of varied accomplishments.'[18] Brailsford promised his friends, somewhat uncharacteristically, to 'get roaring drunk' should he succeed in obtaining the job. As it happened Scott decided to trust to well-worn Oxford channels of recruitment, informing the applicant that there was no full-time work in sight, but that he would be kept in mind for occasional assignments. Without giving up either his fellowship or the intention of completing his lectures, Brailsford accepted a trial appointment as sub-editor of the new *Scots Pictorial*, scheduled to begin

---

[16] Curriculum vitae and testimonial letters, HNBP.
[17] *Magazine*, IX, No. 7 (16 Dec. 1896).
[18] Robert Adamson to C. P. Scott, 24 Jan. 1897, *Manchester Guardian* Editor's file. I have relied on David Ayerst's notes on this letter.

publication in April 1897. In addition to writing the 'Looker On' column and interviewing local notables, he was to assist the editor and correct incoming copy. The first issue carried his plea for the teaching of Gaelic in the schools and a scathing attack on the Scottish Home Rule Association for protesting the dispatch of a Highland regiment to Crete as part of British peace-keeping operations.[19] The weekly had scarcely been launched before he was denigrating it as unworthy of his talents, its gossipy society pages affording little chance to display stylistic flourishes.

His dejection was intensified by the turmoil of his private affairs. He was hopelessly in love with Jane Malloch, but his affection was not reciprocated. The two had met several years before, perhaps as early as 1894. One of six children of a prosperous Renfrewshire cotton spinner, Jane was a headstrong girl with striking looks, 'beautified', as H. W. Nevinson described her, 'by Celtic blue-grey eyes, dark hair, and a smile to soften the heart of any Turk or even of any infidel'.[20] After graduating from Paisley Grammar School, she had enrolled at Queen Margaret's College in 1893 at nineteen and quickly acquired a reputation as 'a great Hegelian'.[21] She studied Greek with Murray, for whom she harboured a passionate attachment, and was the cleverest of Brailsford's students in 1895. Drawn together by a common interest in Idealist philosophy, they also met frequently in the committee meetings of the Fabian Society. He was not alone among his circle in finding her captivating, although none of the others pursued her with his single-minded devotion. Scott, to whom his friends confided tales of unrequited love, reported that Murray had thought her to be 'one of the first women of the century' when he first met her but changed his mind upon futher acquaintance.[22]

Initially Brailsford's infatuation was kept in check by the warnings of his friends, eager to protect him from what they regarded as a fatal attraction. One of them, after scrutinizing her photograph, declared that she had no heart and would never love anyone, a judgement he found difficult to contradict. Scott labelled her a neurotic who would prevent his friend from ever accomplishing anything in literature. To complicate matters further, Brailsford had been more or less engaged to a childhood sweetheart, a Blairgowrie girl to whom he had pledged himself in adolescent innocence. He had long since outgrown the relationship, was bored by her docile faithfulness, and complained to Scott that she lacked any 'inner life, any grubbings about her inside to

[19] *Scots Pictorial*, I, No. 1 (3 Apr. 1897).
[20] H. W. Nevinson, *More Changes, More Chances* (London, 1925), p. 4.
[21] Murray, *Autobiography*, p. 102.
[22] Alexander MacCallum Scott, MS 'Diary', MSP. The quotations that follow in this chapter are all taken from the diary.

report', while he was 'constantly having mental and moral crises'. Guiltily recognizing that his affections were now otherwise committed, he none the less contemplated early marriage to avoid becoming more entangled with his student. Scott persuaded him that such a course of action would be financially imprudent, saddling him with obligations which would compromise his career. Reassured that he was acting in his fiancée's interest, he broke with her only to find himself succumbing to Jane's charm. Her rebuffs, her aura of mysterious unapproachability, merely inflamed his ardour, blinding him to the calculated cruelty of her behaviour. He overpraised her essays and futilely resorted to various strategems to ingratiate himself, but his efforts were rewarded with little more than her photograph. So distracted did he become that he could no longer concentrate on his work, which doubtlessly contributed to his ineffectual classroom performance. Although he admitted that Jane humiliated him, Brailsford could not restrain himself from proposing marriage to her in December 1896, just as she was about to leave for a year at Somerville College, Oxford. To no one's surprise, she refused him.

In her absence he tried to win over her family, lending her sister a book and befriending the youngest of the four Malloch sons, Bruce. He wrote to her in Oxford, sent copies of his *Magazine* articles, and agonized over her curt replies. After more than a year of courtship Jane had become adept at exploiting his vulnerability to gratify her own vanity. Alternately inviting and repelling his overtures, she encouraged him only enough to keep him importunate. His subservience, his readiness to grasp the merest crumb of kindness as an auspicious sign disturbed Scott, who rebuked him for seizing any excuse to write to her. Solicitous about her feelings, he was constantly on guard lest he offend her and cause an irreparable breach. When rumours of their engagement spread around the university, he took steps to refute them, informing Jane's friends that she had in fact rejected his suit.

In April 1897, a week after Jane's return from Oxford, Brailsford announced to Scott that he had made up his mind to go out to Greece as a volunteer if war were declared against Turkey. After seeing an appeal in the *Daily Chronicle*, he had telegraphed offering his services in the Philhellenic Legion then being recruited to help the Greek rebels and expressed his willingness to pay his own expenses. The Greek revolt appealed to his romantic feeling for Hellenic civilization, a sentiment inspired in part by Murray, although he confessed to being more outraged at the conduct of the European powers than enamoured of the Greek leaders. His motives were more complicated than his gesture would have suggested. He saw participation in the Balkan struggle as 'the best possible means of objectifying' himself, of realizing in a

Hegelian sense that identity with a higher destiny outside himself. By committing his life to a noble cause, he would be released from absorption in his own subjective nature, freed from the tedium of the *Scots Pictorial* and his personal tribulations. At the same time the budding journalist in him recognized the adventure as 'good copy', a long-sought opportunity to gain notoriety and prove himself worthy of a first-rate position.

Underlying these justifications was a more compelling reason: Jane, insisting that she would not hesitate if she were a man, had written urging him to go. As Brailsford assessed the situation, he must abandon all hope of ever winning her unless he volunteered. Scott, sceptical about whether there was much reason for hope, remonstrated with him for leaving the editor of the *Scots Pictorial* in the lurch so soon after joining the paper. Brailsford asked his friend Charles Dick to deputize for him, prepared a will, and left instructions with Scott for the posthumous publication of his stories. He conceded that it was 'rather ridiculous for a fellow like me to be going out' and worried about whether he would learn to handle a rifle properly, never having fired one before. His departure was kept secret from his family and even from Murray; only Jane, Scott, Dick, and Joe Menzies, a law student friend, were informed of his plans, a precaution against the possibility of the conflict being settled before his arrival. On 14 April, his last night in Glasgow, he took Jane to the theatre, and later, despondent and more than a little frightened, he called on Menzies. He was trying to persuade himself that he was embarking on a noble and brave course of action, but the more they argued, the more Brailsford came to realize that his motives were less honourable than he pretended. The next day he left for Liverpool to join the British regiment of the Philhellenic Legion, half-convinced that he was behaving foolishly, but resolved to strike a blow for freedom and thereby to win the prize that had for so long eluded him.

III

Comrade-in-Arms (1897–1899)

> 'My best pupil went out to fight for Hellas. My parting gift to him was not a copy of Plato's *Republic*, but a revolver and a hundred Undershaft cartridges.'
>
> Adolphus Cusins in *Major Barbara*, Act III.

Fresh from his classical studies, Brailsford cherished an image of Greece more appropriate to the Periclean age than to the sordid atmosphere bred by intriguing politicians and a discredited court. What misgivings he had at the outset of his venture concerned his own motives for joining the Philhellenic Legion, not the political issues of the moment. To embrace the Greek cause was simply to defend liberty against despotism, but he questioned whether his enthusiasm was as selfless as he pretended, whether he had the capacity for physical bravery needed in actual combat. The scepticism of friends like Scott and Menzies confirmed inner doubts about the wisdom of risking his life in a struggle of which he knew little.

Events had moved so rapidly that by the time Brailsford reached Athens, the situation had become desperate. In what was less a military campaign than a rout, the Greek army suffered ignominious defeats in its initial encounters with the Turks and abandoned Larissa without resistance. Most of the Legion was already at the front, but red tape and rudimentary target practice kept Brailsford in Athens, where warnings of imminent catastrophe were rife. After a seemingly interminable delay, he was authorized to join the British company, then participating in the retreat to Pharsala. He travelled with another group of Legion reinforcements, a motley collection of Italians, Germans, and Scots in the charge of a French officer. Disgusted by their low morale and brutality, he assumed a pose of detachment; he was eager to win acceptance, but at the same time too fastidious to become involved in their drunken quarrels. As he described himself, disguised as young Henry Graham in the autobiographical *The Broom of the War-God*,

He had an air of reserve and shyness which he tried to cover by a show of superiority and cynicism, yet at bottom he had not enough respect for himself to be able to dispense with that of others, and when he spoke he seemed anxious to conciliate. . . . His features were an irregular mass of contradictions—the symbols of a character at war with itself.[1]

[1] *The Broom of the War-God*, p. 7.

It was not so much the lack of refined conversation that troubled him as the lack of idealism among his fellow soldiers. Every physical hardship was magnified into a personal insult by men who had long since forgotten the purpose for which they had enlisted. Despite their tales of Greek treachery, of an undisciplined army on the verge of mutiny, he refused to allow them to undermine his faith or his determination to prove himself worthy of it.

Several days of marching along a road crowded with peasants, fleeing from Larissa with their possessions on their backs, brought Brailsford to Pharsala, where he finally met the British company. The last group to leave Larissa, they had watched the Crown Prince abandon his army and had been obliged to fire upon panicky Greek soldiers trying to displace women from a train carrying civilians and wounded to safety. The bitterness of these veterans dampened the ardour of the new recruit from Glasgow, convincing him that he had arrived merely to witness the collapse of the Greek effort. Aside from a contingent of Cockney volunteers with whom he had little in common save language, he found for the first time at Pharsala a handful of cosmopolitan legionnaires who enjoyed discussing literature. He was drawn particularly to a young Greek called Rodocanachi, only seventeen years old, but 'with a keen intellectual profile and an air of vigour and quiet self-confidence'.[2] Tormented by self-doubt, Brailsford tried to model himself on his new friend, hoping to regain something of the resolve that had faltered during his weeks of initiation.

No sooner had he arrived in Pharsala than the Legion was transferred to Driskoli, several miles closer to the Turkish front. For five days they awaited further orders, subsisting on rations of roast lamb and sour bread and relieving their boredom by frequent baths in the village horse-trough to the wonder of the primitive Evzone troops, for whom anointment with holy oil had obviated the necessity of bathing from baptism to death. When the Legion was at last summoned to action, it was merely to rescue a heavy gun, discarded by the Greek artillery in their flight from Larissa. The next day an enemy spy was discovered in Driskoli, and to the horror of the more sensitive spirits, the Evzones hung their captive from a tree by his heels and were at the point of burning him alive when his fortitude broke and he yielded to their demands for information. After this incident, Brailsford wrote, 'if we felt any satisfaction in our task, it was more because we were fighting against a barbaric despotism than because we bore the uniform of a nation that boasts its freedom and its civilization'.[3]

[2] *Broom*, p. 93. In the novel Brailsford calls him Mavromichali. Cf. *John O'London's Weekly*, 17 Dec. 1937. Rodocanachi was later a leader in the Venizelos revolution.

[3] *Glasgow Daily Record*, 6 July 1897. The incidents are also recounted in Chaps. IX and X of *Broom* and in *Macedonia*, p. 213n.

After several weeks in which military activity consisted of little besides retreat, a small party of English volunteers, Brailsford among them, was sent on a reconnaisance mission across the hills that separated their camp from the plain of Larissa where the Turkish army lay. A search for three spies proved fruitless, and they were about to return when their path was cut off by an oncoming Turkish horde. Exhilarated by exposure to danger, Brailsford was gripped by fear the first time he used his rifle:

> His hand trembled; he dreaded the recoil, though he had already become perfectly familiar with the service rifle at the Athenian ranges. But to fire with the hope and the dread of dealing death was a wholly new experience. When the deafening volley at last rang out, he felt certain that his grip had slackened and his bullet fallen wide of its doubtful target.[4]

Although Greek guns slowed the enemy's advance, the Turks, rushing the hills with shouts of 'Allah', vastly outnumbered them. The Evzones and the British contingent abandoned their position, turning and firing from each ridge until they had exhausted their ammunition. The Turks pursued them, inflicting heavy casualties: four of the sixteen English legionnaires, including Captain Birch, their commander, and Rodocanachi, were wounded. Helping to carry a wounded comrade to Pharsala, Brailsford thought that 'he would have given all the years of life spent in studies and classroom for the muscles of a mason or a carpenter'.[5]

Demoralized by their futile sacrifice, the Legion followed in the wake of the general retreat. Short of food and water, they climbed the mountains that separated Pharsala from Domokos, all semblance of discipline disintegrating under the influence of heat and pilfered cognac before they reached their destination the next morning. For five days they marked time in Domokos, prey to rumours of impending armistice, while desertion began to deplete their ranks as it had that of the Greek regulars. During his free hours Brailsford scoured the local shops for books and read aloud from a prose version of the *Iliad* to the servant of Varatasi, the Legion's commander, who corrected his pronunciation in return for English lessons.

The days of inactivity came to an end on 17 May when the Turks were finally engaged in battle, a poorly co-ordinated affair in which the Legion, occupying a position on the Greek flank, fended off the enemy advance for several hours. In contrast to his first experience of combat, it seemed to Brailsford 'as though this work of sighting, and aiming, and firing had been his daily vocation since boyhood'.[6] When his men

---

[4] *Broom*, pp. 144-5.
[5] *Broom*, p. 155. Also see *Manchester Guardian*, 4 Oct. 1911.
[6] *Broom*, pp. 251-2.

had exhausted their ammunition, he went to report their plight to Varatasi, noting, as he crossed the field, Greek officers abandoning their troops, many of whom cowered behind rocks without firing a shot. In his haste he stumbled over a corpse and, pausing to examine the old peasant face, realized that this was the first Turk he had been near enough to touch:

> In the misery of the retreat which followed our transient victory I understood what this experience meant. I had not known that I was firing at simple peasants. I had been firing at 'the enemy', 'the Turks', 'the Sultan's brutal soldiery', 'the forces of Oriental barbarism', and other names, phrases and abstractions. . . . I understood at length that that military discipline which I had been proud to obey myself, and to impose on others, was the necessary condition of this criminal stupidity called war.[7]

Narrowly avoiding capture, the bedraggled legionnaires, isolated from the main army and with only a few dry biscuits in their knapsacks, undertook the arduous three-day march over the hills to Lamia, arriving only to discover that an armistice had been signed the day before. 'It seemed a fitting close to a futile campaign, to a war in which the Turks had never gained a victory, and the Greeks had never waited to sustain a defeat.'[8] Brailsford himself had been slightly wounded, and by the time he found a surgeon in Thermopylae to dress the injury, it had become septic. He was still limping when he arrived in Athens, his ill-fitting uniform ragged and dirty. It was in that condition that he first met Henry Nevinson, then in Greece as a war correspondent. They spent a memorable evening comparing notes at an Athenian café, the beginning of a friendship that was to endure for nearly forty-five years.[9]

By early June a sadly disillusioned Brailsford was back in England. 'Impotent rage against the powers and disappointment with the Greeks —these are my emotions at present', he wrote to Murray in a letter of apology for his secret departure.[10] Seven weeks in Greece had shattered his ideals, leaving a permanent distaste for the excesses of patriotism and the brutalities of war. At the same time his capacity for survival under fire had been tested, revealing facets of his character hitherto

---

[7] *The War of Steel and Gold*, pp. 176-7. His revulsion against the carnage of war emerges in other writings as well. See, for example, *Daily Herald*, 17 Dec. 1919, in which he recalls, '. . . as I ran forward, I began to feel that it would be physically impossible for me to stick my bayonet into another man's body. The anticipated sensation of doing it made me feel literally sick.'

[8] *Glasgow Daily Record*, 13 July 1897.

[9] *Listener*, 20 Nov. 1941.

[10] HNB to Gilbert Murray, 12 June 1897, GMP, 124, fols. 9-10. This letter implies that Murray was unaware of Brailsford's decision to join the Legion. But Murray later claimed to have given him a revolver, the incident to which Shaw refers in Adolphus Cusins' speech in *Major Barbara*. The character of Cusins is modelled on Murray. Either he offered the gun when Brailsford first discussed going out, at least hypothetically, or Murray's recollection was confused, and the gun was, in fact, given on a subsequent occasion. See Murray, *Autobiography*, p. 97.

Comrade-in-Arms 33

unsuspected. In joining the Legion he had exchanged the trappings of an intellectual for those of the man of action, but his friend Scott found him overly conscious of having left his decadence behind him; the protestations of unworthiness appeared disingenuous in one who believed the League honoured by his presence.[11]

While the adventure, so lamentable in its outcome, rehabilitated his self-image, it did nothing to resolve the uncertainties of his last year in Glasgow. His return brought a request from the *Glasgow Daily Record* for articles on the war, but more prestigious papers rejected his reports on the grounds that they were now stale. A week's holiday hiking in the Border country revived his spirits, and by mid-July he had begun writing a novel, tentatively entitled 'The Philhellenes'. He intended to complete his four lectures on ethics as a Clark Fellow by February, the publication of which might yet secure him a lectureship. Alternatively, if the novel were favourably received, it might pave the way to a job on a serious weekly or daily newspaper. He was, in addition, toying with a long-range scheme which he confided only to Murray. He had met an English clergyman about to start a school in Athens for sons of the wealthy which would 'try to put a little manliness into them and also to teach them Greek which nobody in Greece seems to know'. While giving him an opportunity to improve his command of the language, a job at the school might lead to an appointment at the University of Athens as a lecturer:

The life would not be one that I should choose for pleasure. I have too many friends and interests here, and I feel a decided contempt for the average Greek —though I have met splendid exceptions. In any case I shall take no decided step for a year. I am pretty sure that my desire to immolate myself for Hellenism will be dead by that time for I am a sufficiently selfish animal by nature. It is the thought of going alone—to be received as an adventurer—which deters me.[12]

If going at present meant going alone, he dared to believe that he might be able to prevail upon Jane to marry him within the next year. Until the matter was settled, it was impossible for him to resolve his future plans. No sooner had he returned to Glasgow than he resumed his courtship in the hope that compliance with her wish that he join the Legion would cause her to reconsider her rejection. He hastened to visit her at home in Elderslie, but her cool reception made him regret his impetuosity.[13] As the summer wore on he vacillated between a feeling that he could be happy as long as he saw her frequently and a determination to force some breakthrough in their friendship. When he sent

---

[11] Alexander MacCallum Scott, MS 'Book of Characters', MSP.
[12] HNB to Gilbert Murray, 13 July 1897, GMP, 124, fols. 11-15.
[13] HNB to Alexander MacCallum Scott [9 July 1897], MSP.

her the first draft of his book, she responded curtly that his hero was 'a little too shadowy for a novel'. Partly out of pique and partly because he had come to the conclusion that 'I can't work so long as I keep thinking of her', Brailsford decided that the time had come for a showdown. In an emotional interview on the following day she told him that despite her love for him and eagerness to devote herself to his interests, she could not marry him. This much he recounted to Scott, but he refused to explain her reasons, nor is it clear that they were more than a fabrication calculated to appease him. Her imminent departure for another term at Oxford precluded much intimacy, and the relationship lingered on in a state of suspended animation.

The removal of Jane's distracting presence allowed him to finish his manuscript, which Scott and Menzies criticized harshly. The latter felt that Brailsford, evincing little genuine sympathy for the Greeks, used his experience to display his cleverness.[14] Whether or not he adopted any of their suggestions for revisions, the book, renamed *The Broom of the War-God*, a phrase taken from Aristophanes, was impressive for an aspiring author not quite twenty-four. Unlike his friend Buchan, who had recently published his first novel, Brailsford lacked narrative gifts, but he was able to provide a vivid depiction of the war. The drama of the battle scenes and the psychological insight shown in the treatment of his hero's growing self-awareness stand out in contrast to the sketchy background populated by wooden characters. As a piece of fictionalized autobiography it makes for compelling reading, but it is flawed as a novel, the work of a novice who had not yet learned his craft. None the less it does represent an advance over his *Glasgow University Magazine* stories of the previous year. Not only is it a more sustained achievement, faithful to his own experience, but its economy of style showed that Brailsford had rid himself of the literary conceits so obtrusive in his earliest writings. At Murray's suggestion the manuscript was submitted to Heinemann and promptly accepted. The contract stipulated a flat payment of £50 for the copyright in lieu of royalties, a reasonable, if not munificent reward for a first book, and it seems improbable that the sale of the American rights to the firm of D. Appleton brought the author any additional return. Bearing a dedication 'to my friend J. E. M.', *The Broom of the War-God* appeared in January 1898, six months after Brailsford had begun it, as much a tribute to efficient publishing as to the author's industry.

Although the book was a commercial failure, it helped to establish his reputation as a perceptive commentator on Greece and brought him once again to the notice of C. P. Scott. He had by this time been invited to review occasionally for the *Manchester Guardian*, the editor's way of

[14] MacCallum Scott, 'Diary', 2, 13-14 Sept. 1897, MSP.

keeping tabs on likely prospects. Aside from his familiarity with Greek affairs, Brailsford's politics were not uncongenial to the dominant voice of Lancashire Radicalism, and his Fabian affiliations implied less a commitment to socialism than an identification with the progressive spirit that the *Guardian* tried to embody. When Scott decided in January 1898 to send a special correspondent to investigate the turmoil in Crete, he selected Brailsford, who agreed to leave for the Mediterranean at once and to place himself at the *Guardian's* disposal for a year. As long as he could return before the beginning of 1899, there would still be time in which to fulfil his university obligations.[15]

A European naval blockade and occupation of Crete had failed to relieve unrest that had precipitated the Thirty Days' War. While rejecting the insurgents' demand for union with Greece, the Powers proposed autonomy for the island, but the Sultan held out for an Ottoman governor, against the express desire of the Christian majority and the better judgement of the European authorities. Until a solution could be devised, executive control was vested in an international council of admirals. Most of the island remained in Turkish or insurgent hands, but Italian troops protected Canea and a small British garrison under Colonel Sir Herbert Chermside held the port of Candia, where some fifty thousand Muslim refugees congregated. The virtual partition of the island into armed sectarian camps halted commerce and left much of the population on the verge of starvation.

Brailsford's attitude towards Cretan affairs could hardly be regarded as impartial, and his three-month stay confirmed his prejudices. His Graecophil sympathies predisposed him to favour the insurgents, suffering under the Sultan's yoke, but he reserved his wrath for the European Powers, always ready to sacrifice defenceless people to the interests of the dominant power. His fourteen articles, published from March to May 1898, not only treated his readers to a harrowing account of conditions in Cretan villages, but exposed the failings of the British authorities. As a foreign journalist he enjoyed relatively unrestricted travel and was able to interview priests and village headmen, as well as European officers and consular officials. In the company of a Cretan servant he wandered from village to village on horseback, equipped with a pocket phrase-book to convert his classical Greek into the modern idiom and subsisting on a diet of bread, olives, and cheese. His arrival in a village usually resulted in a meeting at the house of the headman, attended by all the male inhabitants. He listened to their pitiful tales of Turkish snipers, of starvation, of their regrets that the idolized Gladstone was no longer in office.[16] These gatherings underscored the tenacity of

---

[15] HNB to C. P. Scott, 24 Jan. 1898, MGC.
[16] *New Leader*, 24 Dec. 1926; *Manchester Guardian*, 6 Apr. 1898.

the desire for union with Greece. Once when he tried to explain the benefits of automony to a peasant by stressing the fact that the Cretans would not thereby become subject to Greek taxation, the old man pondered the issue and replied, 'We'll find some way of sending our taxes to Athens secretly!'[17]

The graphic descriptions supplied by the *Guardian*'s special correspondent prompted humanitarian action in England. Scott was able to send Brailsford £100 from Manchester for the distribution of barley, and the Grosvenor House Committee appointed him as their agent to distribute sulphur for vineyards destroyed by disease. Left to his own devices, he decided that it would be most effective to provide relief to victims in kind. He hoped to be able to buy grain at wholesale prices from a British firm in Smyrna, to obtain army and navy transport, and to persuade the authorities to remit all duties.[18] Obtaining money, however, proved the least of his worries. With no staff to assist him, Brailsford was obliged to spend nights standing guard at the Candia quay while his cargo was unloaded, since the natives were reluctant to venture out of town for fear of being shot. To make matters worse, the Ottoman officials tried to obstruct his mission, even though it could in no way be deemed political. When they balked at exempting the imported grain from customs duties, he appealed to the Admirals at Canea and won a favourable decision. Chermside, fearing adverse Muslim reaction, denied permission to convey the barley overland across the Turkish cordon, but the navy came to his rescue. His attempt to mitigate distress was only a token gesture, but it earned the gratitude of the Christian community for helping to stave off starvation.

In certain respects Brailsford's dual function hindered his efforts. As the target of repeated criticism in the *Manchester Guardian*, Chermside was disinclined to circumvent obstacles in order to expedite relief arrangements. From conversations with Sir Alfred Biliotti, the British Consul, Brailsford learned that 'the other powers, or at least Austria & Germany, & probably also France and Russia, have constantly worked against England and have done all they could to make our occupation of Candia a failure'.[19] Indeed he reiterated this information in his articles, but acknowledging the restraints under which Chermside operated did not, in Brailsford's view, exonerate him. A determined stand would in all likelihood have overcome the Admirals' ban on the use of British troops along the cordon. Instead a policy of concession to Muslim opinion was pursued, and, despite their complicity in raids, Turkish soldiers had been permitted to extend their cordon to take in

---

17 *North American Review*, No. 181 (Aug. 1905), p. 251.
18 HNB to C. P. Scott, 14 Mar. 1898, MGC.
19 HNB to C. P. Scott, 25 Mar. 1898, MGC.

more territory.[20] Since it would have been a breach of confidence to reveal much of what he learned in his articles, he transmitted sensitive information in letters to Scott, urging the editor to make use of it in leaders or parliamentary questions without disclosing his source.[21]

By mid-May Brailsford's mission in Crete had been accomplished, and Scott agreed to send him to Thessaly to report on conditions since the fighting of the previous year. Somewhat to his surprise, he discovered that the Turks had behaved creditably during their recent occupation. 'Any indignation I have felt,' he told Lady Mary Murray,

> has been against the Greeks. After travelling about & investigating lie after lie to find them all absolutely baseless, I have ceased to wonder at the general reputation of the Greeks among Europeans of the Levant. Cowardice, cringing & lying are bad—but the worst feature of all in Thessaly is the way in which every man of influence, wealth or education has deserted his post.

It was ironic that his tour should have been interrupted by a legal entanglement with the Turkish authorities. In Pharsala he was arrested and treated like a criminal without any explanation given. Despite a swift release, he was subsequently forbidden to visit villages in the interior. The arrest was prompted by the error of an over-zealous petty official acting on information from soldiers in the area who had recognized Brailsford as a former legionnaire. It was not his past activity that led to the restrictions on his travel, but the fact that Europeans were not permitted to wander freely without an escort, and the Turks did not feel disposed to supply one to a journalist who had fought against them and who was regarded as a hostile observer. With his movements circumscribed, it seemed futile to remain in Thessaly. From Athens he bagan a protracted journey home by way of Constantinople, Sofia, Belgrade, Budapest, and Vienna. 'It might be interesting,' he wrote, full of trepidation, from the Dardanelles,

> but so far I only find it dismal. I am quite alone & have no introductions. It is only a feeling that I should regret a lost opportunity which induces me to linger at all on my way home. I am hungry for books & music & civilisation again, & for four months I have not had a talk that deserves the name.[22]

Back in Glasgow, his future still uncertain, Brailsford busied himself with the report to the Grosvenor House Committee, as much an indictment of Chermside and his colleagues as an appeal for additional aid. He attributed distress in Crete mainly to the European blockade and to the refusal of the Admirals to reopen communications between Candia and the hinterland. In addition, he blamed the British commander for

---

[20] *Manchester Guardian*, 25 Mar., 19 and 20 Apr. 1898.
[21] HNB to C. P. Scott, 25 Mar. 1898, MGC.
[22] HNB to Lady Mary Murray, 23 May 1898, GMP, 535, fols. 7-12.

refusing to man the cordon with his own troops and for failing to fix a price at which the grain and sulphur should be sold. In order to refute the allegations, the Foreign Office adopted the unusual expedient of issuing a blue book that was more concerned with discrediting Brailsford than with justifying its own policies.[23] The timing of the blue book undercut its impact: it appeared two weeks after a Muslim uprising in Candia exploded the myth of the success of British policy. His warnings vindicated, Brailsford declared that 'a heavy responsibility rests on the English officials who neglected in the sphere allotted to them to prepare the way for the autonomy long since promised by Europe'.[24] When they ultimately realized that Ottoman rule was doomed, the Muslim refugees, goaded by Turkish connivance and British vacillation, rose in desperation against a scheme which offered no material guarantees to reassure them.

Until the Candia uprising he had been spending a 'lazy and unsatisfactory summer', working in desultory fashion on his lectures and the outline of a new novel and 'doing my duty by my family'.[25] Although an occasional article of his found its way into the *Manchester Guardian*, the *Glasgow Herald*, and the *Scotsman*, he was having difficulty in getting published. Scott could promise no permanent employment, and he had begun to look elsewhere, hoping to establish some connection with a paper in need of a foreign correspondent. The news from Crete unleashed a bout of frenetic activity. *The Times* and the *Glasgow Herald* carried his analyses of the outbreak on the same day, and he was busy with other articles in which he tried to interest several London papers. With his experience of Crete, he believed that he had topical stories to sell, but the demand for his articles did not materialize. On the other hand, the controversy over the blue book, following the crisis in Candia, convinced the editor of the *Guardian* that it might be worthwhile to send Brailsford back to Crete, and in late September he was summoned to Manchester to receive instructions.

This time he was not to travel alone. Acting on a sudden impulse, Jane finally accepted his proposal, and they were married in a civil ceremony in Glasgow on 29 September, a day before they left for Crete. Her motives for this sudden reversal after rebuffing him for nearly two years are not wholly explicable. Her father had died in July —Mrs Malloch had been dead for many years—and the Elderslie house was sold, leaving her essentially homeless. Her uncertain health was a factor in, if not an excuse for, her decision not to return to Somerville, but, lacking independent means, it was necessary at the

[23] See *Manchester Guardian*, 23 Sept. 1898.
[24] Letter to Editor, *The Times*, 28 Sept. 1898.
[25] HNB to Alexander MacCallum Scott, 10 Sept. 1898, MSP.

age of twenty-four to find some means of support. Now that he was gaining recognition as a foreign correspondent, Brailsford must have appeared a more enticing prospect than he had been as an unemployed philosophy lecturer, especially to one so eager to shake the dust of Glasgow from her feet. Ever since her undergraduate interest in the classical world, she had longed for the chance to visit Greece and must have felt a certain vicarious exultation in his military adventures, knowing that he had enlisted to please her. It may be that her advances to Murray had been embarrassingly rejected although one cannot determine whether a professor so attractive to his women students took the infatuation of one of them seriously. In any event he was not informed of the marriage until the ceremony had taken place.[26] Perhaps she deceived herself, as she certainly deceived her husband, into believing that she loved—or would in due course come to love—him. Whatever her reasons, it was a decision that would, once the novelty wore off, bring them both incalculable misery until her death nearly forty years later.

By the time they landed at Suda on 10 October, the tension in Crete had subsided somewhat. Although the Sultan had at last agreed to evacuate the island so that an autonomous regime under Prince George of Greece could be established, there were few signs of the impending change. Despite a formidable array of British naval hardware in Candia harbour, Brailsford noted that 'the troops who vied with the mob in every atrocity are now mounting guard over the ruins of their own making, and the very men who murdered our Vice-Consul are standing solemnly with fixed bayonets at the doors of his surviving colleagues.' While French and Italian forces patrolled the strategic positions around Canea, in Candia, where English soldiers were confined to their quarters, the mechanism of Ottoman misrule went on unchecked.[27]

In the weeks before Prince George's arrival there was little news to report, and Brailsford's dispatches tended either to recapitulate recent events or to forecast the future. By mid-December it was no longer necessary to telegraph articles to Manchester so frequently, and there was ample leisure for touring the remains of ancient civilizations, symbols of a glorious past that stood in contrast to the present degradation. Brailsford spent much of his time interviewing local dignitaries, who plied him with information, but he was also able, for example, to talk to Venizelos, then a prisoner in Canea, but later the Greek Premier. It was an untaxing way to begin married life:

We drink every day 'Vin des Balkans' at lunch and dinner, we dine with the Russian admiral whenever we get a chance, and as a last resort we sit on our

---

[26] HNB to Gilbert Murray, 1 Oct. 1898, GMP, 124, fol. 22.
[27] *Manchester Guardian*, 26 Oct. 1898.

balcony. . . . We are making our first essay in house-keeping under quaint conditions—a little thin house of five rooms—two storeys—very commodious for rats & mice—no carpets no fires, the minimum of chairs & tables, but what compensates for everything a view from all our many windows which would busy a landscape painter for a year. There are snow capped mountains from one window, a valley clad with olive groves from a second, the distant town with Venetian ramparts & Turkish minarets from a third, & then above all the sea, sometimes like glass & sky blue, sometimes storm-tossed, white & green—throw in an island, five distinct ranges of hills, two old castles, & still it is short of our view.[28]

The high point of their visit was the festivities surrounding the landing of Prince George on 21 December, when Christian peasants surged into Canea to welcome their hero and to surrender their guns. Men embraced and exchanged the greeting 'Christ is risen'. But it was, Brailsford observed ominously, a wholly Christian demonstration, not a Muslim daring to expose himself in the streets. He persuaded a French sergeant to permit him to enter the sealed-off Muslim quarter, with its tightly-shuttered houses, and listened in a café to the complaints of persecution and the plans for emigration. The shoe was now on the other foot: he realized that the task of pacifying Crete would involve not merely the imposition of a constitution, but also the reconciliation of the anti-Greek minority, for whom the arrival of Prince George heralded disaster.[29]

While Brailsford immersed himself in Cretan politics, C. P. Scott, impressed by the incisive reports transmitted by his new discovery, was once again pondering his claims to a permanent berth in the Manchester office. He broached the subject to the *Guardian*'s proprietor, J. E. Taylor, who, dismayed by Brailsford's brashness, suggested instead that he be retained only for special foreign assignments. Taylor had also urged his editor to appoint a Paris correspondent, and when reports of an imminent *coup d'état* by Déroulède reached England in January, Brailsford was ordered to leave Crete at once for Paris. This was hardly what Taylor had in mind: he believed that the job required someone with broader professional experience, and once Brailsford's outspoken pronouncements on the Dreyfus case began to appear at the end of the month, he protested the 'want of restraint & judicial sobriety which is very undesirable in a correspt. stationed in a foreign capital'.[30] Judicial sobriety was a virtue more appealing to Taylor than to Scott, but as long as the old man retained control of the paper, attention had to be paid to his wishes, and Brailsford's tenure in Paris turned out to be brief. The passionate Dreyfusard sympathies of those he met in Paris,

[28] HNB to Alexander MacCallum Scott, 16 Dec. 1898, MSP.
[29] *Manchester Guardian*, 2 Jan. 1899.
[30] J. E. Taylor to C. P. Scott, 7 Feb. 1899, MGC.

most notably Jean Jaurès, the Socialist leader and editor of *L'Humanité*, reinforced his own inclinations, and he tended, as he had in Crete, to leaven his reports with personal opinion.

Nor did the Dreyfus affair lend itself to dispassionate analysis, least of all in the vitriolic atmosphere of Paris in 1899. Partisan in tone, Brailsford's commentaries were in fact first-rate journalism, his emotional involvement giving a sense of urgency to his observations. His accounts of meetings and street demonstrations capture the turbulence of the moment, and his dissection of the scurrilous allegations that erupted daily in the right-wing, anti-Semitic press revealed not merely a mastery of the facts of the case, but also the capacity for sardonic invective.[31] Naturally his contacts were all in the Revisionist camp, among men like Jaurès, Clemenceau, Yves Guyot, and Joseph Reinach, who were seeking to reverse the conviction. Like them, he never doubted that the attack on Dreyfus and the subsequent attempts to stifle further investigation represented a conspiracy against the Republic by the forces of reaction. For Brailsford, it was a struggle between the forces of light and the forces of darkness. Little wonder that he, the champion of liberty in Greece, perceived the Dreyfusard cause in terms that transcended French politics.

Much as he would have preferred to remain in Paris denouncing injustice, Brailsford was recalled to Manchester at the end of February.

I should rather like to work permanently abroad [he told Murray] but the *Guardian* which is the only paper whose foreign policy I could adopt doesn't seem to want foreign work. I don't think I could again think of the *Daily News* or the *Chronicle* after Fashoda. I wish Scott would understand that he must have a Paris office if he means to work seriously for an understanding between France & England.[32]

It was not Scott's obtuseness, but Taylor's misgivings that cost him the Paris job. That the editor was reluctant to lose so promising a journalist was clear when he was appointed as a temporary replacement for one of the *Guardian*'s rising stars, J. B. Atkins, who had gone to London to take charge of the parliamentary sketch. Brailsford's first taste of leader-writing, supplemented by an ample diet of book reviewing, enabled him to prove his versatility, but unfortunately the editor held out little hope that the engagement would be extended should Atkins return in the autumn as scheduled. Even if it were to last only for a few months, he could not refuse steady employment on the one newspaper he truly admired. With the deadline for fulfilling the terms of his fellowship having expired, he realized what he had not admitted to himself before, that he would never complete his projected lectures, nor resume an

---

[31] See *Manchester Guardian*, 4 and 10 Feb. 1899.
[32] HNB to Gilbert Murray, 26 Feb. 1899, GMP, 124, fols. 24-5.

academic career. He had, whether deliberately or not, closed the door to philosophy; henceforth he must make his way in journalism.

Although he warned Brailsford in August that it might be prudent to look for another job, Scott was beginning to devise other strategems to retain him. A month before, J. A. Hobson had gone out to report on the deteriorating situation in South Africa, and it seemed likely that a second correspondent might be needed. When he learned whom the editor had in mind, Taylor tried to scotch the proposal:

> I am also somewhat influenced by the feeling that Brailsford is not so good a man as we ought to have. I do not think him judicious or sufficiently calm & even minded. I was not altogether satisfied with him in Crete and since, whether in Paris or in dealing with the 'Affaire', I have not much liked his work. Altogether, he is not a man whom I feel a strong wish to retain. I am sorry that I do not quite concur with you in this matter.[33]

When Atkins was sent to South Africa, Brailsford was offered the chance to replace him for a few weeks as lobby correspondent at Westminster, not the most appropriate position for someone of his temperament and interests. Frustrated by halting progress on the *Guardian*, he concluded that the time had come to try his luck elsewhere. He would attempt, as he had once put it to Murray, 'to rough it' in London. An opening on the *Morning Leader*, whose pro-Boer inclinations appealed to him, was sufficient inducement to persuade him to reject Scott's offer. Although his relationship with the *Guardian* was interrupted, rather than severed, the move meant a turning away from his Northern background. For the next fifty years London would be his home and his professional base. Just as Manchester had symbolized a break with the world of Glasgow Hegelianism, so Fleet Street and the contacts it brought marked a vital turning point. Removed from the citadel of Liberal Nonconformity, Brailsford's political views took a turn leftwards, becoming at once more cosmopolitan and socialist. He was always more advanced in his outlook than the Liberal papers for which he wrote in the years before the First World War, a source of friction with the editors who needed to placate their proprietors. Increasingly sensitive to the plight of oppressed peoples, he used his pen to espouse the cause of national liberation, exempting no government, and certainly not his own, from attack when it infringed upon the political rights of the masses. The period of uncertainty was over: he had found the role for which he was suited and an audience willing to listen.

[33] J. E. Taylor to C. P. Scott, 13 Sept. 1899, MGC.

IV

The Streets of Adventure (1899-1909)

Fleet Street meant steady employment and a mass audience for Brailsford, but at the price of anonymity. Until 1917, when he undertook a weekly column in the *Herald*, his articles were usually unsigned, and his name was unfamiliar to most readers. While this was not unusual at a time when by-lines and even initials rarely appeared in the press, it does make it difficult to identify many of his pre-war contributions, much less to assess their impact. Instead of following the conventional route as a reporter, he built his career in London as a leader-writer, with frequent interruptions for extended periods abroad as a special correspondent. Even when called upon to supply the lion's share of leaders—especially on foreign affairs—he never had exclusive editorial responsibility. While leader-writing offered more scope for personal viewpoint than general reporting did, no journalist could afford to become too independent of his employers, as Brailsford learned to his dismay during his stint on the *Daily News*. His own decided political stand dictated his appointments, since only a newspaper of progressive outlook would be disposed to hire him.

His first venture as a leader-writer was with the *Morning Leader*, a halfpenny daily best known for its cricket reporting. It was, he informed Murray, 'cheap, popular & sometimes vulgar, but it is staunch & loyal, has a good circulation & is preparing to reform itself into as good a paper as one can expect for ½d. As there is no other London paper but the "Westminster" [Gazette] for which I could write just now, I am very glad to be on the *Leader*'s staff.'[1] What suddenly restricted the field was the advent of the South African war, dividing the Liberal press as it had opinion in the country. At the end of 1899 Massingham was dislodged from the editorship of the *Daily Chronicle* after refusing to curb his criticism of Milner's tactics towards the Boers, a reflection of the new jingoist contagion to which few newspapers were immune. Although the *Manchester Guardian* remained steadfast in opposing official policy, the *Leader* was temporarily the only London morning paper with pro-Boer sympathies. Brailsford's leaders, outspoken though they were, could scarcely fill the gap left by the defection of the most prestigious metropolitan Radical organ, which

---

[1] HNB to Gilbert Murray, 11 Jan. 1900, GMP, 124, fols. 26-7.

had boasted not merely Massingham, but such respected journalists as Nevinson, Harold Spender, and Vaughan Nash.

His articles sought to refute the charge that the Boers had provoked war by precipitate arming. Possessing few weapons at the time of Jameson's Raid, they had armed against those conspiring to undermine their independence, not in order to commit aggression against the imperial authority.[2] While deploring the Boer treatment of natives, he felt that the British record of tolerating African slavery gave little reassurance that the black population would benefit by the substitution of British for Boer rule. The fault lay in the 'policy of adventure and provocation' perpetrated by Joseph Chamberlain and the jingoist press, rather than in the self-protective measures adopted by the beleaguered Dutch farmers.[3]

Outnumbered and denounced, opponents of the war banded together in a futile attempt to controvert bellicose propaganda. In January 1900 the South Africa Conciliation Committee was established with the avowed aim of preparing the ground for a just settlement. Brailsford was one of its founders, along with several future colleagues, such as Massingham and J. L. Hammond. Courting unpopularity in order to enlighten the public, they issued a series of leaflets challenging the accepted version of Boer culpability and urging a settlement which would reconcile British and Dutch elements. A month later an even more distinctly partisan group launched the League of Liberals against Aggression and Militarism. Overlapping in membership with the SACC, it sought not merely to promote peace, but to rally the Gladstonian wing of the party against the Rosebery faction.[4]

These activities linked Brailsford more closely to C. P. Scott, one of the League's architects, but also to a coterie of Radical politicians and journalists. The alliances forged during the pro-Boer agitation, Peter Clarke has observed, 'stuck fast, and there was a unique emotional charge behind the feeling of solidarity on this issue.'[5] Brailsford began to write intermittently for the *Speaker*, which, under Hammond's editorship, was acquiring a reputation as a serious Radical weekly, and to mingle socially with pro-Boer politicians, such as Leonard Courtney. An entry in Kate Courtney's diary describes a dinner party which the Brailsfords, Emily Hobhouse, and F. W. Hirst attended:

... the Brailsfords (of the *Morning Leader*)—they for the first time—a non-meat eating couple—he a sturdy, independent-seeming man with a good head &

[2] *Morning Leader*, 30 Dec. 1899. Published as leaflet in Jan. 1900.
[3] *Morning Leader*, 11 Jan. 1900.
[4] Stephen Koss, ed., *The Pro-Boers* (Chicago, 1973), pp. 81-3, 99-104; P. F. Clarke, *Lancashire and the New Liberalism* (Cambridge, 1971), p. 181.
[5] P. F. Clarke, 'The Progressive Movement in England', *Transactions of the Royal Historical Society*, 5th Series, Vol. 24 (1974), p. 166.

judgement. I should say rather moderate in his opinions. We had a good deal of talk. . . .⁶

Brailsford's vegetarianism, so typical of humanitarians in his generation, was of recent origin, although Murray's example cannot be discounted. Some months before the evening at the Courtneys he had become so disgusted at the spectacle of a drunken man dragging a bloody rabbit through a train that he vowed to give up eating meat in the future. Several years later, in a controversy with G. K. Chesterton in the *Daily News*, he defended the vegetarian practice not on moral or religious grounds, but simply because he could not endure the suffering of animals. His extraordinary fondness for animals was a lifelong trait, and several essays of this period allude to friendships with cats. Invariably reserved in human relations, the prospect of rejection making him wary of intimacy, Brailsford found it easier to shower affection on animals, knowing that they would neither disappoint nor betray. His attitude towards animals, reflected also in pleas on behalf of pit ponies and against blood sports, was one facet of a revulsion against suffering that figured consistently in his writing. His early reports on Crete and Macedonia were more than mere eyewitness accounts: they revealed a conscience brimming with sympathy for the degradation of subject peoples. The image of himself as something of an outcast, a sense heightened by the later acrimony of his marriage, made him identify with the oppressed. While it would be a distortion to suggest that Brailsford identified tyranny in the world with that of his father, certainly his own experience of lonely rebellion against unjust authority made him sympathize with similar struggles. It was this affinity for the plight of small nations that linked his pro-Boer sentiments to his concern for Balkan peoples.

A year after the move to London Scott was once again promoting his candidacy as the *Guardian*'s parliamentary correspondent, but Taylor continued to veto the appointment. Brailsford moved soon after to the *Echo*, a progressive halfpenny London evening paper then undergoing reorganization. To prevent its passing into the hands of the Roseberyites, Lloyd George and Hirst induced Frederick Pethick-Lawrence to acquire control and to rehabilitate it as an anti-imperialist journal advocating free trade, conciliation in foreign affairs, and social reform. Hammond, initially its principal leader-writer, found that editorial duties on the *Speaker* did not leave enough time for additional responsibilities, so Brailsford was hired instead in 1902.⁷ When Percy Alden resigned as

---

⁶ Kate Courtney's diary, 30 July 1901, Courtney Papers, Vol. 30.
⁷ Vera Brittain, *Pethick-Lawrence* (London, 1963), p. 37; F. W. Pethick-Lawrence, *Fate Has Been Kind* (London, 1943), pp. 57-8.

Echo editor, Pethick-Lawrence took charge himself, arriving, as he later recorded, at the office every morning at seven o'clock to wait

> for the arrival of Brailsford to settle the leading articles for the day's issue. He generally arrived a little late and somewhat hot and bothered, having bicycled from his home. . . . But when once the subjects had been agreed upon, he was a consummate master of his craft. Sharpening his pencil with a small razor, which he kept unsheathed in his waistcoat pocket, he proceeded to write, with incredible rapidity, faultless English and inexorable logic. In three-quarters of an hour he could write both the main leader of some 700 words and a 'short' of 250 words more. In another half-hour he had corrected the proofs and was on his way home again.[8]

Until advancing years made the journey too taxing Brailsford, an avid cyclist, would brave the traffic and pedal down to newspaper offices from Brunswick Square and later from Hampstead, to the consternation of the less adventurous. 'There is nothing like a cycle ride in a crowded London street,' he once asserted, 'for "simplifying" a mind that has knotted itself into tangles. As you discard your interests, jettison your principles, and smooth out the tangle of your cares, a great peace steals over your soul.'[9] Without ascribing too much credit to the daily ride, it is evident that his growing facility for effortless prose, his capacity for concise summaries of complex issues, with appropriate sarcasm or invective, admirably suited him to composing leaders. The practice of writing to a specific length, once mastered, made revision unnecessary, and his breadth of knowledge enabled him to handle any topic of current interest. Little wonder that editors were eager to retain his talents, even though his inflexibility and volatile temper occasionally proved exasperating.

His association with the *Echo*, interrupted by two trips to Macedonia in 1903-4, was a happy one, lasting until Pethick-Lawrence halted publication in the summer of 1905. The two men shared a common political outlook, and the leader columns in these years took a strong line against the introduction of Chinese labour in South Africa and in favour of the decision by the Labour Representation Committee to compel their candidates to remain independent of other parties. Under Brailsford's influence, the *Echo* alerted its readers to nationalist struggles in Macedonia, in Egypt, and, not least, in Ireland. His pamphlet excoriating British policy in Ireland was published in February 1903 under the aegis of the paper, although the views it expressed were even more extreme than those held by anti-imperialist Liberals like Courtney.[10]

---

[8] Pethick-Lawrence, *Fate*, p. 61.
[9] *Daily News*, 30 Apr. 1907. Reprinted in *Adventures in Prose*, pp. 226-7.
[10] Leonard Courtney to HNB, 16 Feb. 1903, Courtney Papers, Vol. 19, fol. 54.

According to Brailsford, the ascendancy in Ireland rested upon a regime of conquest and class oppression that violated the spirit of English law. Instead of protecting the majority of the people, the Constabulary, military in organization and political in function, operated as an agency of repression. In addition to employing a military police, the British administration was guilty of tampering with justice by packing juries with Protestants and subjecting magistrates to the authority of Dublin Castle. Such methods were 'a negation of every principle and tradition of our Constitution'. Only the prompt concession of self-government could rectify historic wrongs and instil among the discontented a sense of loyalty to the Empire.[11]

If his attitude toward Ireland derived more from empathy than experience, his observations of the Balkans enabled him to speak about its problems with an increasingly authoritative voice. Between 1897 and 1913 he visited the region six times, spending more than sixteen months as a correspondent, a relief agent, and, finally, as a member of an international investigatory commission. As with other publicists of the period, he had a particular focus of interest, Macedonia, which became the touchstone of his interpretation of foreign affairs. He saw it as more than a minor, if intractable, trouble spot bedevilling international diplomacy: it was an explosive tinder-box whose local conflicts threatened to engulf the great powers. Unlike other outposts of the Ottoman Empire, Macedonia defied precise geographic or ethnic definition. Politically constituted into three Turkish *vilayets*—or provinces—of Salonica, Monastir, and Kossovo, it was an enclave in the heart of the Balkan peninsula surrounded by Greece, Serbia, and Bulgaria, each with designs on its territory. Terrorized by aggressive neighbours, most Macedonians recognized no loyalties beyond their villages. In 1893 the Internal Macedonian Revolutionary Organization (IMRO) was created under Bulgarian patronage to foment an uprising against the Turks. With the tacit encouragement of the Turkish authorities, Greece and Serbia retaliated with their own clandestine organizations and brands of militant cultural nationalism.

When Scott suggested in April 1903 that Brailsford go to Macedonia to investigate conditions, he jumped at the opportunity. The arrangements stipulated that he was to be paid £10 a week, the fee rising to £15 in the event of war.[12] Pethick-Lawrence, willing to hold his job open for him, employed MacCullum Scott and Ramsay MacDonald for *Echo* leaders during his absence. After soliciting introductions in the Balkans from Murray and others, the Brailsfords set off by train for the East.

[11] *Some Irish Problems*, p. 13.
[12] *Manchester Guardian* Contributor's Ledger, Vol. 3; HNB to C. P. Scott, 23 Apr. 1903, Editor's file (courtesy of David Ayerst).

Their travelling companion was the *Morning Post* correspondent, H. H. Munro, who became better known as the humourous writer Saki.[13]

As a champion of national self-determination, Brailsford arrived in Macedonia sympathetic to the Bulgarian insurgents, who, by 1903, had consolidated their hold throughout the province, but his enthusiastic reports were tempered by strong recriminations against the use of terrorism.[14] Invariably sceptical about the efficacy of reform under Ottoman rule, he was none the less impressed by his interview with Hilmi Pasha, the disarming Inspector-General. Instead of trusting Hilmi's optimistic forecast, Brailsford, determined to assess the situation for himself, spent the next two months evading restrictions imposed on travel by foreigners. From European consuls in Uskub he learned something of the economic exploitation, that tyranny of Turkish official and Muslim landlord which compelled a peasant to pay out £15 in taxes, rent, and protection money for every £10 he was allowed to retain. Denied permission to visit the hinterland, he contrived a secret meeting in Monastir with the headman of a pro-Bulgarian village which had been the victim of successive massacres by the Turks. Although the village had its own Christian watchmen, as Hilmi's schemes had evisaged, they were not allowed to carry guns and were no match for the well-armed *bashi-bazouks*.[15] Brailsford, managing to elude the spies who stalked his movements, spent several days in Macedonian and Albanian villages. In one the school had been closed and most of the men imprisoned for Bulgarian sympathies; in another the majority of the male inhabitants was forced to work on the roads in remote districts for several weeks because they were unable to pay their taxes. These observations confirmed his impression that Hilmi Pasha's reforms were a travesty, at least outside the immediate confines of Uskub. Even though he found the brutality of the insurgents repugnant, he had begun to comprehend 'the desperation of a rebel in this accursed country who prefers to provoke a swift massacre in the hope of putting an end to the slow process of bleeding to death'.[16]

Brailsford's return to London in July anticipated IMRO's call for an uprising by only a few weeks. For all his prescience, he was caught off-guard by the suddenness of the outbreak, which he interpreted as an attempt to incite Turkish retaliation in order to provoke European intervention. Once the rising had begun, his sympathies were entirely

[13] HNB to Gilbert Murray [Apr. 1903], GMP, 124, fols. 36-7; Jack Lambert, ed., *The Bodley Head Saki* (London, 1963), p. 29.
[14] *Manchester Guardian*, 8 June 1903. The Bulgarian movement, he wrote, 'is as ruthless, as brutal, as unscrupulous as the Turkish government itself'.
[15] *Manchester Guardian*, 29 May 1903. In fact, corruption was so pervasive by 1903 that many Christians bought weapons from Turkish soldiers.
[16] *Manchester Guardian*, 27 May 1903. Also see *Manchester Guardian*, 8 June 1903.

with the rebels, his earlier strictures against their conduct notwithstanding. An invitation to return at once to the Balkans for the *Guardian* was tempting, but he was inclined to believe that events would not reach a critical point until the following spring. In any event it would have been inconvenient to leave the *Echo* again so soon, and he hesitated to resign from it unless Scott could guarantee him steady employment for a year either abroad or in London. Noting that he could speak German, he offered to undertake a series on the condition of German workers or to look into life in Southern Russia.[17] Nothing came of these projects, and Brailsford busied himself with articles on Macedonia and joined the newly-formed Balkan Committee.

The Macedonian uprising was the occasion for the Committee's founding under the leadership of Noel Buxton and James Bryce. Like other groups inspired by national movements abroad, it drew support chiefly from Liberal politicians, Radical journalists, and a sprinkling of academics and clergymen. Its aim was to bring the pressure of informed opinion to bear in the press and in Parliament in order to influence British policy in the Balkans. A spiritual descendant of the 1876 Bulgarian agitation, the Committee, several of whose members had firsthand knowledge of the region, identified with the plight of Balkan Christians and blamed England for restoring Turkish rule in Macedonia after 1878.[18]

The uprising, ruthlessly repressed by the Turks, left Macedonia in ruins. Within a few months the land the Brailsfords had left on the verge of explosion was 'not so much a conquered province as a desert swept by a human hurricane'.[19] Prompted by reports of widespread devastation, a Macedonian Relief Committee was formed in England under the chairmanship of Bertram Christian to furnish practical assistance. Although the group was distinct from the Balkan Committee, there was inevitably considerable overlap in membership. Because of their familiarity with the region, Brailsford and his wife were appointed as relief agents in the province of Monastir and arrived there in mid-October to begin a five-month stint. Intending to combine relief and investigatory work with journalism, he promptly discovered that unless he agreed not to send reports to newspapers, his movements in Macedonia would be hampered. Even so he found himself lumbered with a Turkish cavalry escort, ostensibly to protect his life, but in reality to keep him out of mischief. Travelling among the smouldering villages and assessing their needs, he learned a good deal about daily

[17] HNB to C. P. Scott, 11 Aug. 1903, Editor's file (courtesy of David Ayerst).
[18] See L. S. Stavrianos, 'The Balkan Committee', *Queen's Quarterly*, XLVIII, No. 3 (Autumn, 1941), pp. 258-67; Mosa Anderson, *Noel Buxton* (London, 1952), pp. 33-7.
[19] *Macedonia*, p. 36.

life. The Brailsfords were expected to distribute the relief funds collected in England and to provide food and medical care, supplementing local provisions and organizing aid where none existed. They employed a young Albanian to carry large sums of money over dangerous roads, an ex-brigand who had learned the terrain when riding with a notorious outlaw known as the Falcon.

During their early days in Salonica and Monastir they enjoyed the companionship of Nevinson, who had been sent by the Balkan Committee to corroborate reports of distress, and with whom their lives were to become increasingly entwined in friendship and in a curious professional—as well as romantic—rivalry. They travelled together to Brif, a village where only 14 out of 240 houses remained standing. Brailsford continued on to inspect Drin valley hamlets, while Jane set up a hospital in a ramshackle house in Ochrida, a lakeside village surrounded by mountains.[20] Its isolation had not protected it from Turkish depradation, and by the time the Brailsfords arrived, it had become 'a place of ruins peopled by orphans'.[21] While Jane, almost single-handedly, managed the hospital for wounded local inhabitants, he interviewed headmen in the vicinity and listened to complaints from victims.

In March 1904 Jane contracted typhus, and for twelve days her life was in danger. Forced to terminate their work, the Brailsfords returned to London in early April. They resumed their former life: Brailsford rejoined the *Echo* and published articles on Macedonia in the *Speaker*, the *Fortnightly Review*, and the *Independent Review*. Critical of the ineffectual Mürzsteg reforms, which failed either to give European officials executive authority or to remedy the incompetence of the Turkish bureaucracy, he continued to plead for effective European intervention as the only way to relieve tensions.[22] Protests in periodicals seemed futile, and Brailsford decided to undertake a comprehensive study which would explore the historical and social context and spent much of that summer at the British Museum gathering material.

I am at present [he wrote to Murray] working at a *magnum opus* on Macedonia & Albania which is a sufficiently amusing employment. After five years of journalism the joy of telling the reckless, naughty truth is beyond all measuring. Besides I have no other way of revenging myself on the conspirators who come about me at all hours & in all languages. Today I met a Serb & our house is the public address of the Russian revolutionary organization! The historical part of my book is giving me a good deal of trouble for I do not

---

[20] ND, 30 Oct., 6-8 Nov. 1903; H. W. Nevinson, *Changes and Chances* (London, 1923), p. 149; Nevinson, *More Changes, More Chances*, pp. 9-15.

[21] *Macedonia*, p. 79.

[22] *Independent Review*, III, No. 11 (Aug. 1904), pp. 321-36; *Speaker*, 16 Apr. 1904. Also see Letter to Editor, *The Times*, 9 Mar. 1905.

The Streets of Adventure

even know whom to read. . . . I hope to have the book ready in a month or two.[23]

What seems remarkable is not his underestimation of the time needed to finish the manuscript—it was completed at the end of 1905—but that he managed to find any time at all for it amid the difficulties of the ensuing-months. The Brailsfords were about to move from their Brunswick Square flat, which had become too noisy, to a house in Well Walk, Hampstead. He was again negotiating with the *Manchester Guardian* and was soon to find himself facing conspiracy charges.

In February 1905 Scott offered him a permanent position as leader-writer in Manchester, with the likelihood of occasional foreign assignments. The suggested salary was £500 a year in Manchester and twice that rate for work abroad. Brailsford had written occasional leaders for the *Guardian* in 1903 and again more frequently early in 1905, and its editor had lost none of his admiration for his talents.[24] It was the opportunity for which he had longed ever since Glasgow, but it had come too late. Jane was unwilling to leave London for the provinces, and the counter-proposal of a regular attachment to the *Guardian*'s London office did not appeal to Scott, who preferred to keep an eye on his discoveries.[25] The courtship continued: would Brailsford consider six months a year in Manchester? Brailsford agreed to four months— they compromised at five—if Scott could guarantee him a £7 a week retaining fee on top of his salary for the period in Manchester.[26] Even though he would not leave London permanently, he was willing to spend nearly half the year in Manchester and to give up virtually all his present engagements. The paper would be obligated for £100 retaining fee, plus £250 for five months of regular employment a year, while Brailsford would place himself at the *Guardian*'s disposal for war correspondence and special assignments. At a projected salary of £350 the paper would secure 'an exceptionally good man at a very reasonable price'.[27] Within a week, however, Scott was voicing concern that Brailsford's 'trouble may not prove so serious' that it would 'supply an adequate reason for breaking off our engagement'.[28]

The 'trouble' to which Scott alluded was a summons to appear before a magistrate on 23 May, but its roots lay deeper in the past. Ever since he had begun working in London, Brailsford's sympathy for victims of Tsarist tyranny had involved him with exiled Russian revolutionaries.

[23] HNB to Gilbert Murray [Aug. 1904], GMP, 124, fols. 42-3.
[24] C. P. Scott to HNB, 4 Feb. 1905, MGC.
[25] HNB to C. P. Scott, 20 Mar. 1905, MGC; C. P. Scott to HNB, 23 Mar. 1905, MGC. See David Ayerst, *Guardian: Biography of a Newspaper* (London, 1971), p. 248.
[26] C. P. Scott to HNB, 17 Apr. 1905, MGC; HNB to C. P. Scott, 22 Apr. 1905, MGC.
[27] C. P. Scott to J. E. Taylor, 1 May 1905, MGC.
[28] C. P. Scott to J. E. Taylor, 13 May 1905, MGC.

He was a member of the executive of the Society of Friends of Russian Freedom, an organization which brought Russian revolutionaries into contact with English sympathizers to promote the struggle against Tsarism. The Society published a monthly entitled *Free Russia*, edited by Felix Volkhovsky, collected funds to help émigrés, and engaged in propaganda. Brailsford had become acquainted with Volkhovsky in 1902, when he was still writing for the *Morning Leader*. He solicited articles from him on Finland and on peasant movements and later they collaborated in an effort to rouse English interest in the fate of Michael Gotz, a Russian exile implicated in a political assassination in Italy. A Social Revolutionary, ideologically committed to terrorism, Volkhovsky was a gentle man who spent his leisure writing children's stories. It was through Volkhovsky that he met David Soskice, a former student revolutionary who had settled in England in 1898 and was married to Ford Madox Ford's sister Juliet. In 1905 when Father Gapon fled from St Petersburg after leading an abortive workers' demonstration, he hid for a time at Soskice's Hammersmith home, and Brailsford tried to solicit funds for him among English sympathizers.[29] His other Russian acquaintances in these years included the anarchist Prince Peter Kropotkin, Fedor Rothstein, a Marxist who had left Russia in the 1890s and found employment preparing foreign press summaries for the *Daily News*, and Ivan Maisky, the future Soviet Ambassador, who came to England as a freelance journalist in 1912. As Wilson Harris, a *Daily News* colleague and later editor of *Spectator*, observed, 'On Brailsford anyone who was in any sense revolutionary had an *a priori* claim'.[30]

In the same generous spirit he had acceded to the plea of a Russian friend—possibly Soskice—in October 1904 to secure three English passports which might be used by exiles seeking to return to Russia in disguise. However improper, Brailsford and the Society, which condoned his action, held that opponents of the Tsarist autocracy, who could only return to Russia under false passports, were justified in so doing in order to foment internal subversion. On the understanding that the passports were intended for use by Social Revolutionaries engaged in peaceful activities, Brailsford secured the documents. One passport, issued in the name of Arthur McCulloch, an actor friend, was found on the body of a terrorist who was blown up when his bomb

---

[29] HNB to Felix Volkhovsky, n.d. [?1902], 8 Apr. 1903, Volkhovsky Papers; HNB to Leonard Courtney, 8 Apr. 1903, Courtney Papers, Vol. IX, No. 3; HNB to C. P. Scott, 20 Mar. 1905, MGC; HNB to Gilbert Murray, 5 May 1905, GMP, 124, fols. 44-5; HNB to David Soskice, n.d. [?1905], Soskice Papers, SH/DS/1/BRA/22.

[30] Wilson Harris, *Life So Far* (London, 1954), p. 86. His generosity made him an easy target: one Social Revolutionary swindled him out of a good deal of money, although the details are unknown. See ND, 31 Aug. 1908.

exploded in the Hotel Bristol in St Petersburg in March 1905. When Brailsford learned that inquiries were being made, he wrote to Inspector McCarthy of Scotland Yard, admitting involvement but insisting that the perpetrator of the explosion had not been the man to whom he had delivered the passport. Assured that no criminal action would be taken, he and McCulloch signed full statements, only to find themselves summoned to Bow Street on conspiracy charges.[31]

It was not until mid-May, with the prospect of criminal prosecution looming before him, that Brailsford realized the full implications of what he had done. He was not averse to pulling strings, if that would extricate him, and wrote to Murray:

It seems to me a bare chance that influence might be brought to get the thing quashed altogether. My fall will slightly injure several persons and causes—the Macedonian Relief Fund & the Balkan Committee particularly—& the persons connected with these will not like my being exposed. I wonder do you know anyone who could employ any influence with the Government Front Bench? It might be represented (1) that to trap a man into a voluntary signed statement by a pledge of immunity & then to prosecute him is a most dishonourable trick. . . . (3) If they want to stop Englishmen helping terrorists, they are on the wrong track. We had an explicit pledge that the passports wd not be used for terrorism, so they need not imagine that they are punishing dangerous anarchists.[32]

In the meantime he tendered his resignation to the Balkan Committee, expressing regret lest his indiscretion tarnish the Macedonian cause.[33]

His predicament was graver than he imagined: the Russian government had lodged an official protest, and the Foreign Office was disinclined to condone hostile acts towards a friendly nation. At the hearing Sir Edward Carson, the Solicitor-General, expressed the view that while Brailsford had not given the passport to the maladroit St Petersburg terrorist, such dealings were a dangerous way of assisting a revolutionary movement abroad since the use of passports could not be controlled.[34] In the weeks before the proceedings commenced Brailsford's friends launched a legal defence fund. Murray pressed £100 on him, and Scott offered to lend a similar amount to cover

[31] HNB to Noel Buxton, 19 May [1905], NBP; *Daily News*, 23 and 24 May, 7 June 1905; Rex v. Brailsford, *The Law Reports: King's Bench Division, 1905*, Vol. II, pp. 730-47; Barry Hollingsworth, 'The Society of Friends of Russian Freedom: English Liberals and Russian Socialists, 1890-1917', *Oxford Slavonic Papers*, New Series, III (Oxford, 1970), pp. 61-2.
[32] HNB to Gilbert Murray, 13 May 1905, GMP, 124, fols. 46-9. Murray made overtures on Brailsford's behalf. See Bertrand Russell to Gilbert Murray, 16 May 1905, GMP, 165, fols. 105-6 and James Bryce to Gilbert Murray, 21 May 1905, GMP, 125, fols. 3-4.
[33] HNB to Noel Buxton, 21 May [1905], NBP.
[34] *Daily News*, 24 May 1905.

expenses, so he was at least relieved of worry about costly litigation he could so ill afford.[35]

In the trial, which opened on 26 July before the Lord Chief Justice, Sir Robert Finlay, the Attorney-General, joined the prosecution while John Simon appeared for the defendants. Without pretending that Brailsford was implicated in the bombing, Finlay based his case on the conspiracy to mislead the Foreign Office.[36] Brailsford was advised by counsel not to take the stand, although Christian and Courtney testified as character witnesses. Simon, rebutting the charge that the passport had been wrongly obtained, succeeded in getting the detective's evidence on Brailsford's statement excluded from the testimony and emphasized Brailsford's unimpeachable record. In his summary Lord Alverstone asserted that if the defendants had secured passports knowing they would be used by others, they were guilty of conspiracy, an argument sufficiently persuasive to induce the jury to render a guilty verdict after fifteen minutes of deliberation.[37]

Neither Brailsford nor his friends were surprised by the outcome, but they felt that Simon had mismanaged the defence. Nevinson, watching the proceedings from the gallery with Scott, Barbara Hammond, Hirst, and others, thought that 'Simon niggled away his chances, first trying to get off on technical grounds, secondly trying to maintain innocence, thirdly saying it didn't matter in any case because passports were only forms'.[38] Brailsford's opinion was scarcely more charitable:

I am very much disgusted by the whole proceedings. Mr. Simon had promised to make a political appeal to the jury, but did nothing of the kind & indeed no sort of explanation of my motive was tendered at all. The result is that I have simply been convicted of a petty & unintelligible fraud. I wish I had followed my own instincts, given evidence myself, admitted what I did & justified it.[39]

Simon did manage to delay sentencing pending the reconsideration of several technicalities. When the case reopened five days later before three High Court Judges, Sir Robert Reid (later Lord Chancellor) appeared for the defence. He argued that the evidence had failed to establish an intention of mischief, but the court upheld the conviction,

---

[35] HNB to Gilbert Murray [June 1905], GMP, 124, fols. 50-2. Murray's loan included £30 contributed by Shaw. See G. B. Shaw to Gilbert Murray, 21 June 1905, GMP, 167, fol. 45. Also HNB to C. P. Scott, 30 July 1905, MGC; Ayerst, *Guardian*, p. 359. Both John Simon and Sir Robert Reid waived legal fees.

[36] Rex v. Brailsford, *Law Reports*, p. 730; *Daily News*, 27 July 1905.

[37] *Daily News*, 27 July 1905; Kate Courtney's diary, 31 July 1905, Courtney Papers, Vol. 32.

[38] ND, 26 July 1905.

[39] HNB to Lady Mary Murray [27 July 1905], GMP, 536, fols. 60-1. Murray's view was that Brailsford 'should be kept out of the witness-box himself, as he evidently has serious scruples about the existence of Courts of Law at all'. Gilbert Murray to Lady Mary Murray, June 1905, GMP, 457, fol. 76.

denied the defendants the right to make personal statements, and fined them each £100.[40] None the less, the *Westminster Gazette*, the *Daily News*, and the *Guardian* all published excerpts from Brailsford's undelivered speech, in which he admitted guilt to a minor infraction of the law, but disputed whether a passport was as sacred a document as had been alleged. In defence of those he had tried to help, he contended that their views would be deemed lawful, even patriotic, in any free country.[41] He urged Soskice to distribute his remarks to the Russian underground press so that the revolutionaries would 'know that some Englishmen at least are willing to take some risks to help them'.[42]

What bothered Brailsford most was that he could not afford to bear the consequences of his escapade without exploiting the generosity of friends. As far as his purported crime was concerned, he remained unrepentant. 'It is just because I do not share the general view as to the gravity of my offence,' he told Scott, 'that I committed it at all. My only misfortune is in being judged too soon. If there comes a real transformation in Russia, people will change their minds.'[43] Emotionally drained by the trial, he was gratified by the evident esteem in which friends held him. Nevinson not only took over his *Echo* assignments, but left the Balkan Committee in protest against its hasty acceptance of Brailsford's resignation.[44] Wounded by its lack of solidarity, Brailsford informed Buxton that unless the members wished unanimously to reverse their decision, he would prefer that discussion of his affiliation cease. Buxton sought to make amends, assuring him of the Committee's genuine desire that he remain a member.[45]

The end of the trial coincided with the demise of the financially-troubled *Echo*. Somewhat at a loose end, without regular employment, Brailsford continues to write *Guardian* leaders on a piece-work basis. Less than a fortnight after his trial ended, he even toyed with the idea of compounding his offence, as he told Soskice:

> I have hopes of getting work in the *Daily News*, but nothing can be settled until September. The *Guardian* seems still to be willing to employ me temporarily but not to admit me to its permanent staff. It occurs to me that I might make more money by going to Russia as a special correspondent than in any other way, if I knew when anything important was going to happen and if I could get a false passport.[46]

[40] *Daily News*, 1, 2 and 5 Aug. 1905; Rex v. Brailsford, *Law Reports*, pp. 737-47.
[41] Text of undelivered statement (handwritten), HNBP. Part of the statement is quoted in *Daily News* and *Manchester Guardian*, 5 Aug. 1905.
[42] HNB to David Soskice [9 Aug. 1905], Soskice Papers, SH/DS/1/BRA/23.
[43] HNB to C. P. Scott, 6 Aug. 1905, MGC.
[44] ND, 30 July, 1 Aug. 1905.
[45] HNB to Noel Buxton, 10 Aug. 1905, NBP; Noel Buxton to HNB, 11 Aug. 1905, NBP.
[46] HNB to David Soskice, 18 Aug. [1905], Soskice Papers, SH/DS/1/BRA/14.

Brailsford also approached Scott for a recommendation to Franklin Thomasson, proprietor of the *Tribune*, then being organized to replace the *Echo*. Although Scott did furnish a testimonial, he also tried to forestall Brailsford's defection by obtaining Taylor's permission to invite him once again to Manchester, now that he had 'purged his offense'.47 As Brailsford explained the arrangement,

> . . . after many queer twists & hesitations Scott asks me to go to Manchester from the beginning of October to the end of December. It is still a purely temporary arrangement, but I imagine that since he has gone so far now he will probably want to keep me. I expect he is playing a cautious game with Taylor & really means to retain me.

As gratifying as the *Guardian* offer was, the prospect of a lengthy stay in Manchester was less attractive. Now that the *Macedonia* manuscript was nearing completion, he was caught, as so often during his career, between the practical necessity of journalism and the lure of scholarship. He was toying with an idea for another book and, as usual, sought Murray's advice:

> I have been turning over in my mind a project of a book which rather excites me, and I wonder if you wd think it feasible—a history of humanitarianism, or I shd probably call it a history of pity. . . . To answer [the questions] would need long years of work, & one would have to study the records of legislation, & of monastic orders as well as political & literary history. It's just the sort of work I should like if I can convince myself that the subject has sufficient unity.48

Despite Murray's cautious encouragement, nothing came of the idea.

During the last three months of 1905 he was to write one-third of the *Guardian*'s long leaders, which Scott regarded as the 'prime instrument of policy'.49 The three-paragraph format, consisting of twelve to fifteen hundred words, was a hallowed tradition, and its completion in two hours required quick thinking, logical exposition, and the mastery of the subject. With six years of experience, Brailsford was suited to its rigours, and for £50 a month he also supplied articles, reviews and short leaders.50

No sooner had the Brailsfords settled in Manchester than they were anxious to escape from it. Finding the Lancashire climate and Jane's

---

47 J. E. Taylor to C. P. Scott, 18 Aug. 1905, MGC; also see HNB to C. P. Scott, 14 Aug. [1905], MGC; C. P. Scott to Franklin Thomasson, 15 Aug. 1905 (Copy), MGC.
48 HNB to Gilbert Murray, 3 Sept. [1905], GMP, 124, fols. 60-1.
49 J. L. Hammond, *C. P. Scott of the Manchester Guardian* (London, 1934), p. 305.
50 This discussion is based on Ayerst, *Guardian*, pp. 241, 360. Brailsford's salary was fairly high for the *Guardian*, where the starting rate was £250 p.a. It was comparable to that of Herbert Sidebotham, one of the two principal leader-writers, but less than that of his colleague C. E. Montague, who was paid £1,000 p.a.

gloom dispiriting, he accepted an appointment as leader-writer on foreign affairs with the *Tribune* only a few weeks after his *Guardian* stint began. Subsidized by Thomasson, heir to a Bolton cotton-spinning fortune and to unsullied Liberal principles, the *Tribune* was launched in January 1906 with considerable fanfare. L. T. Hobhouse, another *Guardian* veteran, became political editor, heading an illustrious staff that also included Hobson and Hammond. Shortly after he joined, Brailsford secured Soskice's appointment as *Tribune* correspondent in St Petersburg, a posting which would give his covert activities diplomatic protection, although Brailsford confessed that 'it will be a tremendous wrench to part with you'.[51] Along with Brailsford and G. H. Perris, the foreign editor, Soskice helped to shape its strongly anti-Tsarist tone.

From the outset, however, the *Tribune* was plagued by insoluble difficulties. The decision to fix its price at a penny in the face of competition in a saturated market from the halfpenny *Daily News* and *Daily Chronicle* boded ill for attracting enough readers. Insufficient sales and overscrupulous advertising policy, excluding offensive or fraudulent copy, starved the paper of revenue, and there was a continual attrition of staff, ready to abandon the sinking ship as other opportunities beckoned.[52]

Shortly after Brailsford joined the paper in January 1906, his *Macedonia: Its Races and Their Future* was published by Methuen and promptly acclaimed as the outstanding study of the subject. Although based largely on personal observation, the book, which had taken nearly a year and a half to write, was more than a mere traveller's account. In it he sought to portray the conditions of life for ordinary Macedonians, supplementing his description with essays on the ethnic groups of the region—Bulgarians, Albanians, Serbs, Greeks, and Vlachs—as well as on religion, language, and customs. Less propagandistic than some of his reportage, it was speculative and infused with passionate convictions:

My sympathies and my friendships are not all on one side. The Turk in his shabby uniform, reponsive only to primitive ideals of loyalty and honour, simple, courageous, dignified, and poor, is often a more attractive and picturesque object than the little huckster in European clothes who has called his cafe after Byron. But it is my weakness that I cannot hear the name of Freedom unmoved.

As in Greece in 1897, the loss of romantic illusion in no way diminished his compassion for the oppressed. While he admired individual Turks,

[51] HNB to David Soskice [Nov. 1905], Soskice Papers, SH/DS/1/BRA/13.

[52] This account is based chiefly on Alan J. Lee, 'Franklin Thomasson and the Tribune: A Case Study in the History of the Liberal Press, 1906-1908', *Historical Journal*, XVI, No. 2 (1973), pp. 341-60. Also see Philip Gibbs, *The Pageant of the Years* (London, 1946), p. 63.

he could not condone the misrule that they perpetrated. There might be 'little to choose in bloody-mindedness between any of the Balkan races', but, however reprehensible their behaviour, they at least were striving to emancipate themselves from servitude.[53]

Refuting the outdated notion that Macedonia was administered by the Turks with benign neglect, Brailsford depicted a regime increasingly subject to the centralizing control of Yildiz Palace. Even benevolent provincial officials, such as Hilmi Pasha, were manipulated by telegraph from Constantinople, their initiatives hamstrung by the fanatics and courtiers who had the Sultan's ear. In spite of pervasive corruption and administrative incompetence, the system succeeded in exploiting the Christian population for the benefit of a parasitic class of Muslim officials, tax-farmers and landlords. Previous witnesses had told of spying and police brutality in the cities of European Turkey, but Brailsford was virtually the first to portray conditions in the outlying districts, which bore the brunt of the suffering. Stripped of their meagre resources by rapacious landlords, the villagers, denied even the rudimentary security enforced in the towns, were constant prey to brigandage and massacre.

Devised to prevent the emergence of national consciousness, Turkish tyranny had, in fact, stimulated its growth, each ethnic element asserting its historic claim to dominance. While Greeks and Serbs jostled for Turkish favour, the Bulgarians had seized the opportunity to exploit discontent with the Turkish administration. Inspired, armed, and financed by Bulgaria, the insurgent movement retained a distinctively Macedonian character, to which Brailsford attributed its growing popular support. Outraged by its conspiratorial methods, its enforcement of rigid discipline, its savage reprisals directed as much against Greek teachers and priests as against Turkish officials, he still found much to extol. A genuine movement of national liberation, it was democratically constituted and, at least initially, wary of Bulgarian ascendancy. Yet as an English liberal, even one sympathetic to nationalist ideals, he found it difficult to believe that freedom could be secured through terrorism and assassination. In the end he was willing to judge the revolutionaries not by the civilized standards they violated, but rather by their striving for a better life in the future. Attracted by the heroism, Brailsford was, at the same time, repelled—as he was to be in later years by similar Communist tendencies—by the subordination of individual conscience to collective authority. The Macedonian experience also taught him to distrust nationalist or patriotic zeal, even in the guise of a struggle for liberation.

[53] *Macedonia*, pp. x-xi.

Ruling out either immediate autonomy or partition, he aimed not so much at dispossessing the Turks as substituting direct European control for the Sultan's personal rule, vesting authority in an international board that would enjoy the position of a responsible ministry. Although he believed that the Macedonians were not ready for a parliamentary system, he favoured local self-government through popularly elected village councils. The racial feud would, he predicted, subside, with the Bulgarian element gaining uncontested predominance, once order was restored and economic reforms undertaken.[54]

Macedonia was the central, but by no means the only focus of Brailsford's attention in the decade before the First World War. Ranging widely over the spectrum of foreign affairs, he was almost equally concerned with Russia, with the emerging alliance structure, and with the British ascendancy in Egypt. His sharp criticism of British policy abroad posed occasional problems for conciliatory editors, reluctant to antagonize a ministry with which they were in accord. His indictment of Sir Edward Grey's diplomacy will be discussed later, but some consideration of the way international problems affected his own career is relevant here.

The 1905 revolution in Russia, creating the possibility of constitutional progress, had fired Brailsford's enthusiasm, and he became even more ardent about the future of Russian freedom. During the summer of 1906 he was one of the initiators of a memorial welcoming its people to the brotherhood of free nations. He hoped to join a proposed deputation to St Petersburg to deliver this expression of British solidarity, but his passport application was denied because of his earlier conviction. When mounting opposition at home and in Russia led to the cancellation of the delegation of journalists and politicians, it was Nevinson who ultimately served as emissary.[55]

If events in Russia offered a glimmer of hope, Egyptian affairs cast doubts about the progress of liberty. In June five British officers had attempted to shoot pigeons in the village of Denshawai without obtaining permission from local inhabitants; the incident triggered a riot, resulting in the death of a British officer. The unusually stiff sentences meted out by a tribunal aroused an outcry in England led by the poet Wilfrid Scawen Blunt, a champion of Egyptian nationalism. Brailsford declared in the *Tribune* that 'the vengeance exacted is recognized by every candid man who knows the facts as excessive in conception and barbarous in execution'.[56] His advocacy of the nationalist cause was

[54] *Macedonia*, pp. 321-32.

[55] ND, 22 and 23 July 1906; Nevinson, *More Changes*, p. 182. The incident is described in Barry Hollingsworth, 'The British Memorial to the Russian Duma, 1906', *Slavonic and East European Review*, LIII, No. 133 (Oct. 1975), pp. 539-57.

[56] *Tribune*, 8 Sept. 1906.

prompted in part by Blunt, whose advice he sought in October and whom he continued to consult. But even the *Tribune* was not immune to Lord Cromer's blandishments, and pressure was allegedly put on him to mute his criticism.[57] Alluding to 'disturbing changes' which were going on at the *Tribune*, he told Blunt that 'if the paper does less well for Egypt than it did, the reason lies not in my indifference but in my impotence'.[58]

Brailsford's problems with the *Tribune* management went back at least as far as the replacement of the ineffective William Hill as editor by S. J. Pryor, formerly associated with the Tory *Daily Mail* and *Daily Express*. Thomasson, hoping that a new broom would salvage the paper's waning fortunes, issued an ultimatum to his leader-writers—Hobhouse, Brailsford, and Hammond—whose gist was that 'there is another piont of view to yours'. The day after the thirty-two point manifesto was delivered to them, Brailsford appeared at the Hammonds' house insisting that all three submit resignations:

> The next two days were spent in conferences & telephoning & drawing up letters to vindicate their injured dignities. They carried them about in their pockets & read & altered them every 10 minutes. LTH[obhouse] drew up a letter wh. meant that he *must* go. It reviewed all the misdeeds of Mr. Thomasson & the slights put on himself fr. the beginning. Mr. Brailsford wrote a letter whose sarcasm wld. pierce the thickest skin . . .[59]

Indignation was appeased when the proprietor apologized, but the final clash was simply postponed.

Brailsford's criticism of the Russian loan had irritated several advertisers, who threatened to withdraw their accounts. He also quarrelled with his employers over a series entitled 'The Bitter Cry of the Middle Classes', which seemed to signal a retreat from the crusading radical spirit.[60] By February 1907 he reported to Scott,

> Hobhouse's departure had distressed me very deeply and though I am going to give the new order of things a trial, I am not at all sanguine. Hammond is going too, and that does not make things easier. . . . I feel like a painter who has been engaged by mistake by the manager of a panorama, and some fine day he will discover that my canvases won't move![61]

Once he decided to go, events moved rapidly: three weeks after his letter to Scott he concluded arrangements with A. G. Gardiner to write leaders for the *Daily News* four days a week.[62] Although it involved

---

[57] Blunt Transcript Diary, 6 Oct. and 25 Nov. 1906, BP, MS 8-1975. Brailsford called Blunt 'the most original and attractive human being whom I have known'. *New Leader*, 28 Dec. 1923.

[58] HNB to W. S. Blunt, 15 Jan. [1907], BP.

[59] Barbara Hammond to Gilbert and Lady Mary Murray, 12 Aug. 1906, GMP, 23b. I am grateful to Peter Clarke for a transcript of this letter.

[60] *Property or Peace?*, p. 82; Lee, p. 356.

[61] HNB to C. P. Scott, 1 Feb. 1907, MGC.

[62] ND, 12 and 22 Feb. 1907. Brailsford left the *Tribune* at the end of March.

some financial sacrifice, he had been so bitter during his final months on the *Tribune* that it was a relief 'to have escaped so comfortably'. It had been 'quite impossible' to work with Pryor, whom he dismissed as 'an illiterate mercenary' with 'no intention of leaving me any independence'.[63] It was not lack of principle, but of principal that ruined the *Tribune*; not even the infusion of American cash could prevent its collapse in February 1908. In addition to his *Daily News* appointment the revival of the defunct *Speaker* as the *Nation* in March 1907 promised Brailsford another forum. Its first issue carried Campbell-Bannerman's plea for naval disarmament, which it hoped to follow with an endorsement by Clemenceau. Brailsford, dispatched to Paris to interview him, found the French Premier unco-operative. 'Pas un mot; pas une virgule' was his response to the *Nation*'s appeal; in private conversation he added, 'It's your navy we want, not your pacifism'.[64] The *Daily News* staff, which the *Nation* partly duplicated, included journalists with whom Brailsford had long associated. Indeed Liberal newspapers in the Edwardian period all drew from the same pool of talent, and the same names—Massingham, Hammond, Brailsford, R. C. K. Ensor, Nevinson—recur on a succession of dailies and weeklies.

Brailsford's *Daily News* colleague Rothstein, who belonged to the Menshevik wing of the Russian Social Democratic Party, was involved in arranging its Fifth Congress in May 1907. Denied permission to meet in Finland, Sweden, and Denmark, the 320 delegates, representing different factions of the party, ended up in London at the Brotherhood Church in Islington. An extraordinary galaxy of personalities, including Lenin, Plekhanov, Trotsky, Rosa Luxemburg, Gorky, Stalin, Zinoviev, and Litvinov, took part in the vitriolic debates, which provoked an irreparable breach between Mensheviks and Bolsheviks over revolutionary tactics. Sympathetic observers were not excluded, and Brailsford was able to describe the proceedings in the *Daily News*.

As the interminable debates wore on, the delegates, their resources exhausted, became anxious about securing funds for their return to Russia. Although several of the Russians had British contacts, their financial plight was not known among their sympathizers. Several days earlier a congress deputation had sought Rothstein's help in tapping British sources. Knowing Brailsford's record of assistance, Rothstein approached him on 24 May, informed him of the financial predicament, and urged him to secure the sum needed for return passage. Brailsford, still in debt to Murray and Scott, did not have funds at his disposal but immediately thought of Joseph Fels, the millionaire American soap

---

[63] HNB to David Soskice, 6 Apr. [1907], Soskice Papers, SH/DS/1/BRA/12.
[64] *New Leader*, 20 Nov. 1929; *New Statesman*, 4 Apr. 1936.

manufacturer and philanthropist. Although he had met Fels, then resident in England, only a few times, he was aware of his reputation as a disciple of Henry George and a benefactor of Radical causes. Fels agreed to see Brailsford and Rothstein at once, and, with the encouragement of George Lansbury, the four men hastened by taxi to Islington so that Fels could observe the congress in session. Ushered into gallery seats, they listened in silence for about twenty minutes to Lenin's blistering attack on the Mensheviks. Despite the fact that neither he nor his associates understood any Russian, Fels, impressed by the seriousness of the proceedings, announced that he would lend the money. Protracted negotiations during the next few days between Fels and a delegate subcommittee resulted in a loan of £1,700, to be repaid without interest by 1 January 1908. (Repayment was, in fact, made to Fels's widow in 1922.) On 30 May Brailsford accompanied Fels back to the Brotherhood Church to witness the signing of the promissory note and to receive the thanks of the assembled delegates. Lenin's brusque acknowledgement was in marked contrast to the cordiality of Plekhanov and Trotsky, but Fels, undismayed, pressed a single-tax tract into the hand of the startled Bolshevik leader.[65]

In February 1908 Brailsford went abroad for the *Daily News*, this time to Egypt, then in the throes of transition after Cromer's lengthy benevolent despotism. Blunt, who plied him with introductions, had the impression that 'Brailsford goes with me in believing that a forward policy of strong opposition to the English occupation is the only one likely to have any effect'. Yet Brailsford was not quite the 'sound Nationalist' that he appeared to be.[66] The nationalist intellectuals, who talked to him readily enough, struck him as 'painfully urbanised', knowing 'little of their own peasants & caring less'. Although they agitated for self-government, 'their parties [were] much more rudimentary, & their

[65] Accounts of Fels's loan to the Russian delegates have appeared in several places. Brailsford's version, based on a BBC Third Programme talk in Dec. 1947, was published in the *Listener*, 1 Jan. 1948, and reiterated in his letter to Dudden, 12 Apr. 1953, Fels Papers. Also see Arthur P. Dudden and Theodore H. von Laue, 'The RSDLP and Joseph Fels: A Study in Intercultural Contact', *American Historical Review*, LXI, No. 1 (Oct. 1955), pp. 21-47; Arthur P. Dudden, *Joseph Fels and the Single-Tax Movement* (Philadelphia, 1971), pp. 130-6; Walter Kendall, *The Revolutionary Movement in Britain, 1900-1921* (London, 1969), pp. 79-81; Ivan Maisky, *Journey into the Past* (London, 1962), pp. 140-4; David Garnett, *The Golden Echo* (London, 1953), pp. 116-17.

Brailsford maintained that the sum requested was £500, although the promissory note was for £1,700. It is unlikely that this was simply a lapse of memory on his part, because, as he later explained to Dudden, he did consider whether he and his friends might be able, on their own, to raise £500, whereas £1,700 was clearly beyond their means. What seems probable is that Rothstein initially mentioned £500 to him, but that in Fels's subsequent negotiations with the delegates, the larger amount was stipulated. See HNB to Arthur P. Dudden, 31 Jan. 1956, Fels Papers. Nevinson, reporting a conversation with Brailsford, gave the figure as £2,000. By June 1908 Fels was grumbling about the Social Democrats' failure to repay the loan, for which he blamed Brailsford. ND, 30 May 1907; 12 June 1908.

[66] Blunt Transcript Diary, 12 Feb. 1908, BP, MS 8-1975.

ideas of politics much cruder' than Blunt had led him to expect. Preoccupied with political power, they failed to realize that 'all the spiritual side of nationality, literature art & the rest', was 'in their own keeping, if they only had the energy and steadiness of purpose to cultivate it'.[67]

Nor was Brailsford as hostile to British occupation as Blunt was. Predisposed to question its benefits, he conceded that 'the Englishmen, for all their arrogance, their talk of imagination and their inability to criticise themselves, had a steady devotion to duty'.[68] But if they did not oppress, neither did they inculcate the capacity for self-government. Until the end of Cromer's tenure there had been no effort to train native secondary school teachers, scholarships for able Egyptian students were restricted, and plans for a new university were regarded with disfavour. As a result of this deliberate neglect 'the level of culture [was] incomparably lower and the educated class incomparably smaller than in any other country of the Near East, with which he was acquainted.[69]

Even though the British had reduced taxes and eliminated forced labour, 'the economic tyranny, the exploitation of one Egyptian by another, has yet to be faced'.[70] Beyond peasant poverty was the blight of child labour, for which the British were directly responsible. Brailsford visited a cotton ginnery in Zagazig where he learned that, in the absence of regulation and medical inspection, young children worked for twelve to fifteen hours a day for sixpence. For Brailsford the 'real issue [was] simply that many thousands of Egyptian children [were] being cruelly exploited by a colony of foreign capitalists while British authorities look on inactive'.[71] Imperialism was here revealed—as it was for him later in India—in its most sinister aspect: the prosperity of Lancashire rested on the economic oppression of subject peoples. He was subsequently credited with the elimination of the abuse; owing to his inquiries, a bill was approved the following year by the Egyptian Legislative Council regulating the employment of children in cotton ginning factories.[72]

Amid a rigorous schedule of interviews with politicians, journalists, and officials, he had little time for relaxation and did not even manage to see the Pyramids on this trip. One highlight of the journey was an interview with Osman Digna, a relic of the Mahdist wars in the Sudan.

[67] HNB to W. S. Blunt, 14 Apr. 1908, BP.
[68] *World Tomorrow*, Feb. 1927.
[69] *WSG*, p. 118.
[70] *Daily News*, 21 Apr. 1908.
[71] Letter to Editor, *Manchester Guardian*, 24 June 1908. Also see *Daily News*, 8 Apr. 1908; *Socialism for Today*, p. 52. Brailsford also appealed to Walter Runciman for a parliamentary inquiry into Egyptian child labour. HNB to Walter Runciman, 7 Jan. 1909, Runciman Papers.
[72] *Egyptian Gazette*, 24 June 1909.

Languishing in a Damietta prison, the Mahdi's ex-lieutenant had found consolation in the Koran and had come to conceive of himself as a prophet. His message to Brailsford was that God had sent the British as a scourge to punish the Sultan for ruling according to man-made laws instead of by the Book.[73]

If businessmen at home were profiting by Egyptian child labour, they were even more shamefully reaping the rewards of slave labour in Angola and the so-called cocoa islands. What made this particularly repugnant to Brailsford was that the Cadburys, owners not only of the cocoa firm, but also of the *Daily News*, were among the system's beneficiaries. Nevinson had visited the islands in 1905 and had begun, partly at Brailsford's insistence, to agitate in favour of the boycott of slave-grown cocoa. When H. R. Fox Bourne of the Aborigines Protection Society published a pamphlet denouncing slave traffic in Portuguese Africa, Brailsford threatened to resign if Gardiner, in deference to his employer's sensibilities, soft-pedalled the issue in the *Daily News*.[74]
Cast in the unenviable role of mediator, Gardiner had to contend not merely with Brailsford's self-righteousness, but with a proprietor who angrily accused his leader-writer of being in the pay of King Leopold! Although the disclosures did not damage the Cadburys personally—the report was, in fact, commissioned by British and German cocoa manufacturers—they were wary of unfavourable publicity and reluctant to sanction Brailsford's Angola leader. While his resignation might have disconcerted George Cadbury's Quaker conscience, it was Gardiner's own appeal to the *Daily News* directors for freedom of publication which caused him to relent.[75] Brailsford's 'A Modern Slave Trade', appearing on 6 May, was a model of discretion, excoriating the Portuguese government, while avoiding any mention of British firms. Amicable relations were restored in November, when Cadbury, summoning Brailsford and Nevinson to his office, expressed his belief that it was 'a good thing to rouse public opinion here outside his paper'.[76]

Had Brailsford been permitted to go to the Balkans during the Bosnian crisis in October 1908 as he wished or to Constantinople in April 1909, the editor's difficulties might have been eased, but Grey advised that the Foreign Office would never issue Brailsford a passport. Friction on the paper mounted. On 25 October Brailsford complained that Gardiner had kept him away from the office in fear of what he might

[73] *Nation*, 18 Apr. 1908. Also see *New Leader*, 27 Apr. 1923.
[74] ND, 13 Apr. 1908. Also see ND, 5 Apr., 11 May, and 29 July 1907.
[75] ND, 25 Apr., 1 and 5 May 1908; Nevinson, *More Changes*, p. 86; Stephen E. Koss, *Fleet Street Radical: A. G. Gardiner and the Daily News* (London, 1973), pp. 112-13.
[76] ND, 5 Nov. 1908. Nevinson and Brailsford had both spoken at an Angola meeting on 22 October and also organized another meeting on 4 December.

write about Angola and the trial of the Pankhursts.[77] When Nevinson was ejected from an Albert Hall suffrage meeting on 5 December for attacking Lloyd George, Gardiner suspended him from the paper. Rushing to his ally's defence, Brailsford immediately submitted a provisional resignation on 'trade union principles'. Nevinson was reinstated five days later, but the *Daily News* directors decided to take Brailsford at his word, much to his consternation. He berated Gardiner for revealing a private communication to the board and for misconstruing his intentions, although he intimated his willingness to negotiate if the board apologized.

The crisis over Nevinson's outburst turned into one over Brailsford's intemperate conduct. As far as the Cadburys were concerned, it was the last in a litany of offences. Nevinson could do no less than offer his own resignation if Brailsford's dismissal were allowed to stand; by 17 December the misunderstanding was resolved, despite Gardiner's murmurings about Brailsford's 'suspicious nature'.[78] He carried on as leader-writer, but the rows persisted. Gardiner tried to restrain his fury over the proposed visit to England by the Tsar, and Brailsford again threatened to resign in July if, as he erroneously anticipated, the editor tried to soften Nevinson's leader condemning the proposal for four additional Dreadnoughts.[79]

The break, when it came, was not over foreign affairs, Brailsford's usual province, but over the government's handling of suffragettes. He had discussed militancy with Gardiner at the end of July, when he and Nevinson suspected that the editor 'has been at his old game of cutting and trimming'. Despite their support for more tolerance towards suffragettes, neither Gardiner nor Massingham would publicly disavow the government's recourse to forcible feeding in September 1909. When Gardiner appeared to condone the practice in a *Daily News* leader on the 28th, Brailsford hurried back from a Devon holiday prepared to do battle for the women's cause, although he admitted that he and Nevinson 'appeared to stand almost alone & must be eccentric'. Gardiner found himself in an invidious position: while privately interceding with the Home Office, he was alternately being reprimanded by his subordinates, who thought him too favourable to the government, and by the Cadburys, who found him too lenient towards militancy. As on previous occasions, Brailsford's resignation letter was designed as a threat with which Gardiner might coerce the proprietors. But this time

[77] ND, 25 Oct. 1908.
[78] ND, 5-17 Dec. 1908. Nevinson commented that Brailsford's 'tone towards his superiors was seldom conciliatory'. *More Changes*, p. 324.
[79] Leaders by Brailsford and Nevinson, critical of the naval build-up, provoked a boycott of the paper by estate agents and auctioneers, resulting in an immediate loss of advertising revenue. *New Statesman*, 17 Oct. 1936.

the editor would not yield. Infuriated by the recurrent battles with Brailsford, who, he protested, 'did not run straight', he accepted the letter as final, recognizing that this would provoke Nevinson's resignation as well.[80]

Brailsford's explanatory statement, co-signed by Nevinson, appeared in *The Times* on 5 October and received wide publicity. Denouncing the Home Secretary, Herbert Gladstone, for a vindictive pursuit of the militants, the letter concluded:

> Exasperation begat violence, and with suffering came a bravery and a spirit of self-sacrifice which no penalty can crush. The weeks as they pass are bringing us nearer to the phase of mortal tragedy. To our minds the graver responsibility will fall on the members of a nominally democratic party who have turned their backs upon a gallant movement of emancipation, and, above all, on the 'great leader' whose obstinate refusal to listen to the appeals even of the constitutional women has made at each repetition a multitude of converts to violence.
>
> Lest we should seem in our strictures on Liberalism and its organs in the Press to be guilty of an inconsistency, we wish to take this opportunity of stating that, despite our warm approval of the Budget, we have resigned our positions as leader-writers on the *Daily News*. We cannot denounce torture in Russia and support it in England, nor can we advocate democratic principles in the name of a party which confines them to a single sex.[81]

Brailsford's peremptory departure from the *Daily News* was a momentous personal decision. For the sake of principle he was willing to abandon the position of principal leader-writer on the most important Liberal daily. Not only did it involve serious financial sacrifice, but a turning from the direction his career had followed for a decade. Although he retained his association with the *Nation*—out of necessity rather than ideological consistency—his resignation from the *Daily News* was the first step in his break with the Liberal press. He would never again be employed as a regular staff member of a daily newspaper.

---

[80] This account is based on ND, 26 July, 14-30 Sept., 1-4 Oct. 1909; Koss, *Fleet Street Radical*, pp. 118-22; Nevinson, *More Changes*, pp. 324-5.
[81] *The Times*, 5 Oct. 1909.

V
Conciliation Committee (1909–1913)

No one as concerned as Brailsford was with the struggle of oppressed groups for liberation could ignore the claims of women to equal rights. Just as national movements in Macedonia and Ireland, in Egypt and Russia, were invariably linked in his writings, so too the women's campaign was, in his view, inseparable from wider efforts to extend economic and political power to the disadvantaged. For him sex differences were irrelevant when rights of citizenship were being conferred. In hours borrowed from suffrage agitation, when he found time to write *Shelley, Godwin and Their Circle*, the immediate political conflicts intruded upon his reflections. It was impossible for him to discuss the French Enlightenment without observing that reformers 'who sought to raise the peasant, the negro, and even the courtier to his full stature as a man, were inevitably led to condsider the case of their own wives and daughters. They were not the men to be arrested by the distinction which has been recently invented.'[1]

Brailsford's own attitude towards women was never free of contradictions. The misfortunes of his childhood had led him to identify women's rights with resistance to masculine tyranny, but the failure of both his mother and his sister to support, much less to share, his lonely rebellion against paternal authority made him doubt the self-assertive capacity of women. His feelings towards Jane combined chivalric adoration with intellectual reverence, and their relationship, built on illusions that were quickly shattered, was never one of equal partnership. An emancipated blue-stocking, so hostile to the symbols of feminine inferiority that she refused to wear a wedding ring, she regarded marriage as at once a social convenience and a reminder of the restraints that beset women who sought to flout convention. Quietly enduring the indignities she heaped upon him, he blamed her unhappiness on defects in his own character. An advocate of enfranchisement ever since his Glasgow days, Brailsford did not become directly involved in the women's campaign until Jane's enthusiasm was kindled. His strong commitment may have stemmed in part from the hope that mutual participation would restore their faltering marriage, although he cited the courage of the militants as the 'chief personal motive' behind his participation.[2] Indeed, his self-sacrifice may have been,

---

[1] *Shelley, Godwin and Their Circle*, 2nd ed., p. 136.   [2] *Common Cause*, 5 Sept. 1910.

unconsciously it must be assumed, a form of restitution for his perceived inadequacy as a husband. During the years from 1909 to 1913 they pursued parallel, but never identical, courses and these differences ultimately exacerbated the tensions in their relationship.

Although Jane began as a member of the London branch of the National Union of Women's Suffrage Societies (NUWSS), by 1908, impatient with the gentility of the constitutionalists, she had begun to take part in marches sponsored by the militant Women's Social and Political Union. Failing to persuade her associates to emulate Pankhurst tactics, she shifted her affiliation to the WSPU in July 1909 and plunged immediately into by-election activity in Buxton and Dumfries. With the unrestrained zeal of the convert she wrote:

I have not before been in touch with a body of people so entirely selfless as the members of the Women's Social and Political Union. This absolute devotion to their cause, a devotion that stops at nothing and fears nothing—is acting like a magnet, drawing supporters slowly and steadily from all over the country. Nothing can stop this movement.[3]

If he accompanied her on marches, Brailsford did not share her outlook. Aside from misgivings about militancy, he preferred using his position to exert influence, both by writing in support of suffragettes and by prodding his editors to repudiate the government's policy. When women prisoners resorted to hunger strikes against Second Division sentences (instead of the less onerous First Division confinement traditionally granted political offenders), he signed a letter defending them and chiding Liberalism for 'burying its head in the sand'. Punishment had failed to curb militancy, and an alternative strategy was needed. Either the ministry should provide enough parliamentary time to facilitate the passage of a bill that could secure support from moderates in both parties or it should seek an electoral mandate to extend the franchise to women.[4] In essence, this was his position during the next four years: denouncing the harsh treatment of suffragettes, while attempting to devise a political compromise to resolve the conflict.

The day after his *Daily News* resignation letter was published, Brailsford conferred privately with Lloyd George on possible terms of peace. The conditions stipulated were amnesty for prisoners, a limited bill if it could be determined that a Commons majority favoured one, and a pledge to make the suffrage question an election issue—a plan closely resembling that outlined in the *Daily News* letter two months earlier. While his break with the *Daily News* proved final, on 9 October the

[3] Baroness Stocks to author; letter to Editor, *Nation*, 24 July 1909. Her letter, dated 21 July, was written 'a little more than a week' after she joined the WSPU.

[4] *Daily News*, 4 Aug. 1909. Second Division prisoners were kept in solitary confinement and denied the right to wear their own clothes.

Nation carried a leader, which has been attributed to Brailsford, proposing a solution to the deadlock in terms close to those mentioned in his discussions with the Chancellor of the Exchequer. Critical of suffragettes for their 'suicidal' use of force, for throwing away 'the weapons of truth and right', it went on to call for a suspension of hostilities on both sides. In addition, the *Nation* urged that if a majority of pro-suffrage MPs were returned to the next Parliament, the government should endorse a franchise bill.[5]

While Brailsford was closeted with Lloyd George, his wife was conspiring with Christabel Pankhurst to demonstrate against forcible feeding in Newcastle, where the Chancellor was scheduled to appear. On the very day of the conciliatory *Nation* leader, a dozen suffragettes, including Jane and Lady Constance Lytton, who had travelled up from London on the same train as Lloyd George, carried out concerted acts of violence. Stones were hurled at Walter Runciman's car, and windows were smashed at the Liberal Club and a local theatre. Jane's gesture was more dramatic: shortly after Lloyd George entered the theatre by a back door, she edged her way through the crowd to the heavily guarded barricades, carrying a large bouquet of chrysanthemums. Dropping the flowers to reveal an axe, she brought the weapon down with a dull thud on the barricade, a 'symbolic revolutionary act' that inflicted no damage. Taken into custody, she appeared before the Newcastle Police Court along with her confederates and was sentenced to the Second Division for a month after refusing to be bound over to keep the peace. Most of the window-breakers were sentenced to fourteen days of hard labour.[6]

Although he disapproved of these actions, Brailsford had accompanied his wife to Newcastle and observed the entire proceedings. Her arrest, which had been anticipated, made him frantic with worry, knowing that her determination to refuse food might result in forced feeding. He telegraphed Blunt, imploring him to ask his cousin George Wyndham to intercede.[7] He also sought the help of Mrs Byles, the wife of a Radical MP, urging her to transmit his letter to Gladstone. In recapitulating his wife's actions, he noted that

she did not want to throw a stone, because the public won't believe that it is carefully done. She did want to commit a technical offence. . . . The whole thing was a symbol, a pantomime. It meant 'I strike this barrier with the

---

[5] *Nation*, 9 Oct. 1909. The text closely parallels Brailsford's simultaneous discussions with Lloyd George.

[6] ND, 6-14 Oct. 1909; *Newcastle Daily Chronicle*, 11 Oct. 1909; *The Times*, 11-15 Oct. 1909; *Votes for Women*, 15 Oct. 1909.

[7] HNB to W. S. Blunt, 11 Oct. 1909, BP; Blunt Transcript Diary, 12 Oct. 1909, BP, MS 8-1975.

symbol of violence to protest against the exclusion of women from politics as this barrier excludes them from the Chancellor's meeting.' The main thing was to get arrested. It was like her to do it in this fanciful humorous way. Are you prepared for that 'violence' to see her tortured?[8]

Not only were Jane and Lady Constance spared forcible feeding, but, as the wife of a noted journalist and the daughter of a peer, they were accorded preferential treatment. On the third day of their imprisonment, doctors attested to their weakened condition and they were released from jail, while several of their associates were being forcibly fed.[9]

Brailsford, although relieved that she had suffered so little, shared her resentment at the special treatment. In a letter to *The Times* he observed that his wife was guilty of the same offence as one of the Birmingham prisoners, but whereas Jane was bound over with the alternative of Second Division imprisonment, her Birmingham counterpart was sentenced to hard labour and forcibly fed. Clearly the government, while refusing to concede First Division treatment, admitted a special category of first class offenders.[10] At the end of October he was busily organizing a deputation to the Home Secretary to protest forcible feeding. As he told Scott, 'The worst severities do not & will not deter. This movement could have been killed by kindness at the start and rendered almost ridiculous. It is quite unconquerable now.'[11]

Despite its conciliatory October leader, heated disputes about the handling of prisoners continued to bedevil the *Nation*'s staff meetings. Brailsford and Nevinson steadfastly supported the women, C. F. G. Masterman—by now Under Secretary at the Home Office—W. D. Morrison, and Hirst were hostile, while Massingham, Hammond, and Hobhouse were usually somewhere in the middle, opposed to violence, but dismayed by the indignity of forcible feeding. Whenever the suffrage question came up, tempers flared and friendships became strained. Brailsford clashed so furiously with Lloyd George and Hobhouse two weeks later that Massingham ordered him to refrain from attending the lunches for a while. Enraged at what appeared to be the government's calculated savagery, he remarked on one occasion to Nevinson that

---

[8] HNB to Mrs Byles, 11 Oct. 1909, Viscount Gladstone Papers, Add. MSS 46067, fols. 236-42.

[9] *The Times*, 14 and 15 Oct. 1909; C. F. G. Masterman to Herbert Gladstone, 15 Oct. 1909, Viscount Gladstone Papers, Add. MSS 46067, fol. 245; *Votes for Women*, 22 Oct. 1909. Nevinson noted that Jane 'had told the doctors & gaolers at Newcastle, "If you feed me, I shall either die or kill myself"'. ND, 29 Oct. 1909.

[10] Letter to Editor, *The Times*, 19 Oct. 1909.

[11] HNB to C. P. Scott, 27 Oct. [1909], MGC. The deputation took place on 3 November 1909.

'the feeding itself would be sufficient cause for assassination'.[12] Nor were the disputes confined to the privacy of the National Liberal Club, where the weekly lunches were held. In a letter to the editor Brailsford accused the government of 'cold and deliberate malice' in its use of forcible feeding, which he depicted as 'a degradation which sears the spirit and breaks the will'. In an editorial rejoinder Massingham denied that forcible feeding, imposed to prevent the death by starvation, was intentionally vindictive.[13]

While the *Nation* continued to air its disagreements publicly, Brailsford, with Massingham's help, approached the Home Secretary about the chances for an agreement with the militants. Gladstone, uncomfortable as apologist for the government, had begun to promote the removal of the suffrage question from politics altogether. Prompted by Massingham's report of an encouraging interview, Brailsford undertook to propose a non-partisan solution at Clement's Inn, but all he could say was that at least one minister thought that a private member's bill should be given facilities early in 1910. The WSPU found this all too insubstantial, and Gladstone, fearing that the Cabinet might find itself inveigled into negotiations with law-breakers, quickly dissociated himself from the initiative. Protesting that his intentions had been misconstrued, he was willing to grant Brailsford an interview as long as it was understood that 'nothing else but a public and authoritative statement' would bind the government.[14]

In the weeks that followed Brailsford sought other means of influencing the campaign. Invited by a group of Scottish women graduates to stand as a suffrage candidate in the January 1910 general election, he considered contesting Churchill's seat at Dundee or Asquith's in East Fife, but shied away from what might have been dismissed as a publicity stunt.[15] On the other hand, he held out little hope of achieving anything through the Men's League for Women's Suffrage, on whose executive he played a dominant role. It was not merely that the WSPU

[12] ND, 16 Nov., 4 and 7 Dec. 1909; Alfred F. Havighurst, *Radical Journalist: H. W. Massingham (1860-1924)* (Cambridge, 1974), p. 197. The lunch on 30 November made an impression on Lloyd George: two years later Sir William Robertson Nicoll noted that Lloyd George 'quite agreed with me about those wild beasts Nevinson and Brailsford. He once lunched with the staff of the *Nation*. Brailsford was there, and somebody said something about Female Suffrage. Brailsford insulted him, and Massingham told him never to come back to the reunions again.' Memorandum, 12 Oct. 1911, Nicoll Papers. I am grateful to Stephen Koss for this reference.

[13] *Nation*, 18 Dec. 1909; ND, 18 Dec. 1909.

[14] HNB to Herbert Gladstone, 5 Dec. [1909], Viscount Gladstone Papers, Add. MSS 46068, fols. 8-9; Herbert Gladstone to H. W. Massingham, 6 Dec. 1909 (Copy), Viscount Gladstone Papers, Add. MSS 46042, fol. 67; Havighurst, *Massingham*, p. 197. Also see David Morgan, *Suffragists and Liberals* (Oxford, 1975), p. 61, which claims that Gladstone would not see Brailsford. Nevinson's diary shows that the interview took place on or about 9 December. ND, 9 and 17 Dec. 1909.

[15] ND, 20 and 28 Dec. 1909.

persistently denigrated its efforts, but also that the members, however sincere as suffragists, lacked any sense of the practicable.[16]

Convinced that he could accomplish little through the Men's League, he reverted to his earlier plan of working through the political system for a non-partisan solution. By mid-January he had begun to take soundings about the feasibility of a conciliation committee which would 'undertake the necessary diplomatic work of promoting an early settlement. It should not be large, and should consist of both men & women—the women in touch with the existing societies but not their more prominent leaders, the men also as far as possible not identified officially with either party.'[17] An inclusive body with the controversial personalities left out might be just what was needed to neutralize the conflict. But Mrs Fawcett was quick to remark that the gulf separating militants and moderates could not easily be bridged even with the best intentions. Although recognizing her objections, he assured her that he had

> met with no signs of bitterness among militants (whom I happen to know best) towards non-militants, and did not suppose that conciliation was necessary there. I proposed rather to mediate between suffragists of all sections and the Government. The formula in my mind was 'a settlement by consent', i.e. by the goodwill of all political parties.

Admitting that the WSPU also had misgivings about direct participation, he added that 'this part of my scheme is not essential'. He would 'try to form a men's committee, in friendly touch with the Men's League'.[18]

Prospects for success would be enhanced if the committee were not encumbered by feuding women suffragists, but it could not survive without their tacit co-operation. Mrs Fawcett's followers presented no problem: since 1906 they had kept in contact with sympathetic MPs, welcoming any plan that promised to hasten parliamentary action. The WSPU was inevitably less favourably disposed. Four years of militant tactics had fostered not only a distrust of parliamentary deceit, but the habit of self-reliance. Brailsford's overture, however, came at an opportune moment. By the end of 1909 Christabel Pankhurst decided that 'mild militancy', the harassment of politicians, followed by hunger strikes in prison, was temporarily played out. A pause in the campaign might either avert the necessity of escalating violence or at least allow well-worn techniques to fade from public consciousness, so that they

---

[16] ND, 13 and 16 Jan. 1910; Laurence Housman, *The Unexpected Years* (London, 1937), p. 278.
[17] HNB to M. G. Fawcett, 18 Jan. [1910], FP, M50, Box 10. Mrs Fawcett was the President of the NUWSS.
[18] HNB to M. G. Fawcett, 25 Jan. [1910], FP, M50, Box 10.

could be revived more effectively later on.[19] Unenthusiastic about a private member's bill for limited enfranchisement, the WSPU leaders found it expedient to accede to Brailsford's plea for a spontaneous truce.

Having secured grudging militant backing, he turned his attention to establishing the committee itself. The Earl of Lytton, Lady Constance's brother, accepted the presidency, and by the end of February a dozen suffragist MPs representing all parties had agreed to join, their number rising to twenty by mid-March. During the early weeks additional members were recruited, front bench support for legislative time was solicited, and discussions were held about the proposed bill. 'I am giving all the time I can to it,' Brailsford wrote to Lytton, 'lobbying in the afternoons, and writing letters in the mornings. I shove back my own journalistic work (such as I have left) into the small hours. I can't get rid of the nightmare of forcible feeding again.'[20] Since it was clear that adult suffrage could not be carried without overwhelming government support, he concluded that the best hope for an early solution lay with a simple bill to eliminate the sex disability on the lines of Henry York Stanger's 1908 measure to extend the franchise on the basis of the existing male qualifications. By restricting themselves to a bill that offended no bloc of parliamentary suffragists, an all-party majority might be constructed. In view of hostility by elements within the Cabinet to women's suffrage, a private member's bill was the obvious recourse, but even that required adequate facilities to ensure progress beyond a Second Reading.

In order to avoid earlier pitfalls, Brailsford hoped to ensure agreement on the provisions before proceeding further. The Pankhursts vetoed a suggested proposal to enfranchise only women graduates, but it was the Liberal suffragists who proved the major stumbling-block. According to his assessment,

> they are so sure that the Stanger Bill would be bad for them electorally that they will not stir an inch from the adultist position, though they admit that even if they carry the next election they can't secure adult suffrage under five-years—the more candid say ten.[21]

Here was the dilemma the Conciliation Committee faced: Liberals foresaw electoral disaster if women were given the vote according to the existing frachise. In their view it would give additional votes to the propertied, thus enlarging the hypothetical Tory constituency. An

---

[19] Christabel Pankhurst, *Unshackled* (London, 1959), p. 153. Mrs Fawcett claimed that the truce was secured 'mainly through Mr. Brailsford's influence'. Millicent Garrett Fawcett, *What I Remember* (London, 1924), p. 201.

[20] HNB to Lytton, 7 Mar. [1910], LP. I am grateful to the Hon. C. M. Woodhouse for permitting me to consult his unpublished biography of Lord Lytton.

[21] HNB to Lytton, 3 Mar. [1910], LP.

adult suffrage measure, including a higher proportion of working men and women, was more palatable, but likely to incur resistance in the Lords and among Irish Nationalists, who feared a possible redistribution of seats. With their majority dependent on Irish and Labour votes after 1910, the Liberals would do nothing to jeopardize their tenure, at least until they had implemented certain campaign promises, notably House of Lords reform and Home Rule. Furthermore, there was no unanimity within the Cabinet about universal suffrage, even though its members were committed to enfranchise adult males. Conservatives, on the other hand, perceived adult suffrage as a device to benefit their opponents, and suffragists among them wanted to give the vote only to those women for whose support they might compete. While Liberals feared an influx of wealthy widows and spinsters, Tories were dismayed at the prospect of working-class wives using the ballot box to demand socialist legislation.

In the face of mounting opposition Brailsford considered stating the general principle of the removal of the sex disability, but imposing restrictions to avoid the stigma of plural voting. This might prove to the Liberals that 'the aim was not to snatch an advantage for property'.[22] Further investigation showed that the least objectionable formula would be enfranchisement on the basis of the municipal register.

> I am convinced [he told Lytton] that this is the line of least resistance. The Liberals welcome it because it omits the freeholder and the 'property' and plural vote. Conservatives like it because it does not enfranchise married women, nor does it prejudge the future. There is this also to be said for it (1) that the register exists already and (2) that the Bill could be drafted in a sentence, and need not occupy precious time even in a crowded session. . . . Miss Pankhurst & Mrs. Fawcett would raise no objections to this way of proceeding. They would not *accept* it as their full claim, but they would welcome it as a valuable concession.[23]

Mrs Fawcett, willing to accept any measure with a reasonable chance of success, agreed to secure a public expression of support from her executive committee.[24] The WSPU proved more obdurate: Mrs Pankhurst complained to Nevinson about the exclusion of lodgers and certain propertied women. She had 'objected to HNB, but he had for the moment overborne her'.[25] For the present the WSPU would not publicize its misgivings; to Brailsford's relief, it was 'going to keep silence—which is the best we could expect'.[26]

[22] HNB to Lytton, 7 Mar. [1910], LP.
[23] HNB to Lytton, 17 Mar. [1910], LP.
[24] M. G. Fawcett to HNB, 21 Mar. 1910 (Copy), FP, M50, Box 10; HNB to M. G. Fawcett, 27 Mar. [1910], FP, M50, Box 10; Edith Dimock to HNB, 9 Apr. 1910 (Copy), FP, M50, Box 10. Miss Dimock was an Honorary Secretary of the NUWSS.
[25] ND, 14 Apr. 1910.   [26] HNB to Lytton, 17 Mar. [1910], LP.

The formula devised, he resumed his canvass of MPs. On 15 March he obtained a private interview with Churchill, now Home Secretary, whose more humane regulations for imprisoned suffragettes seemed auspicious. Churchill, despite some reservations, allowed Brailsford to quote him as approving in principle the formation of the Committee and its non-party solution.[27] Encouraged by indications of support—or at least of neutrality—Brailsford was troubled by the pressure of time, the need to elicit some commitment from Asquith before the recess. He warned Lytton,

> My feeling all this while is that our plan is the gambler's last throw. I have not the least doubt that the WSPU will blaze into militancy the moment Asquith says *No* to us, if he does say no. And it will probably be very reckless militancy. It lies with you & me and us alone to prevent that. But no influence or arguments will stop the WSPU if we do get that *No*. The prospect eats me up day and night, till I can think of nothing else.[28]

Should the truce fall victim to the women's disappointment, the chance for a settlement would in all likelihood be lost. This premonition of disaster, the sense that only tangible results would forestall a new outbreak of violence, dominated his thinking in the coming months.

By early May the Conciliation Committee could boast thirty-six members, while Grey, Augustine Birrell, Alfred Lyttelton, G. N. Barnes, and Arthur Henderson had been persuaded to join Churchill in endorsing its objectives. Framed so as to preclude wrecking amendments, the bill emerged as a simple proposal to extend the existing parliamentary franchise to women occupiers. It sought to meet Liberal and Labour fears of giving undue advantage to the propertied by excluding ownership or lodger qualifications. Since all householders would be admitted, even if they occupied only part of a house, the provisions would apply to working as well as to upper-class women. If a married woman qualified on her own, she would receive the vote, but most married women would be excluded since husband and wife could not both qualify on the basis of the occupancy.

When Churchill and Runciman intimated that the Cabinet was not disposed to grant facilities at present, Brailsford suggested to Lytton that they must at least 'manoeuvre so as to get the refusal in the form of

---

[27] HNB to Lytton, 17 Mar. [1910], LP; HNB to Winston Churchill, 13 Apr. [1910], quoted in Randolph S. Churchill, *Winston S. Churchill*, Companion Vol. II, Part III (Boston, 1969), p. 1427. This was confirmed in W. S. Churchill to HNB, 19 Apr. 1910, LP, and in HNB to W. S. Churchill, 21 Apr. [1910], *Churchill*, p. 1434.

[28] HNB to Lytton, n.d. [May 1910], LP. Also see HNB to Lytton, 15 Apr. [1910], LP. Churchill later claimed that he would not have received Brailsford under ordinary circumstances, but did so partly because he knew that Brailsford had sacrificed his *Daily News* position for the sake of principle. Memorandum, 19 June 1910, *Churchill*, p. 1448.

a definite promise for a later date'.29 Although the Pankhursts 'took the line that no pledge for the next session even if sincerely intended was worth anything', he clung to the view that they must proceed cautiously, exploiting the propitious climate of the truce to broaden support for the bill.30 If the militants chafed at the lack of progress, Mrs Fawcett could be trusted not to queer the pitch. Above all, nothing should be done to jeopardize the delicate negotiations on which the Committee leaders relied. He and Lytton drafted a plea to Asquith, pointing out that so simple a measure would require minimal parliamentary time to enact. Two days later Lytton had a disheartening talk with Churchill, who intimated that the bill was not democratic enough.31 Lytton's bleak interview did not dampen Brailsford's spirits; if Churchill proved refractory, there were other ways of approaching the government. He implored Courtney to use his influence with Asquith and Balfour, who stood 'in need of the plain firm kindly speech which men will only take from a senior'.32

Months of uncertainty culminated in a hollow victory for the Committee: the Cabinet agreed on 23 June to allow the bill a Second Reading, but announced that facilities for the later stages would not be forthcoming at that time. Before the debate could take place, the tenuous unity among women's groups suffered a serious setback. At the end of May Brailsford begged Mrs Fawcett to overlook the inflammatory Clement's Inn style and to join the WSPU in a peaceful demonstration. After the Conciliation Bill was introduced, the NUWSS decided to hold a demonstration to which all the principal suffrage societies would be invited. Mrs Fawcett then asked for a WSPU pledge to refrain from militancy until then, and when it was refused, Mrs Fawcett broke off the meeting.33 Anxious to prevent the quarrel from discrediting the campaign, Brailsford secured a WSPU promise to avoid militancy and suggested that the Conciliation Committee sponsor the demonstration. An appeal to the usually tractable Mrs Fawcett attempted to rectify 'this wretched misunderstanding' by showing that the WSPU leaders were really 'generous and large-minded women'.34 Despite his remonstrances, Brailsford found Mrs Fawcett so irate that she could hold out no hope that the NUWSS might reconsider taking part in a joint demonstration even under the Committee's auspices. To make matters worse, Christabel, apprehensive about her promise of

---

29 HNB to Lytton, 2 May [1910], LP.
30 HNB to Lytton, n.d. [May 1910], LP.
31 Lytton to W. S. Churchill, 6 June 1910, *Churchill*, p. 1435.
32 HNB to Lord Courtney, 7 June [1910], Courtney Papers, Vol. X, No. 77.
33 HNB to M. G. Fawcett, 27 May [1910], FP, M50, Box 10; HNB to Lytton, 1 July [1910], LP. Relations between the WSPU and the NUWSS rapidly deteriorated during 1910.
34 HNB to M. G. Fawcett, 30 June [1910], FP, M50, Box 10.

non-militancy, wanted immediately to write to Mrs Fawcett disclaiming any such guarantee. Although Brailsford dissuaded her from so doing, he found the WSPU leaders 'still bent on a free hand' when he saw them, unable to perceive that 'they have been guilty of a breach of faith'. As a face-saving device, he withdrew the invitation to the NUWSS on the grounds that the demonstration would generate more awkwardness than accord.35

In the meantime he continued to marshal support for the Second Reading of the Conciliation Bill, scheduled for 11 and 12 July. Undeterred by Lytton's interview, Brailsford tackled Churchill again. Although the Home Secretary did not complain about the use that had been made of his name in the manifesto, he was concerned about the possibility of 'faggot' voting under the bill's provisions. Confident that he had assuaged Churchill's fears, he wrote several days later to urge him to speak in favour of the bill during the debate.36 By then it had become apparent that Lloyd George 'was going to play traitor' rather than remain neutral, although the tabulation of expected votes augured well for the final result.37

The two-day debate showed how far the bill's proponents had miscalculated. The measure drew fire not merely from hostile politicians, such as Asquith and F. E. Smith, but even from erstwhile friends, such as Lloyd George and Churchill, who alleged that it was 'antidemocratic'. Suffragist ministers based their attack on three ostensible defects: that the bill was drafted so as to preclude widening amendments; that it enfranchised few married women; and that loopholes would facilitate 'faggot' voting. The tortuous effort to achieve a compromise among divergent views had, in the end, alienated influential adult suffragists. The adoption of a restricted title had been deliberate, a device to thwart attempts by opponents to tack on categories which would have established the ascendancy of property. The limitation on numbers of married women qualifying had been a sop to moderate Unionists, whose votes were an essential component of the pro-suffrage majority. The crucial plural vote threat had been eliminated by an amendment preventing husband and wife from qualifying in the same constituency, but it was not tabled until after the division had taken place. Carried on a Second Reading by a majority of 109, the bill

---

35 HNB to Lytton, 5 July [1910], LP.
36 HNB to W. S. Churchill, 8 July [1910], *Churchill*, pp. 1435-6; Lytton to W. S. Churchill, 15 July 1910, *Churchill*, pp. 1442-4. A faggot vote was one deliberately created by the transfer of property to a person not otherwise qualified.
37 ND, 9 July 1910. Even before the vote Brailsford was suggesting to the women that Lloyd George was 'our great enemy in the Cabinet'. Emily Davies to Philippa Strachey, 12 June 1910, quoted in Leslie Parker Hume, *The National Union of Women's Suffrage Societies, 1897-1914* (New York, 1982), p. 127.

was immediately referred, by an even larger majority, to a Committee of the whole House, effectively extinguishing hope of further progress.[38]

The shock of disappointment found expression in bitter resentment at Churchill's apparent reversal. Of those whose names appeared on the Committee's manifesto, he alone had voted against the bill. The day of the division Brailsford wrote to notify him that

> in discussing your conduct in today's debate, I shall be obliged to describe it as treacherous. You knew when you 'welcomed the formation' of the Conciliation Committee the nature of the Bill which it was drafting. . . . If you consider yourself insulted, I am at your service, and will study your convenience in making arrangements for a meeting.[39]

A protracted correspondence, full of mutual recriminations, between Brailsford and Lytton on the one hand and Churchill on the other, followed. The Home Secretary insisted that he had never been fully consulted, that he had intimated his misgivings prior to the debate, and that he had warned that he would not be able to vote for the measure. Brailsford retorted that Churchill, apprised of its terms in several interviews and letters, had never indicated the depth of his opposition.[40] The dispute, creating a painful breach in the Churchill-Lytton friendship, led Brailsford to remark angrily, 'I have spent a great deal of time in my talks with [the militants] in trying to persuade them that they take an unduly cynical view of politicians. You have made me a convert to their bitter reading of human nature.'[41]

The quarrel, which prompted Brailsford to urge the NUWSS 'to make war on the Government as the enemy',[42] was by no means the sole cause for gloom. On 23 July Asquith informed Lytton that earlier pledges to provide an opportunity to resolve the suffrage question did not imply the concession of facilities during that session. Despite the defiant tone of Brailsford's remarks at a WSPU Hyde Park gathering that day and at Men's League meetings, it was clear, especially once Parliament was prorogued at the end of the month, that progress had been stalled.[43] Asquith's failure to mention the Conciliation Bill when he dissolved Parliament brought several hundred militants into Parlia-

---

[38] Letter to Editor, *Nation*, 23 July 1910; *The 'Conciliation' Bill*, pp. 6-7; letter to Editor, *The Times*, 15 Aug. 1910; Andrew Rosen, *Rise Up, Women!* (London, 1974), pp. 136-7.

[39] HNB to W. S. Churchill, 12 July [1910], *Churchill*, pp. 1436-7.

[40] The correspondence is reprinted in *Churchill*, pp. 1436-47. Brailsford's contributions include letters to Churchill on 12 and 13 July and to Lytton on 15 July; Churchill's side is presented in a memorandum of 19 July, which appears on pp. 1447-54. Originals or copies of several of these letters are preserved in the Lytton Papers.

[41] HNB to W. S. Churchill, 13 July [1910], *Churchill*, pp. 1439-40.

[42] *Common Cause*, 15 Sept. 1910.

[43] H. H. Asquith to Lytton, 23 July 1910, LP; ND, 17, 23, 28 July, 3 Aug. 1910; *Votes for Women*, 22 and 29 July 1910; *The Times*, 29 July 1910.

ment Square, where police treated them with unprecedented brutality. Black Friday, as the savage confrontation became known, resulted in the arrest of 115 women, followed by the arrest of another 185 at a demonstration four days later. Brailsford was furious not merely at the Pankhursts for disrupting the peace, but, as Nevinson noted, at the WSPU 'distrust of him & their action against his advice. They have even refused his letter to *Votes for Women* on behalf of the Concil. Comm. & their sudden first raid entirely wrecked his diplomacy with Asquith. He also regards the assaults on ministers as tactical mistakes. He is afraid the WSPU think he is out for ambition.'[44]

The breach with the Pankhursts propelled Brailsford further towards the moderates. After Nevinson had rejected an invitation some months earlier from the North of England Society for Women's Suffrage (an NUWSS affiliate) to contest South Salford against the anti-feminist Hilaire Belloc, the women had approached Brailsford. At that time he turned them down on the grounds that he and his wife were too closely identified with the militants. Approached again on the eve of the dissolution, he claimed at first that he could not stand without the co-operation of his wife, who 'felt bound' to the WSPU. At the urging of Kathleen Courtney, he soon changed his mind and was officially adopted on 21 November by the South Salford Women's Suffrage Association as their parliamentary candidate. His election address focused on the need to enfranchise 'the voteless victims of every form of sweating', for whose sake he implored male electors to put aside party allegiance. The day before the address was published, Belloc retired from the contest, and the Liberals nominated Charles Russell, an avowed suffragist, in his place. Since both Liberal and Tory candidates were now pledged to support votes for women, Brailsford—somewhat reluctantly—withdrew.[45]

Despite Brailsford's premonition that 'Christabel will now oppose the Conciliation Comm^ee & the whole thing will go scuffling on for years',[46] there was a pause in militancy pending the clarification of the government's plans. A 'long and friendly' talk with Mrs Pankhurst repaired the misunderstanding of the previous November; his plan for a Commons resolution calling for legislative action that session allayed her suspicions. 'She will allow us *some* time,' he told Lytton, 'at the opening of the session before she resumes militancy, but I could not get

[44] ND, 29 Nov. 1910. See letter to Editor, *Manchester Guardian*, 5 Dec. 1910, in which Brailsford warned that WSPU actions 'might even jeopardize their case in Parliament'.
[45] ND, 6-8 Apr. 19-25 Nov. 1910. *Salford Chronicle*, 26 Nov. 1910; *The Times*, 28 Nov. 1910; *Common Cause*, 1 Dec. 1910; *Annual Report of the National Union of Women's Suffrage Societies* (1910), p. 27; H. M. Swanwick, *I Have Been Young* (London, 1935), pp. 209-210. Brailsford's election address was published in *Common Cause*, 24 Nov. 1910.
[46] ND, 2 Jan. 1911.

her to say how long. I think she meant me to infer that the truce will be measured by our activity and our success.'[47] Once again the militants were calling the tune, and Brailsford hastened to do their bidding, desperately lobbying ministers in the hope of securing some tangible gain with which to placate the Pankhursts. Aside from parliamentary activity, he had begun, with the aid of Dr Jessie Murray, to gather information regarding the conduct of the Metropolitan Police towards demonstrators in November, an investigation undertaken at the urging of the WSPU.

After a month of collecting testimony, Brailsford and Dr Murray presented their evidence of police mistreatment at a Conciliation Committee meeting early in February. The members, shocked by the findings, instructed Brailsford to draft a formal memorandum and to transmit it to the Home Secretary with a request for a public inquiry. The report, published several weeks later by the Women's Press and extensively quoted in the daily newspapers, documented numerous cases of brutality and indecent assault. The gravity of the charges was underscored by the conclusion that 'the police believed themselves to be acting under an almost unlimited license to treat the women as they pleased, and to inflict upon them a degree of humiliation and pain which would deter them or intimidate them.' The report insinuated that they were acting with the complicity of their superiors, perhaps even of the Home Secretary himself.[48]

The memorandum aroused an immediate furore, not least because it appeared to implicate Churchill. Brailsford told Scott at the beginning of March that the 'feeling here & in the House is strongly against me & the C. C. for our memorandum'.[49] Massingham admonished the Committee in a *Nation* leader for rushing into print with unsubstantiated charges of Home Office misconduct, a suggestion he termed 'quite incredible'. Brailsford remained unrepentant: if the Home Office had not authorized the brutality, then the police had evidently construed Churchill's order to refrain from arrests if possible as justifying the rough handling of demonstrators. Their conduct showed that they 'believed themselves free to do as they pleased, that none of them would be censured for what they might do, and that it was their duty to give the women a lesson'.[50]

Interest in the memorandum waned once the Home Office rejected the appeal for an inquiry, and attention shifted to the second attempt to

[47] HNB to Lytton, 8 Jan. [1911], LP.
[48] *Treatment of Women's Deputation by the Police* (published by Women's Press in February 1911). Excerpts appeared in *The Times*, *Manchester Guardian*, and *Daily News*, 23 Feb. 1911.
[49] HNB to C. P. Scott, 4 Mar. [1911], MGC.
[50] *Nation*, 25 Feb., 4 Mar. 1911. See Havighurst, *Massingham*, p. 212.

secure passage of a Conciliation Bill. Although women's suffrage had been ignored in the King's Speech, Sir George Kemp, who obtained first place in the private member's ballot, announced his intention to sponsor the revised bill. Aside from the elimination of the £10 qualification and the ban on husband and wife qualifying in the same constituency, the Conciliation Bill differed little from the measure introduced the previous year. The statistical canvass, conducted early in 1911, indicated that approximately eighty per cent of those likely to be enfranchised would be working-class women, an estimate calculated to reassure Liberal and Labour opinion.[51] Generating far less heat than its predecessor, the bill, endorsed at meetings throughout the country, was carried on the Second Reading on 5 May by a vote of 255 to 88, a significantly larger majority than in 1910. But Liberals, still viewing women's suffrage as a distraction from vital problems, were not impressed. Three weeks after the Second Reading Lloyd George, informing the Commons that the government could not provide facilities during the current session without jeopardizing its legislative programme, consoled suffragists with the promise of a week for the further stages of the bill after it had been read yet again.

While the WSPU prepared to resume militancy, Brailsford intimated to Grey that a week would suffice to carry the bill through all its stages, and on 1 June the Foreign Secretary stated that the government would provide the time for serious consideration in the next session. Misled in the past by guarantees later retracted, Brailsford hoped to obtain a definite commitment from the Prime Minister, 'a sop', as Scott put it, 'to throw to the militants who were after foolishness again'. On 16 June Asquith, promising to abide by his pledges 'not only in the letter but in the spirit', confirmed Grey's pronouncement, adding that the week envisaged would be interpreted 'with reasonable elasticity'. Her suspicions allayed, Christabel consented to resume the truce and to suspend the WSPU policy of opposition to government candidates at by-elections.[52]

More hopeful than usual, Brailsford never deluded himself into believing that the battle was over. Asquith had, after all, stipulated that the Conciliation Bill must receive a substantial Second Reading majority if it were to be accorded adequate facilities, and Grey repeatedly counselled Lytton on the need for suffragist unity. Over-confidence might lead to the dissipation of parliamentary support, furnishing the government with an excuse to rescind its promises. Nor was Brailsford

---

[51] *Memorandum of the Conciliation Committee for Women's Suffrage* [1911], Women's Suffrage Collection.
[52] Rosen, pp. 148-50. C. P. Scott diary, 15 June 1911, Scott Papers, Add. MSS 50901, fols. 14-15.

deceived by the quiescence of the militants: at the first hint of ministerial duplicity, violence would break out anew, all the more menacing for the expectations that had been raised. While struggling to keep the WSPU in line through 1911, he continued to advocate the Committee viewpoint in letters and interviews with politicians. 'Unity at this stage and indeed all through,' he told MacDonald, 'depends mainly on the opinion of two or three men, of whom you are obviously one.' He appealed to the Labour leader to help close suffragist ranks by resisting any amendments that would widen the forthcoming Conciliation Bill.[53]

If the villain of the 1910 campaign had been Churchill, denouncing a measure he had ostensibly endorsed, it was Lloyd George who almost single-handedly destroyed its chances for success in 1911 and 1912. Only adult suffrage would satisfy him, and he resolved to wait until the Liberal government was ready to introduce it. Too shrewd to sever ties with the moderates, he continually played on their hopes while intriguing behind the scences to discredit the compromise solution in the eyes of his colleagues. Convinced that the Conciliation Bill was not as innocuous as its proponents claimed, he viewed it as a dangerous threat to Liberal predominance which would 'add hundreds of thousands of votes throughout the country to the strength of the Tory Party'.[54]

With an unerring instinct for the appropriate opportunity, the Chancellor made his move just when suffragist unity was disintegrating. By late October Brailsford, exasperated by the WSPU, was again 'becoming very hostile to Christabel', whose services he thought 'were about at an end.'[55] Enlisting Scott as intermediary, Lloyd George proposed a deal to the Conciliation Committee under terms not easily refused. The government intended to introduce a manhood suffrage bill the following year which could be transformed into adult suffrage by means of an amendment extending its provisions to women. If the Conciliation Bill's supporters agreed to endorse it, he in turn would not oppose the Conciliation Bill in the event that the amendment failed to carry; otherwise he threatened to obstruct the bill when it was next debated. Thus the compromise would be kept in reserve, to be resurrected in the event that adult suffrage was voted down. Although Helena Swanwick and

[53] HNB to J. R. MacDonald, 11 June [1911], MacDonald Papers, 5/21.
[54] David Lloyd George to Alexander Murray, 5 Sept. 1911, Elibank Papers, MS 8802, fols. 309-10. Lloyd George's fears were genuine, but historians have been too quick to discount the Committee's estimates of the social composition of the new electorate. Rosen disparages the 1904 ILP survey of women on the municipal register, on which the Committee relied in 1910, but ignores the Committee's subsequent canvass in 1911 which reached the same conclusion. Even if the figures were inaccurate, opponents of the Conciliation Bill never backed up their suppositions with evidence and could only assert that an adultist measure would be more democratic. See Rosen, pp. 34-5; Clarke, *Lancashire*, p. 121n3. Constance Rover, *Women's Suffrage and Party Politics in Britain, 1866-1914* (London, 1967), pp. 130-4, accepts the Committee's estimates uncritically.
[55] ND, 24 and 31 Oct. 1911.

Kathleen Courtney of the NUWSS welcomed the scheme, Brailsford foresaw grave difficulties. None of the seventy-odd Tory MPs who supported the Conciliation Bill would back adult suffrage and might even desert the bill should the Committee become identified with the larger measure. More seriously, the WSPU had 'the deepest suspicion of Lloyd George, and Christabel envisaged the whole suffrage movement in its present phase as a gigantic duel between herself and Lloyd George whom she designed to destroy'. Still, Brailsford doubted that any group of suffragists could resist a scheme to extend the vote to women on the same basis as to men.[56] In view of the 'dreadful threats of the wrecking & obstruction which L. G. will practise against us if we don't agree', the Committee had little choice but to comply. But since it was being asked to risk Tory defections, Brailsford tried to insist that any arrangements be made contingent on the Chancellor's active support for, not merely his neutrality towards, the Conciliation Bill as a second line of action. Meanwhile the negotiations were to be kept 'absolutely secret, even from the WSPU leaders'.[57]

After receiving Brailsford's qualified approval, Scott arranged a meeting between the Chancellor and the Committee leaders for 6 November. 'We must be wise as serpents in dealing with L. G.,' Brailsford warned Lytton. 'The general idea is I suppose to convince him that we are in a strong position and to demand from him the maximum in reason, using the WSPU in the background as . . . much less easy to satisfy than we are ourselves, which after all is the exact truth.'[58] The interview went badly: Lloyd George, elusive as ever, clearly did not regard the Conciliation Committee as a potent antagonist. The next day Asquith informed a suffragist deputation that a reform bill capable of being amended to include women would be introduced during the next session. Brailsford anticipated an immediate declaration of war if the WSPU learned of the Prime Minister's statement without clarification. He pleaded with Lloyd George for permission to explain their conversations to the militant leaders. While rejecting any plan to consider a limited measure before the reform bill was introduced, the Chancellor did consent to what he termed a 'Dutch auction'—a graduated, descending scale of amendments, starting with adult suffrage and ending with some variant of the Conciliation Bill.

That evening Brailsford went to Clement's Inn, where he found Christabel and the Pethick-Lawrences 'furiously angry & very excited'. Decrying Lloyd George's initiative as 'a move against them', they denounced him as an opponent of women's suffrage, whose word could

---

[56] C. P. Scott diary, 26 Oct. 1911, Scott Papers, Add. MSS 50901, fols. 47-8.
[57] HNB to Lytton, 27 Oct. [1911], LP.   [58] HNB to Lytton, 3 Nov. [1911], LP.

not be trusted. When Brailsford pointed out that the agreement guaranteed the success of at least a limited concession, they disavowed further interest in the Conciliation Bill. Although they would have accepted a compromise before manhood suffrage, by now only sex equality would suffice. Describing the confrontation to Lytton, he predicted gloomily that 'they will revert to the anti-government policy, throw over the Conciliation Bill, & militate primarily against L. G. as the arch-enemy. They reckoned on destroying him or bringing him to his knees. They might fail to get the vote for 40 years, but they would be clear of dishonest compromises'.[59]

From the perspective of the militants Asquith's declaration shattered the last hope of compromise. After pledging facilities for the Conciliation Bill in 1912, the government appeared to be acting in bad faith, diverting support from the limited measure to the proposed amendment. By making franchise reform a party question, it split the coalition so assiduously cultivated by the Conciliation Committee and rendered a non-partisan solution unworkable. At the same time its refusal to adopt women's suffrage as a government measure assured that it would be denied needed Liberal support. Rather than secure a partial concession, the women, sacrificed to the Liberal goal of universal male suffrage, might find themselves with no votes at all. Once the government took up votes for all men, a limited women's bill, to which the WSPU had never been irrevocably committed, lost any vestige of appeal. Wounded by their virulent response, Brailsford resigned himself to a breach with the WSPU but refused to abandon his belief that some concession was imminent. What disturbed him most was that the Pankhursts now regarded him as a traitor for having acquiesced in Lloyd George's machinations. 'I found the chiefs of the WSPU so angry & shocked,' he told Scott, 'that they would listen to nothing, and further they are so bitter with L. G. that they will have nothing more to do with me because I have been in relations with him.'[60] The break with the Pankhursts, underscored when Brailsford cancelled his WSPU engagements, was all the more painful in that Jane sided with them. While he remained 'pretty confident about a halfway measure', insisting on 'taking what we can get', she stood out for 'equality or nothing'.[61] Much as he might feign indifference to WSPU abuse, he conceded privately that 'I am not really so inhuman. One feels sore and raw'.[62]

If the Pankhursts' conduct was unfortunate, but hardly surprising, that of the Chancellor seemed altogether inexplicable. After promising support for the Dutch auction on 7 November, he seemed to waver

[59] HNB to Lytton, 7 Nov. [1911], LP.
[60] HNB to C. P. Scott, [12 Nov. 1911], MGC.
[61] ND, 10 and 16 Nov. 1911.
[62] HNB to Lytton, 12 Nov. [1911], LP.

when Brailsford saw him the next day, once again raising the possibility that he might oppose a limited measure even as an amendment.

> He is too unstable for trust; [Brailsford complained] I am bad at dealing with him. I can be businesslike with him when I see him across a desk in his room at the House, but in his own home after lunch he is so genial & elusive & quick that I don't know how to pin him down. On the whole I think he means well. But he does not yet realise that the women *want* the big thing. . . . The WSPU now says it won't look at the small thing! But it seems to me to have lost its head completely. Its opposition to L. G. & its repudiation of the Conciliation Bill strike me as merely insane.[63]

The patience of the WSPU was at an end. On 21 November Mrs Pethick-Lawrence led a deputation to Parliament Square, while another contingent, armed with stones and hammers, smashed windows of government offices, hotels and shops. Two hundred and twenty women were arrested, among them Jane Brailsford, sentenced to seven days in the Second Division. She emerged from Holloway Prison with her faith in militancy intact, still contending that the WSPU was 'the only body one can work with'.[64] Three days after the demonstration Lloyd George told the National Liberal Federation that the Conciliation Bill, so grossly unfair to Liberalism, had been 'torpedoed' by the proposed reform bill. Appalled by the Chancellor's duplicty, Brailsford lamented,

> Within a week of promising to Lytton, C. P. Scott, Miss Courtney & myself that he will support the Conciliation Bill if he fails, he actually declares that our bill has been torpedoed. . . . My confidence in my own judgment (which I am afraid has absurdly misled me) is now so healthily shaken, that I hardly like even to discuss the position with anyone else.[65]

Lloyd George was right. Once the government grasped the initiative, the non-partisan campaign lost its credibility and, with it, its support. Enfeebled by dissension among suffragists, the Conciliation Committee soldiered on, but its gestures seemed little more than a charade. Mrs Pankhurst, regretting that she had ever looked at 'that abominable Conciliation Bill', warned Brailsford in January 1912 that suffragettes would 'never again tolerate anything but a Government measure of full sex equality'.[66]

Ministers, however, continued to misread the signals. Just as they had convinced themselves that the Bill was Tory-inspired, so they held to the view that the majority of the public, perhaps even of women,

---

[63] HNB to C. P. Scott [12 Nov. 1911], MGC.
[64] *Votes for Women*, 24 Nov., 1 Dec. 1911; Rosen, p. 154; ND, 28 Nov., 4 Dec. 1911.
[65] HNB to M. G. Fawcett, 26 Nov. [1911], FP, M50, Box 10.
[66] HNB to M. G. Fawcett, 22 Jan. [1912], FP, M50, Box 10.

were opposed to women's suffrage. Churchill prophesied serious trouble for the party if votes for women were appended to manhood suffrage. In order to forestall electoral disaster, he recommended a referendum to test public sentiment.[67] To Brailsford and the NUWSS leaders the referendum loomed as a fatal obstacle: the women would be at a disadvantage in countering the influence of wealth and prejudice that could be invoked against them. On 25 January Brailsford, breakfasting with the Chancellor, pointed out 'the humiliating position which he and others who had relied on the P.M.'s pledges and dissociated themselves from or denounced the WSPU' would be in if the referendum were adopted. Lloyd George agreed to disavow the referendum but not to threaten resignation or even denounce it publicly.[68]

Despite these assurances, Brailsford could not be sanguine. Even if Churchill's referendum campaign had been checked, the Chancellor warned that votes for women were unpopular among Liberals, some of whom were agitating to substitute a simple plural voting bill for broader suffrage proposals. Too experienced by now to rely on any understanding with Lloyd George, Brailsford began devising other stratagems to defeat the referendum. Recognizing that the Irish Nationalists would resist any such precedent, he urged John Dillon to send a protest to Asquith. At the same time he was 'pulling wires' to induce the ILP to apply pressure to Liberals who sat for industrial seats to vote against the reform bill if women were excluded. He even tried to make peace with Mrs Pankhurst, but their talk was 'the angriest & most painful in my recollection. She reproaches us most bitterly with inventing the Conciliation movement & declares it has been from the first to last a disaster for them.'[69]

In the weeks before the doomed Conciliation Bill made its third and final appearance in the Commons on 28 March, Brailsford kept in touch with Lloyd George but failed to persuade him to allow it to pass unamended before the reform bill was brought in. He also appealed to Mrs Fawcett to rally moderate women of all parties in a declaration in favour of the bill.[70] Such a demonstration of unity could scarcely offset the damage done by the outbreak of violence on 1 March, when scores of women smashed windows in the West End. Anti-suffragists in the Cabinet were heartened by the timing of the escalated militancy, assuming correctly that it would dissuade many waverers from voting

---

[67] W. S. Churchill to Alexander Murray, 20 Dec. 1911, Elibank Papers, MS 8802, fols. 358-9; Morgan, pp. 89-90.

[68] C. P. Scott diary, 23-5 Jan. 1912, Scott Papers, Add. MSS 50901, fols. 60-5.

[69] HNB to Lytton, 2 Feb. [1912], LP. When Nevinson saw Mrs Pankhurst some weeks later she 'burst out with a violent attack on HNB, accusing him of "stabbing them in the back" & hoping he would take no part in protests or demand for privileges in future'. ND, 15 Apr. 1912.

[70] HNB to M. G. Fawcett, 1 Mar. [1912], FP, M50, Box 10.

for the Bill. This time it lost by a margin of fourteen, freeing the government of 'the albatross which had hung around its neck for two years'.[71] As Brailsford had anticipated, the anti-suffragist contingent was strengthened by the defection of Irish Nationalists, who neither wanted to risk Asquith's resignation, nor face the implications for Home Rule of franchise reform with its corollary of redistribution of seats.[72] The vote was anticlimactic: by 1912 most suffragists had ceased to regard the bill seriously. The defeat dealt a blow to the Conciliation Committee from which it never recovered. Lingering for some months in a moribund state, ignored by the Cabinet and despised by the militants, it could do little to affect official policy.

With the defeat of the bill, Brailsford retired briefly to the Isle of Wight to recuperate and ponder the future of the suffrage campaign. In reconsidering the catastrophe, he reproached himself: 'My one ghastly fault was in the lack of tact or sympathy or adaptability which brought about my personal quarrel with the WSPU leaders last November. If I had been cleverer then, we might have got some degree of consideration from them for our Bill.'[73] Nothing more could be expected from sympathetic ministers aside from an occasional speech, and the Conciliation Bill's poor showing in March did not bode well for an adultist amendment. Whatever the government decided to do, the militants seemed determined to wreck the chances for settlement. 'My semi-moderate mind,' he reflected, 'is torn all the while between a personal admiration for the bravery of these women & a growing conviction that their methods are utterly unsuited to the stolid British public.'[74] In view of the Committee's impotence some other mechanism would have to be devised to bring pressure to bear. His idea was to sponsor Labour candidates as the best hope of augmenting the contingent of suffragist MPs.

The decision of the Labour Party Conference in January 1912 to oppose any reform that excluded women provided an opening that Brailsford could exploit. During the weeks after his return to London, he hammered out the scheme in discussions with MacDonald and Mrs Fawcett. A fund committee was formed under Mrs Fawcett, including prominent male sympathizers, such as Laurence Housman and Israel Zangwill. An appeal was made to the WSPU to refrain from militancy in by-elections where support for Labour candidates might dislodge an

---

[71] Morgan, p. 98.
[72] Brailsford maintained that the 'Irish party's treachery [was] the sole cause' of defeat. ND, 29 Mar. 1912. Also see 'Women and the Reform Bill', *The Englishwoman* (Dec. 1911), pp. 241-50 and *New Republic*, 24 Feb. 1917.
[73] HNB to Lytton, 8 Apr. [1912], LP.
[74] HNB to W. S. Blunt, 21 July 1912, BP.

anti-suffragist, but the Pankhursts vetoed the suggestion on the grounds that Labour was not committed to total opposition to the government.[75] By the end of April Brailsford was able to spell out the terms of the arrangement: in recognition of Labour's past efforts to promote votes for women, a fund would be launched to assist Labour candidates, although not in constituencies where the sitting member was a known suffragist. MacDonald was apprehensive about how much say Labour would have as to which seats were contested, the party obviously fearing the loss of autonomy. Brailsford explained that the NUWSS was eager to help Labour, not merely to secure the election of pro-suffrage candidates irrespective of party affiliation.[76]

Labour's response was hesitant at first. Many were reluctant to link the party too closely to the NUWSS, preferring that the fund operate privately. Brailsford advised Henderson that 'the suppression of any reference to Labour candidates in the formal definition of the scheme is to all our minds totally impossible. . . . A vague resolution talking of support for "individual candidates" would . . . be generally interpreted to mean the pursuit of the hopeless old plan of suffrage candidatures—which everyone knows to be a futility.' He warned that NUWSS members would be indignant if they knew that Labour welcomed the women's money, but not their public endorsement:

I believe that in the course of a fighting alliance most of [the suffrage movement] would end by becoming decided and permanent adherents of the Labour Party. But that certainly will not happen if at this crucial juncture women realise that you do not care to avow any cooperation with them, and in effect reject a plan which involves from most of them sacrifices of party ties.[77]

Brailsford never appreciated how fraught with difficulties the plan actually was. Reports of a £500 contribution in June 1912 proved so incriminating that the party felt obliged to refrain from contesting a by-election.[78] The architects of an alliance, however, prevailed, and on 2 July the party executive adopted MacDonald's resolution calling for the acceptance of money and support from the NUWSS for candidates in seats where Liberal anti-suffragists might be opposed successfully. Just how decisive that intervention was cannot easily be determined: in the eight by-elections in which the Election Fighting Fund was

[75] Housman, *Unexpected Years*, p. 280. The Brailsfords differed once again on tactics, she condemning support of Labour by suffrage groups. ND, 4 May 1912.
[76] HNB to J. R. MacDonald, 28 Apr. [1912], MacDonald Papers, 5/22. Also see *The Englishwoman*, May 1912.
[77] HNB to Arthur Henderson, 6 May [1912], Labour Party Archive, LP/WOM/12/14.i.
[78] The Fund Committee had voted to grant up to £500 to a candidate who would contest the Ilkeston by-election, but the party had no intention of endorsing the local candidate. When news of the £500 contribution was leaked to the press, Labour withdrew from the contest. I am grateful to Leslie Hume for information about the Election Fighting Fund.

employed the Liberals lost four seats to the Tories. Labour, despite an increased vote, captured no additional seats.[79]

Nothing in the agreement could prevent Labour politicians from misconstruing its intentions. When one of the party whips declared that Labour did not favour granting the vote to a limited number of propertied ladies, Brailsford protested; this had never been the purpose of the Conciliation Bill, to whose provisions the party was committed in the event that wider amendments to the reform bill were defeated. As long as Labour MPs sniped at the alliance and the militant women showed contempt, its prospects did not look bright. Brailsford pleaded with MacDonald not only to keep his subordinates in line, but to demonstrate good faith.[80] Scarcely less important than the partnership with Labour was the threat of retaliation against Irish MPs for deserting the Conciliation Bill. If MacDonald and Henderson could be won by financial inducements, Redmond might prove equally susceptible to other pressures. Arguing that 'unless we can show Redmond that there are dangers in the course he has followed, the disaster of March 28 will be repeated when the Reform Bill comes up', he persuaded the Conciliation Committee to press for the inclusion of a women's suffrage amendment in the Home Rule Bill. Hostile to the notion of a largely female electorate, Irish Nationalists might be sufficiently alarmed to barter enfranchisement in England for the exclusion of women voters at home.[81]

Nor did Brailsford abandon hope of an amended government franchise bill. He continued to negotiate with Lloyd George and to affirm the merits of the Conciliation Bill as a plausible alternative. If the House was unable to agree on wider amendments, then it was 'morally bound to concede the minimum'.[82] But there was little sign that attitudes were changing. Arson and window-breaking, intensified after the Pankhurst–Pethick-Lawrence split in October, made most politicians feel that their only obligation was to resist any surrender to violence. No longer surprised by Pankhurst megalomania, Brailsford dismissed their ouster of long-standing confederates as 'base beyond pardon', but for Jane the shock was almost unbearable.[83] So emotionally involved had

---

[79] The NUWSS pamphlet *The Election Fighting Fund: What It Has Achieved* lists Holmfirth, Hanley, Crewe, Midlothian, Houghton, S Lanark, N W Durham, and Leith Burghs as the eight contests in which it took part. Mrs Fawcett's account adds Keighley and N E Derbyshire. See Fawcett, p. 208. The NUWSS Executive Committee Minutes, 1912-1914 (Box 83) and the Election Fighting Fund Minute Book, June-Dec. 1912 (Box 85), NUWSS Papers, contain information. Brailsford attended most of the EFF Committee meetings.

[80] HNB to J. R. MacDonald, 14 Oct. [1912], MacDonald Papers, 5/22.

[81] HNB to Arthur Henderson [4 May 1912], Labour Party Archive, LP/WOM/12/13; HNB to Lytton, 8 Apr. [1912], LP.

[82] 'The Compromise Amendments', *Men's League Handbook on Women's Suffrage* (1912), p. 33.

[83] ND, 27 and 29 Nov. 1912.

she become, so convinced that the Pankhursts were unassailable, that her divergence from them now dealt a blow to her faith from which she could not recover. Resigning at once from the WSPU, she seemed to lose that sense of purpose that had given meaning to her overwrought temperament.

Many politicians must have been relieved at the Speaker's ruling that a women's suffrage amendment to the franchise bill would so alter its meaning as to necessitate withdrawal. For a man like Brailsford, who had devoted himself unstintingly to the movement for more than three years at considerable personal sacrifice, the decision was bitterly disappointing. Up to the very end he had been weighing options, seeking a formula that would open the way to the enfranchisement of at least some women. By 1913 the nature of the bill no longer mattered as long as the initial step was taken. 'For me,' he explained to Mrs Fawcett, 'the main problem is & has always been how to manufacture a majority. I am chiefly concerned to study other peoples likes & dislikes.'[84] More accurately than he imagined, this casual remark summed up his approach. Aside from Pethick-Lawrence, no Englishman immersed himself as deeply in the suffrage struggle as he did, not as a politician or an agitator, but as a concerned citizen, willing to subordinate his own professional career to a cause in which he believed. While preferring universal suffrage, he came to feel that only a compromise, enfranchising women gradually, could succeed. Inexperienced in navigating the political currents, he made a number of serious miscalculations. Tactically he wavered between cultivating government support and relying on a coalition drawn from all parties, options that proved contradictory. The Conciliation Bill, seeking to satisfy too many groups, aroused more suspicion than enthusiasm. A non-partisan solution proposed at a time of intense party feeling, it attempted to make a moral issue out of a question with political ramifications. Preoccupied with social legislation, Ireland, the House of Lords, and the worsening international situation, the Liberal Government continued to regard women's suffrage as an irritant that might be ignored until more vital questions had been settled. During the truce the Conciliation Bill acquired momentary credibility, but even then Liberal support was lukewarm at best, and once militancy revived at the end of 1911, the political atmosphere became so charged with animosity that compromise became impossible. As a collection of back-benchers drawn from all quarters, the Conciliation Committee never threatened the government's tenure, and ministers such as Lloyd George and Churchill disregarded it with impunity.

[84] HNB to M. G. Fawcett, 7 Jan. [1913], FP, M50, Box 10.

Discouraged, but by no means demoralized, Brailsford oversaw the demise of the Committee and slipped back into the career he had never entirely abandoned. Throughout he had continued to write for the *Nation*, even while he and Massingham were quarrelling over the suffrage issue, to attend Albanian and Macedonian relief committee meetings, and to publish *Adventures in Prose* and *Shelley, Godwin and Their Circle*. Just before leaving for the Balkans in August 1913 as a member of the Carnegie Commission of Inquiry, he wrote to Scott suggesting yet another device for bringing pressure to bear on the Liberals. He wanted to get the Men's League to abstain from supporting Liberal candidates unless the party endorsed women's suffrage. Such a step might become the basis of a ground-swell, beginning with ILP members in constituencies not contested by Labour and moving to Liberal voters themselves.[85] The campaign never got off the ground, and the anticipated election did not take place, but Brailsford's letter showed that he was still deeply involved, still fighting the battle that had yet to be won.

[85] HNB to C. P. Scott, 13 Aug. [1913], MGC.

VI

A Dissenting Foreign Policy (1906–1914)

'Of the three cardinal points of the Manchester doctrine—Free Trade, non-intervention in the affairs of Europe, and *laisser-faire* in internal politics,' Brailsford observed in 1908, 'only the first remains. It is an evolution which the modern Liberal welcomes in principle. Non-intervention was a sterile and impracticable ideal.' So total a dismissal of Cobdenite doctrine did not imply a repudiation of his political heritage. He, no less than other Edwardian Radicals, retained Cobden's hostility to needless entanglements, his distrust of traditional diplomacy, and his advocacy of a limitation on armaments. Where they differed was in their views of England's attitude towards oppressed peoples, whether victims of imperialism or of native tyranny. To Brailsford, the insularity of 'Little England' reflected a moral indifference to exploitation, a failure to recognize that 'the sympathies of our common humanity went beyond the Channel'.[1] It was the duty of Englishmen to enlist in the cause of freedom by lending their support to national struggles for emancipation, as he had done himself in Greece in 1897, whatever the price in disillusionment. In a 1907 article in the *Daily News* he warned that to adopt a posture of non-intervention in places such as Macedonia, Egypt, or Persia would be to consign these underdeveloped regions to the avarice of the financiers. As an alternative to both isolationism and imperial rivalries, he proposed a restoration of a European Concert, a partnership capable of restraining the appetite of aggressive capitalism and of upholding the ideal of 'worldwide brotherhood'.[2]

Yet Brailsford was trying to do more than revivify outmoded Victorian ideals. To an extent unimagined by his ideological forebears he had come to believe in the right of every people to achieve a national identity unhindered by strategic considerations. The deep-seated humanitarianism which led him to champion women's rights or to denounce cruelty to animals led him equally to defend the rights of small peoples to cultural self-expression. He was partial to the Macedonians, but his writings before 1914 were as outspoken on behalf of the Irish, the Egyptians, the Albanians, the Persians, the Armenians, and the subjects of the Tsar. His early experiences in the Balkans had shown him the perils of nationalist sentiment, the atrocities committed in the name of patriotism, but he continued to believe—at least until

[1] *Nation*, 30 May 1908.   [2] *Daily News*, 23 Dec. 1907.

1914—that national freedom and cultural self-expression were the prerequisites of a peaceful international community. The obstacles to such a development—imperialism and the rivalry of the great powers—might be overcome by an educated public and by governments willing to curb their ambitions.

Governments might acknowledge the principle of international morality, but dissenters like Brailsford genuinely believed that these ideals should determine British foreign policy. Indeed he tended to expect more of his own country, protected by naval and imperial pre-eminence, with no excuse for self-aggrandizement, than of its rivals. Furthermore, its rulers should pursue an 'ideological' foreign policy, favouring nations dedicated to democratic and humanitarian goals. His natural distrust of those in authority was reinforced by the failure of successive Foreign Secretaries to abandon traditional balance of power diplomacy. Just as he felt freer to chastise his own country for falling short of his ideals, so too he was quicker to criticize a Liberal Foreign Secretary, such as Sir Edward Grey, for perpetuating the misguided policies of his predecessors.

Brailsford himself harboured few illusions about Grey's appointment. He recognized that so notable a Roseberyite imperialist would support a strong defence and a spirited role in Europe. With a Foreign Secretary from the 'Right' wing of the Liberal party, that faction might try 'to insist above all things on its guardianship of national interests, and to approach with more caution and less enthusiasm those diplomatic problems which call for purely disinterested action'.[3] Yet Grey initially appeared receptive to outside advice. During the autumn of 1905 Brailsford began to suspect that the European powers were on the verge of encouraging Austria to intervene militarily in Macedonia to overawe the Sultan. Even though unilateral action was not undertaken, he sent a memorandum urging continued international co-operation to the Prime Minister and Foreign Secretary shortly after the Liberals took office.[4] But the accessibility of the Foreign Secretary was no measure of his performance, and Brailsford found little cause to revise his low estimate of Grey's talents. 'He knows absolutely nothing of foreign affairs,' Blunt was informed. 'Grey has only once been abroad and then only to Paris, and he speaks not a word of French or any foreign language. Haldane manages all that for him.'[5] As if this were not enough, Grey was showing himself to be 'quite indifferent to all humanitarian issues'.[6]

[3] *Independent Review*, Vol. X, No. 36 (Sept. 1906), p. 257.
[4] See HNB to Arthur Ponsonby, 8 Jan. [1906], Ponsonby Papers, c. 655, fols. 184-5.
[5] Blunt Transcript Diary, 6 Oct. 1906, BP, MS 8-1975.
[6] HNB to E. D. Morel, 6 Sept. [1906], Morel Papers, F9.

Several months later he published a two-part assessment of Grey's first months in office in the *Independent Review*, a Radical journal launched in 1903. Despite some laudatory remarks about the 'confidence which the new Foreign Secretary inspires', the tone of the articles was decidedly hostile.[7] He had argued previously in the same journal that there could be no solution to the Eastern Question except on the basis of an Anglo-Russian understanding.[8] But the outbreak of revolution had altered the situation: once it became clear that the Russian government was at war with its own citizens, it was incumbent upon the Foreign Office to proceed warily. Instead Grey's initiative had paved the way for an Anglo-French loan, thus enabling the Tsar's government to 'face the Duma with defiance and contempt'.[9] While progressive elements in Russia pleaded with sympathizers abroad to withhold aid until reforms were conceded, the unseemly haste with which the Foreign Office promoted the accord denied to the constitutional movement its weapon of coercion. In Brailsford's view the Anglo-Russian Convention made the Liberal government an accomplice to tyranny. Moreover, Grey seemed prepared to await the gradual enlightenment of Belgian public opinion rather than demand immediate action to curb King Leopold's depradations in the Congo. As Brailsford observed to E. D. Morel, 'when [Grey] talks of waiting for Belgian opinion to move, he means only that he is glad of any excuse for doing nothing himself.'[10]

He was, of course, in good company in denouncing Grey's reticence and desire for continuity in foreign policy. Similar views were being articulated, with increasing stridency, by Hobson, Hammond, Nevinson, and Morel. While it lasted, the *Tribune* condemned the drift of Liberal policy, and, more significantly, the *Daily News* under Gardiner's editorship refused to withhold criticism despite its partisan leanings. It was the *Nation*, however, which offered him the most effective platform from which to expound his views on international relations. First of all, he wrote for it almost every week for fifteen years, even when he found himself in conflict with its redoubtable editor. He had admired Massingham even before he worked for him, an admiration that survived sharp disagreement over women's suffrage and German responsibility for the First World War. As editor of a Radical weekly, Massingham, even more than Gardiner, saw himself as a critic, with 'more than a touch of the troublemaker and wrecker as well'.[11] What made the *Nation* unusual was its collective conscience, its attempt to weld

---

[7] See *Independent Review*, Vol. X, No. 36 (Sept. 1906), pp. 256-71 and No. 37 (Oct. 1906), pp. 58-68.
[8] *Independent Review*, Vol. III, No. 11 (Aug. 1904), pp. 321-36.
[9] *Independent Review*, Vol. X, No. 37 (Oct. 1906), p. 60.
[10] HNB to E. D. Morel, 6 Sept. [1906], Morel Papers, F9.
[11] Havighurst, *Massingham*, p. 175. For Brailsford's estimate, see *New Leader*, 12 June 1925.

together the ideas of a cluster of brilliant individuals, men with an ideological affinity, but with strongly divergent views.

Brailsford wrote most of the *Nation*'s articles on foreign affairs in the pre-war years, but their subjects had to be negotiated beforehand at the weekly staff lunches and had to pass Massingham's scrutiny. Even before stormy sessions during the suffrage agitation, these meetings at the National Liberal Club often became occasions for a good deal of dissension. Nevinson records a lunch in June 1907 at which there was 'violent discussion on Russian entente—B[railsford] backing me up against Massingham & Hirst'.[12] Nor were the disagreements always ironed out in advance. Brailsford complained to Blunt that one of his pieces on Egypt had been 'a bit curtailed and edited in a "statesmanlike" sense'[13] and on another occasion that he 'could not get Massingham to allow me to go so far in the "Nation" as I had done in the "Daily News".'[14]

In contrast to Massingham, Brailsford had, certainly by 1907, ceased to identify with the Liberal Party, and whatever sentimental affinity remained was largely dissipated during the suffrage agitation. A Fabian at university, he had left the Society because of its uncritical attitude towards the Boer War, and his socialist convictions were certainly strengthened once he started to read Marx seriously early in the century. By the end of the First World War he tended to refer to himself as a Marxist, in his case a rather ambiguous designation, since he also called himself a democratic socialist. His indictment of capitalist enormities was bolstered intellectually by contact with Hobson, whose writings on imperialism began to exert an impact in progressive circles after 1900. None the less his decision to affiliate formally with the Independent Labour Party was as much an act of protest as of commitment. During the summer of 1907 Cromer's parliamentary critics, denied the opportunity to debate Denshawai, were once again enraged by Grey's defence of British actions in Egypt. In a *Nation* appeal Brailsford, urging clemency for the prisoners, contended that the judicial procedure surrounding the incident had been 'vindictive' and 'barbarous in method'.[15] But this plea was unavailing, and he later claimed that the government's obduracy had pushed him into the opposition camp.[16]

On the day his Denshawai's leader appeared in the *Nation* he approached Ensor, a recent convert to the ILP, for advice:

I have always been a Socialist—I used to be a Fabian. The I.L.P. does not exactly draw me like a magnet. Still I believe in its possibilities, and whenever

---

[12] ND, 4 June 1907.
[13] HNB to W. S. Blunt, 12 Mar. [1907], BP. The article appeared in *Nation*, 9 Mar. 1907.
[14] HNB to W. S. Blunt, 3 Oct. 1908, BP.
[15] *Nation*, 24 Aug. 1907. [16] *Nation*, 5 Oct. 1912.

I go abroad & meet such men as [Emile] Vandervelde, I feel a little bit ashamed to be quite outside the international movement. But does the I.L.P. really welcome 'bourgeois' members? And above all, is it tolerant enough to allow me to earn my living on Liberal papers? . . . I have never, I think, written a line that was inconsistent with a sane Socialism—nothing to which MacDonald or Vandervelde or Jaurès could take exception. . . . There is further the question of what the attitude of the party really is towards outsiders. If it issued suspicion & coldness, then I do not care to join.[17]

Ensor's reply, which has not survived, must have been reassuring, and there is no evidence that anyone in the party demurred or that his membership discomfited Liberal editors.[18] His early associations with the party were limited to contact with Hardie and MacDonald, and by 1909 he had at their behest begun a book dealing with international politics which was ultimately published as *The War of Steel and Gold*.[19]

Many of his earliest leaders in the *Nation* dealt with the Russian *entente*. He could not fail to admit that the resolution of existing conflicts would bring considerable advantages:

The conclusion of a convention covering the common interests of the two Empires in Persia, Afghanistan, and Tibet, would free India from the menace of invasion, render impossible the frontier rivalries of the past, promote the free development of the newly awakened Persian people, and, above all, by enabling us to reduce our garrison in India, permit us, at the same time, to abolish the battalions which feed it from home.

A purely local arrangement, stripped of the fanfare that would invest it with undue significance, might avoid the appearance of intimacy with Russia's rulers. By this means the British government might 'reconcile its duty to Russian liberty with its loyalty to the cause of peace and disarmament'.[20] The peremptory dissolution of the second Duma in June 1907 confirmed Brailsford's fears that constitutional government was still-born in St Petersburg. England had no business cultivating the favours of a power prepared 'to dye its hands deep in the blood of its people'.[21] Nor was it merely what the Convention implied for the cause of popular freedom, the fact that the oppressive regime received the fraternal blessing of the Liberal government, that was so alarming.

[17] HNB to R. C. K. Ensor, 24 Aug. [1907] (unsigned and incomplete), Ensor Papers. Brailsford joined the Islington branch of the ILP. He had met Vandervelde while reporting on the 1907 Hague Peace Conference.

[18] According to Nevinson, Brailsford thought his position on the *Daily News* insecure because of his socialist views. ND, 20 Sept. 1908.

[19] ND, 14, 20, 22 Mar. 1909. One story, impossible to substantiate, suggests that Brailsford submitted a manuscript to MacDonald for ILP publication, probably under the Socialist Library imprint, but that MacDonald rejected it. If true, this may have been the source of antagonism between the two men. See Stanley Pierson, *British Socialists: The Journey from Fantasy to Politics* (Cambridge, Mass., 1979), p. 131.

[20] *Nation*, 27 Apr. 1907.   [21] *Nation*, 22 June 1907.

Abandoning its traditional, even-handed neutrality, England was moving towards a clear commitment to one side in the struggle for mastery in Europe:

> The plain fact is that the Agreement has been concluded to restore the European balance of power, or, so some would put it, to isolate Germany. To call it a contribution to the world's peace is unconvincing . . . Had peace been our object, we should have sought it rather at Berlin than at St. Petersburg.[22]

Less than a year after the Convention was signed, Radical sensibilities were offended again by the proposed visit of the King to Reval to greet the Tsar and members of the Russian government. The *rapprochement* was to be crowned by formal exchanges of courtesy at the highest level, a prospect MacDonald decried as 'an insult to Britain'.[23] To Brailsford the royal visit was more objectionable, if scarcely as meaningful, than the friendship between the two countries. The Tsar was, after all, not merely Edward's nephew, but 'personally the embodiment of the reaction'.[24] At the beginning of June Brailsford wrote, presumably with Gardiner's blessing, a long signed article for the *Daily News* intended to prove that the Tsar was 'personally responsible for the pogroms. It will be a sort of "*J'accuse*",' he told David Soskice, who was asked to confirm some of the details.[25] In addition to a litany of facts about massacres, political executions, and deportations to Siberia, Brailsford recounted the Tsar's support for the terror unleashed by the military bands known as the Black Hundreds, even to the point of decorating his infant heir with its insignia:

> What we are about to do in Parliament today is to authorize our King, in the name of the nation, to give the right hand of fellowship to a Czar and a Prime Minister who have protected and honoured an organization whose weapons are pillage, lust, and murder.[26]

The Parliamentary debate on 4 June, to which the article refers, gave critics a chance to reiterate Russian crimes, but Grey, threatening resignation if his policy were to be repudiated, carried the day with few Liberal defections. Among the more strident opponents was Keir Hardie, whose speech, essentially ghost-written by Brailsford, closely followed the thrust of the *Daily News* article in stressing the Tsar's culpability.[27]

In the wake of protests over the King's June visit an Anglo-Russian Committee was formed to gather and disseminate information. Unlike the more extreme Society of Friends of Russian Freedom, the new

---

[22] *The Times*, 10 Sept. 1907.
[23] Quoted in A. J. A. Morris, *Radicalism Against War, 1906-1914* (London, 1972), p. 176.
[24] *Nation*, 30 May 1908.
[25] HNB to David Soskice, 2 June 1908, Soskice Papers, SH/DS/1/BRA/9.
[26] *Daily News*, 4 June 1908.
[27] HNB to Keir Hardie, 3 June [1908], Hardie/ILP Papers.

group sedulously avoided revolutionary propaganda, seeking instead to enlighten parliamentary opinion on conditions under the Tsarist regime. Inevitably some of the same activists—Brailsford, Nevinson, and Soskice, for example—figured prominently in both, but the Committee's respectability emerged in its choice of the doyen of established Radicalism, Lord Courtney as President. It was Soskice's idea that they sponsor a pamphlet detailing evidence of continued torture, and Kropotkin, the celebrated anarchist, then living in Highgate, was invited to write it. Brailsford and Nevinson helped him compile the information, but Kropotkin's methods were so chaotic, his house so cluttered with newspapers, that they found the collaboration exasperating at times. Eventually Kropotkin's pamphlet, entitled *The Terror in Russia*, was completed and published by the Committee in July 1909.[28] The Committee later issued Brailsford's own pamphlet, *The Fruits of Our Russian Alliance* in 1912.

To all Brailsford's hopes for Balkan liberation the one inescapable obstacle was the persistence of Ottoman despotism. Indeed, he was inclined to argue that the possibility of reform was directly proportional to the degree of independence of a province from Constantinople. The revolt of the Young Turks which finally ended the tyranny of Sultan Abdul Hamid not only shattered his image of a moribund Turkey, but totally altered his perspective on the Balkans themselves. As the movement spread, his enthusiasm for 'the national and revolutionary movement which is transforming Turkey' grew. He heaped praise on 'the tolerance, the good sense, the mingled firmness and moderation of its leaders', even though he realized that the real test would come when they had to grapple with the claims of subject peoples within the empire. Unless a federal scheme was adopted, they might find themselves once again facing the task of repressing local rebellions.[29]

Despite his espousal of Balkan nationalism, Brailsford felt that a liberalized empire might facilitate the internal development of Macedonia without unleashing centrifugal forces. Could the two forces—nationalism and political liberalism—be reconciled? For the moment he was willing to trust to the latter and wanted the Balkan Committee 'to assure [the Young Turks] that no difference of religion will cause us to be slow in welcoming the essentially Liberal character of their movement'. He now contended, somewhat inconsistently, that England might justifiably barter her special rights of intervention in return for

[28] Lord Courtney to G. H. Perris, 10 Apr. 1909, Courtney Papers, Vol. X, fols. 65-7; ND, 4 and 18 June 1909. See George Woodcock and Ivan Avakumovic, *The Anarchist Prince* (London, 1950), pp. 250-62, 372-3.
[29] *Nation*, 22 Aug. 1908.

a pledge that 'the Christians shall enjoy all the civil and political rights which it guarantees to Ottoman subjects'.[30] In other words, cultural freedom, rather than political autonomy, was sufficient for the self-realization of a people. In part, this attitude reflected a momentary intoxication with the Young Turk movement, a quickening of the emotional response to revolutionary aspirations. Beyond this, his intimate knowledge of Macedonia led him to question its economic and political viability in a context of seething ethnic rivalries. Committed to an ideal of self-determination, he realized that in the Balkans, as later in Central Europe, some transcendent unity, some notion of a federal community, was preferable to the proliferation of small, jealous states.

Not all members of the Balkan Committee shared his optimism. Sir Edwin Pears held out for immediate Macedonian autonomy, hitherto Brailsford's own goal. While on holiday in Ireland, he penned a rebuttal of Pears's views:

Can we now say that Home Rule for Macedonia is the *only* possible condition of a reasonable measure of tranquillity and civil liberty? I think that would be an extreme position. . . . If we can get equal civil and political rights for all Christians, that is an advance so immense, that any further pressure would seem hostile. . . . I would even go to the extreme length of withdrawing the foreign officials from Macedonia, after a term of trial for the new regime, if the Turks were prepared generally to accept European experts in Turkish service, at the centre.[31]

If the Young Turks were not to be stifled by European prejudice, they needed to demonstrate good faith, to prove that they would not merely rehabilitate the antiquated imperial administration, but concede equality to the Balkan Christians. In an interview with Ahmed Riza Bey, the Young Turk leader, Brailsford was assured that the new regime would bear 'no grudges' against those disaffected peoples who had fomented separatism in the Balkans.[32] Yet he was too sophisticated to be misled by the pronouncements of those eager to win foreign indulgence. It would take time before a competent bureaucracy could evolve, before there was a genuine liberal spirit among the middle classes or a rebirth of intellectual vitality. Even after a counter-revolution was launched to topple the Young Turks from power, Brailsford continued to counsel support for the regime, which alone offered 'a chance of union and renaissance'. Whatever their deficiencies by Westminster standards, they had at least 'made security and peace in a desert of chaotic strife'.[33]

[30] HNB to Noel Buxton, 11 Aug. [1908], NBP.
[31] HNB to Noel Buxton, 14 Aug. [1908], NBP.
[32] *Daily News*, 14 Nov. 1908.
[33] *English Review*, II (May 1909), pp. 379-80.

When the Young Turks regained control, they forced the Sultan's abdication and commenced a policy of centralization to crush all opposition. Brailsford had, even before the attempted counter-revolutionary *coup*, argued that the gravest mistake of the Young Turks was their refusal to make any concessions to the non-Turkish peoples.[34] With the massacre of Armenians at Adana in April 1909, and later with the repression of an insurrection in Albania, Brailsford reluctantly admitted that 'there is no more security for Christian life than under the old regime'.[35] By 1910 even sympathizers could not fail to recognize that in the Young Turk revolution efficiency and domination, not liberalism, had triumphed and that it had failed to bring civilized rule to Macedonia and Albania. It was their suppression of Albanian schools and language almost as much as their massacre of Albanian villagers that completed Brailsford's disenchantment. He soon reverted not merely to the encouragement of Balkan separatism, but to support for German economic penetration of Turkey as well.

In the summer of 1911 the Macedonian Relief Committee asked the Foreign Office for permission to send the Brailsfords to Albania to distribute aid. The official who interviewed Bertram Christian was assured that Brailsford would not 'have much opportunity for mischief in Albania'. When a favourable recommendation was forwarded to Grey, he commented that the Brailsfords were 'so emotional there is no saying what they may say or do', but he did not object to the relief mission until Arthur Nicolson, Permanent Secretary, reminded him that Brailsford had been refused a passport in 1906 and 1909. Although the Foreign Office could not prevent his departure, it was not disposed to reverse earlier rulings.[36] In the end he decided not to go to the Balkans, pleading other commitments and the uncertainty of Jane's health.

If Brailsford seemed to endorse Germany's demands before 1914, it was because he recognized the mistreatment suffered at the hands of rivals determined to thwart its expansion overseas. The provocative conduct which repeatedly threatened to disrupt the peace of Europe was Germany's protest 'against the toils of a vast diplomatic intrigue which were gradually hemming her in'.[37] Menaced by territorial encirclement, excluded from the exploitation of Morocco by devious Anglo-French arrangements, an aggrieved Germany could retaliate only by arming militarily, cowing its antagonists into belatedly conceding a place in the sun. He believed that by offering concessions England and

---

[34] *Nation*, 17 Apr. 1909.
[35] HNB to Noel Buxton [July 1909], NBP.
[36] Foreign Office Minutes, 8 Aug. 1911, FO 371, Vol. 1261, No. 32104.
[37] *English Review*, II (July 1909), p. 787.

France could assuage German feelings of victimization and remove the ostensible motive for massive armaments.

In Germany's dispatch of a gunboat to Agadir in the summer of 1911 he discerned not so much aggressive intentions on the part of the Kaiser, but rather the machinations of the financial syndicates. Quick to identify the economic aspect of the rivalry, he tended to ignore other factors, particularly the willingness of the German Foreign Office to exacerbate tensions at whatever cost in Anglo-German understanding. After Agadir Brailsford proposed a bargain which 'need not leave us isolated, though it should end the Franco-German feud'.[38] Since Germany seemed willing to recognize a French protectorate in Morocco, there should be no objection to suitable compensation in West Africa. By facilitating German enterprise, especially in Africa, the barriers to a revived European concert, including a satisfied Germany, would be eliminated. In 1913 Brailsford was ready to accept imperialism as the framework of international relations and to propose a general settlement, consisting mainly of concessions by England. Since the Entente powers had benefited from earlier gains, it was incumbent on them to share territorial spoils with Germany. British support for a German-financed Bagdad Railway could help 'save Turkey as an Asiatic Power, and even restore her to prosperity'. In addition, further compensation in the French Congo or in Portuguese territories would sweeten the settlement for Germany. In return Germany could be expected to apply 'an ungrudging policy of conciliation to Alsace', while France opened her money market to German enterprise.[39]

Russia's exclusion from these proposals was certainly not inadvertent. By 1913 Brailsford was no more reconciled to the Anglo-Russian agreement than he had been at its inception. Indeed most of his apprehensions seemed justified by the turn of events. Although Grey might balk at a German railway in Turkey, he was willing to sanction a joint Anglo-Russian enterprise in Persia at whatever risk to India's security should Russia prove disloyal. Brailsford protested to Blunt that 'Grey is practically selling both Turkey and Bulgaria to Russia, as he sold Persia'.[40] His motive for bolstering a crumbling despotism, was the fear of German hegemony in Europe. Yet, Brailsford argued, not only was the German menace exaggerated: there was no serious danger of Russia's gravitating toward the German orbit. So eager was the Foreign Office to conclude the agreement that they failed to recognize how much more the Tsar needed British financial support than England needed closer ties.[41]

---

[38] *Nation*, 2 Sept. 1911. Also see H. Weinroth, 'British Radicals and the Agadir Crisis', *European Studies Review*, Vol. 3, No. 1 (Jan. 1973), pp. 39-61; *Nation*, 1 and 29 June 1912.
[39] *Nation*, 24 May 1913. Also see *Nation*, 8 June 1912.
[40] Blunt Transcript Diary, 9 Feb. 1909, BP, MS 9-1975.

Here was the root of his criticism of Grey's foreign policy. Misconceived in its choice of allies, inflaming rather than alleviating tensions, sacrificing not merely British honour, but even imperial interests, it left the country weaker than when the Liberals came to power. Instead of an enlightened policy which would have reduced British commitments and championed European concert, the Foreign Office had implicated Great Britain in the power rivalry, choosing as its partner a despotism whose policies were inimical to traditional values. Rather than encourage national consciousness among the small nations, England had allowed it to be stifled in order to gratify the needs of the imperialists. Grey was a convenient symbol of the defects of British foreign policy, although Brailsford believed that the Foreign Office establishment controlled its direction and that international financiers dictated its options. In several articles, and more systematically in *The War of Steel and Gold*, he attempted to analyse the determining factors, but in the *Nation* it was easier to lumber the Foreign Secretary with responsibility. As he confided to Blunt,

If we *do* assail Russia and her Persian policy, our protests are always hurled at Grey whom we blame for his complicity in Russian policy. As for myself, I think a good 25% of all I have written since 1906 has been an attack on Grey for something or other. I admit I am rather tired of it all now. There seems to be no public opinion to appeal to. Latterly I have been trying the effect of arguing that Grey is stupid, instead of the old line that he is wicked. It works rather better. No one cared about the ruin of Persia, but they can be alarmed about the Trans-Persian railway. No one minded the shame of the Russian connection, but they do not like the idea of our being *done* by Russia. All this is cynical, I know. But I want to assure you that it is done consciously, simply because it seems to be the more promising way of damaging Grey and the Imperialists.[42]

To his premise that the stakes in the struggle for a balance of power lay outside Europe, Brailsford admitted one exception. In a *Nation* series which appeared in May and June 1912 under the title of 'The Trend of Foreign Policy' he identified the Balkans as the only region in which territorial changes were likely. Should disputes over the Bagdad railway and the opening of the Dardanelles be settled, the Turks might achieve enough internal stability 'to make spontaneous action to put their house in order'. Such a course might involve ending the political squabbles at the centre, but also recognizing the wisdom of granting Macedonia and Albania 'some qualified form of Home Rule'. The reawakening of Macedonian nationalism under the tutelage of Bulgaria

---

[41] *Nation*, 15 June 1912. The same argument was spelled out in greater detail in Brailsford's pamphlet *The Fruits of Our Russian Alliance*, published in March 1912.
[42] HNB to W. S. Blunt, 21 July [1912], BP.

was the approach that Brailsford had espoused a decade earlier, when he despaired of internecine conflict. But a Balkan League, based though it might be on a common desire to exploit Turkish vulnerability, was full of promise for the future. Since he had come to realize that genuine autonomy for Macedonia was, if not unfeasible, at least impracticable, the idea of partition, particularly within some framework of associated states, seemed objectionable no longer.

Brailsford also offered a third option to place alongside home rule within a liberalized Turkey or partition between Balkan confederates. After long having denounced the selfish pursuit of national interest at the expense of small peoples, like the Macedonians, he had shifted his perspective to one in which, under the right conditions, he could envisage a larger role for a great power, an extension of influence, not its effacement. He envisaged a restructuring of the Austro-Hungarian Empire to create a Serbo-Croatian kingdom equal to the other components. Since the village population of Macedonia was 'undoubtedly Slav', it would be possible, without doing injury to race or nationality, to partition Macedonia between an Austro-Serbian and a Bulgarian system. In this idea of the consolidation of the Balkan Slavs under Austrian hegemony, one can see the roots of Brailsford's later opposition to the break-up of the Hapsburg Empire.[43]

Ultimately all three proposals were to prove untenable, and by October 1912 it was already clear that the Balkan League would wait no longer for Turkey or Austria to transform themselves. Brailsford's initial response to the outbreak of fighting was just what it had been in 1903: without condoning the war, he queried whether the point had not been reached at which the Balkan peoples 'would incur a worse bloodguiltiness by tolerating the oppression of their brothers' in Macedonia and Albania than by resorting to arms. The fault lay with the Young Turks, whose disastrous unification policy had succeeded only in 'uniting against themselves Balkan races which seemed a few years ago to hate each other hardly less than they hated the Turks'.[44]

Brailsford, knowing the terrain as few Englishmen did, provided as vivid an account of the first Balkan war in the *Nation* as if he had been there rather than in London. Anticipating atrocities on both sides, he had not really foreseen the rapidity of the Turkish débâcle. He attributed the initial Bulgarian advances to gallantry and determination, although he soon began to write about the 'complete moral failure' of the Turkish army. By the fourth week he was affirming 'the total incapacity of the Turkish officers' and recalling to his readers that a Young

[43] *Nation*, 22 June 1912.
[44] *Daily News*, 7 Oct. 1912.

Turk leader had confided to him at the time of their revolution that the army was unfit to meet the Bulgarians.[45]

Even before peace negotiations began in London to December 1912, Brailsford feared that the gains of victory would be squandered in disputes over the delimitation of frontiers. Much as he wished the League to 'bury the old feuds in the memory of a stupendous victory for Balkan unity', he knew too well that in Macedonia the legacy of discord would be difficult, if not impossible to surmount.[46] His own affinities were for Bulgaria, not, as Taylor suggests, because he regarded Macedonians simply as Bulgarian peasants, but because he believed that Bulgarian nationalists had secured the loyalty of much of the native population.[47] While conceding the diverse ethnological make-up of Macedonia, he insisted that its political sympathies in the past generation had been 'loyally and uniformly Bulgarian'.[48]

The London peace conference was perhaps the first occasion in which Brailsford found himself applauding Grey's mediating role. He credited England and Germany with having

> kept the peace among the greater nations, guided the course of the torrent that submerged the Balkans, and extracted from the confusion the boon of liberty and independence for a race whose fate must otherwise have been extinction at the hands of its armed and victorious neighbors.[49]

But it was the decision of the powers to establish an independent Albania, with borders including territory originally appropriated by Serbia, that paved the way for the Second Balkan War.

By July 1913, with the crumbling of the Bulgarian military effort against overwhelming odds, he found himself once again forecasting catastrophe. Like vultures around carrion, her neighbours were gorging themselves on a dismembered Bulgaria. Ignoring its own extravagant demands, he blamed Serbia and Greece for precipitating the Second Balkan War by concluding an alliance against their common rival. It was the Serbs 'who committed the real aggression', and if the Bulgarians could also be convicted of atrocities, there was, after all, 'little to choose in humanity among the Balkan races'.[50]

To portray Brailsford merely as a critic would be to distort his multifaceted career during these years. He would not have enjoyed so formidable a journalistic reputation had he not possessed, to quote Nevinson, 'a faculty of writing about foreign kings, leaders, and politicians just as though he knew them personally and could estimate their

---

[45] *Nation*, 26 Oct., 2 and 9 Nov. 1912.
[46] *Nation*, 23 Nov. 1912.
[47] Taylor, *Trouble Makers*, p. 107. See *Macedonia*, esp. pp. 101-5, 120-4 and *Nation*, 26 Apr. 1913.
[48] *Nation*, 23 Nov. 1912.   [49] *Nation*, 10 May 1913.   [50] *Nation*, 19 July 1913.

motives and characters'.[51] But in addition he had the ability to divide his life into distinct compartments, separating public concerns from private misfortunes, solitary writing from collective agitation, finding strength in one area to sustain him in another. Thus he was engrossed in women's suffrage activity during those years in which he was fulminating against Tsarist repression or the 'penning-in' of Germany. In part this was simply the nature of a career which compelled him to write about a host of subjects in order to earn his living. But his success suggests a talent for focusing on divergent issues simultaneously without loss of vitality or coherence. While satisfying the demands of several editors, Brailsford also wrote books, agitated on behalf of the Conciliation Committee, and took part in foreign affairs pressure groups which proliferated in this period. Aside from the Society of the Friends of Russian Freedom and the Balkan Committee, he was active on the Persia Committee and regularly attended meetings on Macedonian relief, Angolan slavery, Russian prisons, the future of Albania, not to mention votes for women. An inveterate joiner of protests and signer of petitions, he believed in the efficacy of the pressure group. Few of the organisations to which he belonged were 'popular' in terms of mass participation. Typically, they were composed of handfuls of prominent individuals, impelled by a sense of duty to enlighten others, regarding themselves as the guardians of liberal principles. Yet they all, Brailsford no less than his fellow members, shared a conviction about the educability of the common man; an informed public would strive for the pacific settlement of disputes and would advocate freedom for small peoples.

In view of his unequalled knowledge of Balkan affairs, it was perhaps inevitable that he would be selected as one of the two British representatives on the Commission, established by the Carnegie Endowment for International Peace in 1913, to inquire into the causes and conduct of the two Balkan Wars. Pressure for an investigation arose after widespread reports of atrocities, and the Chairman of the Endowment's European Advisory Council, Baron d'Estournelles de Constant, a French Senator with international experience, was asked to head the inquiry. A group of eight men, chosen for their disinterestedness and consisting mainly of lawyers and academics, was selected. Drawn from the major powers, the members included F. W. Hirst, editor of *The Economist*, and Professor Paul Miliukov, Russian Cadet leader, as well as Brailsford, who was a friend of both.

After a series of preparatory meetings in Paris in July, a subcommittee consisting of Brailsford, Miliukov, the American Samuel T. Dutton,

---

[51] Nevinson, *More Changes*, p. 215.

and Justin Godart, a French Deputy, was dispatched to the war zone. Brailsford was keen to return to the Balkans, which he had not visited since 1904. Moreover, his painful separation from Jane two months before made him particularly 'anxious to go somewhere'.[52] From the outset the Commission encountered resistance, especially from the Greek and Serbian authorities. D'Estournelles de Constant had taken the precaution of informing Balkan diplomats in Paris of the Commission's intentions, provoking an immediate protest from the Greek Foreign Ministry over Brailsford, who was accused of being a Bulgarophile. His recent articles had certainly deplored Greek designs on Macedonia, but he had, after all, been an advocate of the Greek struggle against Turkey. As the Commission President put the issue:

> Brailsford had been frankly partisan, but for whom? For the Greeks. He took up arms for them and fought in their ranks, the true disciple of Lord Byron and of Gladstone; and in spite of this fact, today Brailsford is held to be an enemy of Greece. Why? Because, passionately loving and admiring the Greeks, he has denounced the errors that bid fair to injure them, with all the heat and vigor of a friend and of a companion in arms . . .[53]

Not that he alone was singled out for attack. Miliukov was denounced as antagonistic to Serbia, and when the subcommittee arrived in Belgrade in mid-August, members were greeted by inflammatory newspaper articles and demonstrations against their visit. The Serbian government, emboldened by its military victory against the Bulgarians, refused to communicate with them, but did not prevent the Commission from gathering evidence. In Salonica the hostile reception was repeated, this time with Brailsford as the target. The newspapers, conveniently forgetting his service in the Philhellenic Legion, recalled that he had distributed relief to Bulgars in Macedonia. Salonica newspapers heaped abuse, publishing fake interviews in which offensive statements were attributed to him.

Despite these impediments, the four Commissioners completed their tour, travelling from Serbia to Greece, Macedonia, Turkey, Thrace, and Bulgaria in the course of five weeks. Wherever possible they took deposition from refugees, officials, priests, and school teachers, sometimes interrogating witnesses in the seclusion of a hotel room, occasionally in the full spectacle of the village square. The commissioners toured military hospitals in Belgrade and Sofia, and, despite the recalcitrance of Serbian officials, were able to purchase copies of General Staff documents through an intermediary. In Salonica they acquired captured letters written by Greek troops, which Brailsford translated, attesting

[52] ND, 13 May 1913.
[53] Carnegie Endowment for International Peace, *Report of the International Commission to Inquire into the Causes and Conduct of the Balkan Wars* (Washington, 1914), p. 7.

to atrocities committed on command of the officers. The evidence proved conclusively that the violence of the war against Turkey paled in comparison with the atrocities perpetrated by the former allies in the Second Balkan War. The worst excesses could be attributed not to the soldiers, but to an unleashing of sanguinary barbarism among the population at large. The war had suspended the restraints of civil life, goading the people to a level of murderous savagery unprecedented even in the bloody history of the Balkans.

When they came to assess the impact of the wars, the Commissioners discovered, somewhat to their surprise, that the economic consequences were far less significant than the moral and social ones. In a region of primitive agriculture, with most of the cultivation undertaken by women, there was little loss of productivity, although the hordes of refugees created serious dislocation. What was more ominous was the breakdown of civil order, the return to vendetta and reprisal as a form of social intercourse. Implying that war itself was the culprit, they were clearly astounded by the degree of butchery encountered in the Balkans and were pessimistic about Macedonia's future. Out of deference to the Endowment's preoccupation with world peace, the report reprimanded the manufacturers of guns for fomenting militarism and urged restraint in exploiting Balkan nations for profit. These were noble sentiments, to which all the Commissioners could subscribe but not entirely germane to the specific issue. However much the region had been victimized by international machinations, the immediate conflict, particularly the coercion of the Bulgarian villages, derived more from virulent nationalism than from power involvement. More than any other event, it was the Second Balkan War that convinced Brailsford that Macedonian autonomy was a chimera. In the face of so colossal a slaughter, partition or a federal scheme under Austrian hegemony seemed preferable to unworkable self-determination.

The Commission report, written chiefly by the subcommittee members and published in May 1914, received scant acknowledgement before most of the copies were consigned to American university libraries. The British press ignored it, although Hirst's *The Economist* hailed it as 'the most searching inquiry ever made into any war'.[54] It appeared one month before Brailsford's own *War of Steel and Gold* and three months before the start of a war neither work had anticipated. Ever since 1909 Brailsford had been writing about the armed peace in terms of a menacing imperialist rivalry, but without a premonition that actual war in Europe was imminent. To be sure, he had never subscribed to Norman Angell's optimistic view that since wars did not pro-

[54] *The Economist*, 18 July 1914, quoted in Carnegie Endowment for International Peace, *Year book* (1915), p. 75.

duce economic advantage for any nation, enlightened statesmen would strive to prevent them. When first reviewing Angell's work in 1909, Brailsford had agreed that no power had anything to gain by conquest. But such a realization did not justify complacency about the prospects for peace. It was essential to drive home the lesson that 'the enemy is not so much the faulty reasoning of the many as the shrewd self-interest of the few'.[55]

It was this conviction that spurred Brailsford to elaborate the ideas delineated earlier in 'The Trend of Foreign Policy' and other articles.[56] The problem stemmed not only from lack of popular control over foreign policy, but also from a failure to realize that 'the potent pressure of economic expansion is the motive force in an international struggle'.[57] Yet if he recognized, as Angell did not, the incentives which stimulated competition in armaments, he did not entirely share the pessimism of economic determinists. If the leaders could not be persuaded, they could be controlled by an educated public to act in the interests of the nation at large rather than of the wealthy few.

The War of Steel and Gold opens on a paradoxical note: civilized opinion regarded war as an obsolete barbarism, yet armaments were on the increase. Although crises had been repeatedly settled in the previous decade without bloodshed, the fact was that 'the more successfully we escape war, the more hotly do we prepare for it'.[58] Besides accumulating munitions, the powers had sought to protect themselves by joining in alliances, none of which had brought security:

Modern conditions have involved us in a rivalry of armaments which is now a conscious struggle to achieve by expenditure and science, by diplomacy and alliances, a balance of power which always eludes us, and because it is always variable and unstable condemns us to a bloodless battle, a dry warfare of steel and gold.[59]

Historically, the search for a balance of power had been a function of a nation's fears of invasion or loss of independence, but European frontiers, at least outside the Balkans, were no longer at issue by 1914. Brailsford was even willing to hazard a prediction that 'there will be no more wars among the six Great Powers'. Aside from Alsace-Lorraine, which had 'entered irrevocably into the German network of commerce and finance', the questions that divided them 'turn on no European controversies, and affect no question of honour, liberty or nationality that touches our own homes'.[60] While England could no longer afford, either economically or morally, to remain aloof from European affairs,

[55] *Nation*, 18 Dec. 1909. See Norman Angell to HNB, 1 Nov. 1910, Angell Papers, C-2-43.
[56] The phrase 'war of steel and gold' first appeared in a *Nation* article, 5 June 1909.
[57] *Nation*, 18 May 1912; *WSG*, p. 42.
[58] *WSG*, p. 16.   [59] *WSG*, p. 308.   [60] *WSG*, pp. 35, 41.

her entry into the Continental system signalled its division into two armed camps. The apparent search for equilibrium concealed the fact that each state wanted to gain predominance, to exclude its rivals from new regions for economic penetration, places in the sun for the investment of surplus capital. It was economic motives, not questions of nationality or political autonomy, that underlay the struggle for a balance of power.

Adopting the analytical framework of Hobson's *Imperialism*, Brailsford argued that capital, accumulating too rapidly to secure a profitable return at home, sought outlets in the underdeveloped parts of the world and then invoked the power of the state for its protection. It was no longer true that trade followed the flag; rather the flag followed investment, with the power and prestige of the state harnessed to win profits for private adventurers. If finance did not invariably determine the course of diplomacy, there did exist a covert relationship between them, stimulating armed competition among the capitalist powers, a war of steel and gold. The fears aroused by imperial rivalry had generated a munitions industry closely linked with financial circles and eager to exacerbate tension among nations for the sake of profit.

Although Brailsford admitted that popular jingoism reinforced the financial pressure towards expansion, he denied Angell's thesis that the problem was merely to persuade the public of the folly of war. Armaments had increased not so much to equip a nation for war as to enhance its prestige and underpin its expansion overseas. Even if one were to accept the risk of war, rather than the unstable 'armed peace', as the greatest danger, pacifist activity had proved less effective a weapon than socialism, 'the most formidable factor in the preservation of the peace of Europe'.[61] Modern nations, obliged to rely on conscript armies, could no longer contemplate unleashing a war without taking into account the anti-militarism of the socialist movement. Even discounting the impact of socialist propaganda, Brailsford claimed that there were limits to the sacrifices a conscript army would make, particularly if it doubted the necessity of a war. This meant that on moral grounds there was 'a time-limit to a modern war'.[62]

To his analysis of the economic basis of international conflict he added five concrete proposals that he believed would pave the way for a reordering of European relations. First, a fundamental change was needed in England's constitutional machinery to secure a more democratic control of foreign policy. He suggested a separation of external from domestic matters by a scheme of federal devolution, leaving the Westminster Parliament to deal with imperial questions. Within the Commons a committee for foreign affairs would be elected on a pro-

[61] *WSG*, p. 195.   [62] *WSG*, p. 191.

portional basis from all parties to supervise the Foreign Office in a manner akin to that of the Senate Foreign Relations Committee.[63] Although the Foreign Secretary would retain executive responsibility, the Committee would be empowered to appeal over his head to the Commons. Second, those who invested capital or sought concessions abroad should, if they wanted the protection of the British flag, restrict their activity to imperial territory. If they chose to venture into areas outside British control, they would do so at their own risk, aware that they had no claim on official protection. In order to safeguard undeveloped regions from ruthless exploitation, a credit bureau—not unlike the later World Bank—might be created to supply financial expertise and to negotiate loans on reasonable terms.

Third, in the interests of peace England should agree to abandon the archaic right to capture an enemy's merchant fleet at sea. If this claim were surrendered, the motive for Anglo-German naval rivalry would be eliminated, facilitating a reduction of expenditure on battleships. Fourth, the manufacture of armaments should be nationalized in all countries to remove the private financial incentive for the accumulation of munitions. Finally, the powers should agree to merge sectional alliances into a genuine Concert of Europe. Once England, France, and Germany resolved their few outstanding differences, there would be no futher obstacle to the establishment of a council capable of mediating all disputes. The one remaining impediment to amity, French sentiment over the lost provinces, would be appeased if Germany conceded local autonomy to Alsace-Lorraine.[64] The basis of a permanent accord would be a resolution that nothing should happen in the world without the consent of all civilized powers. Ultimately, however, a new order in Europe awaited two events: the defeat of the Prussian Junkers by the German masses and the establishment of the Duma's supremacy over the Russian court and bureaucracy.

Brailsford's own conclusions were ambiguous. He had demonstrated that imperialism served the interests of an entrenched group, reluctant to forsake their profits, and expressed doubts about 'whether a principle which has helped in half a century to transform a large part of the earth's surface can be reversed'.[65] He had spelled out necessary concessions but could perceive no readiness on the part of governments to make them. Moreover, the re-orientation of European relations which hinged on democratic evolution in Germany and Russia did not, at least in 1914, seem imminent. At the same time there were hopeful signs in the anti-militarist sentiment among the working classes of a

---

[63] Brailsford outlined this proposal earlier in *English Review*, IV (Dec. 1909), pp. 122-31.
[64] *WSG*, pp. 40, 305.   [65] *WSG*, p. 245.

critical spirit that might deter governments from unnecessary wars. Utopian though his prescriptions were, he was convinced that increasing enlightenment would bring them to fruition:

> Let a people once perceive for what purposes its patriotism is prostituted, and its resources misused, and the end is already in sight. When that illumination comes to the masses of the three Western Powers, the fears which fill their barracks and stoke their furnaces will have lost the power to drive. A clear-sighted generation will scan the horizon and find no enemy. It will drop its armour, and walk the world's highways safe.[66]

Rapidly overtaken by political events, *The War of Steel and Gold* never acquired the notoriety its author sought for his first broadly speculative study. Just as Hobson's essay on imperialism grew directly out of his impressions of the Boer War, so Brailsford's tract was rooted in contemporary experience which made some of his ideas appear instantly obsolete once the war began. If Hobson's work would overshadow it in reputation, Brailsford's was the more daring, offering a penetrating exploration of the relationship between imperial expansion and European instability. Drawing on his own extensive knowledge of foreign affairs, he was able to extend Hobson's analysis of British imperialism to encompass the relations among all the major powers before 1914. That he was mistaken about the likelihood of European war or about the efficacy of socialist pacifism does not detract from the book's merit. If the intellectual tools were Marxist, the rhetoric was Radical, accounting for its appeal to British socialists during and after the war, but also to Lenin, whose own essay on imperialism it influenced.[67] *The War of Steel and Gold* not only explained how finance capitalism had heightened the tensions that led to war but offered a formula for change, including the kernel of Brailsford's later scheme for a League of Nations. It was a work of clarification rather than subtlety, of popularization at its least condescending. Its purpose was exhortation: the culprits were revealed, the imperialist conspiracy against the public interest disclosed, and the signposts for a more harmonious future clearly charted. Although enough of a Marxist to recognize the economic taproots of politics, Brailsford never discarded his old-fashioned Radical convictions. Despite its ringing denunciation of the perpetrators of the armed peace, *The War of Steel and Gold* is a work of hope and affirmation, testifying to its author's faith in the capacity of a democracy to seize control of its own destiny.

[66] *WSG*, p. 317.
[67] See V. I. Lenin, *Collected Works*, Vol. 39: *Notes on Imperialism* (Moscow, 1968), pp. 638-52. I am grateful to Victor Kiernan for bringing Lenin's notes to my attention. Also see V. G. Kiernan, *Marxism and Imperialism* (London, 1974), pp. 5-6, 16.

This inspirational quality attracted a younger generation disillusioned with jingoism. ILP speakers sometimes addressed audiences with *The War of Steel and Gold* close at hand for easy reference. One zealot later recalled signing the names of new ILP recruits at an Ayrshire gathering in the flyleaf of his own copy, and other labour activists readily acknowledged the book's formative influence.[68] Its impact during the First World War was out of proportion to its sales. George Bell and Sons reissued it eight times before permitting it to go out of print in 1926, but total sales barely exceeded 10,000 copies, and its author received a mere £132 in royalties.[69] Like most of his books, timely rather than enduring, its immediacy doomed it to relatively brief circulation. None the less, *The War of Steel and Gold* deserves better of posterity. In a commemorative essay on *Imperialism*, Taylor, never an indulgent critic of Brailsford, called *The War of Steel and Gold* 'a more brilliant book than Hobson's, written with a more trenchant pen and with a deeper knowledge of international affairs'.[70]

Brailsford's disagreement with Angell, begun in a 1909 review, resurfaced in a critique of the latter's essays in the spring of 1914. Arguing that force was not yet irrelevant, he claimed that in the Balkans, war did still produce movements of population and shifts of territory. If war among more civilized participants did not result in enrichment by conquest, the competition among financiers in places such as Turkey and China invariably involved their governments.[71] When Angell reviewed *The War of Steel and Gold* in the *Nation* two months later, he countered that the real problem was that the emotions of the masses were 'grounded in unanalyzed conceptions, vague fears and avidities, inherited prejudices, old political fanaticisms'. In order to confute jingoism, it was necessary to educate the public mind, not to restrain the financiers. Even if Brailsford's diagnosis were correct, how was it possible to control the diplomatic machinery when it was in the hands of those 'whom he represents as helpless puppets of the very forces it has to check?'[72] Angell was attacking Brailsford at his most vulnerable point, and he took pains to respond. It was true that he had insisted that democracy must control the financiers, but he was no less emphatic about the need to educate that democracy. What Brailsford tried to suggest was that under the conditions of modern finance it was essential not merely to persuade the public about the folly of war, but also to strive for 'the

[68] Interviews, Lord Archibald, R. Page Arnot, Dame Margaret Cole, Dorothy Woodman, all of whom confirmed the seminal influence of *WSG*. It was also one of Aneurin Bevan's favourite books in his youth. Foot, *Bevan*, p. 207.

[69] Information furnished by G. Bell and Sons.

[70] A. J. P. Taylor, *Essays in English History* (Harmondsworth, 1976), p. 171.

[71] *Nation*, 18 Apr. 1914.

[72] *Nation*, 27 June 1914. See Weinroth, p. 59.

national control of exported capital, and the constitution of a Concert to regulate the process of expansion'.[73]

Brailsford was merely recapitulating themes articulated in *The War of Steel and Gold*, but if he was able to expose Angell's superficiality, he did not refute Angell's criticism. He could not conceal his scepticism about whether imperialism and its beneficiaries could be thwarted, whether the masses had not already become 'helpless puppets'. Before 1914 he was still confident that the working classes could be mobilized to act in their own interest and that reform could be achieved through the democratic process. This faith was to undergo severe testing in the years ahead, and although Brailsford would never forsake democracy, he grew less and less optimistic about its prospects.

[73] *Nation*, 4 July 1914.

VII

Glimpses of a Marriage (1898–1919)

Despite the risks in speculating about the factors which cause a marriage to fail, the Brailsfords' break-up was too devastating an experience for both of them to be mentioned in passing. Although neither can have been wholly optimistic about their prospects together, their initial separation in 1913 was long in coming and accepted with misgiving. A reconciliation the next year failed to heal the breach, and while they were to remain together for another seven years and married at least in name until Jane's death in 1937, they succeeded only in bringing unhappiness to one another.

The marriage was probably doomed from the start. Brailsford, painfully shy, inexperienced with women, isolated from his family, was no match for the tempestuous woman whom he had courted so ardently. Infatuated as he was, he was not blind to her defects, but grateful to Jane for consenting at long last to be his wife, willing to accept whatever conditions she imposed. Starved for affection and fearing that he was beyond redemption, he would accept her on any terms, but her reasons for yielding remain obscure. Family upheavals, restlessness, the chance of a trip to Crete, momentary impulse—all these may have figured in her decision, though one senses less frivolous reasons as well. He represented, if nothing else, constancy, which may have proved appealing after disappointment in love. There is, to be sure, scant evidence about the extent of her involvement with other men before her marriage—or after it for that matter—yet hints of love affairs cannot be discounted. Brailsford and his university friends were all enamoured of her, but their devotion was innocent and, except in Brailsford's case, led to nothing more than a juvenile flirtation. She was, however, to intimate more illicit relationships in conversations with Nevinson, although such tales could well have been embellished in order to heighten her aura of seductiveness. On one occasion she confessed to him that there were 'others who loved her and one whom she still sees much' and that her life had been 'spoilt by some early love for a married man'.[1] While this merely implied sexual entanglements, something more conclusive might be deduced from her avowal that 'she had given all to the man she loved before her marriage. She loves him still and he her'.[2]

[1] ND, 18 June 1907.   [2] ND, 5 Nov. 1908.

Although she was probably too discreet to identify the object of her affection, there are numerous indications that it was Gilbert Murray. The very fact that Brailsford was Murray's protégé may have goaded her to marry him either because she could not have Murray himself or to spite him by choosing someone of whom he was fond. A comment years later by Bertrand Russell, a close friend of Murray, lends credence to the view that Jane achieved at least a brief liaison. Russell informed Clifford Allen that

She had been a brilliant student of Gilbert Murray's, had fallen in love with him though he was married, and at last wrote that she would go to the devil unless he had an affair with her. [Russell told Murray] that the only way to deal with the situation was to do one thing or the other. Either he must have nothing to do with her or he must agree to her wish. Murray instead merely philandered, and she ultimately married B. . . .[3]

Russell's remarks suggest a relationship that may have been more than flirtatious. On the other hand, Murray was strait-laced in personal morals, an attitude incomprehensible to Russell, who presumed that his friend would behave as he might have done.

If Brailsford knew of her infidelities—real or attempted—he would have been too compliant to object. Certainly he hoped that in time she would grow to love him or at least to become content with a marriage which imposed no restraints on her friendships or the pursuit of her interests. But while Jane exploited the relationship with deliberate cruelty, she did not feel free within it. Disdaining to wear a wedding ring, which she deemed a 'sign of bondage', she continued to regard marriage as a form of subjugation, her home as a 'paddock' that enclosed her.[4]

Vain about her appearance, Jane was haunted by the fear that she would become ugly with advancing years. Nevinson, whom she completely captivated, perceived shortly after meeting her that she was—at the age of twenty-eight—'already terrified of old age'.[5] Her sister-in-law Mabel could recall sixty-five years later her vow to 'kill herself if she ever lost her beauty'.[6] But even this neurotic obsession would not in itself justify her warning early in marriage that should she become pregnant, she would drown herself. Some of this can be ascribed to self-dramatization, but given her repugnance for Brailsford, it is likely that their marriage was never consummated or, in any event, that it was virtually sexless. Russell, hardly the most reliable source on the amour-

---

[3] Clifford Allen Diary, 1 June 1919, quoted in Martin Gilbert, ed., *Plough My Own Furrow* (London, 1965), pp. 133-4.
[4] ND, 15 Sept. 1905.
[5] ND, 9 Nov. 1903.
[6] Interview, Mabel R. Brailsford.

ous foibles of others, claimed that Jane married Brailsford 'on the understanding that there should be no sexual intercourse because of her love for M[urray]'.[7] Were it not for the hints of infidelity, Jane might indeed be presumed frigid, her narcissism manifesting itself in a revulsion against sexual involvement. As if this rejection of the physical side of conjugal relations were not sufficiently humiliating, Jane showed her distaste for her husband by deflating his self-image. She taunted him with being so unattractive that she was surprised he dared to go out in society. For years he had found solace in his cello, but despite her professed enjoyment of music, she would promptly leave the house whenever he began to play. He stopped playing in order to placate her and eventually sold his instrument.[8]

What seems remarkable is that so much of this perverse relationship could be concealed from outsiders. On one occasion she told Nevinson that even 'fraternal relations were not always safe', he noting in his diary that she was 'evidently thinking of her marriage'.[9] Yet in certain aspects it remained a workable partnership. It was Brailsford's earnings as a journalist that supported them, but Jane, who aspired to a literary career, did occasionally publish book reviews in the *Manchester Guardian*. When they went to Macedonia in 1903-4, they were employed jointly as relief agents, Jane running the hospital in Ochrida until she contracted typhus. They also shared common political interests, she becoming no less devoted to Russian freedom than he.

Unlike Brailsford, whose professional life moved from accomplishment to recognition, Jane's efforts to find creative outlets were stymied. Her contempt for her husband derived partly from jealousy for his intellectual gifts and literary facility. Whether she was impeded as a woman or simply because, despite earlier promise, she lacked genuine talent is not clear, but her efforts in these years to build a reputation for herself as something other than an occasional participant in Radical compaigns invariably proved abortive. Everything she turned her hand to seemed destined either to fail or feebly to emulate his accomplishments. She once recalled to Nevinson, somewhat wistfully, 'her joy as a girl in Glasgow when Fabians sent her pamphlets and she felt she was really in touch with the heart of things'.[10] During their stay in Crete Jane was writing a novel, but despite Brailsford's efforts successive publishers rejected it, and the novel never appeared in print. After Jane began to contemplate a theatrical career, he undertook to write a play to display

---

[7] Gilbert, *Plough*, p. 134.

[8] Some years later he wrote, 'I used to play the cello, but that alas is long ago, & my poor instrument now stands in a corner without strings, a constant reproach'. HNB to H. Bräuning-Oktavio, 1 Feb. 1918, BOP.

[9] ND, 6 May 1908.   [10] ND, 3 Apr. 1907.

her acting talents and hired a London hall to perform it, but her stage début failed to elicit contracts.

All this suggests a long-suffering husband catering to the whims of a self-deluded woman. But the relationship was more masochistic than that: Brailsford never ceased blaming himself for her frustration. While his self-reproach may have been rooted in feelings of sexual inadequacy, he believed himself the cause of her unhappiness. Rather than perceive her discontent as neurotic, he attributed it entirely to their marriage, to the bond he has foisted upon her against her own inclinations. Despite his promise to devote himself to her, they grew further apart with the passing years, and she responded to his self-sacrifice with disdain. Nothing he could do would compensate for his failure to bring romance and adventure into her life, for the unfulfilled yearnings. His reputation for brilliance seemed proof of the unfairness of public esteem. She regarded herself as at least his intellectual equal, but to the outside world she was a person of no consequence. More than that, while Fleet Street extolled his integrity and independence, she knew him to be vulnerable, insecure, easily manipulated. Her refusal to live in Manchester cost him a regular appointment on the *Guardian* staff, and their years in London were punctuated by petulant outbursts on her part, after which they would announce to friends their intention of abandoning journalism to live in the country. She was, to be sure, neither wholly malicious nor self-regarding: at some level she found gratification in her husband's triumphs; reflected glory was, after all, better than no glory at all.

The contrast between professional reputation and personal deficiencies may well explain the contradictions in her behaviour towards him: comradeship in public affairs coupled with romantic intrigues with other men. Of these, the most extraordinary was that which developed with Nevinson, Brailsford's friend and journalistic colleague. During the years when he was on the most intimate footing with the Brailsfords, Nevinson, estranged from his own wife, seems to have engaged in several concurrent liaisons. Although their political affinities and literary styles were similar, the two men provide a study in contrasts. Whereas Brailsford was short and stocky, with rimless glasses and bristling hair, Nevinson was a 'handsome man who looked like a soldier and an athlete', tall and well-proportioned and 'Elizabethan' in bearing.[11] The aura of worldly adventure, combined with his striking physical attributes, attracted men and women alike. Despite his gallantry to women —flowers, fulsome letters, courtly gestures—Nevinson was a lonely man, prone to fits of despair when his overtures were rebuffed. Between

---

[11] *Listener*, 20 Nov. 1941.

1903 and 1910 he sought persistently but, for the most part, unsuccessfully to win Jane's favours.

They met initially at a Relief Committee meeting in October 1903 just before they all departed for Macedonia. Ten days later they were together in Salonica, enjoying lively dinners at which Nevinson talked 'chiefly with Mrs. B. who was interested in Yeats and other literature'. Within a few days Nevinson recognized that he had been smitten, and he believed the attraction to be mutual.[12] Although he returned to London several weeks later, the Brailsfords remained in Ochrida, so that Nevinson did not see her again until April 1904. Their first reunion afforded them no privacy, but it rekindled his ardour.

During the weeks that followed a curious pattern evolved. Nevinson would dine with both Brailsfords, conversing sociably as though nothing in their relationship had altered. But each of these evenings ended with a private tête-à-tête with Jane where, somewhat guiltily, he struggled to overcome her hesitations. Just how much Brailsford himself knew of all this—at least at this stage—is uncertain, although Nevinson recorded a walk with him 'discussing everything except the thing in our hearts'.[13] When Jane warned him to keep his distance, Nevinson told her that, love notwithstanding, he would be satisfied merely with her friendship. Yet so aroused had he become that he could not keep his part of the bargain. One explosive evening brought the following riposte from the distraught Jane:

> I feel ashamed when I think—we were together about two and a half hours. Of all that time I can remember nothing we did or said that had about it any suspicion of dignity or anything that has not made war upon one's last refuge—self-respect. All I can remember is one long struggle, your struggle to satisfy your desire, my struggle to resist my own desire. You are not made of stone-wall. I am not an iceberg. I am a 'wild animal'—yes, but with a brain—and because of that I see how degrading it was for both of us. . . . I would be your friend. I might even be more than a friend, but a mere body I will not be to anyone.[14]

For the moment at least she was able to resolve the relationship on her own terms: there was a respite in Nevinson's importunings, although he continued no less attentive. Eight months in Africa did little to dampen his passion, and upon returning in July 1905, on the eve of the passport trial, he renewed his attention. Friendship for Brailsford may have prompted the generous offer of a blank cheque loan for legal expenses, but it did not deter him from seizing the next opportunity to attempt seduction again. Just before the Brailsfords left for their unfortunate stay in Manchester in the autumn of 1905, Jane reiterated her plea to Nevinson:

[12] ND, 12-29 Oct. 1903   [13] ND, 27 Apr. 1904   [14] ND, 3 July 1904.

I want to have a simple happy friendship with you and nothing more. If that cannot be, then, as I said, I shall have to be unkind and that is what I hate.[15]

Friendship perhaps, but simple and happy it could never be. When the Brailsfords returned—living a few blocks from Nevinson in Hampstead—the intimacy resumed, although he now determined to keep his emotions under better control. Jane, reluctant to compromise her position, still relished the flirtation. 'I am glad I did not meet you earlier,' she told him. 'I should have had fewer years of peace.'[16]

As their friendship mellowed, she kept his interest alive by constantly changing her mood, one moment deliberately wounding him and the next showing only tenderness. Nevinson's diary reveals him as perplexed by her mercurial temperament, never knowing what to expect, unable to feign indifference. His disappointment was heightened by Jane's penchant for reminding him of how nearly he had succeeded. In the spring of 1907 she reproached him for 'the apparent purpose of long and secret intrigue that would have ruined her life. . . . At one time she might have given all that; she was much attracted. Is only thankful now she didn't.'[17] Without shedding the trappings of intimacy, they were never again to venture as close to sexual entanglement. In any event they were apart much more in the next few years. Nevinson left for India in October 1907, and when he returned five months later, his friends were in Egypt. By 1909 she had become engrossed in suffragette activities which often removed her from London for weeks on end.

None of this portrays Jane in a very creditable light. Self-indulgent and spoiled, deliberately cruel to those who loved her, neglectful as a daughter and probably unfaithful as a wife, she hardly seems to deserve much sympathy. Yet she was a woman of spirit and sensibility, of creative potential that never found adequate outlets. An emancipated blue-stocking, she could not contain her bitterness at the blows she felt life had dealt her. Nevinson's diary notes not merely her carefully orchestrated coquetry, but frequent illnesses and bouts of depression. For all her spitefulness, she could be ingratiating when the occasion warranted. At their first meeting Blunt found her to be 'a charming woman, very clever and sympathetic'.[18] Men were attracted by her enigmatic beauty, her enjoyment of serious discussion rather than polite banter.

It was the capacity for recklessness coupled with deep-seated frustration that led her to invest so much energy in WSPU activity between 1909 and the end of 1912. Her yearning for a cause to which she could

---

[15] ND, 15 Sept. 1905.
[16] ND, 9 Nov. 1905.
[17] ND, 18 June 1907.
[18] Blunt Transcript Diary, 9 May 1908, BP, MS 8-1975.

wholeheartedly commit herself, her ambition for notoriety in her own right, were satisfied for the first time in the franchise agitation. That sense of exhilaration, of constraints removed, seemed to promise liberation in the company of other militant women never fully achieved in relationships with men. While Brailsford tried to restrain her—without success—from behaving impetuously, he found himself, at least initially, following her lead. The suffrage movement seemed to unite them in a common purpose, but in fact her activities kept them physically apart for long periods, and their disagreement about tactics aggravated existing tensions. Much as her instincts responded to the appeal of militancy, it was her experience of prison in the early months of her involvement that transformed her into a zealot.

I came through so little [she wrote to Blunt] compared to what some of my friends have suffered. I do not know how this detestable government can hold up its head. It is simply driving women who have no particular desire for a vote to revolt from a sense of comradeship. I don't think that I should ever have become 'militant' if I had not seen other women persecuted.[19]

Once committed, however, she could not retreat, and the militant campaign become essentially a vocation for her, her days filled with demonstrations and speeches despite the risk of prison. She never understood her husband's cautious approach, his concern to secure a compromise legislative solution. Even Nevinson, a more consistent supporter of the Pankhursts than Brailsford, was dismayed to find her so 'full of desperate fighting spirit against everyone who even hesitated.'[20]

When Mrs Pankhurst and Christabel expelled the Pethick-Lawrences from the WSPU in October 1912, Jane was shattered. It was not that she had been personally close to the Pethick-Lawrences, but rather that her idols had at last done something she could not condone. While she did not object to heightened militancy, she found intolerable the Pankhurst quest for absolute control. By the end of November she had resigned from the Union, cutting herself off from any organizational base. Profoundly depressed, she fled from London for some months. Her brother Donald's death in December compounded her grief, and Nevinson's diary during these months refers frequently to her absence and 'mysterious illness'.[21]

The situation worsened: clearly overwrought, she quarrelled with Brailsford about militancy and may well have begun the heavy drinking that blighted her later years. By mid-April Nevinson, often oblivious to anyone else's unhappiness, noted after seeing Jane that 'things are evidently at crisis there or strained to breaking'.[22] On 4 May the

---

[19] Jane Brailsford to W. S. Blunt, 2 Jan. 1910, BP.
[20] ND, 29 Oct. 1909.
[21] ND, see e.g. 12 and 13 Jan. 1913.
[22] ND, 17 Apr. 1913.

Brailsfords agreed to separate, and 32 Well Walk was put up to let. Jane told Nevinson that 'there is another woman more beloved',[23] an excuse too implausible to deceive him. In any event she moved into a flat in Warwick Crescent, while Brailsford temporarily found lodgings with the journalist James Bone, his friend from Glasgow, in King's Bench Walk. The separation was provisional, with Brailsford continuing to visit his estranged wife. His departure for three months in the Balkans with the Carnegie Commission left matters unresolved.

Her health—physical and psychological—remained precarious. In April 1914 Nevinson, spending an evening with her, learned that she was 'very ill, has been for 10 weeks'.[24] Apparently her disillusionment with the Pankhursts' leadership precipitated a breakdown, whose effects lasted well into 1914 and probably long after. Nevinson did not see her again until he visited the Brailsfords in their Welwyn cottage at the end of August, but Blunt provides an illuminating account of a visit by Brailsford alone in mid-July, a few weeks after they had retired to the country:

I have had two days with Brailsford and much pleasant talk on literature, politics and philosophy, on all of which we have many ideas in common, but he is more of a pessimist than I am because with very great talents he has produced nothing of much effect. He has achieved little and enjoyed little and will have nothing that will live after him. His marriage has proved a failure and he has no children though it is not true that there has been a separation. But his wife has become a militant suffragette of an extreme type and he finds himself cut off by it not only from his friends but from his bread and butter as a journalist. She will have nothing to do with non-suffragist mankind.[25]

If Welwyn was intended to restore Jane and rehabilitate their marriage, it obviously failed. Their remaining years together only intensified the resentment and recriminations. Brailsford ordinarily spent the week in Welwyn, going up to London only for *Nation* editorial lunches. Friends could not understand why he had become so taciturn; fearing that Jane might be drunk when they arrived, he had gradually stopped inviting any of them to the house. Nevinson, a daily caller when they were Hampstead neighbours, visited the Brailsfords only three times in their five years in Welwyn. His account of an April 1915 trip indicates that the bickering had not abated:

Mrs. Brailsford met me at the Green: has grown very stout and rather deliberately rude and unpleasant in manner. Is probably unhappy in every respect, differing from HNB on all points—peace and war etc. She thinks vengeance

[23] ND, 4 May 1913.   [24] ND, 1 Apr. 1914.
[25] Blunt Transcript Diary, 13 July 1914, BP, MS 14-1975.

for supposed atrocities must be exacted from Germany and supports the 'crushing' policy. He is for easy terms so as to avoid future revenge.[26]

Brailsford escaped from marital miseries by writing and by plunging deeper into political activity, but Jane found little to do. Her brilliance and beauty had been wasted, and now in middle age she had few resources left.

Scarcely anything is known of the Brailsfords in Welwyn—or indeed of Jane at all after 1914—but Allen's harrowing description of his visit to them in 1919 shows that the intervening years had taken their toll. It was his first glimpse of the woman who had once charmed Murray, Blunt, and Nevinson, not to mention innumerable Glasgow undergraduates. She was now forty-four years old:

Had often heard of [Brailsford's] mysterious wife. She had overheard us talking as we came past the edge of the garden when B. had been describing a terrible old witch who had 'squatted' on the piece of common ground a little way from the house. Mrs. B with sparkling and malicious wit asked us whether it was of her that we and her husband had been talking. She seemed to me to be a person with a past, and I wondered whether she had some time perhaps in Macedonia or even elsewhere committed a murder. She is excited, and nervy, anxious to talk much and quickly to avoid pauses for observation; she often sparkles in a quite horribly brilliant way, and then seems almost mad and secretly morose. I could not make out what part sex played in her make up; it might have done so vigorously in the past, but did not do so now. Her relation to B. seemed astonishing and either malicious or totally impersonal. There seemed far more in the ordinary domestic quips that pass between such people than usually appeared. 'Madam' he always called her with a strange emphasis. She was like a haunted figure from some foreign novel . . . I am convinced that there is a good chance of this woman going mad, when the whole tragedy of her life will suddenly flash back on her and then she might well kill Brailsford.[27]

[26] ND, 17 Apr. 1915.   [27] Gilbert, *Plough*, pp. 132-4.

VIII

The Pen Against The Sword (1914–1918)

Brailsford, whose ancestors had fought Charles I and who had, with few qualms, taken up arms to defend the Greek cause in 1897, was neither by temperament nor inheritance a pacifist. Much as he deplored nationalist excesses, he was still able to condone wars of liberation against the Turks, to contend that it was worse to submit to oppression than to rebel against it. His opposition to the First World War, unyielding and consistent, stemmed mainly from a sense that it could have been avoided had there been an effective Concert of Europe or had national motives been less hypocritical. Yet if his writings before and after 1914 tried, above all, to disentangle economic and strategic realities from propaganda, they also reflected a deepening revulsion against war itself. It was the searing vision of carnage during the Second Balkan War that instilled in him an opposition to war that remained unalterable until the Spanish crisis rekindled dormant sentiments in 1936.

Returning from the Balkans in October 1913, the image of devastation indelibly stamped on his consciousness, he completed the manuscript of *The War of Steel and Gold*. In a revealing passage, quoted in part earlier, he described his initiation into battle during his first trip to the Balkans. It was when stumbling over the corpse of a Turkish soldier in Thessaly that he first perceived the 'enemy' as a simple peasant, sacrificed to abstractions whose meaning he probably never comprehended. This early experience, vividly recalled some sixteen years after his Balkan visit, showed him that human kinship transcended the political illusions over which nations fought, but, more significantly, that the process of war itself was dehumanizing:

War is the suspense and annihilation of the individual conscience. It blots out for the soldier the humanity of the men whom he opposes, and blurs them together in one unrealised and unimagined horde which he calls the enemy.

His abhorrence of bloodshed and unswerving allegiance to English liberties were the lodestars of his world, as deeply rooted as his concern for the oppressed. It was the persistence of these values that dictated his opposition to war no less than his recognition that in any European war 'two armies mainly composed of working men would face each other in the service of some capitalist intrigue, and in defence of interests whose chief concern is their exploitation'.[1]

Brailsford's stress on the economic basis of international affairs derived mainly from Hobson's writings on imperialism, but until August 1914 he shared the Radical outlook on war and peace. The personal bonds forged during pro-Boer agitation at the turn of the century had strengthened during campaigns against increased armaments and entangling alliances. Nowhere more than in the columns of the *Nation* was the British government exhorted to uphold the peaceful traditions of Liberalism and to strive for European reconciliation. However its staff clashed over women's suffrage, the *Nation* spoke with a single voice—usually that of Brailsford, perhaps tempered by Massingham—when the peace of Europe was threatened. The advent of war shattered this unanimity and brought to an end the uneasy partnership of Radicals and the Liberal Party. To be sure, Brailsford had never been an unqualified admirer of Gladstone's heirs. But although he had joined the ILP as long ago as 1907 and did not hesitate to attack Grey's diplomacy and Asquith's handling of suffragette militancy, he had not, any more than other progressives, written off Liberalism. The war, however, was to sever his remaining ties and to move him definitively into the Labour camp, a progression other Radicals were to follow after 1918.

He had never denied that the preconditions for a European war existed. Indeed the increase in armaments and the tightening of rival alliances heightened international tension to the point of explosion. But as long as the conflicts were directed towards distant regions ripe for economic exploitation, the likelihood of war had seemed remote. When a war began to loom as an immediate danger, he joined other Radicals in calling for British neutrality. But once the Belgian invasion was made a *casus belli*, many Radicals, including several of Brailsford's *Nation* colleagues, beat a hasty retreat from their erstwhile opposition to war. The violation of Belgian neutrality split the Radicals, with Massingham, Hammond, Hobhouse, Murray, and Gardiner shifting from 'principled support of neutrality to principled support of the war'.[2] Brailsford, formerly more a Gladstonian than a Cobdenite, encouraging at least moral intervention in the cause of national self-determination, came down now on the Cobdenite side. Having contended for more than a decade that the differences among the powers could be settled by mutual concession, he was not swayed by the patriotic outbursts about the rectitude of England's cause. His con-

---

[1] *WSG*, pp. 177-9.
[2] Peter Clarke, *Liberals and Social Democrats* (Cambridge, 1978), p. 168.

tinued vehemence against the war did not deprive him of his livelihood —the *Nation*, to its credit, still provided a forum, however fractious, for divergent Radical views—but he found himself in conflict with many long-standing associates.

The last months of 1914 were a profoundly desolate time for him as, for somewhat different reasons, the start of the Second World War would be as well. The collapse of the European order paralleled his own personal distress, and he had little hope that the pieces could be put together. Removal to Welwyn failed to halt the disintegration of his marriage. In the face of Jane's growing irascibility, he began to shield himself from social contacts and the solicitude of friends. Despite his prolific output and involvement in the Union of Democratic Control, he was lonely, living out of London and reproached by friends for his outspoken anti-war sentiments.

Even though he had not anticipated the coming of war, he was certainly not at a loss to explain its causes. Indeed his writings during the previous decade, concentrating on the seething Balkan cauldron, can serve as an extended inquiry into its origins. Unlike Massingham, whose pre-war pacifism made his later writings seem defensive, Brailsford had no tracks to cover, and his remarks after August 1914 are completely consistent with what he had written before. As an authority on European relations, he saw his task as twofold: first, to determine, free from jingoistic bias, the causes of the war, and, second, to identify the means to end the conflict as soon as possible. Against those who defended British participation in order to avenge Belgium and preserve Europe from Prussian militarism, Brailsford countered that 'no nation save innocent Belgium can come forward with clean hands'. Germany intended 'to win a vulgar blustering diplomatic triumph over [Russia], to weaken her prestige and to break up the Entente—but she hoped to manage all this without war'.[3] Far from blameless, English diplomats had linked the nation's destinies with two restless powers: France, risking the division of Europe into armed camps in order to exploit Morocco, and Russia, scheming to disrupt Austria and rushing to mobilize at the expense of peace. But even if Germany were defeated, militarism would remain:

Every proposal to take German provinces and dismember Austria is a justification of the German belief that the position of the German race in Central Europe is made tenable only by its vast armies, its cult of ruthlessness, and its readiness to subordinate civilian rights to military claims.[4]

Such an analysis was indeed only a variant on an earlier Brailsford

[3] HNB to Francis Johnson, 26 May 1915, Johnson Papers.
[4] Letter to Editor, *Nation*, 29 Aug. 1914.

theme: Germany's mistreatment by other European powers. It was fear and envy that engendered militarism; reconciliation, not conquest, was necessary to transform German attitudes.

In another letter to the *Nation* three weeks later he was to warn against the delusion of a 'fight to a finish' which would bring Germany to its knees. A dictated peace would require 'years of warfare' and would 'decimate the whole manhood of Europe'. What in retrospect proved prophetic contradicted popular assumptions of victory by Christmas 1914. Even if a resounding German military defeat were possible, it would have the disastrous effect of uniting the population 'as it never has been united since the Napoleonic wars' in order to erase the humiliation.

It was therefore essential in the early days of the conflict to articulate principles of a settlement that would not only reconcile the antagonists, but liberate subject peoples. A just and durable peace could only be achieved if principles were applied universally, with the good of one's enemy, not retribution, as the goal. While England ought to forfeit any claim to colonies or compensation, Belgium deserved some indemnity for its suffering. The claims of nationality might be satisfied if all powers pledged to accept federalism, but, failing that, some territorial changes were probably inevitable. Instead of automatically dismembering the Central European empires, plebiscites should be ordered in Alsace, Posen, Galicia, and the Serbian and Italian parts of the Hapsburg Empire. Finally, he argued that negotiations should begin as soon as Germany was prepared to consider general disarmament, not once the Allies had secured their military objectives.[5]

A vital aspect of these early formulations was Brailsford's acceptance of the reality of a war whose occurrence and conduct he never ceased to lament. Refusing to acknowledge Germany as sole culprit, he rendered himself liable to the charge of pro-German sympathies by harping on the need for reciprocity and fair treatment. Massingham, espousing identical views six weeks earlier, now disputed the wisdom of compromise. When Brailsford denounced the clamour for 'a fight to a finish', his editor argued that any war ending in a 'draw' would leave the conflict unsettled.[6] Their dispute broadened into disagreement over the origins of the war. When the editor cited German pride as the source of the conflict, Brailsford retorted that had the Russians been warned that Anglo-French support was contingent on avoiding provocation, the war might have been averted. 'The man who denies that the Allies have any share in this collapse of civilization,' he insisted, 'is the enemy of a better future.'[7]

[5] Letter to Editor, *Nation*, 19 Sept. 1914.
[6] *Daily News*, 21 Sept. 1914. [7] *Nation*, 12 Dec. 1914.

As with women's suffrage several years before, the disputes at *Nation* lunches were even more acrimonious than the published disagreements. Nevinson recorded a 'very distracted' gathering in September, with 'HNB becoming more & more German as the patriot slush rises'. By March 1915 Hobhouse and even Hammond joined in 'attacking Brailsford with unfair & scandalous abuse as a pro-German'.[8] The latter kept his temper under this onslaught and, somewhat ironically, cooled off at military drill in a volunteer club after *Nation* lunches. Too old by several years to be called up once conscription was launched, he did enrol as a Private in the Second Batallion in the City of London Volunteer Regiment from June 1916 to January 1918. Until the *Nation* staff, chastened by the 1916 battle reports and by repugnant conscription, began to advocate a negotiated peace, Brailsford and Hobson found their views decidedly unpopular. Rothstein, acquainted with several of them from the *Daily News*, sneered at leftists who 'abandoned all their principles & swallowed every lie the Government told them. All his friends here in London have done this except Brailsford & one or two others.'[9]

It was at the start of his self-imposed seclusion, amid the welter of recrimination, that Brailsford became involved in one of the most remarkable relationships in his life. In July 1914 Hermann Bräuning-Oktavio, a twenty-eight year old aspiring German critic, came to London intending to study the British theatre. Stranded in England by the war, he sought shelter at a Quaker college in the Midlands before being interned as an enemy alien on the Isle of Man for the duration of the war. At the beginning of 1915, casting about for productive work, he wrote to Brailsford, whose *War of Steel and Gold* had impressed him, to propose a German translation. Despite the fact that such a project was already under way, Brailsford encouraged him to proceed:

To come into any friendly intellectual touch with one of the 'enemy' is quite the best thing that can happen to any of us in these miserable days. . . . I should like to have it translated, not merely because one wants one's ideas to spread, but also because it will help the creation of better relations between our two countries . . .[10]

Little came of the proposal, but the chance contact soon ripened into friendship. Bräuning-Oktavio, the hapless victim of circumstance, became Brailsford's private cause. Feeling himself an alien in his own world, he could respond to the plight of the interned German. It was his way of making restitution, a personal atonement for his country's

---

[8] ND, 22 Sept. 1914, 23 Mar. 1915.
[9] Blunt Transcript Diary, 3 July 1915, BP, MS 15-1975.
[10] HNB to H. Bräuning-Oktavio, 31 Jan. 1915, BOP.

complicity in a war he abhorred. To befriend one of the 'enemy' was to refute his government's indictment of the Hun, to suggest that human contact need not cease because nations were at war.

Although shyness militated against easy intimacy, Brailsford was often impelled to reach out to those in need of help, especially to those exiled because of war. It might be too facile to suggest that, feeling himself cut off from ordinary humanity, he should feel an affinity for the homeless, the uprooted, the political victim. Yet it was to just such people that he extended his deepest sympathy—Balkan peasants whose villages had been destroyed, Spanish and Russian political exiles, Jewish refugees from Hitler's camps. He could identify with their misfortune and, more significantly, believe that he could alleviate it. In some ways these relationships, however one-sided, were more satisfying than those built on equality. After Jane, he tended to seek out women towards whom, because of age disparity, he could adopt a protective manner. So too, his male friends were often much younger, eager for the proffered solicitude and paternal advice he never received from his own father. These were safe relationships from which his battered psyche would receive no unanticipated injuries. Similar tendencies characterized his friendship with Bräuning-Oktavio. The acquaintance was fortuitous, coming when his marriage was dissolving and other bonds were at least temporarily strained. His life with Jane had become intolerable, the two seeming to coexist at Welwyn only by ignoring each other—a breakdown of companionship coupled with enforced mutual toleration. The new friendship filled that void by providing a focus for self-sacrifice that Brailsford craved. Paradoxically, Jane too regarded herself as a prisoner and sought solace in drink and vituperation, against which, by 1914, he had ceased to struggle. Physical distance promoted, rather than hindered, the relationship with Bräuning-Oktavio, giving it an intensity it might not otherwise have developed. In four years the two met only once, when Brailsford visited the Isle of Man in 1916. It flourished because it called for generosity instead of intimacy, enabling Brailsford to assume the role of benefactor without fear of rebuff.

When it seemed likely that Bräuning-Oktavio would be interned in the summer of 1915, Brailsford offered to write to Sir John Simon, once his own defence counsel and now Home Secretary, on his behalf and tried to ease his apprehension:

Personally I would very much rather be put in a Concentration Camp than in solitary confinement in a prison. But I can understand your dread of the promiscuity and coarse fare. None the less, even such experiences have their value for a student. I would not for worlds have missed my experience of life in the Greek Foreign Legion during the war of 1897.[11]

The Home Office appeal failed, although Simon gave assurances that the camp doctor would be instructed to watch the case. Brailsford not only continued to send books but food, underwear, flower seeds, cloth for a coat, and, finally, money every month. He could vent his feelings of isolation without fear of reproach, since it was his antipathy for the war that had alienated him:

Not to feel as a whole nation around one feels—that is the worst & ugliest fate in war & the sense of keeping one's own objective mind clear is no great compensation.[12]

Isolated, but certainly not excluded from the *Nation*, Brailsford soon found opportunities to cast his net more widely and to establish his reputation abroad. In July 1914 he was introduced to Walter Lippmann, an encounter that led to a fruitful thirty-two year association with the *New Republic*, the progressive American weekly launched with funds from heiress Dorothy Whitney Straight, later the wife of Leonard Elmhirst. Lippmann, not long out of Harvard, had been appointed Assistant Editor and was taking advantage of a London trip to discover potential foreign contributors. A provisional arrangement was soon concluded whereby Brailsford would contribute a weekly article on international affairs at a rate of two cents a word. Lippmann told him that the *New Republic* was 'counting on your knowledge of the Near East'.[13] His first two articles, dispatched in mid-October, dealt mainly with the Balkans, but he warned of the risks in writing about that region 'for the situation may alter abruptly any day'. Lippmann's offer proved too generous: almost immediately Brailsford was reduced to an article every other week, and as the war progressed and mails grew less dependable, somewhat less regularly.[14]

Just as with women's suffrage, journalism seemed to him an inadequate vehicle for influencing the public mind, especially once anti-war publications were restricted by the government. He had been excluded, perhaps inadvertently, from deliberations which led to the founding of the Union of Democratic Control, as his letter to Arthur Ponsonby indicates:

I have been thinking spasmodically ever since the war began (& I think you

---

[11] HNB to H. Bräuning-Oktavio, 16 July 1915, BOP.
[12] HNB to H. Bräuning-Oktavio, 21 Dec. 1916 BOP.
[13] Walter Lippmann to HNB, 28 Sept. 1914, Lippmann Papers, Box 4.
[14] HNB to Walter Lippmann, 12 Oct. [1914]. Also HNB to Walter Lippmann, 14 and 16 Oct. [1914], Lippmann Papers, Box 4. 'The Empire of the East' appeared in *New Republic* on 7 Nov. 1914 and 'Turkish Adventure' on 21 Nov. 1914.

have also) that some organization should be formed to intervene at the appropriate moment to stop it. How far off that is I can't guess. But it may come when the German armies are drawn out of France or Belgium. Many people who regard it as in a sense defensive now will be of a different mind when it becomes obviously a war for world power & the crushing of Germany. If even the ILP, the Society of Friends, & the few Radicals who think as we do could act together, there would be a nucleus for action.[15]

By this time a private letter, jointly signed by MacDonald, Angell, Morel, and C. P. Trevelyan, had been circulated among prospective UDC supporters, although news of the organization did not appear in the press until mid-September. The UDC's four point charter, calling for no territorial changes without plebiscite, democratic control of foreign policy, reduction of armaments, and an international council to arbitrate disputes, invoked principles that Brailsford had expounded. Indeed there was little in the charter that Radicals who supported the war could not endorse, although the UDC was soon to be denounced as defeatist.

It was not until 17 November 1914 that the UDC held the inaugural meeting of its General Council, to which Brailsford was named. More important than committee work was his contribution of two pamphlets, the first issued on 7 November in an edition of 10,000. By the time the meeting was held ten days later 6,000 had been sold.[16] *The Origins of the Great War*, published as Union of Democratic Control Pamphlet No. 4 —the first three were by Morel, Angell, and Russell—was in fact a reprint of an article that had appeared in *Contemporary Review* in September. Appended to the essay was Brailsford's *Nation* letter of 19 September, setting forth the principles of a settlement. Its major premise was that the war hinged entirely on conflicts in the East, specifically on the rivalry between Russia and Austria, rather than on German designs on France or desire for naval supremacy. To the German military caste, the waxing of Serbian power in the Balkans was a warning that 'it would sooner or later have to meet a Russian challenge'. If there was moral responsibility for the war, he concluded, it must be 'shared between Germany and Russia'.[17]

A stridently anti-Russian interpretation also emerged in Brailsford's first article for the ILP's *Labour Leader*. Although he reiterated the view that Russia and Germany were mutually responsible, he paid scant attention to Germany's role. Rather he stressed Russia's guilt as the first of the powers to order a general mobilization, since 'she knew

---

[15] HNB to Arthur Ponsonby, 2 Sept. [1914], Ponsonby Papers, c. 661, fols. 10-11. Also see HNB to C. P. Trevelyan, 9 Sept. 1914, Trevelyan Papers, Box 17.
[16] Minutes of UDC General Council, 17 Nov. 1914, UDC Papers.
[17] *Origins of the Great War*, UDC Pamphlet No. 4 (1914), pp. 3-8, 13-14.

perfectly well that war must inevitably follow. There was no blundering, no muddling into war. Russia marched into war, resolutely and with foresight.' If there was a blank cheque offered, it was that given by England and France to their Entente partner.[18]

Unlike those Liberals who gravitated to the ILP as a result of wartime disillusionment with the Liberal government, Brailsford's affiliation antedated the war. Formerly a member of the Islington branch, he acceded to the invitation of Herbert Bryan, the enterprising secretary of the City of London ILP branch, to affiliate in March 1915, warning that he would seldom be able to attend discussions.[19] Brailsford's value lay in the expert knowledge of European affairs, possessed by few contributors, that he could bring to ILP publications. Keir Hardie, who had not hesitated to take advantage of his knowledge of Russia in earlier years, had by this time proposed that he produce a series of pamphlets for party distribution. Several topics were mentioned, among them secret diplomacy, Russian militarism, Belgian neutrality, and the Balkans.[20] Two pamphlets, both subsequently suppressed by the government, did appear in 1915: *Belgium and 'The Scrap of Paper'* and an abbreviated, updated version of his 1912 essay entitled *Persia, Finland and Our Russian Alliance*.

The Belgian pamphlet cast doubt on the sanctity of England's obligations and intimated that German conduct was not without precedent in international history. Belgian security was clearly 'a claim on the honour or her neighbours', but the 1839 treaty, prescribing neutrality, did not compel its signatories to defend that neutrality with arms. More importantly, it was hardly 'straight dealing' not to caution Germany, whose military strategists had plotted the invasion 'without the faintest suspicion that to attack Belgium was to attack us'. Such an interpretation came perilously close to the apologetics Brailsford explicitly disavowed. He was essentially blaming England for not preventing the German invasion, much as he reproached Grey for failing to restrain Russia from mobilizing. Even Belgium could be criticized, at least implicitly, for incurring needless suffering. Once it became apparent that the invasion could not be averted, might it not have been preferable to acquiesce and thus, presumably, avoid senseless destruction?[21]

Brailsford's heterodox views attracted attention, little of it favourable. He did, to be sure, contribute not only to the *New Republic* and the *Labour Leader*, but also to the *Herald*, to Angell's *War and Peace*, and to

[18] *Labour Leader*, 10 Dec. 1914. Also see *New Leader*, 13 Apr. 1923.
[19] HNB to Herbert Bryan, 21 Mar. [1915], City of London ILP Papers, General Correspondence, V.b, fol. 51. Brailsford was elected at the March annual meeting.
[20] HNB to Keir Hardie, 25 Nov. [1914], Hardie/ILP Papers.
[21] *Belgium and 'The Scrap of Paper'*, ILP Labour and War Pamphlet No. 10 (1915), pp. 1-5, 10-11.

the UDC's own monthly. In addition, prominent Liberal dissidents, finding his remarks congenial, recommended him to wavering colleagues.[22] More frequently, his interpretation offended his audience, even those on the left who had once echoed his assumptions. *The Origins of the Great War* elicited a stinging rejoinder from Murray which led to a cooling of their friendship. Murray's polemical *Foreign Policy of Sir Edward Grey* tried not merely to rehabilitate Grey's reputation, but to denigrate critics, especially Brailsford and Russell. It was not enough to label as pro-German their concern 'to state the case for Germany as clearly and as fairly as possible'. Murray charged that the anti-war pamphleteers ignored facts, intending to mislead the public into believing that Germany was blameless and that Grey was 'the central enemy of the human race'.[23] Even within the bounds of permissible exaggeration, such a summary grossly distorted their meaning. Not content with impugning his integrity, Murray went on to recall Brailsford's approval of 'a policy of mere submission' to Germany's extortionate demands. Far from asserting the 'comparative harmlessness of being conquered by Germany', the objectionable passage of *The War of Steel and Gold* simply conjectured that German imperial gains would have left Europe substantially unchanged.[24]

To reject his caricature is not to deny 'pro-Germanism' as Murray initially defined it. Brailsford certainly tried to counter the bias of jingoist propaganda by reiterating the validity of pre-war German grievances and by ascribing equal blame to other powers, notably Russia. But as the war progressed he shifted his attention from the past to the future, contending that Germany, never having desired a universal war, would accept reasonable peace terms. Whatever the pretext for war, its underlying causes related to the growth of German population and restraints on the export of capital, a desire for *lebensraum* expressed in terms of imperial ambitions. Failing co-operative international development of the world's resources, some fair allocation had to be devised to prevent

> such an obvious anomaly as the assignment of an area like Morocco to a Power like France, with a dwindling population, possessed already of two good colonies of the same type (Algeria and Tunis), while Germany with a teeming population has none.

That it was inconsistent to condemn imperialism while advocating that Germany be given her share of its fruits seems hardly to have concerned him. As long as imperialism was the name of the game, Germany

---

[22] See Viscount Morley to Viscount Bryce, 24 Nov. 1914, Bryce Papers, UB 12.
[23] Gilbert Murray, *The Foreign Policy of Sir Edward Grey* (Oxford, 1915), pp. 5-9.
[24] Murray, p. 109. See *WSG*, pp. 33-5.

had a right to be included among the players. What is perhaps more surprising is the undercurrent of social darwinism which subordinated undeveloped regions of the world to the economic imperatives of European civilization. It was just such a perception of the Boer conflict that had driven Brailsford from the Fabian Society, and he had continually reproached those who justified England's role in Egypt or Ireland in similar terms. But with Germany cast in the role of victim, cheated of her share by devious rivals, it seemed somehow less reprehensible to uphold her claims. To be sure, he never regarded her aggrandizement as anything but an expedient to mitigate hostilities, an attempt to cope with the world as it was rather than as it should be. Until there was some advance towards genuine international government, it was essential to 'arrange for the equitable allotment of these exclusive areas of opportunity'.[25]

By the beginning of 1915, with all signs pointing to a protracted war, many Radicals were turning their attention to the organization of peace. Even if the war continued until Germany's defeat, they wanted to forestall a dictated peace and provide for a basic restructuring of international relations. Divisions emerged between those who sought a limited league as a substitute for traditional diplomacy and those promoting international government. But there were tactical differences as well. The Bryce Group, under G. Lowes Dickinson's influence, wanted to avoid antagonizing sympathetic Liberals by taking a position on the origins or conduct of the war, as the UDC had done. Their scheme for a league of limited authority was entirely compatible with support for the war and the defeat of Germany. In contrast, the more extreme advocates, repudiating military victory, envisaged a league as an alternative to Germany's defeat. Whatever their attitude to the war itself, they believed that only a federal union with legislative power, capable of enforcing decisions by military means, would be sufficiently potent to guarantee the peace. To Dickinson, such proposals smacked of utopian illusion. 'Our worst enemies,' he told Ponsonby, an opponent of armed sanctions, 'are really men like Brailsford and Hobson, who go for federation. They won't get that; but they may easily help to prevent our getting what we ask for.'[26] Fundamental as these distinctions were, they did not prevent Brailsford, Hobson, and Dickinson from collaborating in the League of Nations Society, an umbrella organization established to popularize the concept. In 1917 Brailsford, Leonard Woolf, and Dickinson were members of a lecture 'circus' arranged by the Society, following each other at weekly intervals in

---

[25] *War and Peace*, Feb. 1915.
[26] G. L. Dickinson to Arthur Ponsonby, 2 Apr. 1915, quoted in E. M. Forster, *Goldsworthy Lowes Dickinson* (New York, 1934), p. 165.

various towns with lectures sponsored by the Workers' Educational Association.[27]

Brailsford, recently cited as 'the most outstanding advocate of real international government during the war years',[28] joined the debate early and in characteristic fashion. Unwilling to blame the war on German militarism or on 'outbreaks of accidental passion',[29] he was dissatisfied with a league designed merely to inhibit aggression. Modern conflicts were rooted in economic rivalry, and a mechanism had to be devised which could solve economic problems and remove legitimate grievances. But this meant the subordination of national ambitions to a federal authority equipped with legislative and coercive powers.

Some of these ideas were prefigured in his pre-war publications, but it was, significantly, a new edition of *The War of Steel and Gold* in July 1915 that offered their first systematic exposition. He found little reason to amend the original text except to remove the mistaken prediction that there would be no war among the powers. In a postscript he identified the psychological basis of the war as a 'fatalistic belief that fundamental change is possible in Europe only as a sequel to war'.[30] Commitment to an alliance meant forfeiting autonomy without gaining reciprocal 'control of nation over nation'. The only alternative was to fuse rival alliances into 'a single European system with an impartial machinery of mutual control'. Only a 'World-State' could internationalize the export of capital and apportion territorial concessions. Where economic incentives failed to secure compliance, military sanctions might be applied by pooled international forces.[31]

Brailsford returned to these themes several months later in his contribution to *Towards a Lasting Settlement*, a collection of pro-League essays edited by C. Roden Buxton. Although he endorsed Dickinson's proposal for the submission of disputes to an international council, he regarded this as a minimal commitment. A promise to refrain from war was expedient, but it would not remove the temptation to arm even during a moratorium. Only by creating effective international organs, based on economic ties, would it be possible to remedy the deficiencies of a rudimentary scheme of conciliation.[32]

These ideas were increasingly linked with proposals for peace by negotiation, given new urgency with the passage of the Military Ser-

---

[27] David Mitrany, *The Functional Theory of Politics* (London, 1975), p. 6.

[28] Henry R. Winkler, *The League of Nations Movement in Great Britain, 1914-1919* (New Brunswick, 1952), p. 33.

[29] *War and Peace*, Feb. 1915. See Leonard Woolf, *Beginning Again* (London, 1964), p. 191.

[30] *WSG*, rev. ed., p. 315. Also see 'The Organization of Peace', in C. R. Buxton, ed., *Towards a Lasting Settlement* (London, 1915), pp. 151-3.

[31] *WSG*, rev. ed., pp. 323-6.

[32] 'Organization of Peace', p. 173.

vice Act in February 1916. Conscription aroused the opposition of erstwhile war supporters such as Massingham, whose *Nation* had modified its editorial tone. With casualties increasing, talk of defeating Germany dwindled on the left, to be replaced by a demand for a clear statement of war aims. It was in this atmosphere of heightened expectation that Brailsford proposed 'a peace by satisfaction'. Translated into specific proposals, his plan seemed remarkably modest. Instead of restructuring Europe, he suggested little more than a return to the prewar arrangement with the more flagrant abuses rectified. Thus Belgium and Serbia should be restored, France evacuated, and Alsace-Lorraine returned to her. Whatever the attraction of independence for the Poles, reunion within a revivified Austrian Empire offered a more practicable solution for a landlocked state trapped between three rival empires. Internal self-government might be extended to transform the Hapsburg Monarchy into a 'quintuple Federal Empire', consisting of Austria, Hungary, Bohemia, Poland, and Yugoslavia.[33] Germany would not only regain her colonies or be compensated with equivalent territory, but would be permitted closer economic links with Austria and opportunities for expansion in Asia Minor.

Central to the proposals was a determination to avoid punishing Germany for aggression, to admit that the war had been an error, and to find some basis short of total victory for negotiations. Never intended to influence British authorities, these proposals were devised with one eye towards American opinion and the other towards the enemy. Brailsford had long contended that concessions would have prevented war; now he maintained that an even-handed settlement would end it. America, however, represented a new factor in the international balance. Disillusioned with Liberalism at home, British Radicals looked to Wilson to rekindle idealistic hopes for a democratic order. By showing him that there was a substantial body of opinion in England approving a moderate solution, they might encourage him to mediate the conflict. Their views were propagated through American publications, particularly the *New Republic*, to which anti-war writers contributed. During a visit to London in November 1917 Colonel E. M. House, Wilson's confidant, conferred with disaffected Radicals, Brailsford among them, and conveyed their views to Washington.[34]

Certainly in the early months of 1916 Brailsford expected more from

[33] The *UDC*, Feb. 1916.

[34] Laurence W. Martin, *Peace Without Victory: Woodrow Wilson and the British Liberals* (New Haven, 1958), p. 150; Charles Seymour, ed., *The Intimate Papers of Colonel House*, III (Boston, 1928), p. 235. Also see V. H. Rothwell, *British Wars Aims and Peace Diplomacy, 1914-1918* (Oxford, 1971), p. 97. Brailsford met House only once in 1917 but sent him articles and memoranda on other occasions. See *New Leader*, 5 Mar. 1926. He was also in touch with William H. Buckler, special State Department agent, in April 1917. Havighurst, *Massingham*, p. 256.

American initiatives than from the inert Asquithian leadership. Opposed to the introduction of conscription, he was horrified by the ill-treatment of imprisoned conscientious objectors, reported to him by his friend Catherine Marshall. He even contemplated, rather briefly to be sure, joining the staff of the No-Conscription Fellowship and did serve as a member of its Associates' Political Committee. Further contact, however, convinced him that the NCF was 'a blind alley which won't bring us even infinitesimally nearer to peace'.[35]

Although British leaders, suspicious of Wilsonian diplomacy, discouraged American overtures, Brailsford was heartened by the President's apparent support for a league of peace. It was partly in response to Wilson's May 1916 endorsement of a league and of the principle of self-determination that he resolved to incorporate his views into a full-scale, systematic study, his first book since *The War of Steel and Gold*. For Brailsford a league and a just settlement were inseparable: it was futile to establish any international organization unless it could become an 'instrument of fundamental change'.[36] Written mainly in the summer of 1916, *A League of Nations* was completed in October and appeared in February 1917. The book provoked enough comment to warrant reprinting by Headley in April, and a second edition was issued in November. The League of Nations Society, tactically committed to a less ambitious scheme, issued a guide to help readers evaluate the proposals, and Dickinson, cool to Brailsford's hopes for world federation, admitted that it was 'much the ablest book' on the subject.[37] But these were mere ripples in a sea of complacency, its impact lost in the patriotic tide.

The discrepancy between Lloyd George's insistence on guarantees before negotiation and Wilson's appeal for 'peace without victory' discouraged those on the left who anticipated a more conciliatory approach from the new Coalition government. Brailsford, recalling suffrage battles, held out little hope of a peace initiative by the Prime Minister:

He won't like the League of Nations idea, simply because Wilson will be its architect, & the credit of it in history will not go to L. G. I see him keeping a 'torpedo' handy for it—a handy subtle underwater invisible torpedo of the kind that killed the Conciliation Bill.

Nor was there any point in pressing the government for a declaration of terms, since it was obvious that the Allies were committed to 'la victoire

---

[35] HNB to Catherine Marshall, 15 Jan. 1917, Marshall Papers, D/M, NCF Main File, Box 3. See Jo Vellacott, *Bertrand Russell and the Pacifists in the First World War* (London, 1980), p. 36.

[36] *A League of Nations* (1917), pp. 71, 77.

[37] *A League of Nations: A Scheme of Study*, League of Nations Society Publication No. 2; G. L. Dickinson to Viscount Bryce, 7 Mar. 1917, quoted in Keith Robbins, *The Abolition of War* (Cardiff, 1976), p. 129.

integrale', including indemnities, the return of Alsace-Lorraine, dismemberment of Austria, and the expulsion of the Turks from Europe. What was now essential was to persuade the Labour movement of the folly of such a policy.

> I do think we ought to attempt some *destructive* work—I mean enough to make wooly-minded people understand what an outrageous program of conquest this is. . . . I think the only line is to say 'This is pure conquest. It's bad statesmanship anyhow, & it means years of war.'

He looked to others on the left, Snowden or Russell for example, to articulate this position, but after two years of political truce one could have 'little hope of Labour anyhow. Our best hope is now I think in a revolt of the saner middle-class Liberals'.[38]

It was to that audience—and in some sense to Wilson—that *A League of Nations* was addressed. The book, he remarked, was intended 'as much for the U.S.A. as for England. What I write for America just now seems to succeed better than what I write for England'.[39] In contrast to his initial conception of a European league, Brailsford now regarded American adherence as of primary importance. The viability of the League hinged on Wilson's ability to make good his pledge of American support for a new international authority. Uncommitted to either side, disinterested, yet formidable in resources and naval power, America was the obvious guarantor of a settlement. Nowhere does he suggest that American interests, once engaged, might seek to exploit an advantageous position.

Even if the Americans assumed the role of guarantors of a settlement, its viability depended upon a League's readiness to undertake 'radical reconstruction in a spirit of tolerance and charity'.[40] Above all, this meant abandoning any move towards closed markets, prohibitive tariffs, or other measures designed to undermine German prosperity. Instead of promoting a permanent anti-German alliance, Europe should 'make room for German ambitions', encouraging its participation in the development of Turkey and China. Either its colonies should be restored or, if this proved unfeasible, compensation should be made in equivalent African territory. That such a settlement bartered immediate material concessions for pledges of good conduct, rewarding aggressor no less than victim, did not vitiate its appeal.[41]

Considering its length, the book scarcely touched on international machinery. Effective power would reside in an executive council, representing the governments of the major states. All members would

---

[38] HNB to Catherine Marshall, 15 Jan. 1917, Marshall Papers, D/M, NCF Main File, Box 3.
[39] HNB to H. Bräuning-Oktavio, 23 June 1916, BOP.
[40] *League*, p. 25.   [41] *League*, pp. 241-6.

be obligated to submit disputes either to a court of arbitral justice or to a standing council of inquiry and conciliation. Although the League would ordinarily impose its will by isolating a potential aggressor, depriving it of the economic benefits of membership, military sanctions would be applied should economic pressure prove inadequate. An International Council should be formed representing all the peoples, selected by a system of proportional representation. It would reflect ideological rather than national cleavages, much as the latter-day European Assembly is designed to do.[42]

No machinery, however carefully devised, could ensure a durable peace unless outstanding grievances were resolved and economic benefits accrued from membership. He proposed, as an essential constitutional component, a charter of commercial freedom. This would forbid boycotts or differential tariffs, oblige signatories to accord each other most favoured nation treatment, ensure equal opportunity for the export of capital, and provide international supervision for the distribution of raw materials. Here was where Brailsford diverged from most League proponents, who focused their attention wholly on maintaining peace. Yet these bold proposals—and they were less sweeping than he would have liked—merely elaborated his earlier pronouncements, prompting him to describe the book as '*The War of Steel and Gold* applied to present emergencies'.[43]

Although the League must ensure that territorial changes could be achieved without war, Brailsford did not himself advocate widespread reconstruction. He regarded the much vaunted ideal of national self-determination as a barrier to the realization of internationalism. World federation, based on a League of increasing competence, should be the goal towards which the powers should strive. Instead of seeking to rationalize boundaries, the League should set minimum standards for the protection of racial minorities and secure cultural rights for all subject nationalities.

Above all, Brailsford's scheme dispensed with notions of war guilt and retribution. The new international order would rest on mutual concession, which he regarded as the only way to eliminate the causes of war. Instead of continuing the conflict on the economic front, the powers should link political and economic goals, winning support for the settlement by ensuring that all powers enjoyed the economic benefits it conferred. His immediate proposals—an executive of the major powers, pooled armaments, a charter of economic freedom, and guarantees of cultural autonomy—did not go much further than the moderate proponents of the League. They presupposed no restructuring of the

[42] *League*, pp. 313-15.
[43] HNB to H. Bräuning-Oktavio, 23 June 1916, BOP.

capitalist economy, no socialist revolution; they sought to mitigate the excesses of imperialism, not to eliminate colonial rule. In that sense *A League of Nations* was a work of deliberate caution, a manifesto of enlightened liberalism, not a socialist critique.

Although the book was brought to Wilson's attention by Senator Borah,[44] there is no evidence that it had any impact in Downing Street. The League concept was no more appealing to the advocates of revolutionary change. Brailsford found himself defending the limited plan, with which he was himself dissatisfied, against socialist criticism. In an article in the *Herald*, for which he had begun to write in 1917, he warned against dismissing it as 'a league of the governing classes'. So negative an attitude would be 'the most disastrous error which Socialism could commit'.[45] In private, however, Brailsford was much less sanguine. Although convinced that nothing 'so advanced as my scheme of a Federal League could be possible immediately after the war', prospects even for the more moderate Bryce scheme did not appear auspicious. With no illusions about its likelihood, he doubted that 'much will be got without a big international popular agitation, of an almost revolutionary temper'.[46]

The most hopeful portent was the revolution in Russia, the first phase of which coincided with the book's appearance. If his sympathies were immediately engaged, he found the task of interpreting the rapid changes bewildering. His prognosis was often superseded by events as he tried to keep pace with the fluctuations in revolutionary fortunes. At times he appeared as uncertain of his bearings as his readers, trying to fathom events he could not entirely comprehend but wanted to endorse. While reporting the situation favourably he found it impossible to conceal misgivings about the tactics of those he applauded. Although the Russian workers intended neither to abandon their Western comrades, nor to conclude a 'dishonourable separate peace', it was clear that they might not survive a continuing war. Unless the Allies agreed to negotiate, they would imperil 'the greatest triumph which democracy has won since the French Revolution'.[47]

If the Allied Socialist parties could only unite on a moderate peace programme, the International might be reconstituted as an effective instrument. The first step was to get in touch with the Russian leaders. Before the end of March 1917 a Radical group, including Brailsford, MacDonald, Massingham, and Hobson, decided to send a telegram of

---

[44] Cf. Woodrow Wilson to Senator William E. Borah, 25 July 1917, quoted in Ray Stannard Baker, *Woodrow Wilson: Life and Letters*, VII (New York, 1939), p. 194.
[45] *Herald*, 14 July 1917.
[46] HNB to Lord Courtney, 17 Sept. [1917], Courtney Papers, Vol. XII, No. 81.
[47] *Herald*, 28 July 1917.

encouragement to Kerensky.[48] As a result of pressure from the left, in both allied and enemy camps, the balance of opinion was moving toward a 'peace on the basis of the things for which British democracy took up arms—disarmament, arbitration, the rights of small nations'.[49] Behind this surface optimism about the rising socialist tide, he was deeply apprehensive about the course of the war and his lonely stance:

> I get so remote from my fellow men as I write, that I might as well be writing against Cleon or the younger Pitt. I write it every week, in different tones— with increasing boldness for the 'Nation', with entire frankness for the socialist 'Herald' and occasionally with infinite caution for the American 'New Republic' or the French 'Les Nations'.[50]

At the start of the war Brailsford regarded the undemocratic regimes in Germany and Russia as the fatal obstacles to a new era in European affairs. The change of leadership in Petrograd encouraged the development of international institutions and signalled the abandonment of aggressive designs against Poland and Constantinople. He endorsed Kerensky's call for a peace without annexations and never doubted that the progressive forces in Germany, which seemed likely to gain the upper hand, would respond positively as well. Peace was in the grasp of European statesmen, but the allies had first to abandon their 'nakedly Imperialist aims'.[51]

Although his interest extended to all areas of the war, the focus of his concern remained, as it had been before 1914, the Balkans and Central Europe. Willing to subordinate the French stake in Alsace-Lorraine to the need for peace without victory, he never wavered from his long-standing conviction that Bulgaria's claim to most of Macedonia was justified. Here alone was he determined to upset the territorial status quo of 1914, in part because Bulgaria's legacy had been seized upon her defeat in the Second Balkan War. As early as January 1915 he was urging a deal between Bulgaria and the Allies instead of 'leaving everything to the arbitration of the Powers after the war', a procedure which had generally short-changed Bulgaria in the past. In order to entice Bulgaria away from her wary neutrality, the Allies might offer 'much or most of Central Macedonia' as bait, compensating Serbia at Austria's expense. He appealed to Bryce, the best placed of Bulgarian sympathizers, to promote such a scheme and offered to serve as intermediary with Mincoff, the Bulgarian minister in London.[52] Subsequently, after Bulgaria joined the enemy, Noel and Charles Buxton went to Sofia on

---

[48] David Marquand, *Ramsay MacDonald* (London, 1977), p. 207.
[49] *Herald*, 13 Oct. 1917.
[50] HNB to H. Bräuning-Oktavio, 8 Aug. 1917, BOP.
[51] *Herald*, 16 June 1917.
[52] HNB to Viscount Bryce, 17 Jan. [1915], Bryce Papers, UB 23.

an unofficial mission to try to detach her from the Central Powers. In a memorandum for the Buxtons Brailsford asserted that Bulgaria would not desert her new allies unless her Macedonian ambitions were satisfied.[53] Bulgaria's loyalty to the Central Powers, at least until her defeat in September 1918, did not deter him from resurrecting these proposals at the end of the war when the disposition of Balkan territory was being considered.

Brailsford's ambivalence towards nationality as a sufficient basis for a new Europe is nowhere more evident than in his reflections on the future of Austria-Hungary. Never sentimentally attached to the Hapsburg Empire, he became, as the war continued, resolutely opposed to its breakup. In contrast either to *Mitteleuropa* or a string of newly devised states, the Hapsburg Empire did not have to be invented; it already existed, albeit in a ramshackle state, and deserved to be refurbished, not dissolved. As a large free trade area, providing port facilities for landlocked regions, a common railway network and financial infrastructure, it facilitated commerce in an otherwise economically backward area. These advantages would be lost if the Empire disintegrated into a collection of quarrelling states. Independence would prove illusory: a 'half-free Bohemia' would become a 'Russian vanguard and wedge in Central Europe'.[54] Moreover, the inclusion of sizeable German minorities in a Czech or Polish state would perpetuate the ethnic conflict in more virulent form than under the aegis of a tolerant empire. The best way to deal with the problem was to reorganize Austria-Hungary on a federal basis, with territorial home rule for the principal sections and cultural liberty for minorities.

While recognizing that elements within the Empire—notably the Czechs, Poles, and Serbs—wanted full independence, Brailsford argued that the will of the noisiest groups must not be the sole determinant of a future settlement. An independent Poland would rectify centuries of injustice, but was a Polish state viable without either natural borders or an outlet to the sea? A better solution would be absorption into an Austrian federation, in which it would be 'internally independent'. Nor were the more recalcitrant Serbs excluded from the grand design: whatever the commitment to restore Serbian independence, its people should be discouraged from maintaining 'an attitude of aloofness and hostility' towards Vienna.[55]

A negotiated peace, leaving the European map essentially intact, not

---

[53] HNB to Noel Buxton, 11 Dec. [1916] and memorandum on Bulgaria [Jan. 1917], NBP. See Rothwell, pp. 51, 120-1 and Anderson, *Buxton*, pp. 62-74; ND, 2 Jan. 1917.

[54] *The Call*, 25 Jan. 1917. *The Call*, expressing the views of the anti-war faction of the British Socialist Party, had been established as a rival to *Justice* in February 1916.

[55] The *UDC*, Feb. 1916. Also *New Republic*, 10 Dec. 1916 and *League*, pp. 107, 112-13.

only eliminated Austria's motive for continuing to fight; it was essential if the new revolutionary regime in Russia were to consolidate itself. A democratic Russia no longer threatened her neighbours, but only a quick termination of the conflict could save Kerensky. He blamed Kerensky's eventual fall on Allied unwillingness to admit that the price of continued Russian involvement was self-destruction. While recognizing why the Bolsheviks had won, he denounced their tactics as inimical to the socialist goals of the revolution. Instead of trusting to the verdict of the electors, Lenin and Trotsky had seized power, oblivious to the fact that 'their violence would ruin their moral standing'. A Russian government 'may be as boldly Socialist as it pleases, on one condition, that it has the votes of the Russian people behind it'.[56]

Angered by Trotsky's overtures to Germany, in violation of Bolshevik pledges, Brailsford indignantly censured its leaders:

It must be firmly said that they are putting themselves outside the pale of our International Socialist Society. . . . If they attempt to make peace without an explicit assurance that Belgium, Serbia, and Rumania shall be restored, they will cut a sorry figure in the eyes of all honourable men.[57]

On both democratic and internationalist grounds the Bolshevik regime had been found wanting, and even those socialists friendly to the new rulers were morally obliged to take them to task.

Such criticism, however muted, incurred the wrath of Lenin's British acolytes, as it would again in the mid-1930s when Brailsford denounced the purge trials. Even Lansbury's *Herald* refused its editorial imprimatur to Brailsford's views, although it continued to publish them. Robin Page Arnot, distinctly to Brailsford's left, chided him in its letter column for expecting the revolutionary leaders in Russia to honour the Tsar's secret pledges.[58] R. Palme Dutt, who clashed with him over Bolshevik tactics at a Cambridge lecture in December 1917, was only the most notable of British Communists to recall periodically Brailsford's perfidy as proof of the insincerity of his socialist commitment.[59] Indeed, respect for democratic practices, staunchly maintained throughout the post-war years, would earn few plaudits from the denizens of King Street, and no subsequent encomium for the Soviet achievement effaced the stigma of his initial misgivings.

In the final year of the war he became more active in pressing for a Wilsonian settlement. Along with Morel and Woolf, he helped to devise the War Aims Memorandum approved by a Labour conference

---

[56] *Herald*, 2 Mar. 1918.   [57] *Herald*, 1 Dec. 1917.
[58] R. Page Arnot, *The Impact of the Russian Revolution in Britain* (London, 1967), pp. 115-17.
[59] R. Palme Dutt in *New Statesman*, 10 July 1937, *Labour Monthly*, Feb. 1945, and in interview with author.

in December, but he was not ordinarily in London enough to attend committee meetings. He did serve as a delegate to the conference of Allied Socialist parties in August, urging that colonies not yet ripe for self-government be placed under international authority.[60] The revised edition of *A League of Nations*, published in November 1917, did not envisage the end of empire: the powers—including Germany—would retain their colonies, but under restraints. They must respect native property rights, prevent economic discrimination, co-operate in railway investment, and prohibit the raising of native levies. A permanent League commission on African affairs would ensure compliance with these provisions, employing inspectors to handle complaints.[61] No less anti-imperialist than in 1914, he did not yet regard subject peoples, especially in Africa, as ready to govern themselves. Henceforth the powers must be motivated by a sense of responsibility, of trusteeship, not by a competitive struggle for profit.

In pondering Turkey's future Brailsford was no more sympathetic to the nationalist principle than in regard to Austria-Hungary, but for somewhat different reasons. Within the Ottoman domain, nationality was irrelevant: the crucial lines of division were not racial, but religious. He proposed the devolution to the religious community of education, tax collection, and social assistance, leaving to the national government non-contentious issues, such as road building and irrigation. Along with administrative decentralization would be an extension of cultural autonomy, guaranteeing all minorities the right to pursue their own cultural life in secure isolation. Instead of carving Turkey into separate economic spheres of influence, it should be developed by international companies, with German enterprise accorded 'a considerable share'.[62] 'I have done my best,' he wrote Blunt, 'to oppose schemes of partition, but I am afraid without much success. The only direction in which I think I may be able to do something is in suggesting ideas to some of the young men who are preparing President Wilson's dossier for the settlement.'[63] He had already furnished a memorandum on Turkey to the semi-official American Inquiry, and early in the new year prepared another for Colonel House on Albania and Macedonia.[64] Nor did he ignore the British Foreign Office, however unreceptive it was likely to be to his views. In November 1918 he reiterated Bulgaria's right to Macedonia in an interview with Arthur

[60] ND, 28 Aug. 1917; *New Statesman*, 10 Dec. 1949.
[61] *League*, 2nd ed., pp. 283-5. See Winkler, p. 212.
[62] *Contemporary Review*, Vol. CXIII, No. 628 (Apr. 1918), pp. 389-96. Many of the same issues are discussed in *Herald*, 26 Jan. 1918 and *New Republic*, 20 Apr. 1918.
[63] HNB to W. S. Blunt, 5 Sept. 1918, BP.
[64] 'The Future of Turkey': A Report to the Inquiry Committee [Feb. 1918], Inquiry Papers; HNB to Colonel House, 6 Jan. 1919, House Papers.

Nicolson and left with the sense that officials saw his idea of cultural autonomy as 'a way out' of the Balkan morass.[65]

When, early in 1918, the Advisory Committee on International Questions was set up by the Labour Party, primarily to guide the thinking of the leadership in foreign affairs, Brailsford was appointed as one of its members. With the UDC ranks well-represented, he was an obvious choice, especially in view of his special knowledge of Russia and the Balkans. The first major problem that the Committee tackled was the thorny issue of intervention in Russia. In opposition to a memorandum in favour by Rex Leeper, the Foreign Office Russian desk officer, Brailsford submitted one, warning of the dangers of military interference in Russian affairs. While the revolution had obviously produced military difficulties for the Allies, it had also brought a 'moral gain to the cause of democracy and national freedom'. The Russian people had a right to choose their own form of government, even if it were offensive to other powers. He urged the party to disavow a policy whose intrinsic basis was the desire to redeem Tsarist debts. In the end both memoranda were transmitted to the Executive, with G. D. H. Cole, C. R. Buxton, and Woolf appending their signatures to Brailsford's anti-interventionist report.[66]

Unlike other champions of the Russian revolution, Brailsford refused to refrain from criticism while inveighing against intervention. None the less, he cautioned against applying a double standard for socialist governments:

We, who have never dreamed of acting to stop the infinitely more cruel terrorism of the autocracy, and allied ourselves with a Tsardom which denied democracy in any form, have no right now to step in because the new Russian forms of popular self-government err upon the other side.[67]

If for no other reason, it was necessary to restore the workers' International to safeguard an 'uncompromisingly socialist State' from the armed hostility 'of the world's bankers, of small investors of France, and the Anglo-American syndicates of concession-hunters'.[68]

The German offensive in the spring of 1918 made it difficult to argue that pacific influences were gaining the upper hand in Germany, but Brailsford was heartened by signs of a 'passion for peace' in the Austrian camp. Disillusionment with the war was widespread, especially among socialists and Slavs, and it opened the way for pressure

[65] HNB to Noel Buxton, 5 Nov. 1918, NBP. Nicolson, created Lord Carnock in 1916, had retired from the Foreign Office.
[66] ACIQ Memorandum No. 12 and Minutes, 5 and 15 July 1918; *Herald*, 6 July 1918.
[67] *Herald*, 14 Dec. 1918.
[68] *Herald*, 9 Feb. 1918.

from Vienna on Berlin for a 'peace of reconciliation'. There were even signs that the Czechs were becoming amenable to a Danubian Federation instead of seeking to destroy the monarchy. Since security and economic imperatives made a Central European union inevitable, the obvious course was to accept 'the principle of Austria's integrity'.[69]

The controversy flared up across the Atlantic when Brailsford dissented from the *New Republic*'s call for Austrian dismemberment. This was another 'internal' conflict, reminiscent of his dispute with Massingham in the pages of the *Nation* in 1914-15, and was the only time, except for the purge trials in the 1930s, that author and journal aired their differences publicly. He argued that to make dismemberment a war aim would prolong the conflict 'until the last German army had surrendered', something 'no sane being would expect within less than two or three years'. Even if the Empire were dissolved, it would be necessary to compel 'races steeped to the lips in nationalist chauvinism' to coexist amicably. Thus a cumbersome international body would be forced to impose from the outside a solution that a federated Austria-Hungary could achieve on its own.

The editors denied that dismemberment would wreck the chances of securing German consent to a peace settlement. The emancipation of subject nationalities, they maintained, would remove the greatest impediment to a League. A federal solution would, further, give the Slavs enough leverage against the 'German-Magyar ruling class'. As long as it was consistent with national self-determination, safeguarding the Slavic peoples of Central Europe from 'German political and military domination', the *New Republic* did not object to the concept of a Danubian Federation.[70] As far as Brailsford was concerned, a Danubian Federation, while interesting in theory, seemed a dubious proposition. It was, as he reminded the Advisory Committee in an August 1918 memorandum, a 'natural economic unit', but he saw little prospect of all the component parts joining.[71]

In August 1918 Brailsford's League of Nations Prize Essay, entitled 'Foundations of Internationalism', appeared in the *English Review*, the recipient of £100 as the best original essay on the League idea. Later published in America as *The Covenant of Peace*, it asserted that a League of Nations could only function effectively if permeated by a genuine internationalist spirit. Above all, this meant the capacity to ensure timely changes before any people was driven by intolerable grievance

---

[69] *Nation*, 23 Mar. 1918. See Harry Hanak, *Great Britain and Austria-Hungary During the First World War* (London, 1962), pp. 257-8.
[70] *New Republic*, 31 Aug. 1918.
[71] ACIQ Memorandum No. 16. This was written in response to a report by Lewis Namier, ACIQ Minutes, 26 July 1918.

to force changes through war. Ultimately, it was not sentiment, but 'the effective will to make a workable League' that was the first condition of its creation, a determination that would only come about when a measure of confidence and good will among all the major powers had been achieved.[72]

In the final weeks before the armistice Brailsford became fearful that the Allies were raising the stakes. Should the occupation of the left bank of the Rhine become a precondition for an armistice, it would mean war against the German people, not merely their rulers, and would unleash the kind of social revolution that had engulfed Russia. Once the German republic was declared, however, he commended the Social Democrats for avoiding the 'first capital error' of the Russian revolutionaries: they had closed ranks in order to avoid a fratricidal clash between factions. What he predicted was a return to the principles of 1848, with no abandonment of 'traditional Western forms of democracy'. German Austria would seek to affiliate itself, while Alsace, if permitted to determine its own future, might indeed choose to remain 'with the race to which by blood she belongs'. The task of European socialists was to ensure that these developments took place without the interference of 'foreign capitalism'. After his despair at the protracted war, he seemed over-confident about the prospects for peace. Wilson would ensure the adoption of an enlightened settlement, aided in part by the advice of European progressive opinion. What personal exhortation failed to accomplish, the will of the masses would secure. The armistice had unshackled the workers at home; if Labour's demands were ignored, it now had the means to enforce them. Taking a leaf from the book of Continental socialists, he declared, with uncharacteristic militancy, 'If our rulers scheme to destroy the European Revolution, our answer must be the general strike.'[73] Such exultation was premature, and his disillusionment was all the more profound when he found the democratic electorate, no less than the governing classes, betraying his hopes for an enlightened peace.

[72] *The Covenant of Peace: An Essay on the League of Nations* (1919), pp. 17, 20, 22.
[73] *Herald*, 16 Nov. 1918.

IX
The Flawed Peace (1918–1922)

By 1919 Brailsford had earned a reputation as the outstanding Labour journalist of the period. The anonymity of his *Nation* leaders, as well as Massingham's strong direction, had restrained his indignation while elevating his style. Given his post-war mood, the *Herald* was a more appropriate forum in which to vent his pessimism. In his signed columns he was unmuzzled, free to express the white heat of his anger. Further, once he had ceased to write chiefly for a Liberal, middle-class audience, as he had done since his *Manchester Guardian* days, he adopted a more popular tone, with fewer literary allusions and simpler language. It was a style that culminated in his brilliant *New Leader* columns and later in both the *New Statesman* and *Reynolds*. If Brailsford felt more comfortable as an independent dissenter, as a socialist writing for Labour publications, it was an irrevocable move. He would never again work and rarely write for an 'Establishment' journal and was thus cut off from more lucrative journalistic options. Although continuously employed—he never wrote less than two or three pieces a week until he retired—the publications were not always worthy of his talents. It was the price he paid for the right to speak his mind, but it was also his socialist vocation. He was more concerned to inform the popular mind, to make ordinary people think about foreign affairs correctly than to influence those in power. He privately brooded that what he wrote was ephemeral, published in journals read and quickly discarded. The search for permanence kept him writing books, but it was his weekly journalism that probably had the greatest impact.

While removal from London had freed him from the constant round of meetings and demonstrations that he had known before 1914, he did manage to attend *Nation* lunches faithfully during the war and to take part, less frequently, in the activities of the UDC and the League of Nations Society. Almost the only organization he joined not concerned with the post-war settlement was the Family Endowment Committee, established in October 1917 at the suggestion of Eleanor Rathbone. Members, mainly noted suffragists and feminists, included Kathleen Courtney, its Chairman and Brailsford's close personal friend, Maude Royden, Mary Stocks, Eleanor Rathbone, and Emile Burns. Its aim was to deflect public attention from the cry for equal pay for women to a 'national recognition of the mother's work'. In a September 1918 report written at least in part by Brailsford, the Committee proposed the establishment of a national scheme of family endowment along the lines of the separation allowances paid to soldiers' families. It argued in favour of a weekly allowance paid directly to the mother for herself and each of her children during the period while they demanded her full attention. The immediate impact of the report was slight, and although supporters continued to press for the endowment of motherhood, child allowances did not come into effect until 1946.[1]

The qualities that made his journalism so compelling—his breadth of knowledge and his clarity of expression—made him an enlightening lecturer as well. He was much in demand on Labour platforms, at weekend schools, and as a visiting tutor at the Central Labour College in Earls Court, where his students in the 1919 session included James Griffiths and Aneurin Bevan.[2] Here he delivered lectures on imperialism, but he often spoke elsewhere on his observations in Central Europe. In the following years he regularly accepted invitations to address working-class and university groups around the country. Freda Utley recalled him debating with Sir Bernard Pares at King's College, London in 1923 on the merits of the Soviet regime,[3] and a secretary of the Monmouthshire Trades Council recounted in 1968 a visit Brailsford made to South Wales nearly half a century earlier:

> He came and delivered outstanding lectures dealing with international affairs from his usual angle. He was not an orator but his matter was magnificant and he gripped his audiences. On his return to London he wrote to me saying that having witnessed the conditions here at first hand he preferred not to accept his fee. This was not big in any case but it was of great help to us and was not forgotten.[4]

Still unsure of his vocation, Brailsford had not entirely abandoned his parliamentary ambitions. But although he was to become an increasingly esteemed figure in Labour circles and, for the first time, active in the ILP, he was ill-suited to a parliamentary career. Too shy and withdrawn to enjoy political camaraderie, he would have been an ineffective campaigner and hardly likely to sparkle in the Commons. Moreover, the Labour Party, dominated in the inter-war period by trade unionists, was never hospitable to intellectuals, whose views might be assimilated, but who were rarely—Sidney Webb being the exception that proved the rule—rewarded with safe seats. But in 1918, with nearly four hun-

---

[1] Family Endowment Committee, *Equal Pay and the Family* (1918). Also see *Herald*, 31 Aug. 1918.

[2] James Griffiths, *Pages from Memory* (London, 1969), pp. 24-5; Foot, *Bevan*, p. 37; William W. Craik, *The Central Labour College 1909-1929* (London, 1964), p. 171.

[3] Freda Utley, *Odyssey of a Liberal* (Washington, 1970), p. 46.

[4] Willie James to author. Brailsford mentions this incident in *Daily Herald*, 21 Mar. 1922.

dred Labour candidates, it was not difficult to secure a nomination, and Brailsford was chosen to contest the Montrose Burghs, a safe Liberal seat. Although prospects at Montrose were poor, it was by no means implausible for him to contest a Scottish seat. He had, after all, received his schooling in adjacent Dundee, then represented by another transplanted Englishman, Winston Churchill. He had lived in Blairgowrie and evinced a continuing interest in Scottish problems, but the Coalition candidate, J. Leng Sturrock, emphasized his own local roots and secured an endorsement from John Buchan.

Brailsford harboured few illusions about his uphill fight. After having been offered the nomination in June, he spent a week in the constituency meeting local socialists and trade unionists.

> It is a traditional Liberal stronghold, like most Scottish towns, [he wrote] and probably I shall not be elected. One never knows what will happen in these days of rapid change, and this little ancient town [Montrose] with its rich memories of Scottish history feels to me like a very dignified old maiden lady who had been caught unawares on the road to a battlefield & did not quite know what to do.[5]

Labour had never contested Montrose, and party organization was rudimentary. Unlike industrial and mining areas, where ILP and trade union activity had prepared the ground, this cluster of five sleepy towns and fishing villages was changing far less rapidly than needed to elect a Labour candidate. It was 'a troublesome constituency to work, and there was little organization to start with' in the biggest of the burghs, Arbroath.[6] Once he began campaigning in earnest, he was discouraged by the apparent 'indifference there, especially among women',[7] to whom much of his appeal was pitched. His experiences in Bervie, the most northern of the villages, typified the problems he encountered:

> It was a little fishing village with a mill far from town. It had no shows, no cinemas, no distractions of any kind, and I thought in my innocence that B----e would rise as one man when a political meeting broke its dull routine. Six solemn male electors attended my first meeting; twenty-four came to the second and last. My opponent, who followed me, profited by my efforts to arouse B----e. Twenty-five electors listened to his discourse. He had beaten my record by one, but the twenty-four who had listened to me made 96% of his audience. I had the curiosity to count the number of electors on the roll. Rather less than 5% attended a meeting.[8]

Brailsford's election manifesto identified his candidacy closely with Labour while stressing issues of foreign policy. Calling for the abolition

[5] HNB to H. Bräuning-Oktavio, 19 June 1918, BOP.
[6] HNB to Noel Buxton, 5 Nov. 1918, NBP.
[7] ND, 1 Oct. 1918. [8] *New Leader*, 17 Nov. 1922.

of conscription and the creation of a League of Nations, he insisted that the only safeguard against secret treaties was 'the vigilant control by Parliament of foreign affairs'. In addition, he echoed Labour's advocacy of equal pay for women, a graduated capital levy to repay the war debt, and the nationalization of the railways, the mines, and electric power.[9] Handbills, circulated to local textile workers, urged them to vote for Brailsford who was 'himself a Trade Unionist':

> He got a factory Act for the Textile Workers of Egypt. He will work with the same perseverance for you. He means to get a Trade Board for the Textile Trades of the Burghs. That means a Board to fix wages. He insists that 30/-shall be the Lowest Wage that may lawfully be paid to any working woman.[10]

As a prominent suffragist, he targeted his programme to the newly-enfranchised women, warning that 'no woman can today secure the happiness of her own home unless she protects it by sending to Parliament men and women who will watch over her interests'.[11] Nor did he forget the khaki voters, reminding them that he had 'fought as a private in the Greek War against Turkey, and will support every reasonable proposal to improve the soldier's lot'.

From the outset Sturrock, backed by the Tories, joined the popular outcry for a 'severe indemnity' in order to recover war costs and to 'teach the German a lesson which he would never forget'.[12] In rebutting this 'appeal to the irrational instincts of the mob', Brailsford was 'well aware that [he was] staking everything on the cool reasoning power of the Scottish elector'.[13] He asserted that an indemnity could only be paid by a vast transfer of goods that would constitute 'the most colossal, most wanton, most suicidal organization of dumping that the world has ever known'.[14] After his supporters pleaded with him to concentrate on some issue more likely to gain a local hearing, he cited Indian competition as the chief danger to the Forfarshire jute industry, the competition of sweated Asian labourers employed in mills owned by British capitalists who now demanded protection.[15]

While Brailsford continued to stress local issues, Sturrock played the jingoist card to clamorous cheers, declaring at one gathering, 'If Labour was going to say that it was right to shake hands with the Germans, he was perfectly sure he could appeal confidently to the men of Arbroath to refuse support to any gang who would go and sell our

---

[9] Election Address: 'To the Electors of the Montrose Burghs', Nov. 1918, HNBP.
[10] 'To the Textile Workers of Brechin and Bervie' (handbill), HNBP.
[11] 'Women and the Labour Party' (handbill), HNBP.
[12] *Montrose, Arbroath and Brechin Review*, 29 Nov. 1918.
[13] *Herald*, 7 Dec. 1918.   [14] *Montrose Standard*, 6 Dec. 1918.
[15] *Montrose Standard*, 29 Nov. 1918. See *Nation*, 22 Jan. 1921.

soldiers by behaviour of that kind.' As the campaign intensified, Brailsford attacked the Coalition government for calling a snap election 'with the sight of an enemy humbled in the dust'. The nation's leaders, he warned,

> need not be surprised if the working classes turned upon them and told them that that was no representative House, that constitutional democracy had already been destroyed by the Coalition. If they wanted to encourage Bolshevism, to encourage these violent courses, let them support the Coalition.[16]

Brailsford had little outside support for his candidacy, although Helena Swanwick and Maude Royden, both noted suffragists, spoke on his behalf, and Jane joined the campaign in its final week. Royden told a Montrose rally that Brailsford, 'one of the ablest of men and something of a prophet', had given the idea of a League of Nations 'practical application'.[17] In contrast, the local press was markedly hostile. In its endorsement of Sturrock the *Montrose Standard* denounced Brailsford as a carpet-bagger who 'has wooed the constituency as an alien with little knowledge of its individual conditions and requirements'.[18]

Labour's chances in Montrose were not improved by the light turn-out on 14 December. Forty-nine per cent of the electors went to the poll, although local press reports suggested that a high proportion of these were women. Nor were there any surprises in the results: Sturrock received 9,309 votes to Brailsford's 2,940. The Coalition candidate held the seat until 1924, and the Liberals continued to retain it until 1945. Brailsford blamed the outcome on faulty local organization and his advocacy of a 'peace of reconciliation. The unforgivable crime was that I would "shake hands with the Germans" as my opponent put it. That lost me thousands of votes.'[19]

The results of the General Election confirmed his worst fears. British voters, demanding that Germany be punished, repudiated virtually every candidate identified with the UDC—Brailsford, MacDonald, Trevelyan, Ponsonby. That voters were 'inattentive, inexpert, and uncritical',[20] hardly consoled those, such as Brailsford, who expected universal suffrage to be the precursor of socialist internationalism. Internationally-minded Liberals turned increasingly to Labour as the hope of the future, while Brailsford, already committed to socialism,

---

[16] *Montrose Standard*, 6 Dec. 1918; *Montrose, Arbroath and Brechin Review*, 6 Dec. 1918.
[17] *Montrose, Arbroath and Brechin Review*, 13 Dec. 1918.
[18] *Montrose Standard*, 13 Dec. 1918.
[19] HNB to H. Bräuning-Oktavio, 19 Jan. 1919, BOP.
[20] 'Parliaments or Soviets', Supplement to the *New Commonwealth*, 9 Jan. 1920. Also see Swanwick, p. 313.

now gravitated towards the Guild movement.[21] If his involvement was minimal, it was because he was more concerned with European affairs than with political representation at home and was generally less enamoured of trade unionism than were the Guildsmen. Never sharing the pro-Bolshevik affinities which were to lead a number of Guild Socialists into the Communist Party after the movement disintegrated in the early 1920s, he was none the less dissatisfied with parliamentary democracy and more fearful than ever of 'the all-powerful, all-permeating Capitalist system'.

In a lecture to the National Guilds League he admitted the 'instant attraction' of the Soviet system, but he did not regard its application as practical. In Russia it was possible to achieve the dictatorship of the proletariat before organizing industry because of the revolutionary conditions brought on by disillusionment with the government and military defeat. Nothing could be further removed from the post-war situation in England. Instead of an impoverished working class and a disaffected bourgeoisie, there was a ruling class 'elated with the fruits of its victory'. Any attempt to foment revolutionary action would provoke a confrontation that those in power would not hesitate to exploit. If an industrial parliament was to evolve, it must be on the basis of self-government in the workshops and the cultivation of the 'solidarity of all who are engaged in the work of production'.[22]

While seeking to disabuse the Leninists within the Guild movement, he suggested in his *Herald* articles at the end of the war that a harsh indemnity was likely to trigger a violent Bolshevik revolution in Germany. The greatest folly of the Allies was that they were 'strangling German democracy in its cradle. We are visiting the sins of the Kaiser and his Junkers on the people which has cast off its yoke.'[23] British Labour should dissociate itself from a peace of annexations and from foreign intervention in Russia. Until the International was restored and Labour gained power, there was little chance for a genuine League of Nations which would curb 'the predatory appetites of our Junkers'. At the same time he admonished Bolshevik leaders for continuing 'to meddle in affairs beyond [their] borders', a policy calculated to invite foreign retaliation.[24]

In the weeks before the Peace Conference opened in Paris, Brailsford clung to the hope that Wilson could dissuade the European statesmen from their ruinous course. Early in January he spelled out his objections to a League consisting entirely of government representatives in

---

[21] I am grateful to Dame Margaret Cole for bringing Brailsford's brief involvement with Guild Socialism to my attention.

[22] 'Parliaments or Soviets', pp. 2-8. Also *Herald*, 11 June 1919.

[23] *Herald*, 7 Dec. 1918. [24] *Herald*, 28 Dec. 1918.

a memorandum for the Advisory Committee on International Questions. Such an executive body, reflecting only the interests of the ruling classes, would disregard 'the true solidarity of human masses'. He therefore urged the British delegation at the forthcoming International meeting to propose a deliberative assembly, composed of delegations chosen by proportional representation from national parliaments. The pressure of popular opinion could also be brought to bear through a restored International, but for those who rejected 'the revolutionary triumph of the Soviet idea', it was preferable to work for 'the democratic evolution of the League of Nations on the basis of Parliamentary forms'.[25]

Brailsford elaborated his misgivings several weeks later in a discussion of League mandates, which raised issues that went back to his pre-war critique of economic imperialism. Since he felt it premature to appoint an international civil service to administer tropical Africa, it was essential to vest mandatory authority on behalf of the League in a single power. To prevent its abuse, he suggested certain conditions: the inclusion of the United States among the mandatory powers; the grant of a mandate for a limited, but renewable term; a prohibition on the raising of native armies or the employment of forced labour. But he foresaw the risk that a mandate system might provide a respectable cover for exploitation by private syndicates and the exclusion of the enterprise of other nations from areas theoretically held in trust.[26]

He was considerably heartened by the results of the January election to the German National Assembly, which indicated majority support for a democratic republic. The outcome, he contended in an excess of optimism, provided indisputable evidence that 'the social, the political and the economic power of [the Junker] class is effectively and finally broken'. But if the Allies maintained their blockade of Germany and excluded her from the League, they would unleash a general social revolution which would 'destroy in a year what a generation could scarcely build again'. The alternatives were Wilson or Spartacus—a democratic League including Germany or Central Europe in the throes of a Bolshevik revolution which could not be contained.[27]

Except for the special circumstances of his participation in the Carnegie Commission of Inquiry in 1913, Brailsford had been unable to travel on the Continent since 1907. By 1919 not only had the political atmosphere changed, but he had become an established, if somewhat

[25] ACIQ Memorandum No. 44: 'A Parliament of the League of Nations'.
[26] *New Republic*, 22 Feb. 1919. Also see *Nation*, 8 Feb. 1919.
[27] *Herald*, 1 Feb. 1919. See Arthur L. Skop, 'The British Labour Party and the German Revolution, November 1918-January 1919', *European Studies Review*, Vol. 5, No. 3 (July 1975), pp. 293-4.

controversial authority. With European capitals filled with journalists returning to the haunts from which they had been barred during the four years of war, the organs which published his work were keen to take advantage of his discerning eye. Early in February he embarked on a three-month tour of Central Europe for the *Herald*, keen to gain wider readership as a daily paper. Raymond Postgate later recalled that for the sub-editors 'the most exciting messages' were those Brailsford transmitted from Warsaw, Vienna, Budapest, and Berlin, a sentiment shared by *Herald* readers.[28]

On assignment for the newspaper and also as a member of an economic commission sent to Poland in March, he had ample opportunity to observe the devastation at close quarters. Hardly a dispassionate witness, even he had not anticipated the extent of suffering that the continuing Allied blockade had provoked. His reports documented shortages of coal and food, the deteriorating physical condition of the people, the gnawing shame of middle classes reduced to penury and unemployed workers rescued from starvation only by makeshift relief programmes. Malnutrition—he found the Viennese subsisting on half a kilo of bread a week and cabbage soup—sapped the energy of working people, who had little incentive to work, since goods were either unavailable or beyond their means. In mid-February he wrote from Vienna that unless the blockade were raised before the end of the month 'Central Europe will be economically and politically a desert of despair'.[29]

Brailsford's route criss-crossed Central Europe, taking him from the International sessions in Berne to Vienna, to Lodz, Warsaw, Brest-Litovsk, and Pinsk in March, back to Vienna in April (where it was reported that he had been shot),[30] and then to Budapest and Berlin. As part of his official investigation, he took a more extensive look at economic conditions in Poland, beginning with Lodz, once considered the Eastern Manchester. From the moment that cotton ceased to enter Bremen, its mills had been silent, the bulk of the population remaining idle throughout the war. He visited some workers' dwellings where ten people in a single room slept on the floor without bedding, barely surviving on a diet of potatoes and bread.[31] The Economic Mission was soon to recommend the resumption of shipments of raw material in order to revive the textile industry, an objective partly achieved when the Americans began to send cotton in June.

From Lodz, his journey took him first to Warsaw and then to Brest-

---

[28] Raymond Postgate, *The Life of George Lansbury* (London, 1951), p. 188.
[29] *Nation*, 15 March 1919. Also *Across the Blockade*, esp. pp. 40-7.
[30] ND, 4 Apr. 1919.
[31] *Contemporary Review*, Vol. CXVII, No. 651 (Mar. 1920), p. 335.

Litovsk, a mainly Jewish city reduced to rubble in the Russian retreat. Typhus had taken its toll, and the largely refugee population lacked bread, sugar, and milk. Polish officers, convinced that behind every beard lurked a Bolshevik, sanctioned systematic terror against the Jews. Taken to visit refugees from the burned quarter of Brest, he found them living in abandoned barns, ill and untreated.[32]

While much of the Western press hailed the resurgence of Polish nationalism, Brailsford was among the first journalists to document its less savoury aspects. As in Macedonia, he did not rely on official reports, but persuaded village leaders to recount their experiences. In Pinsk, which had fallen to the Poles three weeks before his arrival, the depradations of Polish soldiers exceeded those of the Tsar's troops. The town commandant invited him to be his guest and, amply plied with vodka, admitted that the local population had not taken kindly to the Polish military occupation. He attributed the disloyalty not to the severity of Polish rule, but to the Communist sympathies of the Jews. Brailsford assured him that the Jewish leaders he had met were all old-fashioned liberals, religiously predisposed against social revolution. The commandant, in no way swayed by this appeal, anounced his intention of burning hostile villages and decimating the Jewish and Ukrainian populace. The following day Brailsford took the train back to Warsaw, where, after pulling every imaginable string, he managed to secure an interview with Pilsudski. The President, listening impassively, excused the commandant with the remark 'You civilians cannot understand the mind of a soldier'. When Brailsford replied that he too had been a soldier, Pilsudski grew friendlier, took Brailsford's arm in his, and 'talked with almost effusive cordiality'. But it proved of no avail: the commandant gathered the leaders of the Jewish community in Pinsk ten days later and had thirty-five of them executed.[33]

No contrast could be greater than his response to the Hungarian situation upon arriving in Budapest at the beginning of April. Scarcely a fortnight earlier the liberal aristocrat, Count Michael Karolyi, abandoned his seemingly hopeless task of holding together a coalition of disparate elements, paving the way for the Social Democrats and the Communists to assume control. Bela Kun, prodding the reluctant Social Democrats into setting up a Soviet dictatorship, proclaimed a close alliance with Russia. Brailsford was one of the first Western journalists to arrive in Hungary after the bloodless revolution, and his enthusiasm for what he saw, somewhat ironic considering his coolness towards Bolshevism in Moscow, was almost unrestrained. It resembles

---

[32] *Across the Blockade*, pp. 69-71.
[33] This story is recounted, with minor variations, in *Across the Blockade*, p. 73; *New Leader*, 15 Dec. 1922; *Reynolds's Illustrated News*, 19 May 1935; *New Statesman*, 23 Sept. 1939.

nothing so much as George Orwell's euphoric reaction to egalitarian Barcelona in 1937. Coming from Vienna where he had been haunted by the hungry, dispirited faces, he encountered Budapest in the first flush of revolutionary fever. The city had 'found in Communism the violent stimulus it needed in the hour of despair and defeat'.[34]

A Communist dictatorship in Hungary, covertly sponsored by Moscow, inevitably incurred the opposition of the Entente powers, who imposed a blockade and unleashed Czech and Rumanian troops against the objectionable regime. Although the regime did not collapse until after Kun's disastrous offensive against Rumania in July, it was threatened by hostile encircling powers from the start. The beleaguered atmosphere accounts in part for the extraordinary unity of its early weeks that so impressed Brailsford. As a friendly journalist from the capitalist West, he was warmly welcomed and was able to secure interviews with all the leading personalities. Karolyi, whom he came to know better later in London, told him of the impossible task he faced as the first President of a country denied necessary supplies because of the Allied blockade, its borders overrun by Rumanian troops, its capital crammed with homeless refugees.[35]

Unaware of Bela Kun's links with the Soviet Union, Brailsford tended to see the Hungarian revolution as wholly indigenous rather than fomented by Moscow. He ignored the fact that the manual workers and clerks who were its strongest supporters represented a small segment of the population. Brailsford, invariably attracted by the passion of young revolutionaries, the very qualities that his innate circumspection precluded, was dazzled by the 'vitality and self-possession' of this thirty-three year old dictator. That he admired men like Gandhi and Jaurès and Keir Hardie even more did not lessen his fascination with the men of action. What appealed to him about Bela Kun, aside from his youth and energy, was that the Communist takeover in Hungary had been accomplished without bloodshed or terror.[36]

Among the young intellectuals who comprised Bela Kun's government the most notable was Georg Lukács, the thirty-four year old philosophy lecturer put in charge of the educational system, later to become the most significant Marxist critic of his generation. Meeting Lukács, Brailsford was impressed by his determination to abolish the culture of privilege and to elevate the educational level of the masses. Teachers were transformed overnight into 'the most honoured servants of the state', and a uniform salary, comparable to that of government

---

[34] *Across the Blockade*, p. 12.

[35] Ibid., pp. 16-18. Also see Michael Karolyi, *Memoirs: Faith Without Illusion* (New York, 1957), p. 164.

[36] *Across the Blockade*, pp. 19-21.

ministers, was paid to the village schoolmaster and university lecturer alike, an indication of the value the new regime placed on teaching.

Such glowing praise—and it foreshadowed his initial response to Soviet Russia when he visited it the next year—was not unqualified. He recognized that it was an 'unmixed dictatorship', that even though terror had not been instituted, there was no freedom for the press or for opponents of the regime. Those who did not do 'productive' work had been disenfranchised, and even the apparently free elections were expressions of assent to unopposed party candidates. While an emergency might justify temporary dictatorship, Brailsford warned that 'it will destroy Hungary intellectually and morally if it is continued for more than a few months'. Yet he contended that even if freedom were temporarily eclipsed, it was a justifiable price for the destruction of capitalism and the chance for 'real autonomy'.[37] Such sentiments implied wishful thinking, an unwillingness to recognize that Communist dictatorship was not merely a temporary expedient, but intrinsic to the system.

A more serious misapprehension was his failure to recognize the dimensions of the peasant problem. Visiting a communal farm in Kaposvar, accompanied by Dr Hamburger, the Agricultural Commissioner, he was assured that the collectivized estates were running smoothly. It would be wrong to suggest, as some critics did,[38] that he never questioned the lack of common interest between socialists and peasants. One peasant, whose conversation he recounted, informed him that his fellow estate workers, indifferent to socialist theory, were willing to give the experiment a chance in the hope of material advantages. Brailsford also commended the regime for having avoided the Russian mistake of too rapid collectivization. In Hungary the conservative peasant, owning or renting his own small farm, would be left alone until he was ready for change.[39] As the regime began to founder, he attributed its problems to external threats rather than to peasant disenchantment. Had it not been for the Rumanian assault, he wrote late in April, the government would have consolidated itself.[40] By November he was willing to concede that 'the real problem' for Hungarian communism had been 'the intensely conservative peasantry', whose acquisitive instincts were incompatible with the growth of a socialist society.[41]

When Brailsford moved on to Germany in late April for a three-week visit, he was struck by the penitent mood he encountered. The rejection of the past, signalled by the republican election victory earlier in the year, was confirmed in the general willingness to accept responsibility

[37] Ibid., pp. 32-8.
[38] Interview, David Mitrany.
[39] *Across the Blockade*, pp. 26-30.
[40] *Daily Herald*, 23 Apr. 1919.
[41] *Nation* (US), 22 Nov. 1919.

for past misdeeds. On the steps of the Reichstag he listened to a Socialist deputy telling an acquiescent crowd that the nation must be prepared to pay for Ludendorff's crimes. But what moved Brailsford even more was the 'black abysmal hopelessness' that he observed as a consequence of five months of Allied blockade.[42] Instead of encouraging the infant republic, struggling to win acceptance among its own people, the Allies seemed bent on ensuring its disgrace by compelling the avowedly anti-militarist regime to acknowledge war guilt. Only the threat of starvation and the hope of future revision would induce the German leaders to yield. Even so, the signatories would find themselves branded as traitors, and the government, discredited as well as disarmed, would be incapable of coping with *revanchist* militarism or revolutionary strikes.

For all the lofty hopes aroused by Wilsonian idealism—and even to his surprise by Lloyd George—in Germany no less than in England, the terms of the treaty provided 'an accurate mirror of capitalist Imperialism'.[43] Whatever reparation might appropriately have been exacted to compensate France and Belgium for damage, this extortionate scheme could only be viewed as a 'cold-blooded project for the destruction of a commercial competitor'.[44] A similar pattern could be seen in the blockade of Soviet Russia, intended to establish the British fleet in the Baltic permanently:

It is to make Russia safe for British profiteers that we are trying to impose upon her the rule of a clique of Tsarist soldiers, and to bring back after two years of an intellectual renaissance the dark ages of pogroms and miracles and priest-ridden schools.[45]

His sharpest condemnation was reserved for the territorial changes, especially the cynical dismemberment of the former empires under the guise of self-determination. Although he accepted the inevitable loss of Alsace-Lorraine and Posen, he rebelled against the subjection of the Saar to French military and economic surveillance. While such arrangements were provisional, they might foreshadow the permanent detachment of the region from Germany. As recently as 1917 he had regarded German absorption of Alsace-Lorraine with equanimity, but the prospect of even temporary French control of the Saar was intolerable. Still worse was the manner in which Germany's eastern boundaries had been redrawn in blatant disregard of ethnic demarcation lines. According to his calculations some two and a half million Germans in Posen,

---

[42] *Across the Blockade*, pp. 107-10.
[43] Ibid., p. 146.
[44] Ibid., p. 110. Also see *Daily Herald*, 21 May, 18 June 1919.
[45] *Daily Herald*, 22 Oct. 1919.

Silesia, West Prussia, and Danzig had been subjected to Polish rule without any consideration of their wishes. But this new Polish state, with its large unassimilable population, he predicted, would be 'a reactionary Imperialist, military State, created only to serve French military ends against Germany and Russia, a "ramshackle Empire", rather smaller, but not much more homogeneous, than the Austria which has vanished'.[46]

And what of Austria, that tiny remnant of the old Dual Monarchy, made the 'scape-goat for Hapsburg sins'? Eager to gratify the nationalist longings of Czechs, Serbs, and Poles, the Allies prohibited union between Austria and Germany in 'flat defiance of any honest reading of the principle of self-determination'. To compound the travesty, three and a half million Sudeten Germans, concentrated in an area easily detachable from Czechoslovakia, had been placed under 'foreign rule'. The Eastern settlement had aggrandized nations who were 'relatively barbarous at the expense of one of the world's great civilizations'. These 'raw peoples' might develop in a few generations, but for the present, 'the dismemberment of Austria-Hungary meant the Balkanization of morals and culture over the whole of Central and Eastern Europe'.[47]

Brailsford's tendency to ascribe all of Germany's ills to Allied oppression was hardly likely to gain wide acceptance. M. Philips Price, a British journalist stationed in Berlin, disputed the notion that political unity could be achieved if Germany were treated with greater forebearance. He contended that it was a delusion to imagine that the republican electoral victory meant the eclipse of the old order.[48] To be sure, Brailsford did not so much deny the survival of traditional forces as discount their importance in Weimar Germany. Attributing the ruthless suppression of the Spartacist revolt to the exigencies of the moment, he warned against expecting too much from a new government seeking consensus under the pressure of blockade and Allied demands.[49]

If Wilson had been hoodwinked by devious European statesmen and England fobbed off with commercial advantages, it was France which emerged victorious. By excluding Germany, she had 'wrecked' the League of Nations, encircling her former enemy with a ring of French satellites which included the 'maximum number of millions of subject Germans' in defiance of the principle of self-determination. While

---

[46] *Daily Herald*, 20 May 1919.
[47] *Manchester Guardian*, 3 June 1919; *Nation*, 16 Aug. 1919.
[48] M. Philips Price, *My Three Revolutions* (London, 1969), p. 168. Price, a Communist at the time, was the *Herald*'s German correspondent.
[49] *Daily Herald*, 20 May 1919.

England and the United States monopolized world trade, France would exercise 'military hegemony' over Europe in accord with Clemenceau's plan to make France the dominant military power on the Continent.[50]

For all Brailsford's powers of philosophical reasoning, his understanding of history, his ideological bias against capitalism, it was visual impressions that affected him most of all. His most memorable reporting was based on firsthand evidence, on the images that imprinted themselves on his conscience. The scenes of misery in Central European cities seared his conscience as nothing had before. It would be no exaggeration to suggest that his three-month journey in 1919 determined his attitude for the next twenty years. It was his response to human suffering, no less than his conviction about the unjust settlement, that made him so resolute an advocate of revision. In lamenting the onerous peace and the folly of indemnities, he was hardly unique among left-wing writers. Labour spokesmen inveighed against the treaty from the outset, but Brailsford was in many ways the most consistent and, perhaps, the most eloquent critic. Certainly none of his works was to achieve the notoriety of Keynes's *Economic Consequences of the Peace*, a work he hailed[51] and many of whose insights his own articles had anticipated. What is remarkable about his post-war writings, apart from the compassionate indignation they embodied, is their logical consistency: the outcome had confirmed his predictions about the consequences of unsound policies. Most of what he wrote in 1919 and 1920 confirmed the warnings of his 1914 pamphlet, *The Origins of the Great War*. His prescription for a lasting settlement seemed all the more relevant once the mistakes against which he had fulminated so fruitlessly were enshrined in a treaty. Tirelessly, and somewhat more stridently, he renewed his appeal for reconciliation in 1919: by appeasing Germany, England might rectify the injuries perpetrated at Versailles. Even if the government failed to act, it was Labour's duty to dissociate itself from the settlement, to strive for peace with the Soviet Union, the admission of Germany to the League, and the repudiation of a military alliance with France. There was no time to wait for a gradual process of revision to evolve; unless harsh conditions were promptly alleviated, the European order would 'collapse under the stress of want and revolution'.[52] He rejoiced neither in the breakdown of the traditional order nor in the apparently inevitable Communist revolutions. His own preference was for the peaceful evolution of social democratic regimes throughout

---

[50] *Daily Herald*, 18 June, 2 July 1919. See Henry R. Winkler, 'The British Labour Party and the Paris Settlement', in *Some Pathways in Twentieth Century History*, Daniel R. Beaver, ed. (Detroit, 1969), p. 142.
[51] *Labour Leader*, 1 Jan. 1920.
[52] *New Republic*, 1 Oct. 1919.

Europe, an objective that seemed even less probable in 1919 than before the war.

Brailsford returned from his travels, invigorated, but combative, on 19 May, having been away from England for nearly four months. Nevinson found him 'full of interest on state of Germany' but complaining that 'half his telegrams had been cut out'.[53] This did not prevent him from providing the fullest account of conditions yet to appear in the British press, in addition to interviews with Central European statesmen such as Bela Kun and Matthias Erzberger. Fourteen reports with foreign datelines appeared in the *Herald* while he was abroad, in addition to a number of articles based on his observations in the *Nation*, the *Manchester Guardian*, the *New Republic*, and the American *Nation*. His book *Across the Blockade: A Record of Travels in Enemy Europe*, published by Allen and Unwin in September and based on these articles, represented a return to the kind of reportage that had established his pre-war reputation as a foreign correspondent. He had been so traumatized by what he observed that he felt compelled to impart his views in other ways as well. Clifford Allen, whose regard for Brailsford's ability was soon to have profound implications for his career, met him at a party at Mary Agnes Hamilton's and listened attentively to his reports of Germany and Austria. 'Brailsford,' he recorded in his diary, 'in his usual splendid form, wise, humorous, sincere, passionate.'[54] In June Brailsford was named to a subcommittee of the Advisory Committee on International Questions looking into revision of the peace terms.[55] He also sought the chance to speak at the Southport Labour Party Conference later that month, a request that was evidently denied:

> I have recently come back from a stay in Berlin & Vienna, [he wrote Henderson] my mind very full of the belief that the future there will get out of all control, unless the German Socialists have faith in the will of the British Labour Party to work effectively for the amendment of the Treaty at an early date. . . . If it would be of any use to have first-hand impressions to back an appeal to the Party to work for the revision of the Treaties, I would be prepared if it were of any service to the Executive to speak to the Conference about what I have seen and heard.[56]

During the months that followed, his frustration over the European situation was compounded by the turmoil in his private life. Relations with Jane had not benefited from their separation during his trip, nor

[53] ND, 19 May 1919.
[54] Clifford Allen Diary, 30 May 1919, quoted in Gilbert, *Plough*, p. 132. Allen's visit to Welwyn, discussed in Chap. VII, took place two days later.
[55] ACIQ Minutes, 17 June 1919.
[56] HNB to Arthur Henderson, n.d. [1919], Labour Party Archive, LP/JSM/INT/29.

from their reluctant move from Welwyn to London in October. He was coming to realize that the marriage was doomed, as Jane's drinking worsened, and he sought escape from domestic miseries in foreign travel and, as usual, in writing. In the two years between his return from Berlin and their final separation in September 1921 he wrote three books, largely derived from journalism. It was for him a period of increased celebrity as well as personal reassessment, but until 1922 he was, to some extent, at a loose end.

The dislocated post-war economy and the ineffectual plea for treaty revision filled him with foreboding about the future. That paradoxical faith in the innate reasonableness of liberal societies, a corollary of his pre-war critique of capitalist imperialism, now seemed to desert him. Nowhere in *After the Peace*, written early in 1920 and published in September, can one find even the glimmer of hope that had marked *The War of Steel and Gold*. Appearing two years before Spengler's *Decline of the West*, his gloomy prognosis anticipated its recognition of the breakdown of civilization and the resurgence of primitive values. The blockade had paralysed Central European industry, while the structure of debt spelled 'the economic death of half a Continent'. The impossibility of enforcing the peace except by policing meant the perpetuation of alliances and armaments. 'The image of the future which presents itself,' he prophesied, 'is that of all Central Europe reduced to the condition of a camp of prisoners of war, kept at work for the benefit of their gaolers, by a system of calculated intimidation.' Blaming the settlement for the 'world shortage, the dwindling of populations, the decay of industries, the twilight of civilization', he prophesied:

> Under the pressure of this grinding poverty, sooner or later, unless the decay is arrested, the urban civilization of Europe will be as dead as the culture of Babylon, and there will survive only peasant communities, narrow, reactionary and clerically-minded.[57]

The probable outcome would be either social revolution or militarist reaction, the expressions of despair by the middle and working classes for whom life was becoming unendurable.

So keen had the Allies been to crush their enemies that they ignored Germany's potential contribution to European economic and cultural recovery. Rather than channel German energies towards some mutually beneficial goal, they showered their

> favours on Poles, Roumanians and Jugo-Slavs, primitive unschooled races, not indeed without their own charm and emotional genius, who never, even after generations of experience, are likely to replace the Germans as industrial or intellectual workers.

[57] *After the Peace*, pp. 21, 30, 39, 82.

The Balkanization of Central Europe, with the deliberate reduction of its productive capacity meant 'the ruin of Europe and of our common civilization'.[58]

Admitting that the peace treaties could only be revised by general consent, he was willing to suggest at least some guiding principles that might shape the international thinking of the Labour Party. With France refusing concessions, it was up to England to seize the initiative, sacrificing its spoils in the interests of peace: to cancel inter-Allied debts, to forego its share in the indemnity, to distribute equitably such prizes as Mesopotamian oil, to surrender the unlimited right of blockade, and to reduce the size of its navy.

Typical of Brailsford's style in its economy of language, its use of historical allusion, and its lucid analysis, *After the Peace*, fascinating as polemic, never transcended the fleeting pessimism. Lacking the satirical touch of Keynes, Brailsford's essay was too unrelievedly gloomy to appeal to its readers. Where Keynes attributed the mistakes of the peace conference to human guile and stupidity, Brailsford ascribed Europe's problems to the death-throes of bankrupt capitalism and the malignant influence of France. His prejudices—against the African troops, against the politically and culturally underdeveloped peoples of the succession states—are too close to the surface. Before and during the war his diagnosis of the ills of capitalism had taken second place to prescription; *The War of Steel and Gold* and *A League of Nations*, for all their denunciation of the traditional order, were both rooted in the optimistic conviction that rational solutions would prevail. But his remedies—a revived European Concert, limitation on armaments, co-operative exploitation of mineral resources, an international civil service—had either been ignored or distorted for self-serving ends. The echo of previous proposals sounded hollow in *After the Peace*, as if its author could no longer convince himself that they were plausible. His alarmist judgements about the imminent collapse of Western culture did little to enhance his reputation.

Ever since his arrival in London at the beginning of the century he had carried a lance in 'the stage army of the Good'. He had lent his pen and voice to innumerable organizations, most of them ephemeral, devoted to improving the lot of the disadvantaged of the world. But he was essentially a loner, identifying more readily with causes than with formal organizations. His involvement in the Advisory Committee on International Questions, writing numerous reports and memoranda and even serving for a time as Vice Chairman, essentially ceased early

[58] Ibid., pp. 22-3, 173.

in 1922 and had been punctuated by long absences. Since many of these short-lived pressure groups received little public attention, their activities are difficult to document. Brailsford and Woolf joined H. G. Wells in an informal body agitating for the removal of the hated Black and Tans and for peace in Ireland, which Woolf, another inveterate joiner, dismissed as 'ineffectual'.[59] In March 1920 Blunt inveigled Brailsford into yet another tenuous group seeking Egyptian independence, an issue on which they had collaborated for fifteen years.[60]

Although most of its members disapproved of the efforts of the Third International to foment world revolution, the Advisory Committee tried to urge the Labour Party to adopt a stronger pro-Russian policy. They feared that Allied efforts to subvert the Bolshevik regime would result in a preventive war with the Soviet Union, with Poland as the vanguard. In February Brailsford was the principal author of a memorandum denouncing the Allied blockade of Russia and urging the party to declare its opposition to war between England and Russia.[61] Such a policy was in fact adopted by Labour in August 1920 at more or less the same time that the newly formed Communist Party of Great Britain made its first bid for affiliation with Labour. The movement in general was still fascinated by the regime, and in 1920 Western visitors were becoming more frequent.

Brailsford was keen to go to Russia, an opportunity he had repeatedly missed before the war because of his politics and complications over his passport. By 1920 he was able to secure a British passport to Estonia and a visa to enter Russia without difficulty. In the spring Massingham agreed to release him from his *Nation* duties for three months, and Woolf was hired to write foreign leaders in his absence.[62] Unlike his trip to Central Europe the previous year, he was not intending to send back articles, perhaps for fear of offending his hosts. He was able to travel alone wherever he wished, unhindered either by protocol or surveillance. It was not until after his return in October that he described what he had seen, not only in the *Nation* and the *New Republic*, but more extensively in *The Russian Workers' Republic*, his second book for Allen and Unwin.

Relieved of professional obligations and travelling once again without Jane, he left at the end of July 1920, taking the steamer from Hull

[59] Woolf, *Beginning Again*, p. 193.
[60] HNB to W. S. Blunt, 25 Mar. [1920], BP; Blunt Autograph Diary, 11 Apr. 1920, BP, MS 455-1975.
[61] ACIQ Memorandum No. 126: 'The Russian Situation' (Feb. 1920).
[62] Woolf, *Beginning Again*, pp. 185-6. Virginia Woolf claimed that Massingham, somewhat implausibly, offered Leonard Brailsford's job on the *Nation*, but later changed this to the offer of a position as 'second string in the foreign dept'. Anne Olivier Bell, ed., *The Diary of Virginia Woolf, II: 1920-1924* (London, 1978), pp. 34, 42.

to Helsingsfors. Harold Laski, meeting him for the first time, was convinced that 'his observations are likely to be more accurate than those of any other observer'.[63] Although he had spent some months before his trip trying to learn some Russian, his minimal acquaintance was not a serious handicap, since he found many people who could speak to him in German, if not in English or French. During a stop in Copenhagen he met Maxim Litvinov, travelling in the West in an effort to establish unofficial contacts. Since Brailsford was going to Moscow, the Soviet diplomat asked him to carry a bundle of European newspapers to the Commissariat for Foreign Affairs, which had been largely cut off from regular communication with the outer world. At Reval the Bolshevik authorities confiscated copies of the *Labour Leader* and *L'Humanité*, perhaps fearing contamination by the democratic socialist press, but they allowed *The Times* to pass unimpeded.[64]

Brailsford divided his time between Petrograd, Moscow, Minsk and the Western war-front, and the central province of Vladimir. Having intended to spend a few days in Vladimir, he became so interested in what he saw that he remained for a fortnight, learning more about Russia there than in the other six weeks. Here he was able to observe a provincial Soviet in session. Without deceiving himself as to its influence, he was impressed by the practical experience in self-government. Unlike Moscow, there was little evidence of the 'Extraordinary Commission', whose task was to extirpate the forces of counter-revolution. But here too the Communist dictatorship, much to his regret, prevented any genuine representative system. On the other hand, he was encouraged by the rapid social improvements. Although collectivization was meeting resistance from peasants eager to cultivate their own holdings, those employed on communal farms had 'undoubtedly gained immeasurably by the Revolution and know it'.[65]

Throughout his journey he noted the emphasis on making culture accessible to the masses and especially to the children. The educational strides indicated that the regime was 'ripening the whole Russian people for responsibility and power'.[66] Although the distrust of intellectuals led the government to recruit teachers from the proletariat, the determination to break the barriers of class and poverty pervaded all that he saw. With the proliferation of libraries, theatres, and concerts, the regime might well claim 'a better record in its relations to art and culture' than any other civilized government. Of course the socialization

---

[63] Harold Laski to Maurice Firuski, Aug. 1920, quoted in Kingsley Martin, *Harold Laski* (New York, 1953), p. 47.
[64] Transcript of broadcast in BBC Overseas Service, 17 June 1942.
[65] *Russian Workers' Republic*, p. 61.
[66] Ibid., p. 73.

of publishing constituted an intolerable censorship which could not survive without 'grave detriment to the liberty of thought'.[67]

Brailsford first encountered the Red Army near Minsk early in August. Recently recaptured by the Russians, Minsk had been the scene of a pogrom. The inhabitants of a burnt village nearby crowded around him to inquire how they could escape to America. After harsh treatment from the Poles, Jews and peasants seemed to welcome the Russians, although the Polish aristocracy had fled with the retreating army. At the army headquarters at Minsk, he met Tukhachevsky, a Communist born into the nobility and Chief of Staff at the age of twenty-seven. He seemed a romantic figure, 'curiously modest and youthful in manner, with the air rather of a student than of a soldier', a favourable impression that remained with him years later when Tukhachevsky fell victim to Stalin's purge.[68] He also enjoyed a brief interview with Trotsky in Moscow, the two men conversing in German about the Polish War. In contrast to most officials he met, ordinarily two or three hours late for their appointments, Trotsky was absolutely punctual, 'the only businesslike Russian I met'. His personality suggested 'the driving power of an unflinching will'.[69]

His most vivid experience with the Red Army came later in Vladimir, where he responded to the commander's invitation to speak to a volunteer batallion off to the Crimea to oppose General Wrangel's forces. He knew that some of these young peasants would be killed by ammunition that had been furnished by the British to the anti-Soviet armies. Standing on a platform in front of the ancient cathedral, he told the troops of the dockers' refusal to load ammunition bound for Poland on the *Jolly George* and of Labour's opposition to war with Russia. 'The thrill of friendship,' he later reported, 'went through their ranks.'[70]

Although he applauded the cultural strides, the dedication of teachers, soldiers, and provincial administrators, and the visionary experiments to uplift this backward, peasant nation, he was apprehensive about the exercise of power in the Soviet Union. Whether or not the dictatorship was preparing for its own eventual demise by educating the masses, the party had in the meantime consolidated its position by means of propaganda and intimidation. The hostile environment in which the Bolsheviks had seized power, the resistance to their grandiose plans explained the source of the terror, but 'nothing can excuse [their] cruelty. To save the revolution, [they] are ruining Russia.'[71] He dismissed the doctrine of world revolution as a defensive reflex. Should the capitalist powers

---

[67] Ibid., pp. 88-90. [68] Ibid., p. 128.
[69] Transcript of broadcast in BBC Overseas Service, 22 Aug. 1940; *New Statesman*, 31 Aug. 1940.
[70] *New Leader*, 1 Feb. 1924. [71] *Russian Workers' Republic*, p. 115.

abandon their hostility, the Soviets would willingly turn to the more urgent tasks of education and economic recovery. Despite fears that the regime might come to grief through its suppression of dissent or the recalcitrance of the peasantry, his final verdict was enthusiastic: 'this Revolution will live to vindicate itself in history as the greatest effort of the constructive human will since the French made an end of feudalism'.[72]

It was a judgement to which, on the whole, he clung, although his sympathy was eroded by the ineluctable tyranny he found so repugnant. In a preface to the English edition of Trotsky's *The Defence of Terrorism* he paid tribute to the audacity of the Bolsheviks for making a proletarian revolution in the country whose economic development seemed least prepared for it. He saw their survival amid invasion, famine, and economic collapse as 'a triumph of the unflinching will and the fanatical faith' and praised them for having 'spurred a lazy and demoralised people to notable feats of arms and to still more astonishing feats of endurance'.[73] But when, in 1921, Lenin launched the New Economic Policy, Brailsford wrote that Communism 'if not finally defeated, has executed a comprehensive retreat'. The shift towards moderation indicated that it was not the Bolsheviks who prevailed, but the peasants who had used the Bolsheviks to destroy the landed class and establish peasant ownership.[74] By the beginning of 1922 he was willing to concede privately in a letter to Russell that 'events were going to prove you right over Russia & me pretty badly wrong'.[75] The time had come to ask whether any interest of the Revolution could still justify the retention of dictatorship. Communism, he felt, had been largely defeated by blockade, civil war, and famine, and the problem that remained was not ideological purity, but the restoration of Russian civilization.

In mid-October 1920 Brailsford returned from Russia, crossing again by ship, this time from Oslo to Hull. The highlight of his journey was his encounter with a flock of wrens that had attached themselves to the masts of the ships as though they were tree trunks. Brailsford, whose love of birds surpassed even his affinity for cats, tossed them some of the pine kernels he invariably carried in his pockets, but they ignored him. Even bread failed to attract them. When he sat down to watch their activities, two or three climbed on his deck-chair and over his body, hopping about in his hair, pecking for insects. He later recalled the feel of the birds wandering over his body as one of the most memorable sensations of his life.[76] Shortly after his return he recounted his

[72] Ibid., p. 205. [73] Leon Trotsky, *The Defence of Terrorism* (London, 1921), pp. i-ii.
[74] *New Republic*, 13 July 1921.
[75] HNB to Bertrand Russell, 15 Jan. [1922], Russell Papers.
[76] *Radio Times*, 23 May 1930; Clare Leighton, *Four Hedges: A Gardener's Chronicle* (New York, 1935), p. 42.

adventures at the 1917 Club,[77] and in the next weeks he produced four articles for the *Nation*, five for the *New Republic*, and, by Christmas, the manuscript of *The Russian Workers' Republic*, published in April 1921.

His Russian experiences influenced a review of a new edition of Graham Wallas' *Human Nature in Politics* in which Brailsford contrasted Western democracy with Russian Communism. Acknowledging Trotsky's *The Defence of Terrorism*, he conceded that the pressure employed by the wealthy in a democracy makes its political process an elaborate camouflage for bourgeois dictatorship. The irrational impulses which determined the voters' minds were stacked in favour of property, as Wallas, analysing the power of instinct, understood. Not that Soviet Russia represented an improvement on the failings of Western democracy: the Bolsheviks seemed 'to be strapping a strait waistcoat on to the body of the sovereign proletariat'. Both regimes would become more responsive to the public when the masses were educated to govern themselves, but it was not clear whether that process would be achieved more rapidly in Western democracies or in Russia.[78] His distaste for dictatorship did not inhibit him from working for the Russian Famine Relief Fund in 1921 and 1922. He tried to interest J. L. Garvin of the *Observer* in a proposal to buy grain in Poland and Rumania with British coal, thus providing food for Russia while assisting the unemployed at home.[79]

At the end of February 1921, Brailsford attended the inaugural meeting of the Vienna International, comprising dissident socialists seeking to mediate between the Second and Third Internationals. The ILP endorsed the venture, whose goals were close to Brailsford's rather futile hope of reconciliation within the socialist camp. Here he renewed his acquaintance with Continental socialists, such as Friedrich Adler and Otto Bauer, and met for the first time the young Julius Braunthal, later to become a close friend.

In September the Brailsfords at long last separated, Jane remaining in Ladbroke Gardens, while he moved to a Pimlico flat. It had been eight years since their initial split and reconciliation, but the relationship had only become more embittered in the interval. Once they returned to London from Welwyn, they were rarely seen together, his frequent trips helping to keep them safely apart. Without ceasing to blame himself for Jane's alcoholism, carefully concealed from family and friends, he was at the same time becoming involved with an old friend. An independent-minded, attractive Oxford graduate, Kathleen Courtney had shifted from suffrage activity to the Women's Inter-

[77] ND, 28 Oct. 1920.
[78] *Nation*, 22 Jan. 1921. See Clarke, *Liberals and Social Democrats*, pp. 213-18.
[79] HNB to J. L. Garvin, 26 Jan. [1922], Garvin Papers.

national League and to war-victim relief. Towards the end of the war she and Brailsford collaborated in the work of the Family Endowment Committee. It is not clear when their professional association began to ripen into intimacy, but by 1921, when both were in Vienna for the International congress, he broached the subject of marriage if Jane would concede a divorce. She declined his offer, ostensibly on the grounds that at forty-three she was too old to bear children and that should he remarry, it ought to be to a younger woman. Brailsford did not proceed with the divorce, probably because Jane refused, but he realized that they could no longer live together. Nevinson, adept at sniffing out trouble between the Brailsfords, was, by July 1921, afraid to 'enquire about J. E. M. for fear of some mental disaster said to have befallen her'. Catherine Marshall, intimating that Jane had become addicted to drugs, prodded him to find out 'what had become of Mrs. Brailsford all these months'.[80] Brailsford's comment was full of characteristic self-reproach:

The facts are painful & I have been grossly to blame. I decided last September to live alone & moved to my flat. My wife remained at Ladbroke Gdns. She is still there & I see her fairly often. For the unhappiness which led me to take this decision (as I thought in both our interests) I am alone to blame.[81]

His visits were, in fact, regular and the costs onerous, since Jane lacked other means of support and was no longer employable. There were repeated attempts at reconciliation, the last in the mid-1920s when Jane promised to reform. He went so far as to furnish a new house for them only to find her lying drunk on the floor of her flat when he arrived to collect her. By 1929 she was in need of constant attention and was moved to Kew Road, Richmond, in the care of a housekeeper, where she lived until her death in 1937.

A second blow struck several months later when Edward Brailsford died at the age of eighty. Father and son had become reconciled in later years, although the wounds inflicted in childhood had never really healed. After his retirement to Ilfracombe Edward had busied himself with the Save the Children Fund, with his son's approval. In late November 1921 Brailsford was lecturing in Liverpool when he received a message summoning him to his father's bedside, so that he was able to be with him when he died on 30 November surrounded by his family.[82] Brailsford recalled his sentiments in a letter to Kingsley Martin nearly twenty years later, when Martin suffered a similar bereavement:

I had a sensation as if my roots had been torn up. And in a strange new way I

[80] ND, 11 July 1921, 10 and 12 Apr. 1922.
[81] HNB to H. W. Nevinson, n.d., quoted in ND, 21 Apr. 1922.
[82] Interview, Mabel R. Brailsford.

felt myself alone and unsupported in the world. And this was the stranger because my father had never been a support to me, and, until he was an old man, I had had to fight him.[83]

In the autumn of 1921 Brailsford was one of several British journalists recruited by Paul Patterson to write for the *Baltimore Sun*, a connection which, with brief interruptions, lasted into the 1940s.[84] Along with the *New Republic*, the *Sun* was an important American vehicle for his views, not to mention a welcome source of additional income. His first articles examined the issues at the Washington naval conference, a series which also appeared in England in the *Labour Leader*. In them he encouraged joint economic penetration of China much as he had collaborative Anglo-German ventures in Turkey before 1914. Long an advocate of rationing scarce minerals, he wanted to anticipate potential dangers by admitting Japan's special needs. Under international control of Chinese resources, Japan would be permitted to purchase coal at stipulated prices, a concession that would deflect Japanese aggression and pave the way for disarmament.[85]

The following June he revisited Central Europe in order to determine whether conditions had improved since 1919. His earlier impression of universal poverty was no longer accurate, but although hunger had abated in Vienna, it remained spiritually lifeless. Without the abolition of trade restrictions and the concession of credit, Austria seemed doomed to economic collapse. In contrast, Czechoslovakia, whose birth he had regretted, now appeared 'the one soberly active and creative force' in Central Europe. Although he thought that the skilful statesmanship of Beneš—whom he interviewed—might overcome some of the impediments to Danubian commerce, he was less confident about the government's capacity to resolve racial problems. While the intolerance of the immediate post-war period had subsided, he felt that this 'capable and vigorous Republic can maintain itself only by force', unless it agreed to concessions on a wide range of political and social issues to the aggrieved minority.[86]

In Germany the picture was mixed as well. He found the occupied Rhineland 'a French camp', intended not merely to hold the region militarily, but 'to dominate its life'. While he found little to confirm complaints of French violence, he reiterated charges of 'sexual assaults' by African troops, whose presence was deemed a 'perpetual insult'.[87]

[83] HNB to Kingsley Martin, 8 Nov. 1940, KMP.
[84] I am grateful to William H. Honan for information concerning Brailsford's association with the *Baltimore Sun*.
[85] *Labour Leader*, 29 Dec. 1921.
[86] *Nation*, 24 June and 1 July 1922. [87] *Daily Herald*, 11 July 1922.

When he travelled through Saxony in 1919, he had found not a single chimney smoking; in 1922 the factories were busy, the shops full, and work plentiful. But everyone seemed to be 'living on the margin of a just tolerable existence'. The price of food had risen by more than twice the level of wages, and although workers were no longer suffering privation, they were not adequately nourished. The middle class had been reduced to a proletarian standard of living, no longer able to afford luxuries. In economic terms, he could only conclude that the 'busy prosperity is only a show. The fact is deep poverty.'[88]

Despite the grim forecast of *After the Peace*, Brailsford had to admit that Central Europe had undergone some measure of economic recovery. But the spiritual malaise observable immediately after the war had in the intervening years become a crisis of civilization. In Vienna he once again met Lukács, now a political exile, who attempted to convince him that 'culture, in the sense of an activity which creates and conquers new fields, is dying because the leisured class is sinking to a proletarian level'. Although Lukács did not anticipate immediate social revolution in Central Europe, he believed that the Soviet Union would eventually attack the West, precipitating a conflict which would reduce the Continent to barbarism. Brailsford was not entirely persuaded that the destruction of the class that had transmitted art and science was inevitably fatal to the perpetuation of culture. In Germany he was impressed by the strides made towards diffusing culture among the workers through adult courses and the youth movement. During a visit to Bräuning-Oktavio in Darmstadt he attended a Goethe festival in the woods early one Sunday morning where two hundred young workers sat on the ground listening attentively to a lecture on Goethe's early development.[89] This was the authentic German spirit, that reverence for cultural enlightenment which he had cherished since his student days in Berlin in the 1890s. As long as the words of Goethe or the music of Beethoven could inspire the younger generation, the flame of culture would not be extinguished. It was a conviction even stronger than his belief in socialism; his sense of a tenacious, civilized spirit in Germany survived not only the despair of the early 1920s, but the advent of Nazism. The flawed peace had destroyed the material basis of life, had weakened the will to survive, but there was at least a glimmer of hope for the future.

[88] *Nation*, 15 July 1922.
[89] *Manchester Guardian Commercial*, 4 Jan. 1923.

X
The New Leader (1922-1926)

After a chequered existence during the 1890s, the *Labour Leader*, a weekly begun by Keir Hardie to rival Blatchford's *Clarion*, had been sold to the ILP for £1,500. J. Bruce Glasier, who became editor, was able to raise circulation from 13,000 to 24,000 by 1906 and to 43,000 two years later, when the numbers began to dwindle and the financial losses increased.[1] Between 1911 and 1916, edited from Manchester by the young, ambitious Fenner Brockway, it was a mediocre journal, appealing in the main to provincial working men. When Brockway was imprisoned for anti-conscription activity, Katherine Bruce Glasier took over, and for a time the *Leader* prospered. During 1917 circulation reached 62,000, a factor in the party's refusal to reinstate Brockway when his prison term ended, to his bitter disappointment. Mrs Glasier was retained after the war, but by 1921 the paper was losing money at a rate of £1,200 a year, less perhaps through any editorial deficiency than because of the stiff competition of Thomas Johnston's *Forward,* organ of the Scottish ILP, and of the *Herald*.[2]

The paper's decline paralleled the crisis that threatened to engulf the ILP itself. Although the principal source of policy and leadership before the war, its *raison d'être* was called into question by the individual membership provisions of the 1918 Labour Party constitution and by the ostensible commitment to socialism embodied in *Labour and the New Social Order*. Despite loss of momentum and lack of support among trade unionists, the ILP refused either to submerge itself within the Labour Party or to retreat into a purely propagandist role. That the disintegration of the ILP was forestalled was in large measure the achievement of Clifford Allen, who became party treasurer in 1922. Through his Quaker contacts, cultivated during wartime pacifist activities, Allen was able to tap sources hitherto inaccessible to the party, and during his first year of fund-raising he collected nearly £12,000, much of it in large individual donations.[3] In addition, he attempted to introduce some semblance of efficiency into the amateurish organization by concentrating power in the National Administrative Council

[1] Lawrence Thompson, *The Enthusiasts* (London, 1971), pp. 137-40, 154-5; Philip P. Poirier, *The Advent of the Labour Party* (London, 1958), p. 213.
[2] Fenner Brockway, *Inside the Left* (London, 1942), p. 120; Thompson, pp. 230-2; NAC Minutes, 1921.
[3] Robert E. Dowse, *Left in the Centre* (London, 1966), p. 77.

(NAC) and by appointing full-time, paid officials to manage party affairs. In April 1922 the NAC instructed MacDonald and Allen to visit Manchester, where the *Labour Leader* had been published since 1901 by the autonomous National Labour Press, and to investigate whether it would be feasible for the NAC to acquire the paper directly. By June MacDonald was able to persuade his colleagues that it would be advisable for commercial and editorial reasons not merely to transfer control to the NAC, but to publish in London. A new company, with NAC members as shareholders, was formed to exercise authority.[4]

In the meantime Allen and MacDonald had pursued the task of securing a qualified editor. Allen discounted the claims of Brockway, who was relegated to the position of Organizing Secretary, and resolved to find a journalist whose reputation matched his own lofty plans for the journal. He made it clear that he wanted someone who would devote himself fully to the paper, and he was willing to pay for it, if not from advertising and circulation revenue, then from donations. Impressed by these ambitious schemes, MacDonald had misgivings about turning the *Labour Leader* into a journal of socialist propaganda, especially if it were not subject to his control. What he envisaged was an updated version of the personalized newspapers of the past—Blatchford's *Clarion* and the *Labour Leader* under Keir Hardie—a revival of a familiar formula rather than a new departure in labour journalism. He saw the editor as a 'genial autocrat', interfering as little as possible with contributors and not seeking to put his own imprint on its content. It was clear that he desired a periodical lively enough to attract an audience, but not sufficiently independent to criticize the leader or to seek to influence policy.[5]

To MacDonald's dismay, Allen had a candidate in mind who scarcely fitted this image. Having become acquainted with Brailsford during the war, he admired his literary gifts and astute appraisal of world problems. It was at once an obvious and a risky choice. As a journalist his credentials could scarcely be bettered. Widely travelled, he had a reputation for integrity, and was extraordinarily knowledgeable about world affairs. At the same time he lacked editorial experience and was regarded by many who knew him as irascible, aloof, and prone to self-righteousness. Brailsford's relations with MacDonald, which went back as least as far as 1903, had never been entirely cordial. MacDonald regarded him as something of a nuisance without a redeeming trace of sycophancy.

[4] NAC Minutes, 18 Apr., 12 May, 25 June 1922.
[5] MacDonald memorandum (11 May 1922): 'My ideas of the Leader', AP, Box V. MacDonald edited *Socialist Review* until he became Prime Minister.

Although affiliated with the ILP ever since 1907, Brailsford's membership was nominal until 1921, not from ideological diffidence, but because he found organizational politics uncongenial. His suspicion of its coolness towards middle-class intellectuals was warranted; he always remained an outsider, a recruit from the enemy camp, welcomed, but never trusted by those who deemed middle-class origins as inimical to genuine socialist conviction. Until the 1920s his involvement had been chiefly a literary one, although in 1921 he allowed himself to be nominated as an (unsuccessful) candidate for the National Administrative Council. In the same year he served as an unofficial delegate at the inaugural meeting of the Vienna International and was subsequently named to the Programme and Policy Committee set up at the Southport annual conference to refurbish the party image.[6]

MacDonald attempted to dissuade Allen from his choice, bringing in spurious evidence to bolster his disapproval:

I hope you will think over very carefully the question of Brailsford's editorship. A friend of his talked to me last night and began by remarking upon how tremendously prosperous and successful he was. . . . As my friend knew him out and in I asked how he would do as editor of a paper that was actively propagandist, and the answer was swift and prompt: 'He would do not at all; that's not his line; he would either destroy such a paper or resign within six months.' So I am inclined to be very cautious in pursuing the possibility of his editorship. I think he ought to be enlisted in some way or other and in as big a way as possible, but I cannot see him as editor of an ILP paper.[7]

Much of this was scurrilous gossip—Brailsford could scarcely be described as 'tremendously prosperous'—a smoke screen for MacDonald's apprehension that he might prove insufficiently pliable as editor. Allen, still immune to MacDonald's captivating manner, prevailed, and the two men promptly arranged to 'meet Brailsford to discuss with him whether he would be willing to take over the editorship'.[8]

Naturally apprehensive about his suitability, Brailsford did not hesitate in accepting Allen's offer. His career had reached a plateau: it was unclear whether he could go any further than being a respected columnist. His political views restricted him to the left-wing press, where financial survival was always somewhat uncertain. He had often disagreed with the editorial policy of his employers—with the *Daily News* over forcible feeding, with the *Nation* over support for the war, with the *Herald* over Bolshevism—but he could do no more than argue his dissenting views in his own articles. In personal terms as well Brailsford was ready

---

[6] *Labour Leader*, 31 Mar. 1921; *Report of the 29th Annual Conference of the ILP* (1921), p. 13. Brailsford was placed seventh in the election to fill three vacancies.

[7] J. R. MacDonald to Clifford Allen, 13 May 1922, AP, Box V.

[8] Clifford Allen to Edith Ellis, 15 May 1922, AP, Box V.

for change. The death of his father and the break-up of his marriage had, at least in part, released him from the burdens of his past, opening the way to new ventures. He had come to terms with his private tragedies and ceased to flee from personal intimacy. A gentler, even mellower man by 1922, he was able to command the affection of his staff and to assert his authority far more confidently than might have been possible a few years earlier.

In June 1922 the National Administrative Council invited him to outline his plans at its July and August meetings. He contended that an enlarged format of sixteen pages—the *Labour Leader* had ordinarily published eight or twelve—was essential if the paper was to make its mark, even though this might cost £40 per week in the early months to pay contributors. He expected that advertising revenue would soon eliminate the need for a subsidy and predicted a small profit if 60,000 copies could be sold.[9] Allen, who hoped to limit the subvention to £15 or £20, yielded to Brailsford's estimate.[10] The terms of appointment were for one year from September 1922 at a salary of £1,000 per annum subject to six months notice on either side. The NAC accepted Brailsford's stipulation that the final decision in regard to engaging or dismissing staff, accepting or rejecting articles, would rest with him.[11] Ultimate authority would be vested in a company, chaired by Allen, whose shareholders would include NAC members. What was surprising, in view of subsequent carping, was that the NAC did not balk at the proposed salary, an amount far in excess of what his predecessors had received.[12] On the other hand, £1,000 was exactly what Massingham had been paid when he launched the *Nation* in 1907 and was no more than the salary of a leader-writer on a national daily.[13] While Brailsford's income had fluctuated over the years, there was no obvious financial inducement in the job, his previous earnings having probably matched or even exceeded the stipulated salary. To be sure, the Rowntree Trust could afford to be more generous than the ILP, but it was absurd to expect Brailsford to sacrifice his livelihood to propitiate those who deemed it immoral for party employees to receive adequate remuneration. No previous *Leader* editor possessed Brailsford's credentials, and if the ILP were to reap the benefits of his appointment, it would have to pay accordingly. When he accepted the editorship, it

---

[9] NAC Minutes, 26 June, 21 July, 10 Aug. 1922.
[10] Clifford Allen to J. R. MacDonald, 21 June 1922, AP, Box V.
[11] Clifford Allen to HNB, 14 Sept. 1922, Johnson Papers.
[12] When he assumed the editorship in 1905, Glasier received two guineas a week; Bertram Carter was paid £450 p.a. in 1921-2. Thompson, p. 140; NAC Minutes, 26 May 1921.
[13] Havighurst, *Massingham*, p. 143. Massingham was getting £1,500 p.a. at the time he left the *Nation* in 1923.

was with the understanding that he would abandon other professional activities—even unpaid ones.

Defeated over the editorship, MacDonald convinced Allen that they should impose Mary Agnes Hamilton as sub-editor, although she was presented to the NAC as Brailsford's appointee. Despite guarantees about his authority over appointments, the selection of his deputy was removed from him. It proved a disastrous choice. Daughter of philosopher Robert Adamson (who had blocked Brailsford's academic career in Glasgow) and herself a Cambridge graduate, she was one of MacDonald's most unflagging admirers. Brailsford, who regarded her quite rightly as the Leader's watchdog, treated her with ill-concealed antipathy, a sentiment that was cordially reciprocated. Mrs Hamilton saw his criticism of her reviews as belated revenge for her father's ungenerous treatment and resigned from the staff within a year. She continued to speak maliciously of Brailsford, missing no opportunity to fan the flames of MacDonald's enmity.[14] A more auspicious choice was that of the twenty-one year old Leslie Plummer, whom Allen discovered in the advertising department of the *Herald*, as general manager. His business acumen, compensating for Brailsford's ineptitude in financial matters, was to prove crucial in keeping the paper on a sound footing.[15]

Brailsford refused to view the *New Leader* merely as an official organ, though the conditions governing his appointment made it clear that he held office on party sufferance. He saw in the editorship an opportunity to create what the British labour movement had never possessed—a journal of literary distinction. The advance of socialism was for him far more a matter of education than of political mobilization; in Soviet Russia and Communist Hungary it was the experiments in the dissemination of culture that won his approval, not the repression of dissent. Indeed, the *New Leader*, despite its distinctive ideological bent, celebrated the diversity of progressive thought. Brailsford believed that working-class consciousness and education had developed to the point at which many would welcome a serious weekly: the *New Leader* would bridge the gap between the quality periodicals and the popular press. Like the *Nation*, which remained his model, he believed that a journal should give its attention not merely to political issues, but to the arts, music, poetry, and science. MacDonald, seeking to keep the paper as a docile platform for the party leaders, complained that the prospectus for the *New Leader* gave the 'impression of a magazine with special highbrowed contents' and failed to make clear that 'the active people in

---

[14] Hamilton, *Remembering My Good Friends*, pp. 146-8 offers a jaundiced view. ND, 2 July 1926, records Mrs Hamilton's remarks on Brailsford 'whom she has always detested'.

[15] Plummer, later Sir Leslie, had an illustrious career in newspaper management and as a Labour MP from 1951 to 1963. His wife became a Life Peeress in 1965.

the party are to contribute regularly'.[16]

The difference lay, perhaps, in the interpretation of 'the active people'. MacDonald meant leaders such as himself; Brailsford meant the creative intellects in the socialist movement—and even outside it. 'I have large ambitions for [the *New Leader*] as a possible engine for raising the whole intellectual standard of the Labour movement,' he told Keynes. 'I do not want to confine contributors narrowly to party members.' Since he planned to include essays on literary classics, he invited Keynes to write an article on Malthus' *Essay on Population* or on *The Wealth of Nations*.[17] One of the hallmarks of the *New Leader* was its illustrations. No issue appeared without drawings and woodcuts by artists such as Jack Yeats, Muirhead Bone, Käthe Kollwitz, and Clare Leighton, as well as the political cartoons of Will Dyson and Phil Mendoza. From the outset he invited artists to submit their work, especially those who had not yet made their reputation and would not balk at the three-guinea fee.[18] As to literary quality, Brailsford was determined not only to draw upon prominent political figures, but also to solicit contributions from the best authors of the day. Thus in addition to topical articles by Angell, Hugh Dalton, Hobson, Oswald Mosley, and E. F. Wise, he published literary essays by Nevinson, stories by T. F. Powys, poems by Frances Cornford, and science features by Julian Huxley. During his four years he also published nearly a dozen poems, essays, and reviews by E. M. Forster. Shaw contributed occasionally, and H. G. Wells serialized one of his books. His initial approach to Wells in 1922 reveals both the editor's hopes and his adroit manipulation of an author's vanity:

> We want a leader, not in the routine business of making party speeches and writing leading articles, but in the far bigger job of thinking out and giving life to a programme, until people really come to feel it as part of their historic destiny. I'm more of a Marxist than you are, yet I do believe in this sort of personal force. I look around and see no one but you has got it. I want you to give me the chance of convincing you that the new paper will be a vehicle for your thoughts worth using.[19]

Like all weekly newspapers, the *New Leader* functioned on a rigid schedule. Each issue was planned at a Monday editorial lunch at the 1917 Club, attended by regular contributors like Nevinson, Angell, Dalton, Russell, or Ponsonby, and by others connected with the paper, such as Allen, MacDonald (before 1924), and Ernest Hunter. These

---

[16] J. R. MacDonald to Clifford Allen, 5 Sept. 1922, AP, Box V.
[17] HNB to J. M. Keynes, 23 Aug. 1922, Keynes Papers, L/22.
[18] HNB to William Rothenstein, 5 Aug. 1922, Rothenstein Papers.
[19] HNB to H. G. Wells, 21 Aug. 1922, Wells Papers. Wells's first article appeared in the opening issue of the *New Leader*, which also serialized *The Story of a Great Schoolmaster* in 1923.

occasions also provided an opportunity to meet the editor's foreign guests and to open a channel of communication between politicians and journalists. Although many features and reviews were commissioned well in advance of publication, topical stories and leading articles had to be completed between the Monday gathering and Wednesday, when the paper was set up for the printer. While Brailsford was preoccupied with the content of the paper, Plummer busied himself with securing advertisements, chiefly from publishers, banks, co-operative societies, and patent medicine manufacturers, and with boosting circulation.

Unlike editors he had known, he saw his function not merely to cultivate a distinguished roster but to express his own opinions. Although he had learned, often painfully, the virtue of handling authors tactfully, he was, above all, a journalist, not an administrator. The *New Leader* became a personal paper in a sense very different from Scott's *Manchester Guardian* or later Martin's *New Statesman*. It was not that Brailsford dictated policy—indeed he interfered as little as possible with his contributors—but rather that every week he provided much of the copy himself. In addition to leaders and signed political articles, he wrote the political notes at the beginning of each issue, a London Letter, and reviews of books, plays, and even concerts. The London Letter, either unsigned or bearing the pseudonym 'The Journeyman' tended to be entertaining, with recollections of people and places he had encountered, while his 'Politics and Work' column was more serious in tone. It was here that Brailsford tended to expound his view of socialism and his prescription for the world's ills. His middle pieces generally analysed international affairs, much as his *Nation* and *Herald* articles had done, although he now began to tackle economic questions more readily.

Writing as much as he did himself, it was inevitable that Brailsford placed his own imprint on the paper, but he did so in various ways. He offered informal, self-revealing letters that delighted his readers. Shy as he was, he found it easier to talk about himself under the veil of anonymity than in direct contact. In the first number he described his exhilaration at returning to the press room:

> . . . I used to think that digging, or better still, planting seedlings, with one's fingers spreading out their roots in the soil, was the ideal of human work—on a day, for choice, when the swallows have just returned, and the rhythm of their ecstatic prose blends with one's own movements. But now I hesitate. There is much to be said for the foundry.[20]

On later occasions he rhapsodized over his intimate friendship with a cat named Griffin or over the robin that flew down and ate his bread

---

[20] *New Leader*, 6 Oct. 1922.

offering during his last visit to Wilfrid Blunt. It was this mingling of human interest and political rhetoric with which he sought to infuse the *New Leader*, to make it more than a dry rehash of industrial news and ideological preaching. It must appeal to the mind and the spirit, to uplift its readers while plumbing the economic structure of society.

During its first year, coinciding with the Ruhr occupation, the *New Leader* devoted considerable attention to European affairs, reflecting Brailsford's interests, if not the more provincial ones of the ILP. He had repeatedly attributed unemployment at home to a peace settlement which left the French as 'the armed dictators of Europe'[21] and imposed a prohibitive indemnity on Germany. Therefore to emphasize international politics was not to divert attention from domestic problems; it was a precondition to a proper understanding of them. His sense of outrage blinded him to the genuine fears which motivated French intransigence, but he could recognize its folly. Germany could pay reparations only if she were allowed to recover economically and given access to foreign markets. Instead the French chose to invade the Ruhr, reduce the Germans to near starvation, and incorporate the rich coal and steel area into a French economy, thus endangering the survival of the fragile German democracy.

What one fears is the rapid growth in Germany of an inflamed militarist patriotism, which will one day attempt the overthrow of the Republic, because it alone stands in the way of a policy of revenge. . . . The fact is that every violence, every insult, every unreason exercised on the prone body of Germany is a blow to the Republic. . . . One day all Europe will pay for this insanity.[22]

What could be done to divert Europe from catastrophe? Since it was impossible to reason with French militarists and financiers, the British government should appeal directly to the people. More concretely, it must offer an alternate means for the French to obtain some tangible sum for reconstruction as well as greater security. In return for ending the Ruhr occupation, the British should agree to cancel French debts to England, surrender their share of the indemnity, and use British credit to back an international loan to Germany in order to facilitate the payment of scaled-down reparations. Should these concessions fail to loosen the French grip on Germany, the *New Leader* proposed a unilateral repudiation of the Versailles treaty.[23]

As he became increasingly doubtful about the efficacy of the League, he held out hopes for the reconstituted International if the split between social democrats and Communists could be healed. The Vienna

[21] *New Leader*, 9 Feb. 1923.
[22] *New Leader*, 6 July 1923.
[23] *New Leader*, 9 Feb., 26 Oct. 1923.

International, to which the ILP affiliated, refused to admit that cleavage as permanent despite Lenin's contempt for the non-revolutionary European left. While the headquarters of its secretariat was in London, Friedrich Adler, the Secretary, and Oscar Pollak, sometime editor of the *Arbeiter Zeitung*, brought him into closer contact with Continental socialists. Like his friendship with Julius Braunthal, many of these relationships blossomed during the Second World War when prominent German and Austrian socialists were exiled in London. Flying for the first time in May 1923 to Hamburg, he served as an ILP delegate at the meeting of the International and as a *rapporteur* for the commission on the struggle against world-wide reaction. His speech to the congress on 25 May denounced the crimes perpetrated by reactionary regimes in Italy and Hungary, but recognized moral pressure, especially through the press, as the only valid response. Protesting against terrorist methods in Russia, he urged the delegates to recognize that 'the excesses of the revolution are a result of the policies of capitalist governments'.[24] Such conciliatory statements, oblivious to the realities of Bolshevik rule, neither propitiated the Russians, nor endeared the Vienna International to the more moderate—and anti-Soviet—elements among European socialists. Brailsford's qualified partisanship—admitting defects, while absolving the Russians from blame—was intellectually reprehensible, but typified the left commitment to a *rapprochement* with the Communists, a plan doomed no less by Soviet enmity than by Western reluctance.

Despite this impassioned loyalty, a sense of the practical ordinarily infused Brailsford's ardour, and his advice tended to be cautious. Sympathetic to the plight of the unemployed, he was contemptuous of those who exploited social grievances for political ends. While opposing the exclusion of Communists from the Labour Party, he ridiculed the CPGB for exhorting the TUC and Labour to carry the revolutionary message to the armed forces. Such tactics, rather than foster a workers' revolution, would only 'stimulate recruiting for the Fascisti'.[25] He could not accept the Communist view that socialism was unattainable without violent revolution. His introduction to Trotsky's *Where is Britain Going?*, published after the disheartening experience of the first Labour govern-

---

[24] *Protokoll des Internationalen Sozialistischen Arbeiter-Kongresses in Hamburg, 21 bis 25 May 1923* (Berlin, 1923), pp. 77-80; Julius Braunthal, *History of the International 1914-1943* (New York, 1967), p. 269. Brailsford spoke in English at the conference but addressed an open-air rally in German.

[25] *New Leader*, 21 Aug. 1925. The *Workers' Weekly* (25 Aug. 1925) described Brailsford as 'a Right Wing Labour source' and accused him of giving 'encouragement to Fascism'. He did however sign an appeal for left unity and against the exclusion of the Communists from the Labour Party. See James Klugman, *History of the Communist Party of Great Britain*, Vol. II: 1925-1926 (London, 1969), p. 54.

ment, cited Trotsky's failure to appreciate the democratic and Nonconformist heritage of the labour movement. Since the parliamentary tradition and the 'instinct of obedience to the majority' were deeply rooted, it might be possible to alter the economic structure fundamentally once Labour obtained an electoral majority. If the propertied class defended its privilege by force, then it was preferable to fight with Parliament on the people's side rather than arrayed against them.[26]

Collaboration with Communists was one of the issues on which he continually differed from the Labour leadership. MacDonald's return to the party leadership in 1922 seemed a hopeful portent after the stolid trade union domination, and Brailsford's personal estrangement—more evident after MacDonald tried to block his appointment—did not vitiate *New Leader* editorial approval. Even MacDonaldite zealots could scarcely have improved on a tribute some months later:

> He is the one possible leader. His personal distinction, his intellectual power, his stature as a man and a thinker rank him among the greatest of our assests. Whatever weakens his position is an injury to the Socialist cause.[27]

That Brailsford did not personally believe this—these words were written to reprimand Scottish MPs for disrupting the Commons—does not detract from their affirmative tone. He found himself subject to conflicting pressures within the ILP at this time. Allen warned, in terms similar to Brailsford's own comment, that 'if someone else should become leader, then the party will almost certainly break up'.[28] In contrast, Clydesiders, such as John Wheatley, who were also members of the *New Leader* board, were growing restive under MacDonald's supine command. During the internal struggles in 1922-3, the editor practised unimpeachable loyalty to MacDonald, a stance moderated only after Labour came to office.

By dissenting publicly from the parliamentary tactics of NAC members, Brailsford forfeited their good will, although other factors heightened tension. When financial problems were raised at a June 1923 NAC meeting, Allen tried to soothe his colleagues by promising further economies. As a concession the editor agreed to allocate more space to news from the branches. In order to ensure that the promise would be implemented, the board decided early in 1924 to place the ILP head office, instead of the editor, in charge of those pages dealing with party activity.[29] Dissatisfaction had surfaced at the annual conference even though the official report praised the *New Leader* as 'a greater

---

[26] Introduction to Leon Trotsky, *Where is Britain Going?* (London, 1926), p. viii. See Isaac Deutscher, *The Prophet Unarmed: Trotsky, 1921-1929* (London, 1959), pp. 221-2.
[27] *New Leader*, 6 July 1923.
[28] Clifford Allen to HNB [1 July 1923], Johnson Papers.
[29] NAC Minutes, 8 June, 7 Sept. 1923, 23 Feb. 1924.

success than even the most optimistic of us anticipated'. When Brailsford was hired, he was made responsible for its entire content, but voices were now raised demanding 'some plain matter that would enable them to appeal effectively to the men in the workshops'. As if this were not enough, a Sheffield delegate protested that to pay an editor £1,000 a year was 'against the whole tradition of the ILP'. Allen, reminding the delegates that 'they owed Comrade Brailsford an enormous debt of gratitude', urged them to be 'generous-mooded', adding that the ILP was actually losing less money with the *New Leader* than when they had paid an editor half Brailsford's salary.[30]

To struggle against anti-intellectualism and snide allusions to his salary was merely one of the editor's difficulties. Scarcely less irksome were MacDonald's persistent efforts to undermine his position, intensified once Molly Hamilton left in November 1923. Barely a month after Brailsford chastised MacDonald's detractors, the latter confided to Allen:

The *New Leader* troubles me. It will not do, and wherever I go, I find people are dissatisfied with it. It must be losing piles of money. . . . It also lacks the spirit of the ILP. . . . More than ever do I feel that anyone who is to edit it successfully must do so as an ILPer. H. N. B. unfortunately seems to grow more rather than less detached from us.[31]

The unanticipated result of the 1923 general election temporarily stilled internal wrangling. Nevinson reported a *New Leader* lunch in early December at which a jubilant MacDonald pronounced himself 'in favour of taking office & trying to get something done before turned out'. Brailsford 'seemed dubious, about the lack of specific objectives, and Allen expressed misgivings about taking office 'unless unemployment could be allayed'.[32] As he informed MacDonald, Brailsford's doubts were reinforced by his sampling of rank and file opinion at an ILP meeting in Clapham:

It was no use to talk of anything else, so I discussed the question of taking office fully. I thought it had educational value, so I gave all the pro's & con's, so far as I could see them, quite fairly. This was easy because I was in great doubt myself & well aware of the case on both sides. A long discussion followed. Nearly all the speeches were intelligent. There was keen interest & the chairman had to extend the time, to let in more speakers. *Every single speech was against taking office*. This may be of use to you as a test of rank & feeling.[33]

MacDonald was in no way dissuaded, and the *New Leader* loyally

[30] *Report of the 31st Annual Conference of the ILP* (1923), pp. 25, 98-9.
[31] J. R. MacDonald to Clifford Allen, 17 Aug. 1923, AP, Box V.
[32] ND, 10 Dec. 1923.
[33] HNB to J. R. MacDonald, 10 Dec. [1923], MacDonald Papers, 5/33.

endorsed the decision to form the first Labour government. 'If conditions allow a fair trial'—an important if—Brailsford insisted that 'it is our duty to accept.' Even in a brief term in office, socialists might convince respectable opinion that they intended neither 'the erection of guillotines in Whitehall, nor the pillage of their homes'. Debarred from radical measures, they could at least begin to alleviate unemployment, bring Russia and Germany back into the European community, and lay the foundations for the extension of public control in mining, banking, transport, and electric power. 'If we take office,' he declared, 'we must be prepared to live dangerously, and to lay it down as boldly and as promptly as we take it up.'[34] Brailsford thus endorsed the decision to take office, but in terms unpalatable to the new Prime Minister, who was more concerned with proving Labour's competence to rule than with setting a socialist course.

A clash between the two could not long be averted. In December Christian Rakovsky, the Soviet Chargé d'Affaires, approached Brailsford and others to intercede on his behalf with the Labour government. Eager to serve as intermediary, Brailsford conveyed the gist of his conversation to MacDonald, whom he invited to lunch with Rakovsky in order to negotiate the restoration of amicable relations.[35] Although the Prime Minister insisted that he favoured granting diplomatic recognition—and did so unconditionally within days of taking office—he was wary of the editor's involvement:

I suppose you and [Rakovsky] are aware of the terribly awkward situation in which we should find ourselves if we recognised a Government which came to grief immediately afterwards. The papers are again full of rumours. At the same time, if we recognise them and then find that they are cheating us on details that have to be straightened out, it would bring us down in disgrace.[36]

To MacDonald's irritation, Brailsford was not so easily deflected from his mission. He suggested opening immediate negotiations between Rakovsky and MacDonald or his representative with the aim of settling debts and compensation claims. Everything, he wrote,

depends on whether we can take our stand side by side with them as a Socialist Government; this we should do, if our first act were to recognise them as a matter of simple right. On the other hand, if our first official act is to take up the City's case, all the enthusiasm and good feeling latent in the other process may be dissipated.[37]

[34] *New Leader*, 14 Dec. 1923.
[35] *New Leader*, 11 Feb. 1927; *New Statesman*, 4 Aug. 1945; Hugh Dalton Diary, 21 Feb. 1924, Dalton Papers, Vol. IV; Havighurst, *Massingham*, p. 312.
[36] J. R. MacDonald to HNB, 22 Dec. 1923, MacDonald Papers, 5/33.
[37] HNB to J. R. MacDonald, 4 Jan. 1924, MacDonald Papers, 5/33.

A week later Brailsford told MacDonald that the French were only insisting that the Russians respect existing treaties and acknowledge pre-war debts in return for recognition. He urged MacDonald to act promptly since 'the Russians immensely prefer to come to terms with us first'.[38] MacDonald had in the mean time reproached Brailsford for interfering, expressing concern lest the government be implicated by his communications with Rakovsky. He refused to see Rakovsky, although he did authorize Ponsonby, Under-Secretary in the Foreign Office, to meet with the Russian representative in Brailsford's presence.[39] At the *New Leader* lunch on 28 January Brailsford complained that the Prime Minister 'was spoiling a good opportunity and missing the chance of a great gesture'. The next week MacDonald attended the lunch—his final appearance while in office—in order to reprimand Brailsford, 'whose line on Russia &c has been irritating him', but the editor was in Marseilles attending the French Socialist Party Congress.[40]

Disregarding these warnings, he continued in his unofficial role of trouble-shooter. From Marseilles he relayed a message from Blum and Vandervelde requesting an interview with MacDonald. Indeed he went so far as to ask Blum's advice as to the tactics the Labour government should pursue in Europe, doubtlessly galling to the Prime Minister, who wished to be the architect of his own foreign policy. Blum urged the British cabinet to proceed cautiously in dealings with Poincaré until after the forthcoming French elections. Brailsford recounted his own speech at the delegates' banquet in the name of the ILP.

'You see, you are no longer faced by a foreign government: this is a government of your comrades,' [he told the assembled delegates.] They would not let me go on for several minutes—round after round of applause. While they are pleased about Russia, the 8 hour day, &c, the thing that really wins their wildest enthusiasm is the prospect of our accepting obligatory arbitration.[41]

While Brailsford met foreign politicians in a spirit of socialist fraternity, MacDonald felt it improper to grant an interview to the leader of the French opposition. With an election imminent, such a gesture might 'give rise to serious misrepresentation'.[42] Still more unusual, if not more irritating, was Brailsford's transmission to Ponsonby of a summary of the alleged secret clauses of the Franco-Czechoslovak treaty, forwarded to him from Friedrich Adler, who had obtained it through espionage channels. Harold Nicolson, the official who minuted the

[38] HNB to J. R. MacDonald, 11 Jan. 1924, MacDonald Papers, 5/33.
[39] *New Statesman*, 4 Aug. 1945.
[40] Hugh Dalton Diary, 4 Feb. 1924, Dalton Papers, Vol. IV.
[41] HNB to J. R. MacDonald, 3 Feb. 1924, FO 800/218.
[42] Foreign Office Memorandum, 14 Feb. 1924, FO 800/218.

document, found the Czech guarantee of the passage of twenty French divisions to Poland in the event of war between France and Germany implausible and dismissed it as 'too clever to be taken seriously'.[43]

In general the editor gave MacDonald high marks for his conduct of foreign policy. However grudging a concession, recognition of the Soviet Union was significant, even courageous. In his determination to maintain good relations with France, he had proved himself 'plain-spoken and decisive'.[44] While helping to create an atmosphere of confidence, he had been able to clear away the worst encumbrances of reparations and to fix a time limit for the occupation of the Ruhr. But the *New Leader* did not hesitate to criticize the revival of coercion in India or the perpetuation of Tory policies in Iraq, Cyprus, and Egypt. Europe might follow MacDonald 'with fewer reserves if somewhere on the world's surface, he were to prove that Labour's advent to office had altered something in our conduct of our Empire'.[45] His most unstinting praise was for MacDonald's role in promoting the Geneva Protocol, under which signatory nations would pledge themselves to settle disputes through the League arbitration machinery. The *New Leader* proclaimed a 'new chapter in the history of civilisation',[46] but in a memorandum for the Labour and Socialist International Brailsford was more circumspect: the Protocol merited support only if certain other changes took place. The corollaries of outlawing war were the revision of the peace treaties, the admission of Germany to the League, a reduction of armaments, and a curtailing of economic imperialism.[47]

Throughout his term as editor the *New Leader* tried to focus public attention on the need to eliminate unemployment. ILP opinion was fragmented between those, such as Wheatley, who stressed the under-consumptionist argument to explain the economic crisis, and the UDC faction, who fastened on the inadequate post-war recovery of overseas markets. Brailsford attempted to mediate between these points of view, adopting Hobson's analysis without rejecting an internationalist one. In response to David Kirkwood's blinkered complaint about Labour politicians who were 'eternally giving prominence to the Ruhr, or Montenegro, or Timbuctoo, when their prime duty is to emancipate the British working class', he reproved Scottish colleagues for advocating insular nationalism in the guise of socialism. It was the height of folly to contend that if the mass of British wage earners enjoyed

[43] HNB to Arthur Ponsonby, 29 Feb. 1924; Minute by Harold Nicolson, 11 Mar. 1924, FO 371/9673/C3885/41/12.
[44] *New Leader*, 18 Apr. 1924.
[45] *New Leader*, 5 Sept. 1924.
[46] *New Leader*, 10 Oct. 1924.
[47] Draft of memorandum on Geneva Protocol (Dec. 1924), Labour and Socialist International Papers, 1715/33.

adequate incomes, the rest of the world could be ignored. So long as Britain depended on imported food and raw materials, it needed to find markets for its manufactured goods abroad.[48]

It was the inept domestic policy of the Labour government, its adherence to deflationary monetary schemes, that evoked the strongest *New Leader* recriminations. In March 1924 Brailsford lamented that it was 'distressing to find ourselves, as one urgent problem follows another, compelled to put forward interim and inadequate solutions, where we have bolder proposals of our own which are both workable and overdue'.[49] Instead of innovative programmes, ministers postponed action in order to buy time, thus forfeiting the chance to inspire popular imagination. He suspected a failure of will at the top as the explanation for indecisiveness and urged the Prime Minister to delegate one of his ablest Cabinet ministers to devise, with the aid of a general staff drawn from relevant departments, a bold plan based on community control of coal and electricity.[50]

Long before Labour left office, the Prime Minister had become exasperated with what he regarded as Brailsford's carping attacks, not to mention the licence the editor gave to others such as Morel, who was certainly no friend of MacDonald's. During delicate negotiations with the French over reparations in July, the *New Leader* published Morel's letter denouncing British 'subserviency' to the French. MacDonald, infuriated by such sabotage in the Labour press, warned Brailsford that 'if I find that the French have hardened against me and trouble me with some of the things in Morel's letter, you will have to bear your share of the reponsibility'.[51] Grumbling about the 'nasty small spirit' in the party, he told Allen:

As to the *New Leader*, frankly I have lost all interest in it. It is not the kind of paper that does any good to anybody. It has neither weight nor place and its egotistical aloofness would kill any movement. . . . I ventured to protest against Morel's letter being published *at the moment it appeared*, and got such a reply from Brailsford as closed everything. There is no arguing with, or explaining to, these people. They have no spirit of comradeship and no consideration for the large issues of action. The team spirit is not in them.[52]

Allen, quoting this letter at a *New Leader* lunch on 22 September, pleaded for restraint, but Hamilton Fyfe, editor of the *Herald*, and Brailsford both refused to be intimidated.[53]

[48] *New Leader*, 30 Mar. 1923.
[49] *New Leader*, 28 Mar. 1924.
[50] *New Leader*, 30 May 1924.
[51] J. R. MacDonald to HNB, n.d. [July 1924], copy in Angell Papers. Morel's 'Revolt of the Back Benches' appeared on 25 July 1924.
[52] J. R. MacDonald to Clifford Allen, 16 Sept. 1924, AP, Box V.
[53] ND, 22 Sept. 1924.

MacDonald, secretive and suspicious, viewed publicly aired misgivings as treacherous, not merely to himself, but to the movement. Brailsford confessed to Scott in November 1924 that for ten months he had neither seen nor communicated with the Prime Minster, who resented suggestions made in the *New Leader* when he came to office.[54] While praising MacDonald's 'superb record' in striving for peace in Europe, he cautioned against Labour 'regarding itself as an alternative governing party in the old sense—altering nothing fundamental and content itself merely with giving a slight working class bias to legislation'.[55] By the time the ministry fell, he could be numbered among those working behind the scenes to replace the party leader.[56] The breach was permanent: a year later MacDonald, still 'furiously angry' at Brailsford, described him as 'an Anarchist Communist and incapable of comprehending parliamentary government'.[57]

As disenchantment with the leadership spread, the *New Leader* became the forum for alternative policies, the symbol of the ILP determination to pursue a programme distinct from the inert parliamentary leadership. Brailsford reiterated a long held conviction that the Parliamentary Labour Party was 'drifting into opportunism. It has no plan for realising Socialism.'[58] This was the task he set himself: to expound specific remedies for economic ills that would galvanize the movement into action. If the front bench refused either to educate the rank and file or to give expression to the hope of radical change, then the *New Leader* would do so, however much its dissident role was denounced by the party leaders. Although Brailsford himself had written remarkably little in the decade before 1922 that was not directly concerned with foreign affairs, he now emerged as principal publicist for the ILP's domestic programme. As editor of the official party newspaper, he found himself inevitably appointed to policy committees, speaking at party conferences, and participating at the ILP summer schools. Indeed for the first time he now became an active committee man, able to impose his own views and shape policy directives. It became difficult to distinguish ILP thinking from Brailsford's personal

---

[54] C. P. Scott Diary, 27 Nov. 1924, Scott Papers, Add. MSS 50907, fol. 125.

[55] *New Leader*, 14 Nov. 1924.

[56] Francis Williams, *Ernest Bevin* (London, 1952), p. 122; Alan Bullock, *The Life and Times of Ernest Bevin: 1881-1940* (London, 1960), p. 258; Carl F. Brand, *The British Labour Party* (Stanford, 1965), p. 116; Carl F. Brand to author. Brand suggests that Brailsford's choice to succeed MacDonald in 1924 was C. P. Trevelyan, then a relatively junior figure. He told the author of a conversation about the leadership when Brailsford came to lecture at Stanford. Since that visit took place in February 1933, it seems likely that Brailsford was promoting Trevelyan's candidacy after 1931, not 1924.

[57] Sidney to Beatrice Webb, 28 Sept. 1925, published in Norman MacKenzie, ed., *The Letters of Sidney and Beatrice Webb*, III (Cambridge, 1978), p. 247.

[58] *New Leader*, 11 Sept. 1925.

opinions, so close an identity did they achieve in the *New Leader*.

The term 'living wage' was by 1924 familiar in the ILP thanks largely to Brailsford's popularization of the concept in the *New Leader*. From its inception he associated the *New Leader* with Hobson's underconsumptionist argument that under capitalism productive capacity outstripped the rate of consumption. For Brailsford, no less than for Hobson, the way to restore a faltering home market was to increase 'the purchasing power of consumers' through the redistribution of income.[59] While Hobson stressed more steeply graduated taxation, he gave equal attention to the levelling up of wages and to monetary reforms. Although he had advocated international control of raw materials even before 1914, his understanding of the connection between price stabilization and the regulation of the supply of raw materials derived from his reading of E. M. H. Lloyd's study, *Stabilization*.[60] Furthermore, in contrast to Hobson, he believed that unemployment was as much a consequence of deflationary banking policy as of income distribution. Even before Mosley directed Labour's attention to the efficacy of credit control, Brailsford urged that banking be nationalized. Influenced by Keynes' writings on monetary reform, he suggested a contracyclical policy of restricting credit at the first sign of boom conditions and expanding it before a slump occurred.[61]

Misgivings over Labour's handling of the economy, muted while MacDonald was in office, erupted after the government fell. The disregard of Allen's appeal for a national minimum wage policy or for bold initiatives despite Labour's minority position heightened the tensions caused by the ILP's wavering allegiance. The resolution at the Gloucester ILP conference in April 1925 calling for a national commission to determine a living wage was a sign that the ILP rejected Labour's orthodox policy for coping with unemployment. Few of his readers could misconstrue his target when Brailsford warned that 'a party which rejects revolution, and imagines that it has endless time in which to achieve its end, may soon cease to work for it at all'.[62]

To emphasize the ILP's self-appointed duty to provide a socialist blueprint, a series of inquiry commissions were set up to devise policies on industry, India, parliamentary reform, and other vital questions. The sixth of these commissions, whose charge was to explore the speedy abolition of poverty and the realization of socialism, was destined to

[59] *New Leader*, 16 Nov. 1923.
[60] Brailsford discussed the work in *New Leader*, 6 July 1923.
[61] At the Labour Conference Brailsford moved a resolution proposing the nationalization of the Bank of England. *Report of the 24th Annual Labour Party Conference* (1924), pp. 165-6.
[62] *New Leader*, 27 Feb. 1925 and *Socialism for Today*, pp. 68-9.

become the most controversial. The group, consisting of four members, Hobson as Chairman, Brailsford as Secretary, E. F. Wise, a wartime civil servant and economic expert, and Arthur Creech Jones, research officer of the T&GWU, sprang from Allen's mind, rather than the NAC, and its composition showed the extent to which Allen, by now ILP Chairman, had espoused the underconsumptionist thesis. It may well have been Brailsford's commitment to a peaceful transition to socialism that induced Hobson to join the Commission, giving it the imprimatur of respectability it might otherwise have lacked. Certainly the presence of Brailsford and Wise, reassuring to ILP militants, was guaranteed to alienate MacDonald. Creech Jones was appointed as a link to the trade union movement and more particularly to Ernest Bevin, his own General Secretary, an outspoken critic of Labour's performance in 1924. Throughout the year and a half of the Commission's deliberations Brailsford was its linch-pin, reporting its activities to a cautiously approving NAC, propagandizing for the living wage in the *New Leader*, expounding its principles at ILP conferences and ultimately incurring the brunt of MacDonald's wrath.

As initially perceived, the living wage was less an immediately practicable aim than an inspirational target, a half-way house on the road to the socialist commonwealth. The defect of previous Labour programmes was their focus on short-term incremental palliatives, effective perhaps in mitigating the rigours of capitalism, but incapable of mobilizing a movement. What was needed was a single rallying cry for the masses. To articulate such a demand would require 'splendid audacity' because it could not be met without significant economic changes. Indeed it might seem to be 'asking for the impossible', since to 'demand a living wage, is, in plain words, to demand Socialism'.[63] Whether managed welfare capitalism could provide a living wage or whether it was feasible only under socialism was never settled. Brailsford himself alternated between the two, depending on his audience, but seemed increasingly disposed to maintain that the living wage need not await a complete socialist transformation.

In January 1925, several months before the ILP formally endorsed the living wage, Brailsford began to publish a series of articles in the *New Leader* under the general heading *The Socialist Case Restated*. An implicit criticism of Labour's record in office, it represented his first systematic approach to an alternative programme for the transition to socialism. To attempt such a general synthesis would not have been possible for him until the 1920s, when he began to ponder economic questions more seriously and to assimilate the prescriptions of Keynes,

[63] *New Leader*, 3 and 17 Apr. 1925.

Lloyd, Wise, and Hobson. *Socialism for Today*, as the book derived from the series was called, belongs to the tradition of *Merrie England*. Like Blatchford, he was trying to put the case for socialism succinctly and in terms any manual worker could grasp. Much of it was inevitably general, with actual figures kept to a minimum, but it offered as lucid an exposition of democratic socialist doctrine as could be found in the 1920s.

While accepting the underconsumptionist argument that a living wage would increase demand, stimulate production, and create jobs, Brailsford placed primary emphasis on the need to socialize banking. Not only would the regulation of credit keep prices stable and mitigate the fluctuations of trade, but it would be possible to direct the flow of credit in line with desired social policy. In order to give the community control over the industrial sector, two further steps needed to be taken. To ensure that the price of transport and power were kept low, the coal mines, electrical power, and the railways should be nationalized promptly. Finally, it was necessary to eliminate the profiteering middleman and guarantee the supply of food and raw materials by concentrating the nation's buying under central direction. With chartered corporations invested with the sole right to import wheat, wool, cotton, oil and other commodities, prices would be kept steady, speculation abolished, and adequate supplies assured through bulk purchase on long-term contracts.[64] While offering few hints about the institutional aspects of economic planning, he did confront the thorny issue of how to set up a nationalized industry, 'the most difficult problem which Socialists have to solve'. Skilfully navigating between the Scylla of bureaucratic centralization and the Charybdis of guild structure, he stressed the workers' right to share in managing the semi-independent Industrial Corporations. While half of the directing board might be chosen by organizations of workers and technicians, an equal number should be selected for their administrative abilities by parliamentary and consumer groups. Complementing these structural changes, he proposed a more steeply graduated income tax and heavier inheritance taxes to supply funds needed both for communal services and to compensate owners of nationalized property.[65] By the time *Socialism for Today* was published in October 1925 the Living Wage Commission had embarked on its investigation, but Brailsford's own views, previously expounded in the *New Leader*, strongly influenced the direction the Commission followed. It would not be unfair to suggest that, with some shifts in emphasis, especially over nationalization and the relation of taxation to income distribution, the scheme which emerged first in

---

[64] *Socialism for Today*, pp. 100-5.   [65] Ibid., pp. 86-92.

Socialism in Our Time and in amplified form in *The Living Wage* was essentially an elaboration of *Socialism for Today*. Although the theoretical basis owed much to Hobson and Allen, the proposals bore Brailsford's imprint more distinctly than that of his colleagues. The vagueness about detail and timing, the ambiguity in formulation, represented a deliberate effort to reconcile conflicting objectives, to advance socialism without a catastrophic collapse of capitalism.

Even before the interim report, *Socialism in Our Time*, was unveiled and enthusiastically endorsed at the Whitley Bay conference in April 1926, MacDonald had begun to denigrate the ILP programme. Despite his sympathy for Hobsonian economics—and affection for Hobson—he resented efforts by the ILP to foist its visionary policy on the Labour Party as a whole and immediately perceived Brailsford as the culprit. It was not so much the underlying analysis as its implicit criticism of his leadership that galled him. Impatient with gradualism, the ILP seemed prepared to force the pace of socialist advance with little concern for the parliamentary ramifications. Dismissing the proposals as 'flashy futilities', he warned that they would be 'millstones' around the parliamentary party's neck. MacDonald later admitted that he had lashed out even before examining the report: apparently he took offence at the title *Socialism in Our Time* which he saw while reading the *New Leader* over someone's shoulder in a train. 'I suppose it is hard,' he wrote caustically, 'for an editor with no executive responsibility to refrain from telling us how he would act if he were King, Lords and Commons combined, the head of every Department of State and all the Under-Secretaries as well.'[66] When MacDonald returned to the fray several weeks later in his *Forward* column, arguing that socialism was not going to come by the legal declaration of a minimum wage and the nationalization of bankrupt industries, Brailsford accused him of distorting their intentions.[67]

Socialism in Our Time set forth the central argument for the living wage. The workers were being paid 'semi-starvation wages', intolerable in itself, but more importantly 'the immediate cause of extensive unemployment'. Since the labouring population had the 'first claim upon the wealth of the nation', the ILP believed that socialist policy should be concentrated upon the elimination of poverty. Thus the argument was couched in both ethical and economic terms; the socialist goal was clearly stated and the need to accelerate the pace emphasized. In order to determine a living wage, the report proposed the establishment of a commission representing the whole Labour movement

[66] *Socialist Review*, Mar. 1926; Fenner Brockway, *Socialism Over Sixty Years* (London, 1946), p. 229; Marquand, *MacDonald*, pp. 453-4; John Paton, *Left Turn* (London, 1936), p. 235.
[67] *New Leader*, 2 Apr. 1926.

which would assess the needs for a 'minimum standard of civilised existence'. Although there was no reference to compulsion, the ILP was urging the Parliamentary Labour Party to assert its intention of implementing a living wage as fully as possible when it next took office. To render the policy more effective, the ILP recommended the establishment of a national banking system, with control of currency and credit, state control over the import of food and raw materials, the nationalization of railways, mines, and electrical generation, and the public ownership of land—all items contained in *Socialism for Today*. In a separate addendum the report went on to propose a system of family allowances, paid out of direct taxation, a plan Brailsford had endorsed ever since he had participated in the Family Endowment Committee.[68]

Speaking on behalf of his motion, Brailsford declared that the living wage was put forward as the guiding principle of their strategy because it 'would be intelligible to the simplest man or woman on the verge of politics'. With a nod to the underconsumptionist argument, he declared that the cure for poverty was 'the steady flow of purchasing power which would turn the wheels of industry again'. Finally, the living wage offered an issue on which the trade union and political movements might unite. Neither could achieve it alone: industrial action to achieve higher wages was useless unless they could guarantee that prices could be stabilized. Once the Living Wage Commission fixed a figure, it would have to be implemented by some authority empowered to identify those industries paying less than a living wage and undertake their reorganization. This was not to suggest the nationalization of decrepit industries, but to put financial powers in the hands of the state to enable it, whether through subsidies or amalgamations, to promote a living wage throughout the industrial sector.[69]

In the ensuing discussion critics were as outspoken as proponents. Several anticipated difficulties in arriving at an agreed figure for a living wage, while others felt that the report downgraded the fight for the nationalization of industry. Emanuel Shinwell, then still a stalking horse for MacDonald, contended that a living wage could not be attained under capitalism and that the proposal should therefore be referred back to the committee. Extolling the benefits of an 'interim dividend', Wheatley claimed that there was no reason to wait until all industries were nationalized before insisting upon a better distribution of wages. Mosley questioned the feasibility of a living wage until a socialist credit

[68] ILP, *Socialism in Our Time* (1926), republished in *Report of the 34th Annual Conference of the ILP* (1926), pp. 76-7. See also Brailsford's *Families and Incomes* (1926) which suggested that a five shilling per week allowance for children under fifteen would cost £125 million.
[69] *Report* (1926), pp. 78-80.

policy had been introduced, and his ally John Strachey faulted the report for its lack of a clearly articulated credit policy.[70]

Despite—or perhaps because of—its enthusiastic endorsement by the ILP, *Socialism in Our Time* immediately encountered trade union hostility. Bevin, who felt the ILP had no right to encroach upon the union function of pay negotiation, told Brailsford, 'I stand four-square against political interference with wages'.[71] There was a general fear among trade unionists that the declaration of a minimum wage would impede bargaining by better organized unions and that the payment of family allowances would only take away what might be paid in wages to workers. Brailsford tried to deflect trade union opposition by insisting that the state's role was 'to create conditions in which unions may press for a Living Wage with every hope of success'.[72] Although he had emphasized the class struggle in speeches and articles in 1925, warning against violent resistance by the employers, his tone on the eve of the Margate Labour Party conference was far more conciliatory. The increased purchasing power from the living wage, he told an ILP summer school at Easton Lodge, would generate a wave of prosperity 'in which even the capitalists would have their share'.[73]

The Living Wage, the Commission's final report, published as a pamphlet in September 1926, was more comprehensive than anything offered earlier. It provided a full explication of underconsumption theory and of the contracyclical credit policy, to which Brailsford had alluded in his own writings. There were, however, several additional features barely outlined in the earlier formulation. While it advocated nationalizing banking, the mines, electrical supply, and the railways, the report opposed immediate public control of low-paying trades, notably agriculture, engineering, and textiles. In the first stage only 'key' industries should be nationalized, the government asserting its authority over the rest of the economy through an Industrial Commission 'armed with large powers of reorganization'. Throughout the process of reorganization the Industrial Commission would work closely with trade unions so as to confer on workers a 'genuine measure of control'.[74]

MacDonald, sniping in the *Socialist Review*, acquitted Hobson of

[70] *Report* (1926), pp. 80-6; *New Leader* Conference supplement, 9 Apr. 1926; *New Leader*, 9 Oct. 1925. See Adrian Oldfield, 'The Independent Labour Party and Planning, 1920-1926', *International Review of Social History*, Vol. XXI (1976), Part I, p. 25; Robert Skidelsky, *Oswald Mosley* (London, 1975), p. 150. Mosley, travelling in America during the winter of 1925, had little influence on living wage deliberations.
[71] Ernest Bevin to HNB, 7 June 1926, Bevin Papers, MSS 126/EB.
[72] *New Leader*, 13 Aug. 1926.
[73] *New Leader*, 20 Aug. 1926. See *Daily Herald*, 11 Aug. 1925.
[74] *The Living Wage* (1926), pp. 37-40.

responsibility for its supposed excesses. Privately admitting that it was 'an admirable economic document', he did not, he assured Hobson,

> believe for a moment that you were supporting the use that is being made of it by Brailsford. The politics that have become associated with it are really deplorable. I do not know what has possessed our friend; the only word I can use . . . is that he has become cranky.[75]

At the Labour Party conference at Margate the ILP proposal was diluted in a composite resolution, which Brailsford moved, calling merely for an inquiry commission to consider what a future Labour administration might do to establish the principle of a living income. Although it urged such a commission to consider the part that the socialization of credit, transport, power, and the importation of raw materials might play in the reorganization of the economy, it neither attempted to commit the conference to the conclusions of the ILP report, nor implied any criticism of the Labour government.[76] The committee of inquiry, although appointed, took almost a year to organize itself and then decided to consider only the secondary issue of family allowances, effectively torpedoing the living wage concept.

At least one objective of its proponents had been achieved: discussion of more innovative solutions to economic problems was stimulated, not merely in the socialist, but in the Liberal camp. Brailsford sent a copy of the final report to Keynes, who identified one of its fundamental weaknesses, an uncertainty as to whether increased wages were to be the initial or ultimate step in the process and doubted whether the concrete proposals to recharge the economy would in fact provide enough resources to pay the bill.[77] Beatrice Webb, who found it 'a useful propagandist document', remarked to Keynes that 'the lines on which it proceeds are far more hopeful than the old slogan of the Labour Party—the nationalisation of the means of production, distribution and control'.[78]

Frustrated by the hostility the living wage evoked even among enlightened trade union leaders, Brailsford became less resistant to collaboration with Liberals. In 1920 he had warned that a Liberal-Labour coalition would precipitate an ILP breakaway.[79] When Keynes, now

[75] J. R. MacDonald to J. A. Hobson, 8 Oct. 1926, quoted in Marquand, *MacDonald*, p. 455. Brailsford insisted that the programme owed 'its whole theoretical basis' to Hobson. *New Leader*, 6 Dec. 1929.

[76] *Report of the 26th Annual Conference of the Labour Party* (1926), p. 260.

[77] J. M. Keynes to HNB, 27 Oct. 1926, Keynes Papers, L/26.

[78] Beatrice Webb to J. M. Keynes, 3 Oct. 1926, published in MacKenzie, ed., *Letters*, III, p. 271. She was much more critical of *Socialism in Our Time*, which she termed 'a monument of this combination of conceit and ignorance'. Beatrice Webb, *Diaries, 1924-1932* (London, 1956), p. 89.

[79] Letter to Editor, *Nation*, 28 Feb. 1920.

reconciled to Lloyd George, broached the idea in February 1926, Brailsford was no longer as dismissive. He still regarded the former Prime Minister as 'an utterly impossible ally', but he agreed to support negotiations with a group 'who think to any extent' the way Keynes did. Sharing the latter's misgivings about obstructive unions, he observed, 'Our Trade Union people are so barren of ideas outside their own limited area of action that they always sooner or later follow the intellectuals in the Party.'[80]

In retrospect, the living wage policy seems far more plausible than its detractors would allow. After 1945 the Labour government enacted family allowances and the nationalization of key industries, including banking, and employers, admittedly in a period of low unemployment, found it possible to pay a living wage even in depressed trades. The New Deal attempted to stimulate mass purchasing power along lines similar to the proposals of the Living Wage Commission, and Keynes began actively to promote a contracyclical policy, although he had found its version inflationary. To be sure, Brailsford and his colleagues exaggerated the possibility of insular self-sufficiency, as did Mosley and proponents of protectionism. England needed to export because it needed to import, and higher priced goods might have worsened its competitive position. Nor did the Commission pay enough attention to private and public investment in industry, to productivity, and to the impact of monetary policy on international currency movements. Unlike the Labour Party leaders, preaching a utopian gospel while practising Gladstonian economics, the advocates of the living wage did, however, offer a serious plan for the transition, hoping to advance towards the socialist goal in their own generation rather than await evolutionary progress. Without denying class conflict or the likelihood of capitalist recalcitrance, they looked to an organized working class, exercising its vote and flexing its industrial muscle, to secure its objectives without recourse to violence. Although the ILP lacked the popular base needed for so ambitious a campaign—and in any event incurred opposition from much of the labour movement—the living wage represents the most constructive response to British economic problems by any political group in the inter-war period.

The ILP not only misjudged the temper of the movement, its reluctance to respond to initiatives from unwelcome quarters, but was the victim of unfortunate timing. The spring of 1926 found organized labour preoccupied with the General Strike, which took place inconveniently

[80] HNB to J. M. Keynes, 26 Feb. 1926, Keynes Papers, L/26. Nevinson was surprised to find that Brailsford 'hesitated' about considering Lloyd George as a potential Labour Party leader. He, Dalton, and Wise were 'strongly opposed'. He attributed Brailsford's wavering to 'his violent enmity to Ramsay Mac.' ND, 31 May 1926.

between the Whitley Bay ILP conference and the Margate Labour meeting. When the TUC placed an embargo on coal transport in July 1925, the *New Leader* had applauded the defensive stance against wage cuts.[81] The following March Brailsford warned that if the Samuel Commission's advice to end the subsidy were followed, it might be 'the prelude to the greatest industrial war of our generation', and he urged 'uncompromising resistance' by the unions.[82] Recurrent disputes with union officials made him doubt whether they would be as steadfast in the miners' cause as he was himself. His distrust was heightened when the General Council withheld permission for the *New Leader* to publish during the General Strike despite Brailsford's appeal on behalf of a journal that could refute official propaganda.[83] It was, therefore, no surprise that when the *New Leader* resumed publication on 21 May, its editor lashed out at the General Council for 'deplorable' leadership. Still more provocative was the appearance of a tendentious two-part analysis of the strike by A. J. Cook, the miners' leader, which disparaged the General Council's role.

In response to Creech Jones's appeal for the loyal suspension of criticism until the facts had been ascertained, Brailsford replied, somewhat disingenuously, that he did not believe 'a journalist can withhold a judgement on a matter which is of vital concern to all his readers'. If he had misstated the facts, he was prepared to admit his error, but the search for truth was hindered by the General Council's refusal to state its case.[84] The *New Leader*'s anti-TUC bias infuriated Bevin, its most prominent member; when Brailsford asked him for a statement as soon as the General Council abandoned its rule of silence, he retorted angrily:

One did except some sense of obligation to the industrial movement from a paper which in the main is circulated among our own people. I read your articles with some amount of dismay whilst your attempt to exploit Cook I regard as most ill-considered.[85]

Brailsford tried to remonstrate with Bevin: those who refused to cooperate had 'no right to blame me, when as a result of this silence, my version of events fails to meet with their approval'.[86] Unappeased, Bevin accused him of discarding the 'trait of loyalty' in favour of the

---

[81] *New Leader*, 7 Aug. 1925.
[82] *New Leader*, 12 Mar., 16 Apr. 1926.
[83] HNB to Bertrand Russell, 4 May 1926, Russell Papers; Margaret Morris, *The General Strike* (Harmondsworth, 1976), p. 241.
[84] HNB to Arthur Creech Jones and Harold Clay, 8 June 1926, Creech Jones Papers, MSS Brit. Emp. 5332, Box 7, File 1, fol. 49.
[85] Ernest Bevin to HNB, 7 June 1926, Bevin Papers, MSS 126/EB.
[86] HNB to Ernest Bevin, 8 June 1926, Bevin Papers, MSS 126/EB.

muddy side of casting doubt and suspicion. That is and always has been my whole complaint against the so-called 'intelligencia' and their 'superior' attitude of mind. With regard to our refusals to talk to you and people in your category in the movement, believe me we have very good reasons: the 'superior class' attitude is always there in relation to the trade union leader who comes from the rank and file and we feel it.[87]

Nor could Bevin have been gratified to see Brailsford launch the *Miner* at the beginning of June as a propagandist weekly for the striking MFGB, editing its first four issues before handing the paper over to Strachey.

Bevin's well-known animosity towards intellectuals was the least of the editor's problems in June, the very month in which he tendered his resignation. The union leader's reproof would not have jeopardized his position any more than MacDonald's hostility, but both were symptomatic of his isolated, vulnerable position in the movement. Far more ominous was Allen's retirement from the ILP chairmanship in October 1925. Amid the triumph of his speech and the fanfare over the Living Wage campaign at Whitley Bay, he had written to Allen, 'I wish I could convey to you how lonely I have felt during the last six months. Half the pleasure of working for the paper has gone since you disappeared.'[88] So long as Allen's friends had pumped money into the ILP, the *New Leader* was able to withstand attacks from hostile NAC members. But when the Maxton-Wheatley faction dislodged Allen from the leadership, Brailsford lost his principal patron. From the moment of his appointment as editor he had been regarded by the Scottish contingent as Allen's protégé. Although his ideological position was closer to Wheatley's than to Allen's MacDonaldite views, there was little rapport between the Catholic Wheatley and the agnostic editor. Brailsford's warmest supporters were the Liberal recruits—men such as Russell, Ponsonby, and Trevelyan, none of whom carried weight in the party. Thus he became a convenient scapegoat in the Scottish reaction against the middle-class, intellectual orientation of the Allen regime.

The basic problem was a financial one. Although the instantaneous success of the *New Leader* had helped to reduce the ILP subsidy, it was expensive to maintain. Writers were paid at prevailing periodical rates, and the editor refused to reduce the size of the paper as an economy measure. The rise in circulation testified to a growing audience, yet there was ample evidence that ILP branches were slow to promote it, especially in Scotland where the *Forward* retained its hold on working-class allegiance. By December 1923 sales were twice as high as in the final days of the *Labour Leader*, and the following May they reached

[87] Ernest Bevin to HNB [June 1926], Bevin Papers, MSS 126/EB.
[88] HNB to Clifford Allen, 8 Apr. 1926, AP, Box VII.

a peak of nearly 70,000, surpassing that of any other weekly review of the time. Losses were cut from £3,800 in the first year of publication to £1,150 in its third, although losses then began to mount again.[89] Unfortunately, the *New Leader* needed sales of at least 60,000 a week to break even, a level achieved only during the spring of 1924, after which circulation hovered around 50,000 for about a year. Furthermore, for a quality periodical, the price of the paper was comparatively low, twopence an issue as compared with sixpence for the *New Statesman* or the *Spectator*. The need to provide a workers' journal at an affordable price reduced potential revenue, creating the need for a continuing subsidy. Reports at annual conferences and appeals in the columns of the *New Leader* noted the narrowing gap between loss and solvency, but it proved impossible to bridge.

Brailsford's problems were personal as well. He had clashed frequently about the style of the paper and his authority over appointments with the ILP shareholders, especially P. J. Dollan. Murmurs of discontent over his salary and complaints about inadequate coverage of party activities had provoked his resignation in October 1924 (when his difficulties with MacDonald were at their peak), but this had been refused, although the motion assuring continued NAC confidence was only carried 8-3, with 2 abstentions.[90] The ineradicable deficit and intellectual tone provided ammunition for Brailsford's critics, alarmed as well by his propensity for alienating the movement's leaders. He rarely took the directors into his confidence once the paper was launched, which raised problems, for example, when he committed the ILP to sponsoring the *Miner* in June 1926 without informing his colleagues.[91] He attributed his woes to the rivalry of *Lansbury's Labour Weekly* in 1925-6, but Plummer confided to Nevinson that 'the party was displeased with HNB as editor, partly for the literary articles and general high-brow tone, but chiefly for his quarrel with JRM and his repeated pinpricks of attack upon him'.[92] Allen, still a member of the *New Leader* board, was too ill in 1926 to intercede, as he had often done in the past. In any event he was now a somewhat discredited figure in the ILP, his influence vitiated by his loyalty to MacDonald. The controversy over the *Miner* precipitated Brailsford's offer to resign in June, but other factors prompted his reluctant decision. 'After enduring for four years a paper which I think they never liked, the governing body of the Party

---

[89] NAC Minutes, 18 May, 1 Dec. 1924; *Report* (1926). The *New Republic* was subsidized to the tune of $100,000 per year by Dorothy Whitney Straight (Mrs Elmhirst). Ronald Steel, *Walter Lippmann and the American Century* (Boston, 1980), p. 62.
[90] NAC Minutes, 6 Oct. 1924.
[91] NAC Minutes, 6 June 1926.
[92] ND, 25 June 1926. Also ND, 5 July 1926.

was determined to have something different,' he told Lippmann. 'I did not feel inclined to make any large changes.'[93] Much as he might insist that he could not 'go on under a committee of his enemies',[94] it is clear that he was forced out. He had functioned as editor for years with minimal support from the NAC and would have continued, despite the persistent feuding, had he been permitted. Though disposed to accept his resignation, the NAC deferred final action until October, pending the report of a Reconstruction Committee examining the future of ILP periodicals.

When the NAC convened at the Margate conference in October, the Reconstruction Committee proposed Strachey's appointment as editor of the *New Leader*, the *Miner*, and the *Socialist Review*. He was already editing the latter two journals, and Plummer was managing all three, so that further consolidation might reduce the costs to the ILP. A two-day discussion ensued, at which Brailsford made a full statement. Kirkwood, a familiar antagonist, reiterated his objection to anyone receiving a high salary from the ILP while Clydeside engineers were paid less than three pounds a week. What was sufficient for them should be sufficient for the editor of the *New Leader*. Brailsford, often subjected to such abuse, had never intimated that it rankled. This time, his bridges already burned, he rose to reply with 'the detached, explanatory air of a professor about to demonstrate the solution of a problem to a not too intelligent class'.[95] He too was attracted by the idea that all those who serve socialism should take a vow of perpetual poverty. But Kirkwood seemed to single out only the editor of the *New Leader* for self-sacrifice while other servants of the movement—including Kirkwood himself—might continue to draw Parliamentary salaries and trade union subsidies, not to mention speaking fees. This silenced Kirkwood but did not dissuade other critics, especially Dollan and Elijah Sandham, from again flailing the *New Leader* for not embodying the appropriate proletarian temper. Brockway, now ILP Political Secretary, had revenge for having been twice passed over for the editorship when he agreed that the rank and file would prefer a different kind of journal. After prolonged debate the NAC accepted Brailsford's resignation on the grounds that they desired 'a more popular type of paper', voting 8-4 to retain him as a contributor. Brockway was named interim editor, his tenure confirmed some months later at an annual salary of £500.[96]

Although Brailsford's 'inflated' salary loomed large in the discussion, it was only a pretext used by those who wished to force him out. A

---

[93] HNB to Walter Lippmann, 22 July 1926, Lippman Papers, Box 4.
[94] ND, 9 Aug. 1926. [95] Paton, p. 242.
[96] NAC Minutes, 9-12 Oct., 18 Dec. 1926.

month before Margate, Norman Leys, a physician and expert on Africa, wrote to Maxton to protest against Brailsford's imminent departure. The Chairman, conceding that Strachey would not make a suitable *New Leader* editor, told Leys that he had formed a 'very high opinion of Brailsford's courage, literary skill and editorial ability' and would gladly have retained him were it not for his £1,000 a year salary. That was 'the sole problem about Brailsford'.[97] As Maxton might have discovered, Brailsford had already voluntarily reduced his own salary by £200 and offered to cut it by another £100. The *New Leader*'s financial predicament was less bleak than it appeared, because the NAC did not apportion costs fairly among its sponsored periodicals. Since management was shared, the liabilities of the *Socialist Review* might inadvertently be ascribed to the *New Leader*. At the 1927 ILP conference Maxton restated his view that the ILP was 'not prepared to pay for the luxury of a thousand-a-year editor', although he could by then have enlightened himself as to actual expenses. What seems curious is that Brailsford was kept on as principal contributor at £300 a year, which, coupled with Brockway's editorial salary of £500, matched Brailsford's pay at the time of his dismissal.

In braving Brailsford's indignant admirers, Maxton also claimed that the editor 'demanded a complete autocratic control'.[98] The circumstances surrounding Molly Hamilton's appointment and the later surrender of control over reporting of party affairs refute this allegation, but it comes closer to explaining the source of conflict than does the disagreement over salary. Correct though he had been in his dealing with the NAC, Brailsford had refused to follow the dictates of men whom he believed narrow-minded and philistine. His testy independence lay at the heart of his conflict with Dollan and Kirkwood. His remoteness and disdain for easy *bonhomie* exacerbated tensions between the editor and the politicians whose confidence he needed. But it seems unlikely that his enemies would have prevailed had they not been encouraged by an eager aspirant to the editor's chair. In 1926 there was a power vacuum at the top: Allen had ceased to participate actively, and Maxton, misinformed about ILP developments, was too ill even to attend the Margate conference at which Brailsford's fate was settled. Kirkwood and Dollan despised the editor, but it was Brockway who contrived his removal in order to take his place. Brockway later claimed that he was merely reflecting the wishes of the members for a paper 'not so much for the armchair as for the factory and the street' but he

---

[97] Norman Leys to HNB, 11 Sept. 1926, HNBP. Leys was a Glasgow University contemporary and friend.

[98] HNB to Norman Leys, 2 Oct. 1926, HNBP; *Report of the 35th Annual Conference of the ILP* (1927).

wanted the editorship, knew he was likely to be asked to succeed Brailsford, and foresaw that his 'motive would be questioned'.[99] While he may not have actually conspired, he certainly took advantage of opportunity to satisfy his previously thwarted ambition. When his editorship ceased at the end of October, Brailsford was amused at the fulsome tribute offered by his successor, 'the man who had done most in turning me out'.[100]

The unstinting praise that followed his retirement helped to soften the blow. R. H. Tawney assured him that he had 'made it much the best paper that the Labour movement has yet had', while Russell interpreted his resignation as a sign that 'the Labour Party has no use for honest men'.[101] But it was the letters from people he did not even know that were the most moving. Whatever Brockway's estimate of rank and file opinion, many shared the sentiments voiced in an irate protest to the NAC:

> In the interests of Socialism you have autocratically decided to silence the pen of its most powerful and persuasive exponent. You are destroying the *New Leader* and you must know it. Your excuse can only mean that in place of logic and understanding, instead of trying to educate men and women to the finer planes of reason and beauty, the greatest Socialist organ is now to foster more misunderstanding, lower itself to clamouring mediocrity and employ invective and cheap sensationalism in an attempt to convince those who think differently from us. Both I and my friends are young, and I tell you that it is Brailsford and the *New Leader* that have drawn us into the movement.[102]

The grumbling was slow to subside. At the Leicester ILP conference six months later delegates denounced the NAC's action, one of them declaring that 'when we got rid of Mr. Brailsford we lost one of the most brilliant journalists in the Labour movement'. Although Maxton had not been fully involved in the decisions, he accepted personal responsibility. Rebutting the charge that 'we kill our prophets and then we praise them', he noted that the ILP had retained the editor's services, had sent him on a special mission to Russia, and was prepared to send him to China. Brailsford, he continued, was unquestionably a 'brilliant journalist, whose work is easily worth in the general market perhaps two thousand a year. But as far as I am concerned he will have to go into that general market to get the price'.[103] That he had been willing to serve as editor at scarcely more than one-third that sum did not seem to Maxton important enough to mention in exonerating his colleagues.

[99] Brockway, *Inside the Left*, p. 187. Interview, Lord Brockway.
[100] HNB to Evelyn Sharp, 25 Oct. 1926, Evelyn Sharp Papers, c. 277, fol. 112.
[101] R. H. Tawney to HNB, 19 Oct. 1926, HNBP; Bertrand Russell, 7 Oct. 1926, HNBP.
[102] C. N. Freeman to NAC, 25 Oct. 1926, HNBP.
[103] *Report* (1927); *New Leader*, 22 Apr. 1927.

At the beginning of 1927 Brailsford tried to launch a new journal, to be called the *Phoenix*, as a 'vigorous organ of intellectual socialism'. Prospective collaborators included Russell, Nevinson, Hobson, Wise, Ponsonby, and Dalton, all of whom he had brought onto the *New Leader*.[104] Allen, initially consenting to help raise capital, subsequently withdrew when he decided that it was not a sound financial venture.[105] Reluctantly abandoning the project, Brailsford continued his contributions to the *New Leader* until the ILP disaffiliated from the Labour Party in 1932. There was, perhaps, some element of belated revenge in 1933 when he dissuaded his friend Dorothy Elmhirst from subsidizing the financially precarious journal:

It has degenerated in quality so terribly that it does not deserve to be helped. Its circulation and advertisement revenue have fallen so continuously, that it can have no prospect of becoming self-supporting. Apart from all of this, the ILP in my opinion is following a foolish (and unsuccessful) strategy.[106]

The paper did manage to survive as the *New Leader* until 1946, mostly under Brockway's direction, gradually losing both its readership and reputation. If its spirit became more proletarian, it also increasingly reflected the sectarian squabbles tearing the ILP apart.

Only during Brailsford's brief editorship did it aspire to become something more than a parochial weekly for the ILP faithful. What made it 'the best Socialist publication in the world', to quote Otto Bauer,[107] was its editor's commitment to a journal of literary excellence and socialist conviction that might appeal to all elements in British society. Refusing to restrict its audience to the trade union branch or the ILP committee room, it sought to extend the intellectual horizons of its readers, providing a periodical which consciously blended politics and the arts, the class struggle with cultural enrichment. Its exhaustive analyses of world affairs and economic problems reflected a determination to subordinate entertainment to education at whatever cost in popularity. Never professing to be an original thinker, Brailsford was ideally suited to the popular exposition of economic theories and the disentangling of diplomatic complexities. With a gift for the evocative image, he could reduce complicated issues to essentials, enlightening unsophisticated readers without sacrificing the gist of a theoretical argument. He offered alternatives to the timid respectability of the Parliamentary Labour Party, and his receptivity to innovative

---

[104] HNB's pencilled notes on *Phoenix*, HNBP.
[105] Clifford Allen to HNB, 7 Jan. 1927, HNBP; HNB to Clifford Allen, 9 Jan. 1927, AP, Box VII.
[106] HNB to Dorothy Elmhirst, 22 Mar. [1933], Elmhirst Papers.
[107] *New Leader*, 18 May 1923.

ideas belies clichés about the sterility of English socialist thought in the 1920s.

The editorship provided him with a personal forum, and in so doing transformed Brailsford into one of the most influential and widely-read of European socialist writers. Few could challenge his achievement in creating the *New Leader*, nor rival his reputation. Even his successor was keen to enjoy the reflected glory of his contributions. The loss of the paper was a bitter blow from which neither he nor his career entirely recovered. Never again to be personally identified with a periodical, though he wrote for several in the next two decades, he felt himself reduced to being a freelance pundit, admittedly one whose columns informed a large body of readers on three continents. As editor he had been able to combine his interests and his talents: as a writer expounding ideas, as a teacher shaping the socialist convictions of his audience, as a political gadfly prodding politicians to act. Cut adrift from his editorial mooring, he found it difficult to practise these skills simultaneously or as effectively. Neither travelling, nor lecturing, nor writing books—all of which he did in succeeding years—quite filled the gap. It was the culmination of his career, his crowning achievement, but it ended after only four years, more than three decades before his death.

XI
Candide Returns to Earth (1926–1932)

As long as Brailsford could find a steady market for his articles, the loss of the editorship, painful as it was, did not have to entail a serious reduction in income. Writing had provided an adequate livelihood before 1922, partly derived, to be sure, from a regular association with the *Nation* that had long since dissolved. The continuing link with the *New Leader* was worth about £300 a year, but he still needed to earn at least as much again in order to maintain his standard of living, however modest, and to support Jane, now living in seclusion. The *New Republic* willingly received more frequent contributions, dividing London reports between him and S. K. Ratcliffe.[1] Until the Second World War made regular transmission difficult, he supplied the *New Republic* with eight to ten articles a year on average at $30 each, written in long-hand and sent by ship so that they generally appeared some three weeks after being posted.

By 1926 he was much better known in the United States than he had been twelve years earlier when Lippmann recruited him for the *New Republic*. Oswald Garrison Villard, whose American *Nation* had termed Brailsford's resignation as editor a 'calamity',[2] was keen to obtain his services if that did not conflict with his *New Republic* commitments. His reputation and contacts among Continental socialists were such that both the Austrian *Arbeiter Zeitung* and *Der Kampf* were keen to have him write for them. Given his political leanings, it was less plausible for the liberal capitalist weekly *Der deutsche Volkswirt*, German counterpart to *The Economist*, to be interested in a continuing arrangement. Yet between 1927 and 1931 he contributed some twenty articles, about half of which dealt with Anglo-Indian relations, while the rest analysed British foreign policy. These pieces, written in English, were translated by the editor's wife, Toni Stolper, who found it a 'welcome task to render Brailsford's splendidly written articles in German'.[3]

Since none of his books made substantial amounts of money, he needed to write at least two articles a week in order to pay his way and usually averaged close to 150 a year. Between 1916 and 1922 he had managed this by writing for the *Nation* and the *Herald*, a task that involved some ideological dexterity on his part; after 1932 he worked in

---
[1] Steel, *Lippmann*, p. 68.
[2] *Nation* (US), 10 Nov. 1926. See HNB to O. G. Villard, 10 and 17 Dec. 1926, Villard Papers.
[3] Dr Toni Stolper to author.

tandem for fourteen years for *Reynolds* and the *New Statesman*. But between 1926 and 1932 he was obliged to be enterprising, to exploit his international reputation in order to place an inexhaustible supply of articles. For the most part he succeeded; several of these arrangements, not least his thirty-two year association with the *New Republic*, proved remarkably durable. An early piece for the American socialist review *The World Tomorrow*[4] foreshadowed a stint as a regular columnist and associate editor from 1932 to 1934. Aside from these, there was a good deal of ephemera. Scattered over the years were articles and reviews for the *Radio Times, Time and Tide, Harper's,* and *Current History*. Several of these publications were American, prompting him to remark, as he had during the war, that he found himself 'writing more and more for America and less and less for England'. This he attributed to 'the growing prejudice in our Press against anyone who stands in the Left Wing of the Labour camp'.[5] The causes were, in fact, as much economic as ideological. Progressive American journals, usually Anglophilic, paid better than their British counterparts.

The United States also offered almost limitless opportunities for foreign lecturers in the 1920s, especially among universities and foreign policy associations. Persistent isolationism notwithstanding, the war had made educated Americans thirsty for the kind of analysis of international affairs that Brailsford was adept at providing. When Alvin Johnson invited him to deliver a series of lectures at the New School for Social Research, he agreed to come for a two-month visit and used Villard, Johnson, Lippmann and other American contacts to help arrange lectures and meetings. But before he could begin what was to become an almost annual lecture trip to the United States, he was looking forward to collecting his ILP consolation prize—six weeks in the Soviet Union. The fact that the party was paying for his trip in no way precluded his writing about it in the *New Republic* and the *Baltimore Sun* and, more extensively, in *How the Soviets Work*. The only one of his books not published in England, this political textbook *cum* travel report appeared in November 1927 in an American series entitled Vanguard Studies of Soviet Russia and went through two printings.

During the mid-1920s Brailsford's writings were markedly ambivalent toward the Soviet Union. Loudly as he deplored the crushing of free speech 'as ruthlessly as [under] any Tsarist or Fascist dictatorship', he hailed the Communists 'as men who are on the same side of the dividing trenches as we are'.[6] If capitalism was the enemy, socialist

---

[4] *World Tomorrow*, Feb. 1927. Article incorporated into Chap. 8 of *Olives of Endless Age*, pp. 277-83.
[5] HNB to H. Bräuning-Oktavio, 11 Oct. 1927, BOP.
[6] *New Leader*, 16 Apr. 1926, 14 Nov. 1924.

unity was imperative, but its realization was hampered by the 'perpetual follies' of the Comintern 'in pursuit of the mirage of world revolution'. As long as the Russians fomented unrest abroad and retained a formidable apparatus of repression at home, even their advocates in the West would be wary.[7] Never oblivious to the defects of the Soviet regime, he felt an obligation as a socialist, as a critical admirer, to cast it in the most favourable light possible. If he did not knowingly distort the facts, he was selective in what he reported, 'shutting one eye and opening the other', as a similarly inclined friend described it.[8] Like many on the left, he was willing to condone in Russia what would have been deemed intolerable at home. Unlike some of them, however, there were limits to his tolerance, especially in the 1930s. His first visit had fired his enthusiasm, but he questioned whether the revolutionary impetus—or indeed the regime itself, beset by economic and military crises—would survive. These doubts had been dispelled by the time he returned to Russia six and a half years later, determined to be impressed by what he saw.

Above all, it was the improved living conditions, the easing of the stern puritanical tension of the civil war, that he noticed. In Moscow, where vodka once again flowed freely, the people were no longer subsisting on herring broth and potato parings. The change was even more remarkable in Vladimir, the high point of his earlier trip. In 1920 shops had been open only a few hours a day until their meagre stocks were exhausted; now the windows, crammed with goods, beckoned customers. The Sobinka factory, with barely enough cotton to keep the workers busy in 1920, had been replaced by a vast new mill, well-equipped, powered by electricity, and humming with activity.

Brailsford was no less struck by evidence that the regime had won acceptance from the people. In the factories he visited the works council seemed to have gained full control over the social institutions, and the distinctions of the past had been eliminated. The contrasts were just as sharp in villages, such as Bogomolova, where the landlord had vanished and with him the arrogant pretensions of the superior class. The village managed its own affairs through an elected Soviet, an indication that its people were 'realizing the earliest and simplest conception of democracy'.[9] He was not so naïve, however, as to imagine that the dictatorship permitted more than rudimentary grassroots democracy in the village and factory.

Two factors appeared to explain the wide support for the regime, apart from intellectuals and other malcontents. There was a general

---

[7] *New Leader*, 9 Jan. 1925.
[8] Interview, Naomi Mitchison.
[9] *How the Soviets Work*, p. 51.

conviction that the sense of predestined inferiority of the worker had disappeared, that there was widening opportunity especially for women and children. Second, when he travelled to Kazan on the banks of the Volga, he was able to observe the Tartar republic, one of the ostensibly autonomous states within the Soviet Union for the formerly subject races. Since the republic had come into being, an educational system had been launched, with libraries, books, and newspapers dedicated to elevating the masses and fostering the Tartar language. He became convinced that the cultural autonomy would within a generation bring 'not the picked few but the broad masses of these neglected Eastern races within the circle of civilization'.[10] Even more than in his assessment of local self-government, Brailsford took the appearance for reality. That the regime provided a framework for democratic criticism, that it perceived itself as a federation of socialist republics, did not prevent a centralized, totalitarian state from emerging.

As in 1920, he refused to restrict himself to tourist sights or to rely on propaganda to form his impression. Unlike many British visitors, he was familiar enough with life in Eastern Europe to appreciate the contrasts with pre-revolutionary conditions. Yet, he allowed his enthusiasm to shape his judgement. The genuine social gains obscured the rigours of dictatorship; his credulity allowed him to believe that the promise would be fulfilled. Not only did he misconstrue, with well-intentioned optimism, the course of social change in the Soviet Union, he failed to anticipate the temper of Stalinism. Although Trotsky had been dropped from the Politburo, his expulsion from the party was still some months in the future. His conflict with Stalin is depicted in *How the Soviets Work* as though comparable to that which had raged between Asquith and Lloyd George or between MacDonald and ILP. Although Brailsford had interviews with friends, including Rothstein, Karl Radek, and Litvinov, then Vice Commissar for Foreign Affairs, he was oblivious to the dynamics of the power struggle within the Communist Party. He perceived the dispute mainly in terms of economic policy, arguing, despite his personal admiration for Trotsky, that Stalin's insistence on the viability of socialism in one country was not only 'right on grounds alike of economic and political wisdom', but equally a 'triumph for Russian public opinion'.[11] It is of course possible that he was deliberately concealing the tensions that had riven party circles, but it seems more likely that in 1927 he misread the signals. With the defeat of Trotsky and the rejection of any co-operation between Communists and Social Democrats, his misgivings increased. As he told a Dutch acquaintance after the sixth Comintern Congress jettisoned the policy

[10] *New Leader*, 1 Apr. 1927.   [11] *How the Soviets Work*, p. 163.

of peaceful coexistence, 'There was a time in my own development when Moscow attracted me more than it does today. But it seems to me that its rigid ideas have less & less application to the actual world, & certainly in our own struggle in England it has had nothing useful to contribute.'[12]

Brailsford often described his books as 'big' ones or 'little' ones, a designation having perhaps less to do with length than content. His travel books, their polemical intent notwithstanding, were of transitory importance, a record of impressions for contemporaries rather than for posterity. As he grew older, he was troubled by a sense that too much of his writing was ephemeral, forgotten almost as soon as it was published. He did not, after all, write merely to make a living, but to explain international politics to his readers. But of his earlier books only *Macedonia*, *The War of Steel and Gold*, and *A League of Nations* were clearly 'big' books, reflecting not merely a response to immediate concerns, but more considered expositions whose significance transcended the moment of composition. Since the end of the war he had been too busy to undertake a major work, and, in any event, *After the Peace* betrayed a profound despair about the state of the world that deterred him from another systematic exploration. But having polished off *How the Soviets Work* in scarcely more than a month, he was ready to attempt something more substantial—'a big book on the idea of International Unity —political and economic'.[13] He took greater pains over it than almost any of his books and thought it 'the best written'.[14] The title, poorly chosen for the sake of sales, was culled from a Shakespearean sonnet, but sounded to one acquaintance as though it smacked of 'yesterday's cocktail party'.[15] The first of two works dedicated to Clare Leighton, who engraved an olive tree for the frontispiece, *Olives of Endless Age* was published both in England and the United States by Harper, which had issued the American edition of *The Russian Workers' Republic* seven years earlier. It was also the only one of his books expensively produced, with spacious margins and quality binding. Despite his expectations, critical acclaim in the usual quarters outstripped commercial recognition.

Olives of Endless Age begins on a whimsical note: on a train journey from Moscow to Geneva (like the one Brailsford had taken in March 1927) its author encounters a young man who turns out, improbably, to be Candide himself. Instead of earthquakes in Lisbon, his misadventures belong to the troubled post-war world: typhus epidemics,

---

[12] HNB to W. Van Ravesteyn, 8 Nov. 1928, Van Ravesteyn Papers, Vol. 5.
[13] HNB to H. Bräuning-Oktavio, 11 Oct. 1927, BOP.
[14] HNB to H. Bräuning-Oktavio, 15 May 1928, BOP.
[15] Interview, Dame Margaret Cole.

the burning of Jewish villages in Poland and of Chinese cities, revolutionary terror in the Soviet Union. His survival, mainly as a soldier of fortune, confirms for Candide the wisdom of his teacher's philosophy, that this was the best of all possible worlds. Just as Voltaire mocked Enlightenment illusions about human perfectability, so Brailsford was attempting to shake the complacency of latter-day Candides. Although the concept of a League had been 'a titan's step in the development of mankind',[16] it failed to realize its potential because it ignored the primacy of economics and stereotyped the power relationships confirmed at Versailles. Despite the constructive humanitarian work of League officials, its sessions were futile exercises by cynical politicians determined to maintain a peace settlement 'littered with injustices, which have erected on every frontier their fingerposts to the next "inevitable" war'.[17]

The task for the present generation was to give what he termed 'the Great Society of mankind' a political form which fit the facts of economic and cultural interdependence. In this larger conception nationalism was the enemy of civilization, an obstacle to achieving the desired unity. Its legitimate function was as guardian of inherited culture, perpetuating the diversity of the human inheritance in a world that had become 'inextricably one'.[18] Provided that the rights of minority peoples were protected by a charter which guaranteed cultural liberty, neither a national state, nor a policed frontier was necessary for protection. The guiding principle in promoting the good of the Great Society must be the subordination of a smaller group to a larger, a notion popularized a generation earlier by such Fabian social imperialists as Shaw. To Brailsford, however, it implied the exact opposite of imperialism. It must involve the subordination of the sovereign national state—economically and militarily—to the international community.

In *The War of Steel and Gold* Brailsford had argued that the lack of any mechanism to bring about political changes peacefully in 1914 made war inevitable. The way to prevent war in the future was to establish an international legislature powerful enough to impose changes. It would take charge of all dealings between states, all trade across frontiers, and contacts between the advanced economies and the underdeveloped world. The subordination of national prerogatives to the good of human society would end the age of imperialism, the League substituting its own agencies for imperial power. The mandate system, closely supervised to avoid exploitation for profit, would be extended to all non-self-governing colonies in Africa and the Pacific. The emergence of a democratic federation, representing the population of all

---

[16] *Olives*, p. 132.   [17] *Olives*, p. 68.   [18] *Olives*, pp. 404, 53.

independent states and uniting opinion across frontiers, did not preclude regional groupings. His forecast of a Western European economic community, separate from both the United States and the Soviet Union, in which resources would be pooled but political distinctness retained, was a generation ahead of its time.

Olives of Endless Age was a passionate work, a plea to his generation to save itself from the abyss. Although it argued that economic trends were the most significant factor in promoting closer ties, the book was less a straightforward economic interpretation than *The War of Steel and Gold*. If commercial rivalry was the source of international conflict, a more intractable obstacle to unity was the persistence of national sovereignty. Brailsford, recovered from the pervasive gloom of *After the Peace*, was still too realistic to imagine that imperialism or national sovereignty would be lightly discarded, however palpable the benefits for humanity. Once again he was banking his hopes on the awakening political consciousness of the masses. Gentler and more reflective than his polemical works, *Olives* was a secular sermon intended to move men's minds on the subject, to quote the book's subtitle, 'of this distracted world and the possibility of international unity'. He never doubted that international unity could be achieved; the question was whether the message would reach enough people who cared.

Brailsford knew little of America before he arrived there in January 1928, and, despite six visits in the next thirteen years, he 'never got his finger on the pulse of American life'. Politically unsympathetic, he found the naked materialism of the 1920s, the lack of cultural refinement, uncongenial. Aside from brief lecturing forays, one of which took him as far as San Francisco, he moved mainly along a New York-Washington axis, hospitably cared for by wealthy patrons. In New York he generally stayed at the Elmhirsts' Park Avenue penthouse, fully staffed even in their absence. His trips, ordinarily lasting six to eight weeks, were a welcome supplement to his income. Crowded with lectures, each commanding about $100-$150, these visits proceeded at a frenetic pace, exhausting, but lucrative, enabling him very nearly to double his income during the years he came to America.[19]

The arrival of a prominent English publicist was newsworthy in the 1920s, as extensive *New York Times* reporting of his visit demonstrated. While Brailsford was still in transit from Liverpool, Villard's *Nation* hailed him as

an odd recruit in the army of English lecturers. He despises bunk; he does not soft-soap his own empire; he dares to criticize his own party. His editorship of

---

[19] Interview, Clare Leighton.

the *New Leader* made it a force in international thinking in three continents; and his realistic analysis of post-war Europe has been a force of sanity.[20]

During his first six weeks in America commitments at the New School prevented his venturing far afield. His lectures, delivered as a two-evening-a-week course, ranged broadly over the European political scene, with particular attention to the League and the emergence of Fascism and Communism in the post-war world. His opening remarks struck a note frequently repeated in his talks—the need to overcome American isolation. Only through affiliation with the League and disarmament efforts could the United States foster peace.[21]

Between lectures he found the opportunity to make important new contacts, a valuable aid in sorting out his disparate American impressions. He lunched with the *Nation* and *New Republic* staffs and was the honoured guest at a Washington dinner with several progressive Senators, arranged by Villard, who also put him in touch with several political hostesses at the time of his lectures at the Robert Brookings Graduate School.[22] But he relished even more the informal meetings with students at International House in New York and at Yale, where he delivered the Dodge Foundation lecture on Russia and China.[23]

His articles about the United States evinced a fascination with its vibrant culture, but deep misgivings about its more inhuman features. Washington, with wide streets and harmonious public buildings, reminded him of a moderate-sized German provincial capital, but New York had the power 'to terrify and allure'. After six weeks he complained that he 'never felt at home' in the city and found it difficult to sleep.[24] American business leaders, generous towards universities and museums, lived 'graceless and unaesthetic lives'; the 'cramped and untidy' workers' houses made him long for an English village with thatched roofs and orderly gardens.[25]

When he returned to England at the end of March, Clare Leighton was waiting to greet him on the train platform. They had originally met four years earlier when, encouraged by her aunt, Sarah Leighton, a spinster of literary inclinations, she had brought her portfolio for him to see. It was an auspicious meeting. The editor, instantly entranced by both the artist and her artistry, fostered her career by providing the visibility she needed at this stage to gain recognition.[26] Striking, rather than beautiful, with a somewhat flamboyant manner, she radiated

[20] *Nation* (US), 28 Dec. 1927.
[21] *New York Times*, 4 Jan. 1928.
[22] HNB to O. G. Villard, 19 Dec. 1927, 5 Feb. [1928]; O. G. Villard to HNB, 9 Feb. 1928, Villard Papers.
[23] *New Leader*, 3 Feb. 1928; *Yale News*, 7 Mar. 1928.   [24] *New Leader*, 9 Mar. 1928.
[25] *New Leader*, 30 Mar. 1928.   [26] Interview, Clare Leighton.

vitality and creative energy. That she was twenty-five years his junior made him wary of any serious attachment, but it did not prevent his falling in love with her. In April 1924 he published the first of nine of her wood engravings that appeared in the *New Leader*. Entitled 'The Malthouse', it was a powerful evocation of rural labour, a group of men loading sacks of malt onto a wagon. This early work already exhibited those traits that would make her one of the most distinguished engravers of the century—an affinity for the rhythms of nature, a strength and economy of line in depicting men and women at work, a sensuous vibrancy that the black and white medium seemed to enhance.

Born in London, Clare was the daughter of Robert Leighton, successful author of boys' adventure books, and Marie Connor Leighton, who wrote melodramas and romantic serials for the Northcliffe Press. The Leighton household, a haven of genteel bohemianism in St John's Wood and later at Lowestoft, revolved around Mrs Leighton's deadlines and the throng of male admirers, her long-suffering husband resigned to the disordered frenzy to which his wife was addicted.[27] Her favourite among her offspring was the eldest, Roland, who was to achieve posthumous fame as the fallen hero and lover in Vera Brittain's memoir *Testament of Youth*. Educated at home by governesses, Clare later attended the Brighton School of Art and the Slade. During the twenties she was living alone in Bloomsbury, teaching drawing at St Monica's School, and shifting from painting to wood engraving. When Brailsford met her, she was already a consummate artist—enormously industrious, passionate about her work, cherishing her independence.

During the first years of their friendship, Brailsford tried not to monopolize her social life, and, indeed, Clare very nearly married someone else. But in 1928, when she was ill and overworked, he prevailed upon her to move to a flat around the corner from his own in Belsize Park Gardens. It was a compromise: they lived separately, but alternated dinners at the two flats and shared a housekeeper. He was extraordinarily solicitous, arriving early in the morning to light her fire and accompanying her by bus across London when she left for work.

While maintaining separate accommodations, they began to travel abroad together on holiday. In September 1928, after a busy summer in which he spoke at Dartington Hall—the first of many visits to the progressive school begun by the Elmhirsts—attended the Brussels Labour and Socialist International Congress, and gave three lectures at a summer school sponsored by the Women's International League for Peace and Freedom, Brailsford and Clare departed for several

---

[27] See Clare Leighton, *Tempestuous Petticoat* (New York, 1947).

weeks in the Dordogne and the Pyrenees, where they visited the prehistoric caves.

For many years he had been profoundly interested in the discoveries being made by anthropologists and archaeologists about ancient civilizations and primitive peoples. From early *Speaker* 'middles' to *New Statesman* reviews forty years later he turned regularly to these subjects, writing about the books of Frazer or Malinowski or the findings of Flinders Petrie or C. L. Woolley. Despite his avowed rationalism, he retained a mystical reverence for places of worship—English cathedrals, the ancient church of St Cornely in Carnac, Brittany, druidical stones, and the prehistoric Whiteleaf Cross in the Chilterns. Again and again in his reading and in his travels he returned to rites of worship, rituals concerning death, the uses of magic, not to denigrate them, but out of a kind of spiritual bond with the past. Having wrenched himself from his own religious roots, he embraced the study of religion as a tolerable substitute for faith itself. What began as an avocation soon became a scholarly passion. By 1930 he could write that

all the time I can spare from journalism I give to the study of anthropology. I'm working at a book on the origins of the ideas and institutions of the Australian natives, which may have a good deal in it that is original. But it will take me several years still to finish.[28]

Lack of professional training and field work hampered his investigations, but he pursued it until late in life. Its focus was the 'upside down' concept, the idea, according to primitive peoples, that 'everything in the other world is done the wrong way round. When the dead go downstairs, they go head first'.[29] He found examples of reversals or opposites not merely in funerals and burials, but initiation rites, carnivals, and buffoonery.

Brailsford always found solace from personal anxiety in music. Having long since abandoned the cello, he attended concerts frequently and, once he had obtained an EMG phonograph with an enormous papier-mâché horn and bamboo needles, become an avid record collector. His preferences ran to German classics, particularly Mozart, Beethoven, and Brahms, and he liked especially to listen to music at meals.

Music was a frequent theme of his 'World We Listen In' columns for the *Radio Times*. Often linked to some forthcoming broadcast, his pieces covered a wide spectrum of topics from his attachment to birds, to Chekov and Hardy, to English cooking, or to the analysis of a piece of music. 'I've just sweat blood over the IXth Symphony,' he wrote of

[28] HNB to H. Bräuning-Oktavio, 13 Feb. 1930.
[29] *New Leader*, 9 Aug. 1929. Also see *Plebs*, Mar. 1929 and *New Leader*, 31 May 1929.

one such article, 'cutting out all the little discoveries I thought I'd made. But if I've written a trite article, at least I know one symy as I never knew one before. I sometimes doubt if one knows anything till one writes about it.'[30] Although limited in formal musical training, Brailsford had a good ear and the ability to recall long passages of music. As in the case of his anthropological study, the lack of professional experience never inhibited him from writing about the subject.

His 1929 American tour, arranged by William B. Feakins, a well-known agent, began just after New Year's Day with a six-part series at the New School, an abbreviated version of his 1928 course on European politics. After lectures at Cornell and Princeton, Brailsford was introduced to the Middle West, where he spoke at universities in Minnesota, Wisconsin, Illinois, and Iowa. The college towns he visited 'corrected the tyrannous impression' of New York; it was a homelier world, more like England, except for 'the stimulating cold outside the house and the stifling heat within it'. Once again he noted the absence of gardens, a serious defect in the American sensibility. The Mid-Westerners he met seemed conservative, more concerned with advancing themselves in 'business administration' than with social progress.[31]

Being away from Clare for three months made Brailsford aware of the depth of his attachment. They discussed marriage, but Jane still refused a divorce.[32] He then broached the idea of their living together: he was planning to spend part of the summer in Devon and wanted Clare to join him:

I keep day-dreaming about our cottage. Do think about it, dear Mate. Time for you is measured with generous and spacious milestones. My pocket ruler is graded to inches. If the Queen is ready to come to her 'keeper's' garden & be pampered, why shouldn't we act at once and enjoy some of this English summer in it? He won't forget that she's a wild animal. His garden has no bars or locks to it.[33]

The final allusion struck a familiar chord from earlier discussions: she was hesitant to surrender her freedom, since her affection, though genuine, had not yet ripened into love. She wished to keep her options open, not least because Brailsford was obviously not free to marry.

His frequent trips abroad, the dreary weekends in Amersham with his mother and Mabel, then writing a life of William Penn, the lonely London flat all made him long for his own country cottage, preferably

---

[30] HNB to Christopher leFleming, 11 Sept. [1930].
[31] *New Leader*, 15 Mar. 1929.
[32] ND, 13 June 1929.
[33] HNB to Clare Leighton, Easter 1929, CLC.

with Clare, on which to lavish attention. During his last visit with Blunt in Sussex the dying poet had given him the first daffodil of the season for remembrance, and in his will asked that Brailsford choose something from his house 'to remember him by'. Brailsford, recalling the daffodil, asked for a few bulbs, which ever since had flourished in Mabel's garden. He hoped to transplant them if ever he acquired his own house in the country, along with an autumn gentian which he brought from the stone circles of Carnac in Brittany and kept in a window box in Belsize Park.[34]

It was during 1930, before his departure for India, that Clare consented to share his home. Still afraid of 'being caged', she felt protected by him and was increasingly susceptible to his 'hypnotic power'.[35] He was planning, mainly with his American earnings, to build a country house for them in a newly developed area outside the village of Monks Risborough in the Chilterns. It was designed according to her specifications, with a studio, and would serve as a retreat for both of them from London. They would create the garden they both wished for and be near enough to his aged mother to satisfy filial obligations. But before Clare was to move in Brailsford was scheduled to go to India and, later, the United States, where they would meet and return to England together.

In 1914 Brailsford had been among the first group of politicians, academics, and publicists to join the Union of Democratic Control. Although he continued as a member of its General Council throughout the interwar period, he had not been an active participant for many years. In March 1930, however, he and Laski established a research group to study international problems, with the intention of sponsoring a series of studies on the prevention of war. It was to be a Radical counterpart to the Royal Institute of International Affairs. Of the two dozen or so peace activists invited, fourteen attended the initial meeting at the London School of Economics on 21 March. An executive committee was appointed, consisting of Brailsford, Laski, Woolf, David Mitrany, a Rumanian-born journalist and expert on international organizations, and Will Arnold-Forster, until then Lord Robert Cecil's assistant, the latter two serving as joint secretaries of the Peace Research Group. Ten co-ordinated studies were projected, Brailsford and Lowes Dickinson collaborating on an introductory volume on the elements of a stable peace. Other volumes on cultural co-operation, the renunciation of war, disarmament, and international law were proposed, the authors

---

[34] *Radio Times*, 5 Sept. 1930. Brailsford lived at 37 Belsize Park Gardens from 1927 until 1952. A GLC commemorative plaque was placed there in 1983.

[35] Interview, Clare Leighton.

to include Woolf, Hobson, Angell, and other prominent internationalists.[36]

From the outset they were plagued by problems. Despite a vow to avoid duplicating research performed elsewhere, the group appeared to upstage the redoubtable Chatham House, an obstacle to fund-raising, especially from foreign benefactors. In his appeal for £5,000 from the Rockefeller Foundation, Mitrany stressed their goal of providing studies of international organization for the general reader.[37] The initial enthusiasm waned, partly through lack of financial support and partly through the failure of members to follow through on contributions. By early 1931 the now renamed International Peace Group, still lacking the proposed manuscripts, decided to sponsor a single volume of essays focusing on the problem of national sovereignty. Even this more limited plan proved abortive, and eventually Leonard and Virginia Woolf published Brailsford's essay by itself under the aegis of the New Fabian Research Bureau in 1932.[38]

Essentially a condensation of *Olives of Endless Age, If We Want Peace* was another plea for international government. While the League of Nations was a step in the right direction, its effectiveness was limited by its deference to national sovereignty, a doctrine inimical to peace 'since it forbids any radical approach to the problem of organic change'.[39] What Brailsford had in mind was the opening of Australia, for example, to the influx of immigrants from over-populated Southern Europe or Asia. Such encroachments on national sovereignty would become possible when the League ceased to assume merely police functions and began to foster mutual dependence by stabilizing prices, regulating the production of essential commodities, and controlling monetary transactions. Once the benefits conferred were recognized, disobedience would involve for rebellious states a 'relapse into economic anarchy'. Mutual defence would evolve slowly, perhaps only after the victory of 'a violent fascist romanticism' among dissatisfied powers raised the spectre of war which would 'yield only to a visible superiority of organised force'.[40] He looked to the League to adopt the principle of co-operative defence as it became a more tightly organized, less exclusive community. But until the League became more inclusive, there seemed little alternative to reliance on the traditional alliance structure against which he had so long fulminated.

[36] Brailsford and Laski letter, 20 Mar. 1930; Minutes and draft statement of Peace Research Group, Mitrany Papers, Box V.
[37] David Mitrany to Raymond Fosdick, 6 Aug. 1930, Mitrany Papers, Box V; Mitrany, *Functional Theory*, pp. 39-40.
[38] International Peace Group Minutes, 10 Feb. 1931; Leonard Woolf to David Mitrany, 2 Aug. 1931, Mitrany Papers, Box V.
[39] *If We Want Peace*, p. 24. [40] Ibid., pp. 56-7.

Considering his subsequent staunch advocacy of Indian liberation, it is remarkable how infrequently Brailsford wrote about India before 1930. With some exceptions—Egyptian problems the most notable—his articles were almost wholly preoccupied with Europe until the late 1920s. Brailsford was a member of the ILP advisory committee which urged Labour in March 1926 to endorse India's right to self-determination,[41] but he was at first exceedingly cautious, demanding only an 'instalment of self-government' and more rapid 'Indianization of the Civil Service'.[42] He did not yet regard immediate independence, to which Congress militants were committed, as either feasible or enlightened. Nor was he yet convinced that Gandhi, 'speaking for three-fifths of the Hindu Congress party, can be voicing the will of the majority of the Indian population'. As long as there was unrest, the British would be obliged to maintain order, which meant that police and defence would need to remain under imperial control.[43]

During the months before the first Round Table Conference in November 1930 civil disobedience flared up again with a new intensity. MacDonald's failure to guarantee a dominion constitution led Congress to boycott the London meeting, leaving native representation to the princes and the more conservative elements. Despite an appeal for non-violence, rioting accompanied defiance of the law, and Congress leaders, including Jawarhalal Nehru and Gandhi were imprisoned, the Mahatma's arrest triggering a *hartal* (or work stoppage) throughout the country. By June 1930 India was in full revolt, hardly an auspicious omen for the forthcoming conference. It was in that context that Brailsford resolved to visit India in October, remaining for most of the period in which the conference would be in session. 'The project means much to me,' he wrote to Lippmann, appealing for a *New York World* subvention. 'India's fate will then be decided. Even if things on the spot are calm, India will be "in the news", and views gathered there should have value.' He anticipated no difficulty in securing information since he was well known, the Indian newspapers quoting 'everything I write'.[44] Estimating his expenses at £300, he needed several subsidies, and, in fact, his firsthand observations were subsequently carried by the *Nation*, the *Manchester Guardian*, and the *New Leader* in England, the *New Republic*, the *New York World*, and the *Baltimore Sun* in America, *Der deutsche Volkswirt* in Berlin, and specialized magazines such as *Forum* and *Asia*, circulation sufficiently extensive to ensure that he suffered no financial loss. In addition, two Indian papers, the *Bombay Chronicle* and

[41] *Justice for India: An ILP Report*, reprinted in *New Leader*, 12 Mar. 1926.
[42] *New Leader*, 3 Jan. 1930. See Georges Fischer, *Le Parti Travailliste et la Décolonisation de l'Inde* (Paris, 1966), pp. 101, 201, 252.
[43] *New Republic*, 14 May 1930.
[44] HNB to Walter Lippmann, 18 July 1930, Lippmann Papers, Box 4.

Advance, a Calcutta daily, published several of his pieces. While at Dartington Hall in July 1930, he learned a good deal from Leonard Elmhirst, who had established a department of rural reconstruction at Rabindranath Tagore's International University at Santiniketan in the early 1920s. Elmhirst put Brailsford in touch with the Bengal health director and other Indian acquaintances.[45] He sought the name of William Rothenstein's Benares guru and 'anyone else you can recommend to me as an antidote to the hot politics. My fear is that amid nationalism I may miss India.'[46] He also had a talk with Lord Lytton, his erstwhile suffragist colleague and former Governor of Bengal.

After a farewell Soho dinner which Nevinson gave in his honour,[47] Brailsford sailed on the P. & O. liner *Narkunda* on 25 September, delighted to discover among his travelling companions the eminent Bengali scientist Sir Jagadhis Bose, who promptly offered hospitality in Calcutta. His plans called for him to spend about seven weeks in India, fly back with a stopover in Palestine to London before sailing to the United States, where he would remain until March 1931. His journey was hardly begun before he witnessed the clash of civilizations at close quarters. An English fellow passenger, resident in Poona for eighteen years, attributed Indian insubordination to the fact that 'the Government won't let us beat our servants. It's the only thing they understand.'[48] Such arrogance, almost a caricature of the sahib mentality, helped to explain the hostility he encountered from Indians, who hurled epithets and nationalist slogans at him from windows of buses in Bombay.[49]

Upon his arrival Brailsford granted an interview at which he affirmed the view, derided by Indian militants, that the Labour government genuinely wished to concede dominion status rapidly. Once British proposals emerged at the Round Table Conference, he changed his tune, becoming ever more critical of the narrow concessions. With his usual candour, he made the tactical mistake of reproving Congress for boycotting the conference, much to the indignation of the nationalist press. Bombay was a revelation to him, changing many of his preconceptions about the popular mood. The city seemed to obey two governments: the Europeans, the Indian *sepoys*, and the older generation of Muslims were still loyal to the British, but the rest of the population had transferred allegiance to Gandhi and the Congress leaders. When Congress proclaimed a *hartal*, a weekly occurrence, the factories closed and the streets became silent. In the European quarter Indian women took up positions daily at the doorfront of shops to protest against the

---

[45] HNB to Leonard Elmhirst, 19 Sept. [1930], Elmhirst Papers.
[46] HNB to William Rothenstein, 19 Sept. [1930], Rothenstein Papers.
[47] ND, 18 Sept. 1930. [48] *Rebel India*, p. 210. [49] *Subject India*, p. 185.

purchase of foreign cloth.[50] While he was in Bombay such demonstrations were tolerated, but by the end of October more stringent regulations were applied, protest marchers were lashed by the police wielding *lathis*, and sixty thousand were imprisoned for political offences. When Brailsford met less militant Indians—Muslim barristers, moderate Liberals from Poona—he discovered that even they discounted England's good faith. This 'chasm of distrust', the unabated repression and the incarceration of the popular leaders, made the forthcoming conference 'a waste of time'.[51] But although the Indians were no longer acquiescent, they continued to adhere to Gandhi's exhortation to nonviolence, facing the police brutality as willing martyrs:

It was in this readiness to suffer that the moral power of this movement resided. When thousands will go gladly to prison, tens of thousands will give money, and hundreds of thousands will obey. It reminded me, in its temper and outlook, of the militant suffrage movement in England, save that it avoided even the minor acts of violence in which these forerunners indulged.[52]

He was also compelled to change his opinion about Gandhi's influence. While he was in prison, Congress ruled the masses in his name. There was scarcely a shop in the Hindu section of Bombay that did not exhibit his photograph, and Brailsford was to see it wherever he went, even among the poorest tribesmen.

Bombay also initiated him into poverty so devastating that it staggered the imagination of even so seasoned an observer. In the tanneries on the periphery of the city labourers were crammed into sheds surrounded by garbage. Ramshackle huts made of galvanized iron, barely ten feet square, housed six to eight persons, with only three water taps available for some four hundred inhabitants. His description of 'the empire's slums', reminiscent of Engels' sketch of Manchester in the 1840s, is, if anything, more gruesome. Never before exposed to tropical climate, he was struck by the acute discomfort, brought home to him by the inaccessibility of water for the masses. After ten minutes in the sun, his own shirt was wet through, and he managed to survive the heat only by taking four cold baths a day. His skin, he remarked, told him what life felt like for the Indian workers.[53]

From Bombay Brailsford moved north for five days in the villages of Gujarat, where the nationalist movement was strongest. In this relatively prosperous region, where Gandhi was a familiar local hero and saint, the peasant proprietors were resisting the land tax. Those who refused to pay were beaten and often imprisoned, their cattle and

[50] *New Leader*, 7 Nov. 1930; *Living Age*, Jan. 1931.
[51] *Nation*, 22 Nov. 1930. Article also appeared in *New Republic*, 10 Dec. 1930.
[52] *Rebel India*, p. 8.
[53] *New Leader*, 20 Feb. 1931; *Rebel India*, pp. 74-9.

belongings seized. He visited a Borsod jail where eighteen prisoners, awaiting trial, were kept in a cage day and night, allowed out only for three quarters of an hour once a day. When he visited Baroda refugee camps, where several thousand defiant Gujarati farmers, exchanging palm leaf huts for their brick cottages, congregated, a woman told him, 'We'll pay no taxes till Mahatmaji and Vallabhai [Patel] tell us to pay.'[54]

Viewing the conflict no less as an economic struggle against the landlords than as a nationalist revolt against imperialism, he identified with the left-wing Congress leaders, particularly Jawaharlal Nehru, whom he interviewed for two hours in an Allahabad prison. More obviously than any Indian he met, Nehru possessed 'the fire and imagination that make a daring leader'. Disavowing Gandhian mysticism, he saw no way to improve the peasants' lot without a struggle over the division of wealth and did not shrink from a battle with the landlord class, however entrenched that group was within the Indian National Congress.[55] He was encouraged too by what he saw in Calcutta, where the brilliant, but erratic, Marxist mayor, Subhas Bose, was charting the course of social progress, supplying milk to Calcutta's infants, building schools, and establishing clinics.

In seven weeks he had criss-crossed India from Bombay to Delhi to Calcutta and back to Karachi, moving from city to village, from Hindu to Muslim areas, mixing with Indians of all classes and political persuasions. He saw a country inflamed by anti-Bitish feeling, with tax resistance and the boycott of British goods spreading from the politically sophisticated to the ignorant masses of the Ganges valley. Although he had not realized how slight the preparation for self-government had been, he now believed its time had come. 'No sane man who has seen India during this year of turmoil,' he declared, 'supposes that the grant of responsible government can be delayed without irreparable damage, moral and economic, to its people and ourselves.'[56] For those who feared that concession was premature, he recalled the experience of two groups who had removed the 'stamp of inferiority'—women in England and workers in Russia. In India too, liberation would bring about 'a great release of creative energies' that would compensate for the inadequate preparation for freedom.[57]

Brailsford saw no easy solution to the problem of Indian poverty: the persistence of the caste system, the ingrained Hindu passivity, the staggering inefficiency of Indian agriculture, posed almost insuperable obstacles. But he did not hesitate to attribute blame to England for India's ills no less than to exploitation by princes, landowners, and

[54] *New Leader*, 30 Jan. 1931; *Rebel India*, pp. 37-8.
[55] *Rebel India*, pp. 125-7.   [56] *Nation*, 10 Jan. 1931.   [57] *Rebel India*, p. 217.

moneylenders. It was not as an interpreter of Indian society, however sympathetic, but as an implacable foe of British imperialism that he made his name as an advocate of the Indian nationalist cause. It was because the British had failed so abysmally to improve the conditions under which most Indians lived that he believed they had forfeited their right to rule.

Brailsford's return flight afforded him his only opportunity to visit Palestine, then still reeling from the Arab attacks on Jewish settlements. Two months earlier the Passfield White Paper, seeking to mollify Arab feelings, advocated restricting immigration, a policy Brailsford himself sanctioned in 1929. But even then his sympathies, in contrast to those of British officials, were largely on the Jewish side. As far as he was concerned the validity of the Jewish claim to Palestine lay not in prior possession, but in the fact that, unlike the decadent Arabs, they were ready to lavish wealth, science, and dedication to build a homeland in Palestine. If he was willing to limit Jewish immigration in order to lessen Arab fears, it was because he believed that they would in any event influence political and economic development out of all proportion to their numbers.[58] By the following spring, when the official Palestine Commission issued a distinctly pro-Arab report, he became even more critical of Labour's betrayal of the ideal of a national home. He favoured withholding self-government until the Arabs consented to the principle of a Jewish home, stressing the necessity of cultural autonomy and communal self-government rather than a Jewish or an Arab state.[59]

The visit itself confirmed his prior judgement: Jewish colonization was 'a double miracle, a victory over nature and history'. His memories of Warsaw and Minsk, 'where a whole race was doomed to live in narrow streets by petty trade', had not prepared him for these enthusiastic cultivators. And, best of all, it was the realization of socialist ideals: the land was farmed in common; equality was the rule in the *kibbutzim* where women were released for productive work, and children were raised free from the shadow of ghetto degradation.[60]

His Indian trip and the ensuing articles immediately ensured Brailsford prominence as a spokesman for the nationalist cause. In May 1931 he addressed a conference called by the Commonwealth of India League and when, in 1932, Krishna Menon transformed that organization into the India League, committed to total independence, Brailsford served on its executive.[61] He expanded his Indian articles into a book entitled

---

[58] *Menorah Journal*, Vol. XVII, No. 3 (Dec. 1929), pp. 209-18.
[59] *Menorah Journal*, Vol. XVIII, No. 5 (May 1930), pp. 389-98.
[60] *New Leader*, 26 Dec. 1930, 2 Jan. 1931.
[61] P. S. Gupta, *Imperialism and the British Labour Movement* (London, 1975), p. 255.

Rebel India, published by Leonard Stein in England and by the *New Republic* in America. One of his lesser efforts, it attracted little attention in the press, but he admitted to one friend,

> It is a hurried, superficial bit of work, which deals solely with politics. In one sense it was a great mistake to visit India at such an exciting moment. I could never get away from the one absorbing topic.[62]

It was, however, accorded the singular tribute of an enthusiastic review by Tagore, who praised Brailsford's 'perfect honesty' and 'sober judgment'.[63]

During Gandhi's stay at the Kingsley Hall settlement in the East End, Brailsford had a frank talk with him and urged him to get away from the London slums, to take his message to more influential quarters, the universities and Westminster. It became apparent during their exchange that Gandhi viewed himself as representing the entire Indian nation, healer of communal strife and saviour of the Untouchables. Brailsford, harbouring no illusions about British benevolence, implored him to seize whatever opportunity provincial autonomy afforded to liberate the peasantry from servitude to landlord and usurer. Admitting the defects of a constitutional scheme burdened with communal electorates, propertied franchise, reserved budgetary items, and nominated seats for the princes, he still regarded it as a distinct transfer of power which should not be rejected out of hand.[64]

Once Congress reaffirmed its demand for total independence, Brailsford ceased to proclaim even the limited virtues of the scheme. By 1932 he had so far revised his stance as to denounce the proposed constitution as 'an elaborate conspiracy against India's workers'. He continued to harp on the problem of separate electorates: as long as they were retained, a progressive party appealing to a national, rather than a sectarian, constituency could not emerge. Despite admiration for Gandhi and the Congress leaders, he blamed Hindu obscurantism no less than Muslim fears for India's troubles. He looked forward to 'a militant rationalist revolt' against all Indian religions, of which Hinduism was 'the most cramping'.[65] In addition to upholding the nationalist cause in his writings, he remained on close terms with Indian leaders, proferring tactical advice and serving as liaison between nationalists and Labour politicians.[66]

[62] HNB to William Rothenstein, 18 Sept. 1931, Rothenstein Papers.
[63] *Modern Review* (Calcutta), Vol. 53 (Jan. 1931), pp. 2-3. I am grateful to Hugh Tinker for bringing this review to my attention.
[64] *Manchester Guardian*, 13 Oct. 1931; Broadcast, 23 Aug. 1956 (recording, courtesy of BBC Sound Archives); *Subject India*, p. 103; *Mahatma Gandhi*, pp. 191-4. Gandhi visited Brailsford at Four Hedges.
[65] *New Clarion*, 1 Oct. 1932.
[66] Fischer, p. 114; T. J. S. George, *Krishna Menon* (London, 1964), p. 76.

India notwithstanding, it was Europe and the breakdown of the postwar settlement that remained his principal concern in these years. As long as reparations were exacted from Germany, the harm imposed at Versailles could not be undone. By the late twenties he was less concerned with the odium of war guilt that clung to the financial provisions of the treaty than with its economic ramifications. Forced tribute of this kind must inevitably depress German wages, and once low-cost German items competed in neutral markets with British products, England lost any competitive advantage.

The economic slump and the emergence of the Nazis as a major force in the 1930 Reichstag elections made the need for treaty revision seem even more urgent. By subordinating the interests of peace to the designs of the capitalist powers, the League was courting disaster, delaying 'the disarmament of the victors, until Germany rises up against the hypocrisy which keeps her disarmed, while her neighbors ring her round with steel'.[67]

Since the end of the war Brailsford customarily blamed the victors for Germany's misfortunes, accusing them of having conspired to discredit the republic, crippling it with ruinous obligations. But as Germany began to flounder in the morass of economic chaos, he began to ponder, perhaps for the first time, 'whether the assumptions of classical liberalism, which Social Democrats swallowed whole, will work at all in an epoch that calls for fundamental change'.[68] In Germany the timorous socialists who assumed control after the war had left the class structure intact, their enemies dominant in the army, industry, and the bureaucracy. Too cautious to challenge the traditional ruling class or to incur the displeasure of the Allies, the Social Democratic leaders were content to fortify themselves 'behind a frail political barricade ... defending not socialism but liberalism'.[69] But was this crisis of confidence in democratic institutions unique to Germany, or had democracy become, like international conciliation, another of Candide's illusions? Brailsford was coming to believe that capitalism and democracy were no longer, if they had ever been, compatible. The events of 1931 in England confirmed his fears that bankers and industrialists would impede any movement towards socialism, manipulating democratic safeguards if it served their class interest.

After his futile battles with Labour's leadership over the living wage programme, he expected little from a minority government headed by MacDonald, whom he had long ago written off as a charlatan, intended by nature, if not by birth, for the leadership of a Conservative party.[70]

[67] *New Leader*, 19 Sept. 1930.
[68] *New Clarion*, 17 Sept. 1932; *World Tomorrow*, 28 Sept. 1932.
[69] *New Republic*, 17 Aug. 1932. [70] *Harper's*, Vol. 154 (May 1927), pp. 696-702.

When Labour fell from power in August 1931, he found deeper causes than iniquitous leadership. The government had, throughout its existence and with Snowden's connivance, been 'in the grip of the City', a bar to any policy of expansion or development. The lesson was no less alarming for being so blatant: the City had no intention of tolerating even 'the mild quasi-Liberal reformism' of MacDonald's government.[71] The experience of 1929-31 showed that any 'honest' Labour ministry would be compelled to 'engage in a struggle to the last extremity' with the Bank. But Labour needed to understand that the Bank could not be socialized as a result of a few days of parliamentary wrangling: to nationalize banking meant 'to seize power, to seize it as literally as Lenin did when he bombarded the Winter Palace'.

In his summons to renewed battle for socialism Brailsford was no less militant than those ILP MPs who had defied Standing Orders by voting against a Labour government. But while they flaunted their unsullied ideological virtue, he wanted to restore unity in a party which had sloughed off its treacherous leaders. With the culprits safely in the enemy camp, the remedy for disunity lay 'not in tight discipline, but in honest leadership'.[72] But this was to ignore the deeper problems of the ILP's increasingly anomalous position, which had reduced it to impotence by 1929. No longer the source of leadership or policy, the ILP, its socialist virtue intact, deluded itself into believing that it might compete with Labour for working-class support. Seeing no alternative to further compromise under Labour's wing, Maxton and Brockway endorsed disaffiliation, which was only narrowly—and temporarily— defeated at the March 1932 ILP annual conference. Brailsford, certain that schism was a short cut to oblivion, pleaded against 'our tiny group' standing apart when the post-1931 remnant of Labour MPs faced 'overwhelming hosts'.[73]

Even as he wrote these exhortations, he knew that the cause was lost. The March 1932 conference, defeating unconditional affiliation by a large majority, endorsed an untenable compromise. Should Labour revise the Standing Orders to facilitate voting according to conscience rather than dictation, the ILP would remain, but it was obvious that no party could remain united in the face of frequent breaches of discipline. On the eve of a special conference, whose decision was a foregone conclusion, Brailsford argued the case for continued affiliation in the *New Leader*. If the ILP broke away, it would face the same uphill battle that the Communists had been waging, and, like the Communists, would discover the difficulty of training 'its guns simultaneously on the capi-

---

[71] *New Leader*, 28 Aug., 11 Sept. 1931.
[72] *New Leader*, 9 Oct. 1931.
[73] *New Leader*, 25 Mar. 1932, 6 Nov. 1931.

talist enemy and on the Labour Party'.[74] After the overwhelming vote in favour of disaffiliation at a special 31 July Bradford conference, Brailsford promptly resigned from the ILP along with Wise, Frank Horrabin, and several other prominent members. Mutual recriminations continued throughout the summer. When John Paton announced that Brailsford was expected to lecture, as usual, at the summer school, he immediately wrote to say that he would 'have nothing further to do, whether as writer or speaker, with an organization that has behaved with such conspicuous silliness'.[75]

During the winter of 1930-1 Douglas and Margaret Cole and several friends founded the Society for Socialist Inquiry and Propaganda in order to infuse the labour movement with a renewed sense of socialist purpose. Eager to avoid ILP divisiveness, Cole insisted that neither SSIP, nor the New Fabian Research Bureau, which he was instrumental in launching several months later, should affiliate directly with the Labour Party or sponsor candidates. SSIP was a coalition of disparate Labour elements: Attlee and Lansbury from the PLP, young Oxford intellectuals such as Hugh Gaitskell and Evan Durbin, left-wingers including Brailsford, William Mellor, Ellen Wilkinson, and Raymond Postgate, as well as Cole's prize catch, Bevin, who had been persuaded to serve as Chairman.

Stymied in their campaign to prevent the ILP from breaking with Labour, Brailsford and Wise established a National ILP Affiliation Committee after the Bradford conference. While regarding Labour as the only party with a chance of achieving socialism in England, they felt that the left should maintain a distinct identity, providing a rallying point for dissidents and prodding party leaders to abandon their cautious reformism. The two men began negotiations with SSIP with a view towards its amalgamation with the ILP affiliationists in a new socialist body. Brailsford, hoping the new organization would supplant the ILP as the ILP sought to replace Labour, wanted it to be free to engage in parliamentary activity, but Cole feared that such a policy would deflect SSIP from its original aim of inquiry and propaganda. The ex-ILP members, recognizing the need for concessions, promised to abandon the idea of sponsoring candidates, but they insisted that the new organization must affiliate with the Labour Party, against Cole's preference for detachment. Moreover, they were determined to impose Wise as Chairman of the new group in place of Bevin, towards whom Brailsford and Wise had nursed a grievance ever since his contemptuous dismissal of *The Living Wage*. Once agreement was reached, Brailsford drafted a constitution for the new Socialist League, and SSIP members

[74] *New Leader*, 15 July 1932.   [75] *Manchester Guardian*, 8 Aug. 1932.

were invited to an inaugural conference on 2 October. Although the League's founders intended to avoid the ILP's mistakes, it was clear that many of them were itching for battle, suspicious that Labour's new-found militancy might prove transitory. It was not ILP ideology, which they had helped to formulate, but its suicidal tactics that they repudiated.

Resignation from the ILP inevitably cost Brailsford his *New Leader* salary, but his reputation was such that he had little difficulty in finding new journalistic berths. The first proved temporary and, in view of the enmity between him and Bevin, somewhat ironic. In 1932 Bevin persuaded the TUC General Council to invest £2,000 to rehabilitate Blatchford's *Clarion* as an independent socialist weekly. Publication of the *New Clarion* began in June 1932, and Brailsford became a regular contributor during the twenty-one months of its existence. Much duller than his *New Leader* had been, the *New Clarion* encountered the same circulation problems, failing to reach the level needed to avoid a deficit.[76] In September 1932 he became a weekly columnist for the popular Sunday paper, *Reynolds' Illustrated News*. Sydney Elliott, its young editor, brought Brailsford onto the paper after terminating contracts of several regular contributors. Elliott, aiming to make *Reynolds* a working class *Sunday Times*, succeeded in doubling circulation to 500,000, providing him with perhaps the largest regular audience he ever received. The editor regarded Brailsford's column, for which he was paid six guineas per thousand words, the high point of the paper, the article readers turned to first. The other attachment, even more durable than his tie with *Reynolds*, was slower to develop. Shortly after Martin became *New Statesman* editor, Brailsford broached the possibility of writing for the weekly and in the course of the next two years established himself unofficially as principal leader-writer, interspersing occasional long essays with many of the short political comments that filled the *New Statesman*'s front pages.[77]

In many ways, personal as well as political, 1932 marked a significant turning point. The failure of the Disarmament Conference shattered hopes of European conciliation, while the Lytton Report destroyed the ebbing faith in the League. The disaffiliation of the ILP severed Brailsford's ties with the party and with the *New Leader*. That break with the past might well have been symbolized for him by the announcement in the Honours List of a peerage conferred on his former patron, Clifford Allen. Although in sharp disagreement ever

---

[76] Brailsford contributed 21 articles between September 1932 and February 1934, most of them on foreign affairs. See Bullock, *Bevin*, pp. 505-6.

[77] Interviews, Sydney Elliott, Kingsley Martin. Marked copies in the *New Statesman* archive indicate that Brailsford wrote 35 articles in 1933 and at least that number every year between 1934 and 1945.

since Allen allied himself with MacDonald, nothing underscored their divergence more clearly than Allen's elevation to the House of Lords. Brailsford's response to the peerage, greeted in socialist circles with derision, was expressed more in sorrow than in anger. His profound debt made him wish to congratulate Allen wholeheartedly, but he could not conceal his misgivings:

I have strongly wished in recent years that the Gov[t] had used your great powers in such ways as are possible, given your physical disabilities. I realise that a peerage may help. . . . You will realise that with my own strong sense of the class war & my old-fashioned objection to the monarchy & all that lumber, I don't like any Socialist to take a peerage, unless he must. . . .[78]

It was an honest letter, testimony to genuine affection, but it signalled an inevitable breach, concluding a chapter of his life. More than ever a man of the left, Brailsford would continue to follow his principles without compromising his integrity through the challenges that lay ahead.

[78] HNB to Clifford Allen, 21 Jan. [1932], AP, Box VIII.

XII

In the Nightmare of the Dark (1933-1938)

The early 1930s were, paradoxically, the happiest period in Brailsford's life, an interlude of contentment before his world was engulfed by darkness. With his reputation at its zenith, he had finally come to terms with his own limitations as a writer. Comfortable in his new arrangement with *Reynolds* and the *New Statesman*, he had become reconciled to not being an editor or producing monumental works. He was now an elder statesman in the socialist movement, respected, even more abroad than in England, but essentially unencumbered by institutional ties. When he spoke or wrote, he represented no viewpoint but his own. Even in the Socialist League, which he had helped to launch, he took a back seat, preferring, as was his style, to propagate ideas rather than assume administrative duties. Although his writing pace never slackened, the routine of his life—half the week in London and half in the country—seemed to leave more time for non-journalistic projects. *Property or Peace?*, his 'big' 1934 book, took much of the previous year to compose. It was the fruit of deep reflection, not hastily compiled from published articles as some of his earlier books had been. It was followed the next year by his favourite among his own works, *Voltaire*, a sequel to the Home University Library volume, *Shelley, Godwin and Their Circle*.

In the companionship of Clare Leighton he found a reprieve from the haunting loneliness he had known most of his life. Her exuberant spirits, her creative energy were the perfect anodynes for his brooding introspection. She helped him overcome his shyness and softened the asperity of his nature. It was Clare who began calling him Noel instead of Harry, who made him shed stiff-collared white shirts for more informal blue, who encouraged him to wear shorts and to sunbathe in the nude. If their relationship never entirely bridged the age difference, she brought sunlight into his life for the first time. She was his 'multiplier of delights', although those facets he cherished most—her youth, her talent, her vitality—later aroused his jealousy.[1] They were both engaged in arduous work: Brailsford chiefly in the ceaseless torrent of articles, Clare in commissions for books and posters.

Their partnership found expression in creating the garden at Four Hedges which provided the basis for her celebrated book of that name.

[1] Interview, Clare Leighton.

Here Brailsford could indulge his passion for gardening, frustrated since leaving Welwyn in 1919, his love of birds, and his need for privacy. So devoted did he become to his rustic retreat that Clare began to find it difficult to extricate him. He no longer had the same zest for foreign travel once he reached sixty, while she, hungering for new vistas after finishing a project, felt the constraints of domesticity.

With Clare, too, problems were never very far below the surface. Brailsford was highly-strung and prone to self-dramatization. His protective manner towards her, his tendency to put women on a pedestal and to treat them with 'old-world courtesy' may, as Martin suggested, have concealed 'an embarrassed disdain' for them.[2] Much as he would parade his egalitarian notions, he wished to dominate Clare as he had been unable to dominate Jane, and it seems clear that his involvement with successively younger women was a way of confirming his superiority. But self-doubt was not so easily submerged. Unlike Jane, avenging her own sense of inadequacy by belittling him, Clare was a professional success, hailed by critics as a major practitioner of her art. His pride in her accomplishments was coupled with envy: the monuments to her talent would, he suspected, outlast his evanescent contributions. Nor could he help but feel that her career would make her more independent of him, financially and socially, that their arrangement, never solemnized by law, would dissolve. At first she found in his gentle solicitude and perhaps even in his vulnerability a substitute for the doting father she had never had, for the elder brother she had lost. But once she began to spread her wings, to fulfil herself creatively, her need for him lessened, and the disparity of age loomed more menacingly. Life between them, as one friend observed, was 'never easy',[3] but for almost a decade it satisfied an emotional craving on both their parts.

The gardening and literary work, interspersed with music and travel, were only one side of Brailsford's life. Jane still lived in Kew in a state of 'complete degeneration',[4] a constant drain on his income and psychic energy. He usually visited her twice a week, but was in a nervous state anticipating a visit and dejected after it. Although he harboured a good deal of rancour against her, especially for denying him a divorce, he continued—until Clare prevailed upon him to desist for the sake of his own sanity—to inflict these self-torturing visits on himself, as though needing reminders of her alcoholic misery to spur his guilt feelings. But aside from her wretchedness, his own health was beginning to deteriorate. He suffered constantly from insomnia, exacerbated during periods of overwork or after visits to Jane, but refused at first to take sedatives. Over-exertion, whether from the strain of work

[2] Martin, *Editor*, p. 133.   [3] Interview, Leonard Elmhirst.   [4] ND, 27 Jan. 1933.

or the effort to keep pace with Clare when they cycled, induced a day or two of what he termed his 'malaise', presumably an intimation of angina that worsened in his later years.[5]

In January 1933 Brailsford arrived in the United States for his fourth lecture tour, which took him to California and to the Southwest during a five-week stay. He found Americans on the eve of the New Deal sunk into 'a blacker pessimism' than any he had witnessed since touring Central Europe in 1919. Cautiously approving Roosevelt's initial steps, he perceived the American desire for strong leadership. If the average American was still wary of socialism, he had at least been liberated from his obeisance to the idols of capitalism. Brailsford was sceptical about whether the new administration could control the economy without 'an experienced and trustworthy Civil Service',[6] even though Congress seemed willing to confer virtual economic dictatorship on the President. Roosevelt's first hundred days dispelled some of his doubts, and by July he was ready to hail him as a man of 'unusual courage and resource'.[7] His estimate of Roosevelt's achievement was to oscillate wildly during the next few years, alternately viewing him as the most audacious leader outside Russia or as a 'simple-minded Liberal' afraid to tackle Big Business.[8]

When he returned to England in late March 1933, he was contemplating a trip to China the following winter, but by the end of the year his health had broken down completely. He had had to give up an assignment to cover the Reichstag fire trial in Leipzig to George Catlin[9] and abandon any thought of going to China. Early in 1934 he was under medical orders to cease working altogether and to go abroad for an extended rest, even suspending his *Reynolds* column for six weeks. Settling on the Austrian Tyrol, he no sooner arrived than civil war broke out in Vienna between the clerical-Fascist government and the socialists, many of whom were old friends. Although forbidden to exert himself, he announced early one morning that he was going to Vienna; he could not, he informed Clare, 'let the comrades down'. Her pleas finally induced him to leave Austria instead and spend the remainder of their holiday in Corsica.[10]

These domestic incidents and physical infirmities, significant biographically, provide a backdrop to the public events with which he was

[5] Interview, Clare Leighton.
[6] *Reynolds*, 19 Feb. 1933; *New Statesman*, 18 Mar. 1933.
[7] *New Clarion*, 22 July 1933.
[8] *Property or Peace?*, p. 114; *Reynolds*, 13 May 1934.
[9] Interview, Sir George Catlin. Vera Brittain suggested that Brailsford withdrew because he was already 'suspect' in Germany and feared that his movements would be impeded. Vera Brittain, *Testament of Experience* (London, 1957), p. 98.
[10] Interview, Clare Leighton.

preoccupied. Until the Spanish Civil War the private and public spheres did not entirely converge: Hitler's accession to power did not impinge on life at Four Hedges, although his new radio allowed him to listen to Nazi rallies without even leaving his Chiltern garden.[11] By 1936 that detachment was no longer possible for him. For fifteen years he had warned what might happen if the peace treaties were not revised, if reparations were not scrapped, if European governments continued to pursue deflationary policies at the cost of millions of jobs, and although he took little comfort in his prescience, he was by 1933 more or less resigned. But the assault on the Spanish republic was something unanticipated, its impact on him so devastating that it was to affect not merely his perspective on European affairs, but his personal life as well.

Brailsford's initial verdict on Hitler was perhaps even less perspicacious than his prediction of peace in the spring of 1914. Confident that the regime would come to resemble its Hohenzollern predecessors more than its Fascist neighbours, he expressed doubts 'whether there will be fewer Jews in a more Nordic Germany when Hitler's reign is over than there are today'. Instead of consolidation of Nazi rule, he expected that the workers would be driven into some kind of 'uneasy, unorganised unity of action to resist this offensive of the old ruling class'.[12] Nor was there any reason to perceive the new Germany as a military threat. With its virulence directed against socialists and Jews, Nazism was 'a phase of the German class-war', attacking trade unions and democratic parties in order to crush the working class. Since his 'sadist nationalism' could be 'fully satisfied at home', there seemed no reason to doubt that Hitler would pursue a 'prudent' foreign policy, much as Mussolini had.[13]

These sanguine assumptions he partly retracted in *The Nazi Terror*, a Socialist League pamphlet written in April 1933. Based on information derived from *The Times* and *Manchester Guardian* and from press cuttings accumulated by Nevinson, it documented attacks on socialists, Communists, and Jews, offering some of the first allusions to the Dachau concentration camp to appear in England. Yet here, and later in *Property or Peace?*, he was concerned not so much to condemn as to explain how Nazism had gained a foothold. As the 'conscious enemy of rationalism', it appealed to the frustrated and the insecure, who had seen their savings vanish along with their hopes.[14] If Germany was in 'an abnormal mental condition', its opponents needed to discover a

---

[11] See *New Republic*, 21 June 1933.
[12] *World Tomorrow*, 1 Mar. 1933.
[13] *New Statesman*, 25 Mar. 1933; *World Tomorrow*, 12 Apr. 1933.
[14] *Property or Peace?*, pp. 47-8; *The Nazi Terror* (1933).

cure; punishment would merely aggravate the persecution mania on which it fed. Enemies of Fascism should make clear their disgust at 'this madly nationalist, persecuting, reactionary, Jew-baiting, militarist dictatorship', but any attempt to apply external coercion would only

rally the greater part of the nation behind Hitler, and even when he fell under foreign pressure would leave it in such a state of mind that no internationally-minded government, whether Liberal or Socialist, could possibly maintain itself.[15]

Until Hitler actually assumed power, Brailsford had intended to visit Germany to observe the situation at first hand. He turned down an invitation from Bräuning-Oktavio, a convert to Nazism, who wrote extolling the new regime. 'I am a Marxist,' he replied,

an internationalist and a writer. If I had been a German my books would have been publicly burnt, and I should have spent this summer in a concentration camp. Am I to visit a country which has treated many of my friends in this way? There is also the difficulty that I could not bring myself to give the Hitler salute and that might cause me to be beaten by any storm trooper who saw me.[16]

The unsolicited letter from his wartime protégé, their first communication in several years, gave him a startling insight into the German response to Hitler, which he immediately imparted to *Reynolds* readers. He described Bräuning-Oktavio—called 'Dr. A.' in the article—as 'a born enthusiast, emotional, sensitive, incapable of self-seeking, but not very stable in character'. Since he would never see the article, Brailsford felt himself able to write frankly. Until January 1933 'Dr. A.' had been hostile towards the Nazis. Now, to Brailsford's horror, he was cursing himself 'for his failure to understand Hitler's greatness'. The letter helped him comprehend the emotional state of the German people, to realize that Nazi speeches could fire the enthusiasm even of a man with such 'generosity of mind', although he could only assume that 'Dr. A.' knew nothing of 'the beastliness of concentration camps' or what was happening to Jews and trade unionists.[17]

Somewhat to Brailsford's embarrassment, the *Reynolds* piece came to the attention of Bräuning-Oktavio, who indignantly denied the charge that he was deluded about Nazism. Brailsford, in a lengthy reply, insisted 'that in *thousands* of cases Socialists and others have been cruelly beaten in the Brown Houses and in the Camps, merely because they were Socialists'. Because of censorhip, it might be awkward to transmit

[15] Letter to Editor, *New Statesman*, 21 Oct. 1933.
[16] HNB to H. Bräuning-Oktavio, 1 Nov. 1933, BOP.
[17] *Reynolds*, 5 Nov. 1933.

documentary proof to show that 50,000 were imprisoned without trial, but he had ample evidence from American, Austrian, and Dutch sources, as well as from F. A. Voigt, the *Manchester Guardian* correspondent. Nor would he allow Bräuning-Oktavio to claim that charges of mistreatment of Jews had been exaggerated:

> What is not disputed—since the decrees have all been published—is that it is now impossible for the greater number of Jewish professional men, lawyers, doctors, teachers, journalists, musicians, to earn their bread in Germany. I could forgive a few outrages done in hot excitement. But this cold-blooded sentence to death by starvation is a terrible blot on the record of a great nation.[18]

While it became ever more apparent that Hitler's was a 'diseased mind', he did not feel that the Germans would begin to see 'the disadvantages of keeping a madman as dictator' until they overcame their sense of inferiority.[19] Candid about Fascist evil, he doggedly urged, at least until 1936, appeasement as the most effective antidote to Nazism:

> To me it seems axiomatic, that however much one may loathe this Nazi movement, the first element of a cure is to remove Germany's wrongs. It is unfortunate that Europe will have to concede to Hitler what the Allies refused to Rathenau, Stresemann and Brüning. But to persevere in injustice, because our victim has begun to look repulsive in the convulsions of his resentment, is neither right nor wise.[20]

Allied statesmen who might balk at the invidious task of submitting to a dictator's ravings had only themselves to blame. Instead of yielding to Hitler's demands, it would be better to anticipate them; by removing the causes of grievance, the Allies would atone for their sins, showing the German nation that equitable treatment was possible without recourse to violence.

Aside from renewed appeals for disarmament, Brailsford could only counsel patience until the German people were ready to shed the Fascist incubus. Although his attitude towards resistance to Hitler's demands stiffened dramatically later in the decade, he contended from 1933 until after the Second World War that Germans alone could determine their fate and that elements within German society remained uncontaminated by Nazism. He had faith in the resilience of democratic impulses, especially among the young, and was heartened by contacts with members of *Neu Beginnen*, a left-wing underground organization, impressed by their opposition to Hitler rather than their ideological

---

[18] HNB to H. Bräuning-Oktavio, 1 Feb. 1934. Brailsford saw him twice in London, during business trips in 1935 and 1936, but the correspondence ceased.
[19] *New Statesman*, 11 Aug. 1934; *Reynolds*, 18 Nov. 1934.
[20] *Property or Peace?*, p. 291.

viewpoint. His preface to the English edition of their manifesto, affirming the 'debts of comradeship' that the British labour movement owed to the German working class, warned that 'until it stands on its feet again, there is no secure future for us'.[21] To Brailsford, Nazism was a malignancy which had afflicted a desperately misguided nation, an aberration which disrupted historical traditions, not their logical fulfilment. A middle class demoralized by defeat and economic insecurity, a working class trapped in internecine quarrels, were too enfeebled in 1933 to offer more than token resistance to Hitler, but, given time, the German spirit would heal itself.

As long as Hitler's ambitions did not appear to exceed revision of the peace terms, Brailsford was loath to condemn. Indeed so repugnant was that settlement that he actually endorsed its violation:

> For my part, I should deny that Germany could be guilty of a moral aggression. Any physical act of revolt or protest would be an outbreak against the iniquitous Treaty of Versailles.[22]

It was not transgressions against a bankrupt settlement that aroused his misgivings, but the realization that making amends might consign more innocent victims to tyranny. This 'hideous dilemma' became all too apparent when the Saarlanders were subjected to intimidation in the months before the 1935 plebiscite. Despite the obligation to hold the plebiscite, he shuddered at the prospect of 'placing any additional millions under this despotism'.[23]

Brailsford had clearly not yet taken Hitler's full measure. Anticipating a substantial negative vote in the Saar by workers and Catholics, he surmised that such a result, dealing 'a heavy blow to the prestige of the Nazi regime', would move Hitler 'to greater caution and moderation'.[24] That it failed to materialize in no way shook his confident assumptions. Admitting that the return to conscription several months later violated the treaty, he urged the League to refrain from censure:

> One wishes that the Allies had themselves spontaneously revised this miserable Treaty many a year ago. They lacked the wisdom to do it. Let us, then, have the frankness to say plainly that the Germans were justified in breaking it so soon as they had the will and the power.

By 1935 he was impelled to explain to his readers why he was 'arguing for tolerance and sanity' towards Hitler instead of lining up with the Soviet Union against this 'enemy of the whole working class movement'. What was the alternative? Collective security on British terms

---

[21] 'Miles' [pseud. of Walter Löwenheim], *Socialism's New Start: A Secret German Manifesto* (1934), pp. 7-10. The pamphlet was published in England by the National Council of Labour Colleges. Also see *Reynolds*, 28 Dec. 1941.

[22] *Property or Peace?*, p. 297.   [23] *Reynolds*, 21 Jan. 1934.   [24] *Reynolds*, 6 Jan. 1935.

could only mean an alliance with men like Mussolini to fight for 'the sanctity of the Versailles treaty', rather than for the interests of the workers.[25] He would refuse to believe that England sincerely desired reconciliation until its representatives boldly offered Tanganyika or South-West Africa to Germany or offered to scrap its battleships on a reciprocal basis.[26]

When Brailsford counselled against ILP disaffiliation in 1932, he expressed the belief that Labour had, after the experience of MacDonald's betrayal, 'abandoned the old gradualist, reformist tactics'.[27] Admittedly under left-wing pressure, Labour accepted the case for nationalizing joint stock banks as well as the Bank of England, a clear sign that the party had at last 'embarked on a struggle for economic power'.[28] But the honeymoon between affiliationists and the leaders of the party and the trade union movement was fleeting. By the time Brailsford returned from America in the spring of 1933, the Socialist League had come to be regarded as a disruptive clique of left-wing intellectuals, seeking to foist an extreme policy on a party edging back towards the middle ground. Just as Labour's leaders feared that the League might become an electoral handicap, so he and others revised their estimate of Labour's avowed commitment to socialism. Denigrated by the NEC and the trade union leaders, the League found itself cast in the same factional role that had recently bedevilled the ILP.[29] While redoubling propagandist efforts, with lectures and pamphlets throughout 1933, League spokesmen, including Brailsford, sought to avoid ILP mistakes. What gave a new stimulus to this activity was Hitler's rise to power over the virtually inert bodies of the German left. It was in order to prevent a similar fate in England that the ILP forsook its isolation, calling for unity with the Communists in order to combat Fascism. Such a solution, he felt, had 'singularly little relevance to our British problem'. With nothing separating it from the Communists 'save a doubt in the invariable wisdom of Muscovite leadership', the ILP was destined to fade slowly from the scene, those members not joining the Communists escaping extinction by returning to the Labour fold.[30] The prognosis of Strachey's *Coming Struggle for Power,* which Brailsford reviewed while still in America, seemed to him even more suicidal. A simplistic application of the Marxist dialectic to England, the naïve belief in the receptivity of British proletarians to revolutionary doctrine, was misguided. The existence of 'the ancestral memory of

[25] *Reynolds*, 24 Mar. 1935.
[26] *Reynolds*, 12 May 1935.
[27] *New Leader*, 15 July 1932.
[28] *World Tomorrow*, 2 Nov. 1932.
[29] See Ben Pimlott, *Labour and the Left in the 1930s* (Cambridge, 1977), pp. 48-54.
[30] *New Republic*, 31 May 1933.

a revolutionary parliament' offered hope that England would not have to follow the Russian model.[31]

It was just this problem to which Brailsford turned in 1933: the achievement of socialism without violent revolution. His writings sought a *via media* between the supine constitutionalism of the German Social Democrats and the dogmatic subservience to Moscow, between the unimaginative gradualism of Labour and the bastard Leninism of the born-again revolutionaries. Yet he was unsure of his own position, doubtful about whether a peaceful transition to socialism was possible even in England. Much as he might dispute the simple polarity posed by Strachey and others, who saw Communism as the only alternative to Fascism in the West, Brailsford feared that England was at least 'moving into a fascist climate'.[32]

His own confusion emerged in letters to Victor Gollancz, who had suggested a book linking capitalism and war to complement Strachey's controversial tract. 'The main difficulty', Brailsford told his prospective publisher,

is (1) my deep scepticism as to my whole political orientation—in short how far am I a Communist & if not, why not? So (2) while this perplexity lasts, I incline to concentrate on some positive work, & I am engrossed in a most intriguing study of primitive religion. . . . If I do the book, I think it will be a rather broader subject than you suggest—the necessity of socialism, with the argument about war as a main part of the case.[33]

In fact, he could not let the subject alone: rather than devote his time to primitive religion, he plunged into writing *Property or Peace?*, his most avowedly Marxist work. Grounded in dialectical reasoning, yet laced with impassioned idealism, it occupied him for the rest of the year, and he was not able to deliver it to Gollancz until early in 1934. That his health suffered was perhaps as much the result of mental anguish during its composition as of physical deterioration. The most tightly organized of his books, it was to make little impression on the left. In contrast to *The War of Steel and Gold*, which opened the eyes of socialists disenchanted with Liberal foreign policy, *Property or Peace?* struck a discordant note of independent leftism. Flying in the face of fellow-travelling orthodoxy, exemplified by Strachey and later by the Left Book Club, Brailsford could be dismissed too easily as a bourgeois apologist. That he continued to praise parliamentary democracy, to criticize terrorism and enforced orthodoxy in the Soviet Union, gained him few friends among those proclaiming the primacy of socialist unity.

[31] *World Tomorrow*, 15 Mar. 1933.
[32] *New Republic*, 22 Aug. 1934.
[33] HNB to Victor Gollancz, 19 Mar. 1933, Gollancz Papers.

While writing *Property or Peace?* Brailsford also contributed to a series of pronouncements by Socialist League members and published in August 1933 under the collective title *Problems of a Socialist Government*. In defining a socialist foreign policy, he disavowed the 'catastrophic' approach which endorsed a 'useful war' to promote world socialism. Even if some gain might be anticipated, every attempt should be made to avert war in the knowledge that there were 'values in life superior even to the interests, or supposed interest of Socialism'. On the other hand, he insisted that patriotic scruples should not prevent a socialist party from exposing 'exploitation by the capitalists of its own country', even if it seemed to put ammunition in the hands of foreign critics.[34]

Property or Peace? extended this analysis to show that democracy could only be attained within a socialist society. Weimar had failed because the republic had never possessed those 'strategical keys to power' which the Bolsheviks had seized promptly in 1917. Victimized by fastidiousness, the Social Democrats had relied on the illusory security of the constitutional mechanism, convinced that the electorate would rally to the republic. The moral of the German experience was that 'democracy will go down helpless to defeat, if it has left in the hands of the owning class land and the main sources of private wealth, legal authority and the armed forces'.[35] The democratic state turned out to be 'an imposing facade behind which the real forces of Property work undisturbed for their own purposes',[36] diverting tax revenue into military appropriations to safeguard overseas investment, using legislative devices to frustrate the efforts of the working class to curb the rapacity of business. Nor did Brailsford believe any longer, as he had when writing *Olives of Endless Age*, that the impetus was towards greater internationalism; instead economic forces were reinforcing nationalism and the goal of self-sufficiency. The vision of federation, to which he had clung ever since 1914, now seemed remote and disarmament a hopeless undertaking as long as nations clung to the myth of sovereignty.

Order in economic life and in world affairs, then, awaited the abolition of private property, and the immediate crisis dictated prompt action. The elements of control he articulated were familiar, sketched out in *The Living Wage* and ILP programmes during the late 1920s. In contrast to Labour, which concentrated on utilities and transportation, he argued that the encroachment of public control should continue until all important industries and services had been socialized. This would contribute to the single purpose of eliminating private property and securing community control over the economy. Once achieved,

[34] 'A Socialist Foreign Policy', in *Problems of a Socialist Government* (London, 1933), pp. 252-86.
[35] *Property or Peace?*, pp. 41, 46. [36] Ibid., pp. 226-7.

'we can afford to compromise, to soften the rigours of the transition, to deal tenderly with harmless survivals'.[37]

There was little in this critique to set Brailsford apart from Strachey or from Laski at his most polemical. Not even Dutt would fault his stringent indictment of private property or of the partnership between capitalism and imperialism. Where he differed was in his prescription for the future. Half-measures must yield to the assumption of total control over the economy, but this should be done by constitutional means. Despite obstruction by the owning classes, the obstacles to military victory in a civil war launched by socialists would be overwhelming. It was preferable to allow property owners to resort to arms first, so that should a physical struggle ensue, the workers would be fighting with a parliamentary majority behind them.

His plan for implementing the economic programme echoed Socialist League advocates, especially Stafford Cripps. Since the traditional legislative machinery was too cumbersome, Parliament should limit itself to general economic planning, leaving details to technical authorities. Anticipating resistance from financial interests, a majority socialist government would be obliged to obtain emergency powers from Parliament and abolish the House of Lords to prevent obstruction. He also asserted that nationalized industries should be under the control of the responsible minister, allowing the widest scope for initiative from the technical staff, but with workers represented only on consultative bodies. More concerned to obtain the best managers rather than satisfy demands for worker control, he was willing to sacrifice participation to professionalism.

In his aspirations for a classless society he looked approvingly at the Russian model while rejecting Soviet methods. The danger of suppressing dissent, whether in the press or parties, was that it would precipitate civil war. But there was a deeper risk in adopting the Soviet pattern: however disinterested the motive, 'we should ourselves degenerate if we came to fear criticism, even rabid and disingenuous criticism'. In the name of social justice, terror could all too easily become institutionalized, and repression, hesitant perhaps at first, grow progressively easier. 'One begins by suppressing Mensheviks: one ends by suppressing Trotsky.' At that point a revolutionary movement became a dictatorship. Nothing showed his ambivalence more clearly than his concluding assertion that

the world may one day come to join in the honours that Russians pay to Marx. But the world will then be a medieval monastery, unless, while it honours him, it is free to doubt and deny every word he uttered.[38]

[37] Ibid., p. 245.   [38] Ibid., pp. 312-14.

In walking a tight-rope between democratic liberalism and Marxist regimentation, Brailsford satisfied few readers. The nucleus of his new world order would be socialist Britain and Communist Russia, but he shied away from proposing federal union because their traditions were too dissimilar. He warned that the propertied classes would resist expropriation, but sought to retain parliamentary institutions and the electoral process. He looked towards a new democratic society, but it would be one in which experts and professionals made the crucial decisions. When Allen criticized him for advocating a socialist alliance as an alternative to the League and for implying that freedom was a societal rather than an individual trait, Brailsford reproached his old friend for deserting the cause in which they had both once believed:

Your whole difference from us 'Marxists' (I don't mind the name, tho' it's not wholly accurate) is that you now repudiate the class struggle, ignore the dynamic structure of society, and fall back on a flat 18th century intellectualism.[39]

It was perhaps merely a coincidence that he chastised Allen for '18th century intellectualism' when he was himself embarking on a study of Voltaire, the quintessential Enlightenment intellectual. He had been commissioned to write a brief life of Ferdinand Lassalle for a projected Hamish Hamilton series entitled 'Makers of the New World'. After a few volumes were published—including Dutt's *Lenin* and H. L. Beales's *Early English Socialists*—the project was abandoned for lack of sales.[40] Instead of Lassalle, useful for Brailsford's long-term scheme for a history of socialism, he turned, somewhat surprisingly, to a suggested volume on Voltaire for the Home University Library. As a student *Candide* had made little impression on him, its references to the savagery of war and slavery more relevant to a bygone age. He rediscovered it in a Greek bookshop in Monastir in 1903 and read it amid burned villages that made it seem a contemporary document. But if its pertinence in a Macedonian setting made *Candide* seem alive, it was his admiration for Voltaire himself that prompted him to write the book and to edit an anthology for Everyman's Library.

Brailsford's *Voltaire* is the most perfect piece he ever wrote. In less than 150 pages he surveyed his entire corpus, attesting to the merit of some works, underscoring the defects in others. What seems extraordinary is that he found time to read the collected works of so prolific a writer, plays as well as histories, and to provide a vivid account of

---

[39] Lord Allen of Hurtwood, *Britain's Political Future* (London, 1934), pp. 65, 130; HNB to Clifford (Lord) Allen, n.d. [?Oct. 1934], AP, Box XII.
[40] Interview, H. L. Beales.

Voltaire's life and times. Voltaire's personal frailties were never denied, but it was the ways in which he transcended the values of eighteenth-century French society that attracted Brailsford—the disinterested passion for justice, the affirmation of rationality against intolerance and supernatural religion, the relentless war against cruelty and fanaticism. Like Brailsford, Voltaire had liberated himself and made his own career by rebelling against a religious father; like Brailsford, he rejected nationalism and the authority of monarchy and church, encompassing all of humanity—or at least enlightened humanity—in his cosmopolitan aspirations. Brailsford could appreciate as well Voltaire's affinity for British institutions and for the spirit of tolerance, inquiry, and freedom he had encountered during his exile in England. Hailing him as the first historian of modern Europe, Brailsford, writing in 1935, found it impossible to absolve him for failing 'to face the crude issue of power. The old order would not reform itself till it was forced to yield.'[41] Even Voltaire's clarion call, *écrasez l'infâme*, however liberating, suggested something of the misplaced emphasis of Enlightenment thinkers. 'Were dogma and fanaticism,' he speculated with Marxist hindsight, 'really the exciting causes of all these cruelties and oppressions, or were the dogmas rather the symbols in a savage war of classes?'[42] If Voltaire's historical perspective was limited, his commitment to freedom and tolerance constituted a timeless legacy to his intellectual heirs, among whom Brailsford counted himself.

With the manuscript of *Voltaire* completed in August 1935, he prepared to leave for his fifth American lecture tour. During his absence in America *Reynolds* published his seven-part series on a socialist foreign policy, extending ideas put forward in early Socialist League publications. Several months earlier he had written in the *Socialist Leaguer* that 'the whole police mechanism, known as collective security, is merely a means of perpetuating the dictatorship of the Versailles victors'.[43] Since then his views had begun to change very slightly. While continuing to insist that no socialist party should consider a League decision as sufficient grounds for participation in war, he now conceded that if a Tory government or the League were supporting the Soviet Union in a defensive war, 'we ought to back them—albeit with our eyes open'.[44] By the end of 1935 he had begun to advocate collective action by socialist states acting within the Geneva framework. Such a plan, presupposing socialist or Popular Front governments in England and France, was later extended to include Spain and Scandanavia, but its basis was unity with the Soviet Union.[45]

[41] *Voltaire*, p. 64. [42] Ibid., p. 120.
[43] *Socialist Leaguer*, May 1935.
[44] *Reynolds*, 24 Nov., 1 Dec. 1935.
[45] *Reynolds*, 8 Dec. 1935.

It was the Abyssinian crisis that persuaded him that the Fascist threat might have to be met by military action. Neutrality, which he had once advocated for socialists, seemed no longer a viable option. Yet it would be an exaggeration to attribute consistency to Brailsford's articles in 1935-6. He was confused, unsure whether peace could be salvaged and under what conditions. He castigated the League as the tool of England and France, but appealed for collective League action against Mussolini. Even as he defended the liberal tradition against cynical Marxists, he thought it ill-advised to 'pretend that Tory England is arming to defend democracy against Fascism'. The purpose of the escalating arms budgets, which he opposed, was 'to maintain the gains of the last war' and preserve investment and trading monopolies overseas.[46] Alternately pleading for restraint and resistance in dealings with Hitler, he appealed for disarmament while contemplating a military response by the forces of a socialist alliance. While his position on Abyssinia was unambiguous, it was not until the start of the Spanish Civil War that he ceased to advocate appeasement and to call for military measures even at the risk of war. In his progression from support for concessions to Hitler and mass resistance to war to encouragement of a broad Popular Front and even of conscription, the major signposts were Abyssinia, Spain, and Munich. He did not willingly become a patriot or endorse a war that Communists would continue to denounce as imperialistic, but it seemed the only way to uphold the values he had never abandoned.

Brailsford's initial response to Mussolini's designs on Abyssinia was deliberately cautious. He found little to admire in 'this backward people', a country where life was 'cheap and cruelty common'. Once it became clear that Mussolini would not be deflected, Brailsford's stance toughened: the Italian threat to Abyssinia was a direct challenge to the League of Nations.[47] For the first time he began to see the ramifications of a Fascist success: Mussolini's unimpeded advance was an open invitation to Hitler. What seems remarkable is Brailsford's shift in attitude towards the League: in May he advised socialists to abstain from League punitive action; by September he was urging the League Council to prevent a breach of the Covenant by applying 'the whole weight of its sanctions at least in the economic field'. Only if the League took up the challenge, using 'its overwhelming strength and authority', would it be able 'to rid Europe of a dictator whose insane recklessness is a menace to the world'.[48] If his strong pro-League

[46] *Reynolds*, 23 Feb. 1936.
[47] *New Statesman*, 16 Feb., 6 July 1935. According to the magazine's chronicler, Martin had commissioned Brailsford to make clear Europe's choice: Mussolini or the League. The *New Statesman* editorial view was strongly pro-League throughout the crisis. Edward Hyams, *The New Statesman* (London, 1963), p. 153.   [48] *New Statesman*, 7 Sept. 1935.

stance was prompted by Martin, he qualified his position a few weeks later in *Reynolds*. Here he reiterated the view that the labour movement should be wary of unreserved support of the League of Nations. But he now regarded it as a 'mistake to oppose or resist sanctions on principle'.[49]

With Mussolini's victory Brailsford not only reverted to strictures against the National government and the League, but revived proposals to appease Hitler. The Rhineland reoccupation in March 1936 dramatized the issue in all its perplexity: Hitler had been undeniably 'violent and unscrupulous', but had he any alternative to a unilateral revocation of the Rhineland clauses? 'If he has broken a treaty,' Brailsford declared with maddening even-handedness, 'did not the victors break their solemn, written promise to reduce their armaments to the Versailles level?' Hitler's recklessness showed the urgency of negotiations between 'the sated Empires and the hungry Powers' over the divisive issues of closed markets, fields of investment, and raw materials—the substantive questions that lay at the root of economic conflict.[50] He was less certain than he had been the year before that it would be 'a good thing merely to pass chunks of the British Empire over to Fascist Powers', but it was imperative for the victors to take the initiative in resolving outstanding differences.[51] He opposed Anglo-French military conversations as an 'obstacle to appeasement', deploring military measures against Germany 'when there is no reason to suspect her of any aggressive intention'.[52] His Marxist interpretation of capitalist war and his estrangement from proponents of collective security within a League context can be seen at its most egregious in an article entitled 'Resist War: Defend Socialism', in which he asked,

Will you fight to maintain the right of Czechoslovakia to hold three million German subjects against their will? Will you lead English and French workers to the shambles to maintain a clerical-fascist dictatorship in Vienna?.... The survival of most of these States in their present form does not appear to me to be a Socialist interest, and I would pledge no worker's blood to defend them.

At the same time he argued, somewhat contradictorily, that if Baldwin continued 'retreating before the Dictators, democracy and Socialism will go down undefended in Europe as they did in Germany'.[53]

This article, cloaking its author's ambivalence in rhetorical invective, appeared in the autumn of 1936, ironically just when his views were undergoing rapid revision. Much of his writing during the spring and summer had intimated the need for a new departure, a 're-orientation'

[49] *Reynolds*, 22 Sept. 1935. [50] *Reynolds*, 15 Mar. 1936.
[51] *New Statesman*, 4 Apr. 1936. [52] *Reynolds*, 5 Apr. 1936.
[53] *New Fabian Research Bureau Quarterly*, No. 11 (Autumn, 1936), pp. 35-7.

in thinking about European security. In May 1936 he was still calling for mass resistance to 'any capitalist-imperialist war, even if Geneva should bless it', while proposing a kind of contingent collective security. Vigilant detachment was essential under capitalism, but once a socialist government was elected, it would be possible to build a 'Federation of Socialist and like-minded States' with the Soviet Union as 'our chief partner'.[54] In a lengthy pamphlet published by the *New Statesman* under the title *Towards a New League* he traced the League's failures during the previous sixteen years. As he had argued ever since the war, a federal solution was the only way to build a lasting peace, but that involved abandonment of national sovereignty. The impossibility of achieving it made his proposal for an 'inner League' more relevant. Rather than quit the League, it would form 'a resolute vanguard, bent on using every lever of its machinery to keep the peace'. Instead of defining the group in exclusive ideological terms, he called for a People's Front, consisting of those European countries prepared to renounce imperialism and lay the foundations of an international Federal Union.[55]

The appeal of a Popular Front, sparked by the new coalitions in France and Spain, placed Brailsford in a dilemma. Ever since 1932 he had been a staunch proponent of socialist unity, to which the Socialist League was committed. A broader alliance, violating the doctrine he had repeatedly defended, raised the possibility of a breach with political allies, as he indicated in a frank letter to Cripps:

Through the last month or more my mind has been moving, at first reluctantly, but in the end decidedly in favour of a Front Populaire in this country. At first I thought I'd keep silence & let it happen—if it does, without participating. Now I find I can't keep silence much longer. . . . I realise that if I take this line I may have to resign from the S. L.
Now for my reasons,
It's the international situation that moves me. I see no hope of avoiding war, or of saving Russia if it does come, unless we can soon create a firm defensive alliance of England, France & Russia, plus some smaller 'Left' States. But only a Left Government in this country would enter such an alliance with Russia. . . . How then to get this Left Govt? . . . I argue that the formation of a People's Front would be a new event so startling that it would (1) interest the apathetic elector (2) win by-elections and (3) shake the Govt so severely that it might fall. I'm relying more on these psychological effects than on the numerical weight of the Liberal & Communist & ILP votes. Finally I assume that we should secure men like Keynes, [Sir Arthur] Salter etc, some Left Tories & many non-party men, whose experience & abilities would give us the team we need for administrative efficiency.

As to programme, my big hazardous assumption is that all three parties can

[54] *New Statesman*, 9 May 1936.
[55] *Towards a New League*, *New Statesman* pamphlet (1936), esp. pp. 60-3.

be won for this alliance with France & Russia within the League.

I should stipulate at home for some measure of socialisation covering coal, electricity, railway, armaments & perhaps land. . . .[56]

Cripps's reply has not survived, but if he encouraged the initiative, it was for the moment to no avail. During that summer he and Mellor had been negotiating with representatives of the ILP and the CPGB with the aim of achieving greater unity. Cripps shared the Communist preference for a French-style coalition but the ILP, backed by Mellor, prevailed, and a broad-based alliance was scrapped in favour of an exclusive united front of working-class parties.[57] For several months Brailsford continued to advocate a Popular Front, but he gradually yielded to Socialist League pressure. Thus in the coming weeks he reiterated the view that 'the one expedient that may save us' is the formation of 'an international People's Front', the first step towards which would be the establishment of a Popular Front in England to save 'our menaced democratic civilisation'.[58] But by the end of 1936 he had trimmed his sails, calling for unity with the Communists and the ILP, but not with the Liberals.

The Unity Manifesto of January 1937, which Brailsford endorsed, demanded resistance to Fascism, opposition to rearmament, closer union between Great Britain, France, and the Soviet Union, as well as measures of socialization at home. It was correctly perceived in Labour circles as yet another Communist attempt to penetrate the party. For Brailsford, the Unity Campaign was 'an effort to bring new and vital forces into the official movement, so that we may all oppose a united front to Fascism and Imperialist war'. But while few would dispute that the Labour Party had by the mid-thirties 'ceased to be the national vehicle for the emotions and aspirations of the masses', there was little sign that an isolated and ineffective ILP and a miniscule Leninist party had any more appeal for the mainstream of the working class.[59] In any event the Labour leadership proved intransigent: on 27 January 1937 the NEC resolved to disaffiliate the Socialist League, placing those, like Brailsford, who had always opposed fragmentation in something of a quandary.

The same view of Labour's bankruptcy and the need for socialist unity led to the formation of the Left Book Club in May 1936. Like *Tribune*, launched eight months later, it hoped to appeal to a large audience receptive to socialist propaganda without falling prey to sectarian divisiveness. The literature to be disseminated would be avowedly anti-

[56] HNB to Stafford Cripps, 31 July 1936, Cripps Papers.
[57] See Pimlott, pp. 94-9.
[58] *New Statesman*, 15 Aug. 1936. Also *New Republic*, 23 Sept. 1936.
[59] *Reynolds*, 24 Jan. 1937.

Fascist, but contributors would form a kind of intellectual Popular Front, including Liberals, socialists, and Communists. Brailsford's experience revealed the LBC to be distinctly more sympathetic to the Communist line than it admitted publicly, less because of Strachey's Marxist affinities than because of Gollancz's reluctance to sponsor works critical of the Soviet Union. Shortly after the LBC was formed, Gollancz suggested that Brailsford undertake a history of socialism, a proposal not only suited to his scholarly inclinations, but to the Club's desire for books that helped its members respond to the exigencies of Fascism, war, and poverty.

In June 1936 Brailsford agreed to a 75,000-word book, which would include some socialist theory, but focus mainly on the highlights of working-class history—the Commune, the post-war revolutionary attempts in Central Europe, and, above all, the Soviet revolution. He expected to complete it by the end of 1936, after clearing his desk of smaller projects such as *Towards a New League*.[60] Within a few weeks, however, he began to have misgivings about the enforced brevity. Instead of the original plan, he proposed two volumes, dividing the history in 1914. Alternatively he broached the idea of a short book on international policy, less theoretical and more descriptive than *Property or Peace?*[61] This alternative appealed to Gollancz, then projecting an educational series to be called the New People's Library, a kind of left version of the Home University Library.[62] Without retracting the suggestion of a history of socialism, Gollancz invited Brailsford to contribute a short volume on 'why capitalism means war', the dominant theme in his writings ever since *The War of Steel and Gold*.

If Brailsford cooled to the original scheme because of the difficulty of compressing so vast a subject, Gollancz became apprehensive about his heterodox views on the Soviet Union. Although he had always praised the Soviet experiment while deploring repression, it was his outspoken condemnation of the purge trials in August and September 1936, only weeks after the LBC proposal, that perturbed Gollancz. Until then Brailsford's criticism of Soviet justice had been sufficiently muted to pass almost unnoticed by its defenders. Thus when six British engineers were arrested in Russia in March 1933 on charges of sabotage and espionage, the brunt of his attack fell on the British government for retaliating by imposing an embargo on Russian goods.[63] After the wave of purges that followed the December 1934 Kirov assassination, Brailsford tried to intercede privately with Maisky, a friend from

---

[60] HNB to Victor Gollancz, 2 June 1936, Gollancz Papers.
[61] HNB to Victor Gollancz, 28 July [1936], Gollancz Papers.
[62] Cf. John Lewis, *The Left Book Club: An Historical Record* (London, 1970), pp. 80-1.
[63] *Reynolds*, 23 Apr. 1933.

pre-revolutionary days, but the ambassador could have done little even had he been inclined to risk his own career.[64] These misgivings, rare though they were on the British left, in no way vitiated Brailsford's support for an international socialist front against Fascism, nor did it prevent his affiliation with the Congress of Peace and Friendship with the USSR in 1935. When Stalin proposed a new constitution the following year, Brailsford hailed it as evidence that the dictatorship was transforming itself into a genuine parliamentary regime.[65]

Yet within two months of this encomium to incipient Soviet democracy, Stalin struck at Zinoviev, Kamenev, and other Trotskyists. After openly confessing to the allegations brought against them, sixteen were immediately executed. In his only *New Statesman* leader on the purges during these years, Brailsford dismissed the trial as 'wholly unconvincing', the evidence consisting solely of 'worthless confessions'. Even if there had been a conspiracy, a possibility Brailsford never discounted, the judicial proceedings reflected as badly upon 'the state which employs them as upon the victims it condemns'.[66] Then and later he went much further in *Reynolds*, where single-handedly, he 'stripped aside the curtain of lies and saved the honour of Socialist journalism', as Michael Foot has acknowledged.[67]

Brailsford based his denunciation on three factors. First, convictions derived from extorted confessions could not be regarded as legitimate. Second, several of the accused, notably Radek, the young military hero Tukhachevsky, and the diplomat Rakovsky, he had known and respected. Radek, ironically one of the authors of the 1936 constitution, had welcomed him on his two Russian trips, while Rakovsky, who may have been an acquaintance long before in Macedonia, had enlisted him as an emissary to MacDonald in 1924. Unlike most other Englishmen, Brailsford had understood the factionalism of the Russian revolutionary movement before 1917 and endorsed attempts by Rothstein, Radek, and Maisky to accommodate themselves to the triumphant Bolsheviks. Agreeing with Stalin in the ideological dispute with Trotsky, he never doubted the loyalty of the Old Guard, their commitment to a regime for which they had repeatedly risked their lives. Finally, the accusations simply did not make 'plausible history'.[68] It was incredible that all these highly-placed, successful men had conspired with the Fascist enemy, plotted the defeat of their own country, and betrayed every principle on which they had staked their careers. The evidence seemed to suggest two alternatives:

We may believe that the governing ranks of the Soviet Union are honey-

[64] ND, 20 Jan. 1935.   [65] *Reynolds*, 28 June 1936.   [66] *New Statesman*, 29 Aug. 1936.
[67] Michael Foot in Elizabeth Thomas, ed., *Tribune 21* (London, 1958), p. 7.
[68] *Reynolds*, 7 Feb. 1937.

combed with treason and moral depravity; or we may believe that Stalin is a despot who has destroyed every man of distinction and independence round him by an incredible 'frame-up' in order to rule the rest of his party by terror.[69]

Stalin's brutality 'confirmed the worst that any friend of Russia had dared to think. Under him it has become a bloody tyranny ruled by terror and lies.'[70] Behind the scenes Brailsford also tried to apply pressure to save at least one of the victims. He urged Ponsonby to use his influence on behalf of Rakovsky, but an appeal to Maisky was curtly rejected.[71] Rakovsky, sentenced to twenty years imprisonment, died in a labour camp, and Brailsford's friendship with Maisky rapidly cooled.

Such blatant criticism of the Soviet Union during the Spanish Civil War and at the height of Popular Front sentiment, much of it fostered by Brailsford himself, was unwelcome on the left. The socialist press tried to temper or even to withhold anti-Soviet publicity, while the *New Republic* (virtually disavowing a piece by Brailsford in its own pages) eased its conscience by insisting that it was 'almost impossible' for anyone outside Russia to comprehend what was happening.[72] Retrospectively, Foot apologized for *Tribune*'s cowardice during the trials, and a recent critic has faulted the *New Statesman* for 'an exhibition of dithering evasiveness and moral obtuseness rarely displayed by a reputedly responsible publication'.[73] Brailsford found himself the target of vilification from predictable quarters. Arnot, in the *Daily Worker*, likening Brailsford's description of Russian justice to the 'gloomy tints' of the 'Fascist paint pot', reproached him for 'doing harm to all that the working-class stands for'.[74] Dutt followed with an article on the 'Blindness of Brailsford', accusing him of being a 'Liberal waverer who is unable to face the hard realities of the class struggle'.[75] In a letter to the *New Statesman* Dutt warned that 'this high-minded idealism, when not accompanied by political consciousness of real class forces, can become grist to the mill of the Edens and the Hitlers'. Brailsford retorted that he had once risked imprisonment for the Russian cause, devotion that might have been confirmed by several old Bolsheviks had Dutt's masters not liquidated them. Without denying that some of the victims might have been implicated in anti-Stalinist activity, he found the idea that these former leaders 'wrecked trains by the thousand, poisoned

---

[69] *Reynolds*, 20 June 1937.
[70] *Reynolds*, 27 June 1937.
[71] HNB to Lord Ponsonby, 1 Mar. [1938]; Ivan Maisky to Lord Ponsonby, 4 Mar. 1938, Ponsonby Papers, c. 680, fol. 27.
[72] *New Republic*, 28 July 1937.
[73] Hugo Dewar, 'How They Saw It: The Moscow Trials', *Survey*, 41 (Apr. 1962), p. 94. For an alternative view, see Hyams, pp. 196-7. It is clear that Martin, though personally loyal to Brailsford, steered him away from writing about the Soviet Union in these years.
[74] *Daily Worker*, 21 June 1937.   [75] *Daily Worker*, 28 June 1937.

cattle with cholera germs, plotted scores of murders without ever managing to fire a shot' to be simply 'melodrama'.[76]

While denigration by party functionaries could have been anticipated, it rankled none the less. So strong were Brailsford's sympathies that he would gladly have overlooked Stalin's crimes had his conscience permitted him to do so. After all he had written to extol the revolution, it was not easy to find himself breaching socialist solidarity. Even though he reaffirmed his faith in the Soviet experiment, the purges caused him anguish, not least because Russia seemed the only European friend of the beleaguered Spanish republic. Nor was it only the Communists who repudiated his candour. When Gollancz read the manuscript of Brailsford's *Why Capitalism Means War* in September 1937, he took exception to anti-Stalinist remarks and urged the author to eliminate them. 'My own view,' he explained, 'is that support of the Soviet Union at the present juncture is (as the one hope of averting war) of such overwhelming importance that anything that could be quoted by the other side should not be said.'[77] Although Brailsford agreed to moderate the tone of the offensive section, he refused to omit it:

> It seems to me useless to argue that 'capitalism means war' unless one can also persuade the reader that 'socialism means peace'. There Russia, for good & ill, is in the path and one can't walk round her. I've often spoken at meetings on this theme without mentioning Russia, and always someone in the audience has put the inevitable question.
>
> I have, after all, mixed eulogy with criticism—the former much more hearty than the latter. The circulation of the booklet won't be affected, for the C. P. will boycott it anyhow, as they always boycott anything I write. Also you'll have an answer to people who say that you only publish orthodox Communist dope.

Brailsford foresaw much sharper editorial disagreement when he came to write the history of socialism for Gollancz. He felt it ludicrous to exclude an assessment of the Soviet experiment, even if it offended uncritical admirers. 'I'm not Trotskyist,' he added, 'but neither am I Stalinist. And I've become highly sceptical about C. P. propaganda generally. I'm working all through to a far from orthodox Marxist position—though Marx will stand out as the giant in the history . . . I confess that I shudder at Stalin.' He rejected Laski's suggestion that he conclude the book in 1914 on the grounds that 'all socialist history culminates in Russia'.[78]

Gollancz, having reluctantly swallowed Orwell's *Road to Wigan Pier* a few months earlier, now dug in his heels. If Brailsford refused to stop

---

[76] *New Statesman*, 10 and 17 July 1937.
[77] Victor Gollancz to HNB, 6 Sept. 1937, Gollancz Papers.
[78] HNB to Victor Gollancz, 19 Sept. 1937, Gollancz Papers.

at 1914, then the Left Book Club triumvirate believed 'it would be better to abandon the book if you felt necessary to continue it so as to cover the Soviet regime'. While decisions about LBC selections were taken collectively, the Educational Series was Gollancz's sole responsibility. Brailsford's objectionable views convinced him that he should reject the manuscript of *Why Capitalism Means War* two months after its submission.

> It is really a matter of two conflicting consciences, [he wrote to Brailsford.] You feel that you have to say what you say in that last chapter: I feel that, by being the instrument through which that chapter is given publicity, I am, to put it pompously, committing the sin against the Holy Ghost.[79]

Brailsford, reluctant to discard a completed manuscript, appealed to Laski to mediate, and a compromise was worked out. Gollancz honoured his commitments in regard to *Why Capitalism Means War*, and Brailsford revised his proposal for a socialist history. Instead of a comprehensive survey, ending with Soviet Russia, he would limit his scope to the period from More to Marx.[80] Commissioned in 1936 and written the following summer, *Why Capitalism Means War* was not published until August 1938. Its thesis was that capitalism rested on inequality, and that any society based on inequality must rely on force to protect its economic interests at home and abroad. In a world of sovereign states, reliance on force sooner or later led to war. His comments on the Soviet system were confined to a few brief paragraphs which concluded that a democratic system, whatever the constitutional formulation, would not work normally 'until organised pacific opposition by persuasion is held to be compatible with loyalty'.[81] Like ordinary LBC selections, the New People's Library titles were issued monthly, but in editions of about 5,000, with no opportunity to reprint. Brailsford continued to harbour a grievance, complaining later that 'Victor buried it in oblivion, because it contained some very mild criticisms of Stalinism'.[82]

In a broadcast shortly before his death, celebrating Martin's twenty-fifth anniversary as *New Statesman* editor, Brailsford recalled his Spanish Civil War articles as one area in which he made a distinctive contribution to the weekly. On no subject did he write as frequently or as passionately or—in the end—as fruitlessly. In regard to Spain he felt that his views were identical with those of the rest of the *New Statesman* staff, which was certainly not the case with the Russian trials or Munich:

[79] Victor Gollancz to HNB, 10 Dec. 1937, Gollancz Papers.
[80] HNB to Victor Gollancz, 14 Feb. 1938, Gollancz Papers.
[81] *Why Capitalism Means War*, p. 89.
[82] HNB to Kingsley Martin, 28 July 1957, KMP.

I think what was in our minds about the Civil War, apart from our direct personal sympathy with the Republicans, was that this was the first bitter battle of a war that might sooner or later engulf us all. But we hoped that if the Republic won, if the dictators were defeated in Spain, that then we might have been spared the Second World War.[83]

In his first piece on Spain, hailing the 'dauntless courage' of the workers, he perceived the wider implications of the conflict. While the democracies denied arms to Republican Spain, the Fascists supplied the rebels. It was 'class prejudice' that explained British neutrality, the fear that the Republic was controlled by workers, and, perhaps, even by the Communists, an allegation he repeatedly denied.[84] The Spanish cause was that of workers everywhere in Europe: 'if these Spanish workers can be massacred and defeated by Nazi and Fascist bombing planes, not even we in our island are safe'.[85]

By October 1936 he had concluded that the Baldwin government, while not overtly pro-Fascist, was by its policy abetting the Fascist cause in Spain. It was therefore incumbent upon the Labour Party to disavow the hypocritical commitment to non-intervention, and he urged the party to reverse the support its Executive had given to the one-sided arms blockade. At its annual conference in Edinburgh the party, fearful of any association with the Communists, first reaffirmed support for non-intervention and then resolved to restore to the Spanish government the right to purchase arms should it become clear that non-intervention was being violated. To Brailsford such timidity was conclusive proof of its 'moral bankruptcy', a clear sign that 'as an effective political force it has ceased to exist'.[86] It was the Edinburgh Conference that really marked the parting of the ways for him: five years earlier he insisted that affiliation with Labour was the only way to bring about socialism in England. Although he could not join the Communists, he no longer felt that a party which endorsed 'this treason of neutrality' was worthy of support. In the sharpest invective he ever applied to his erstwhile political allies, he thundered:

When [Fascist violence] reaches our own shores, these leaders who have offered up Spanish democracy as a sacrifice to peace will lie down flat as the Germans did. A movement which has in its creed nothing worth fighting for might as well disband its legions. . . . Thirty years ago, as a young man, I joined the I. L. P., for under Hardie it had courage and faith. . . . This slouching leadership, this parasitic attitude towards the Government of the other class, could attract no young man.[87]

[83] Transcript of broadcast in BBC Home Service, 18 Dec. 1956.
[84] *New Statesman*, 1 and 15 Aug. 1936. Also see *New Republic*, 23 Sept. 1936.
[85] *Reynolds*, 16 Aug. 1936. [86] *New Republic*, 2 Dec. 1936. [87] *Reynolds*, 11 Oct. 1936.

While excoriating Labour for complicity in the betrayal of the Republic, his own views were undergoing a reversal as a result of the Spanish conflict. He had urged resistance to Mussolini in Abyssinia in the belief that Italy could be stopped without war, but throughout 1935 and most of 1936 he continued to advocate concessions to Germany partly to undo the wrongs of Versailles and partly to appease Hitler. Spain was the turning point, revealing to him the aggressive designs of the Fascist powers. It was time for collective action, for a 'firm alliance of all the nations in which the working class is still free'. Only a few months after asserting that the survival of Czechoslovakia and Austria was not worth the blood of European workers, he told readers:

Certainly if we always retreat, if we always yield to threats and even to bluff, if we adopt a policy of peace at any price, we shall not get peace and we shall sacrifice all that we hold dear. . . . Men who will not fight for what they hold dear deserve to go under.[88]

If the National government and the Labour opposition refused to defend Spain, then British workers should take the initiative. He appealed for unity among those sections of the movement 'which wage the class struggle relentlessly, whether it be instinct or theory that guides them'. Such an alliance of dissident Labourites and Communists would supply the vitality that Labour had lost.[89] Thus did he hurl his defiance at the party leadership, for whom any link with Communists was anathema. But it was also ironic that his exhortation appeared in the *Labour Monthly*, edited by the very man who had denounced him as a false friend of the working class five months earlier. As long as he shared their views on Spain, the CPGB welcomed him as a contributor to their publications, but he was certainly there only on sufferance. It was the Spanish question more than anything else that precipitated the Unity Manifesto in January 1937, whose signatories included Brailsford, Dutt, Cripps, Aneurin Bevan, Laski, Brockway, Maxton, and Harry Pollitt, just as it was factionalism in Spain which dissipated that unity within a few months.

Yet even the flow of articles and participation in the Unity Campaign seemed an inadequate gesture. 'The question that confronts us,' he wrote in December 1936, 'is whether we have the manhood to defend ourselves. The alternative is to sit still and await the signal for self-destruction.'[90] What this article did not indicate is how subjective his judgement was. Ten days before, Brailsford had announced to Nevinson that 'he is going to Spain to fight for the Govt as he is urging

[88] *Reynolds*, 18 Oct. 1936.
[89] *Labour Monthly*, Vol. 18, No. 12 (Dec. 1936), p. 729. Also see *Spain's Challenge to Labour*, Socialist League pamphlet (1936).   [90] *Reynolds*, 20 Dec. 1936.

others to go, and so must go himself'.⁹¹ Writing to Dorothy Elmhirst to solicit funds for the International Brigade, which he intended to join, he explained his motives:

Two considerations chiefly move me; (1) that we in this country must be shaken out of our indolence & security, and wakened up to action. In short, I think the Brigade, if we back it wholeheartedly, can save our souls as well as the soil of Spain. (2) If the Republic goes down, the whole Spanish Left will be massacred. . . . Can any pacifist principle answer the argument that by fighting we may save hundreds of thousands from massacre, to say nothing of Spain's happiness and our security?⁹²

To Brailsford's dismay, the International Brigade imposed an age limit of forty on volunteers—he was sixty-three—and, despite a last-minute appeal to Maisky, rejected his offer to go to Spain as a political commissar, probably because his heretical views on the purge trials made him suspect.⁹³ He was in a state of turmoil, determined to fight for democracy, yet full of trepidation. Clare, eager to dissuade him from foolhardy risks, enlisted Martin and Maisky to reassure him that his duty was as a journalist.⁹⁴ Torn between conflicting loyalties, he would, she confided to a friend, 'wake during the night in nightmares about it all'. Their flat was 'a noisy hell, with men from the North, hundreds of letters, our telephone (which was being tapped by Scotland Yard) ringing every other minute'.⁹⁵ Reluctantly persuaded to remain in England, at least for the time being, he plunged into recruitment for the Brigade. 'Because in my own youth I did this same thing,' he explained in the *News-Chronicle*, 'I venture to appeal directly to young men.'⁹⁶ He followed up articles with direct appeals to potential donors of funds for the Brigade and letters of introduction for volunteers and others, like Orwell, *en route* to Spain.⁹⁷ By raising money and counselling volunteers, he helped to assuage his own sense of guilt for remaining behind.

After the disaffiliation of the Socialist League, Austen Albu, Patrick Gordon Walker, and other moderate Labourites formed the Socialist Clarity Group to generate activity, especially with regard to Spain,

⁹¹ ND, 10 Dec. 1936.   ⁹² HNB to Dorothy Elmhirst, 11 Dec. 1936, Elmhirst Papers.
⁹³ HNB to Dorothy Elmhirst, 8 Jan. 1937, Elmhirst Papers.
⁹⁴ Interviews, Clare Leighton, Frank Hardie; Clare Leighton to Vera Brittain, 30 Dec. [1936], Brittain Papers; ND, 16 Dec. 1936.
⁹⁵ Clare Leighton to Christopher leFleming, n.d. [Jan. 1937].
⁹⁶ *New-Chronicle*, 30 Dec. 1936. Also see *Reynolds*, 20 Dec. 1936.
⁹⁷ HNB to H. G. Wells, 18 Jan. 1937, Wells Papers. Wells did not contribute; Dorothy Elmhirst did, but only on condition that her donation would not be used for a fighting brigade itself. Brailsford used the money for groundsheets for volunteers. HNB to Dorothy Elmhirst, 8 Jan. 1937, Elmhirst Papers.
   Orwell carried a letter from Brailsford to John McNair, the ILP representative in Barcelona. Peter Stansky and William Abrahams, *Orwell: The Transformation* (New York, 1980), p. 237.

among constituency parties. They persuaded Brailsford that only grassroots opinion might alter the direction of official policy. The Labour Spain Committee, an offshoot of the constituency party reform movement, was established in March 1937. Its first chairman, Charles Garnsworthy, was soon succeeded by Brailsford, who chaired the Committee until its demise on the eve of the Second World War. Its leading members were Joe Pole, its secretary, Albu, the treasurer, and Sybil Wingate, who had briefly served as a nurse in Spain.

The Labour Spain Committee tried to rally the rank and file to a genuine confrontation with the National Executive, whose attitude it considered scarcely less ineffectual than that of the government itself. Within the NEC it could count on limited support from Cripps and Laski, but it made little headway against the trade unionist majority.[98] At the inaugural conference in March 1937 delegates representing nearly eighty constituency parties expressed dissatisfaction at the failure to implement the Edinburgh pledge to re-examine non-intervention. A resolution summoned the Executive to call a conference of the entire labour movement and to initiate a nationwide campaign in favour of restoring the Republic's right to buy arms. It also urged Labour to take steps to co-ordinate all anti-Fascist activities relating to Spain into a single movement, a tacit endorsement of a united front.[99]

Unable to enlist as a soldier, Brailsford was determined to visit Spain, all the more so once he assumed control of the Labour Spain Committee. He and Clare spent most of April in the French Pyrenees making preparations, and during the last week of the month he crossed the border, arriving by train in Barcelona just before the rising, and proceeding by car to Valencia, where he spent a remarkably quiet May Day. Plagued by misfortune which led him to miss every notable event during his Spanish trip, he was in Madrid when he received news of the insurrection in Barcelona. Much of his information was necessarily second-hand and tended, unlike Orwell's, to reflect ministerial and Russian diplomatic opinion. A strong defender of the Popular Front, he criticized POUM for remaining aloof and even more for complicity in the insurrection. Without swallowing the Communist accusation that POUM was led by Fascists in disguise, he believed the suppression of the rising was necessary in order to 'disarm the rear' and 'fuse the party militias into a regular army'.[100] Madrid, temporarily quiet, had been shelled for three weeks before his arrival. Although courage had

---

[98] This description is based on historical notes written in 1966 by Joe Pole, Labour Spain Committee Collection, and on information provided by Austen Albu, Joe Pole, and Sybil Wingate.

[99] Report of Conference of Constituency Labour Parties, 13 Mar. 1937, Labour Spain Committee Collection.

[100] *Spain's Challenge to Labour*, p. 6; *Reynolds*, 16 May 1937.

not flagged, the dead and wounded numbered in the hundreds, and when he visited the workers' suburb of Tetuán, he observed rampant starvation. He felt most comfortable with Germans of the Thaelmann Brigade, which he visited near Guadalajara, and the British battalion on the Jarama front. Conceding that the international volunteers had helped to save Madrid, he was realistic enough to recognize that the future depended on the capacity of the Republican units.[101]

At the same time that the NEC rebuffed the overtures of the Labour Spain Committee, it decided in no uncertain terms that Socialist League members would henceforth be ineligible for party membership. Some wanted to expel advocates of an alliance with Communists, over Spain or any other issue, but the majority were reluctant to alienate Brailsford or Cripps. The League had to decide whether it was worth maintaining its defiance for the sake of a unity that was proving ever more elusive. By the spring of 1937 the ILP and the Communists were quarrelling openly, the former defending POUM from vilification by the *Daily Worker*. Both Cripps and Pollitt felt that the League should be disbanded, and since both the League and *Tribune* depended on Cripps's munificence, his views prevailed. The dissolution conference was held in Leicester on 17 May 1937, while Brailsford was in Spain, but the acrimony of the gathering was heightened by his telegram resigning from the League and denouncing the dissolution as a 'political blunder of the first magnitude'. Only a minority shared his view, and by the time he returned to England the Socialist League had ceased to exist. For a few months the pretence of a Unity Campaign was maintained, but it too was jettisoned after the Labour annual conference decisively repudiated a United Front.[102]

Even so, United Front sentiment persisted, if not organizationally, then at least in periodicals and informal activity. The *New Statesman*, for example, rejected an Orwell piece favourable to POUM, but welcomed Brailsford's two-part feature on anarchists and Communists in Spain. No longer dismissing POUM as Trotskyist, he castigated them for behaving 'with reckless, partisan folly'. He explained the conflict as a struggle between reformism and the will to make a proletarian revolution, and his sympathies were clearly with the Communists, eager to win peasant and middle-class support and to avoid antagonizing Western democracies. What Brailsford did not concede was that the Communists, fearful of an ultimate anarchist victory, wanted not simply to delay, but to prevent revolution. While he referred to the Barcelona rebels, assailing socialists with weapons 'stolen from Government arsenals', as extremist 'gunmen' who had to be 'weeded out',

[101] *Reynolds*, 23 and 30 May 1937.
[102] Pimlott, pp. 102-6.

he ignored Communist atrocities.103 Thus while condemning the Russian purges, he applauded Communist policies in Spain, contributing to the miasma of Popular Front sentiment as he helped to dispel left illusions about Stalin.

The controversies continued to percolate, and Brailsford often found himself in the middle of them. Shortly after his return from Spain, Orwell read Brailsford's *New Statesman* articles, which seemed to typify the distortions in the British press about the Barcelona fighting. He told Raymond Mortimer that the story of POUM attacking the government with stolen guns and tanks was 'absolutely untrue'.104 In response to Orwell's inquiry, Brailsford admitted that his source had been the Russian Consul-General, who struck him as 'a fair-minded man' who was 'less prejudiced than most Communists' about POUM. Although hoping that he had not been 'unwittingly unfair', neither he, nor the *New Statesman* published any retraction.105 When Brailsford demanded an 'unequivocal statement' that unless the Fascists withdrew their weapons, England and France would begin to supply the Spanish government, his militancy infuriated Keynes, then a *New Statesman* director, who charged that Brailsford's leader would only foster an 'impression of drivelling irresponsibility'.106

In April 1938 the Labour Spain Committee convened an emergency delegate conference to consider action to compel the National Government to end the farce of non-intervention and supply arms to Spain. Brailsford also urged the establishment of a fund to buy arms for Spain, an activity in which he was himself covertly involved. Immediately after the conference he had a talk with Attlee in the hope of persuading the Executive to intervene more directly, but the NEC again rejected a proposal for an emergency conference to mobilize the entire labour movement.107 A month later he sounded out the Spanish ambassador about his proposal for the Labour Party to defy the government ban and procure arms for Spain on its own initiative. The ambassador seemed enthusiastic about the plan, although, of course, there was little prospect of its being implemented.108

Earlier that spring Elliott had proposed a United Peace Alliance in *Reynolds* as a way of unseating the National government. Its

103 Martin, *Editor*, pp. 215-16; *New Statesman*, 22 and 29 May 1937. The same articles appeared in *New Republic* as 'Impressions of Spain', 9 and 16 June 1937.
104 George Orwell to Raymond Mortimer, 9 Feb. 1938, in Sonia Orwell and Ian Angus, eds., *The Collected Essays, Journalism and Letters of George Orwell*, I (New York, 1968), p. 301.
105 HNB to Eric Blair, 17 Dec. 1937, Orwell Archive.
106 *New Statesman*, 3 July 1937; J. M. Keynes to Kingsley Martin, 4 July 1937, KMP.
107 Miscellaneous Papers, Labour Spain Committee Collection; interview, Joe Pole.
108 HNB to Stafford Cripps, 27 May 1938, Cripps Papers. Cripps's own discussions with Azcárate led him to conclude that the Ambassador did not favour the proposal. Stafford Cripps to HNB, 30 May 1938, Cripps Papers.

international objectives were to strengthen the League, guarantee Czech independence, and combat Fascism in Spain. The idea, promptly endorsed by the Labour Spain Committee and the *New Statesman*, revived faltering Popular Front sentiment, and members of the Labour left, both on and off the NEC, responded enthusiastically to the initiative.[109] Brailsford, who had never wholly deserted the Popular Front movement, took up the cry once again. When Eden resigned as Foreign Secretary, he went so far as to suggest him as 'the figure round which such an enterprise must rally'.[110] If Hitler was to be checked, the working class would have to be mobilized for the coming struggle:

> An attempt to buy Hitler out by offering him colonies elsewhere would only confirm him in his belief that everything can be won by audacious violence. The more we retreat, the further will he advance. The time to consider concessions will come when the democratic Powers have demonstrated their unity and their will to resist.[111]

Yet after all he had written during the previous two decades, he found it hard to grieve over the *Anschluss*. Incapable of economic survival on its own, Austria was hardly worth mourning. The real tragedy was that union with Germany, harmless, perhaps even beneficial, when both republics were democratic, was now achieved by force as part of a plan to dominate Europe. But if it was too late to salvage Austria, there was still time to curb Hitler's ambitions in Czechoslovakia, where the case for resistance was 'dictated by prudence as well as by principle'. An 'unambiguous statement' that an attack on the Czechs would mean war and a declaration of solidarity with France and Russia would incur 'less risk than a repetition of the uncertainty of 1914'. But even while calling for firmness, he continued to urge the revision of that arrangement which attached several million Germans to 'this Slav state'. His solution in the spring of 1938 was to couple 'a prompt and public promise of British support' with an appeal to the Czechs to erase this 'bolt' either by ceding territory or by cantonal autonomy.[112]

When *Tribune* began in January 1937, the Unity Campaign was just getting under way, and Mellor, its editor, was one of its instigators. By 1938 not only had unity foundered, but *Tribune* had to be rescued from financial disaster by infusions of cash from Cripps and G. R. Strauss. As Cripps shifted back towards support for a Popular Front of all progressive elements, he came into conflict with Mellor, still loyal to the earlier objective of an exclusively working-class alliance. Under the

[109] Interview, Sydney Elliott; Pimlott, pp. 152-3.
[110] *New Statesman*, 26 Feb. 1938.
[111] *Reynolds*, 3 Jan. 1937.
[112] *New Statesman*, 19 Mar. 1938. See Hyams, p. 207.

influence of Gollancz, Cripps, edging closer to the Left Book Club's pro-Communist orientation, engineered Mellor's dismissal and tried to replace him with Foot, the assistant editor, hoping that the younger man would prove more pliable. But Foot, loyal to Mellor, refused the editorship and left *Tribune* shortly afterwards to join Beaverbrook's *Evening Standard*. Although their acquaintance was slight, Brailsford took it upon himself to dissuade Foot from leaving, proferring generous advice that its recipient would never forget. Foot's gesture, reminiscent of his own impetuous resignations, prompted him to caution:

> As to Mellor, I should agree that if you & he had been standing together against the proprietors on a matter of policy or principle, you would in honour have to go with him. But that I gather wasn't the fact. . . . Secondly, as to Victor Gollancz, like you I distrust him and am highly critical of the Left Book Club. (I have reasons drawn from personal dealings with him). But why capitulate in advance? I assume that you would enjoy full editorial discretion. In that case the worst to fear is that VG would make things difficult for you at Board Meetings. . . . I had to face a motion demanding my resignation at almost every Board Meeting through four years, when I edited the *New Leader*. It wasn't pleasant & in the end I was defeated. But I had the satisfaction of making what I, anyhow, thought a pretty good paper.
>
> One may be too subjective—that's in the Liberal-Nonconformist tradition —and forget that to run a good paper matters more than to perform prodigies of conscience. (I too came out of that tradition, & it has poisoned most of my life. One never wholly liberates oneself. It is a great inheritance—to throw away).[113]

When Foot justified his stance, Brailsford conceded that there was a strong case for resignation. No longer involved in *Tribune* affairs, he saw the removal of Mellor and Foot as an indication that 'the Socialist Left is allowing itself to be driven from all its strategical positions by the C. P. With great sublety it drove the Socialist League to suicide, & now it is capturing the *Tribune*.'[114]

His articles during 1938 show ever greater support for collective security, but for him it meant a defence of human rights, not of imperial acquisitions. His earlier ambivalence towards the Prague regime diminished as the outlines of Chamberlain's policy became clear. By the end of May, recognizing that Sudeten autonomy would pave the way for German expansion, he contended that the Czechs had now granted all that Germany 'can reasonably ask' in terms of cultural autonomy.[115] Again and again in the following months he linked the fate of the

---

[113] HNB to Michael Foot, 6 Aug. 1938; interview, Michael Foot. See Michael Foot, *Debts of Honour* (London, 1980), pp. 78-9, 146; Pimlott, pp. 107-8.

[114] HNB to Michael Foot, n.d. [Aug. 1938]. Brailsford had been a founding member of the *Tribune* board but soon ceased to be active.

[115] *Reynolds*, 29 May 1938.

Czechs and the Spaniards: Hitler must be halted on both fronts; if Prague fell, the loss of Barcelona would follow inevitably. Indeed it was Brailsford's commitment to the struggle against Fascism in Spain that strengthened his resolve to thwart Hitler on the Danube. On the other hand, as long as the British government connived at Italian intervention in Spain, he opposed co-operation with Chamberlain: 'That we loathe the record, the spirit and the ambitions of Nazi Germany is no reason for placing ourselves under the banner of British capitalist-imperialism.'[116] Implicit in this argument was a contradiction he was reluctant to admit. Until Labour was strong enough politically to supplant the National government, Chamberlain would have to be tolerated, even encouraged, if there were to be a show of solidarity at home and firmness abroad. For Labour to withhold support as a way of undermining the Prime Minister was neither practical nor provident. To be sure, Brailsford was hardly alone on the left in demanding arms for Spain while refusing to condone rearmament at home. The fact that Cripps, Bevan, and Laski shared these views did not make them any the less reprehensible. Although inclined to interpret the Prime Minister's policy as an attempt to employ Fascism in the class war against Communism, he ultimately concluded that socialists could no longer afford to be fastidious about their allies.

It was Munich, above all, which discredited appeasement, inspiring Brailsford to the sharpest indictment of Chamberlain's policy to appear in the non-Communist press at the time. The search for justice through revision had been betrayed. 'Two Great Powers flinched from their duty to this little State,' he wrote in *Reynolds*. Had they stood firm, in association with the Soviet Union, there would have been 'neither war nor surrender'. Those who found solace in the reprieve should face the fact that 'we have saved our skins and lost our honour. We have gained our ease and jeopardised our safety with our freedom.'[117]

Through all the hysteria over Czechoslovakia the Labour Spain Committee continued to apply pressure to the NEC, but to no avail. Within the Executive Laski tried to persuade his colleagues to agree to an emergency conference, but Dalton was opposed, and the Committee finally decided to defy NEC opposition. On 23 October, less than a month after Munich, delegates from more than 120 constituency parties and a number of unions met in London under Brailsford's chairmanship. Resolutions were passed demanding, yet again, the lifting of the arms embargo and the dispatch of food and supplies to Spain. The delegates also endorsed the efforts of the International Brigade Depen-

[116] *Reynolds*, 4 Sept. 1938.
[117] *Reynolds*, 2 Oct. 1938.

dants Aid Committee, to which Brailsford belonged, and launched its own fund drive for food ships for Spain.[118]

The occasion was notable for two reasons: first, it was the only time a major conference was organized within the Labour Party against the wishes of the NEC. Second, what Brailsford and his associates had achieved was a rallying of an alternate opposition, which had lacked focus since the dissolution of the Socialist League a year before. Although the organizers had sought collaboration on the single issue of Spain, the constituency delegates moved the conference in a much bolder direction by calling for 'a People's Government, led by the Labour Party, based upon a broad union of all the progressive forces in the country'. To Brailsford, this was an indication of mass support for an alliance with Liberals and Communists on a common basis of policy at home and abroad.[119] Thanking C. P. Trevelyan for addressing the gathering, he admitted,

> I had been in great fear of this Conference. But the moment I met it, that vanished, & I realised that we had been if anything too cautious. . . . It is bound to have some effect of stimulation on the Labour Party. There is something worth leading in the ranks. Do you remember my incitements to you, now several years ago, to grasp this leadership? I still feel strongly that you are the only adequate person to do it.[120]

Trevelyan's refusal to emerge from political retirement filled Brailsford with foreboding. It seemed to imply that

> if we want a leader, we must look for a bad man—someone who will enjoy the intrigues & the petty egoisms of committee life. And then, when we've chosen him & pushed him, he will betray us.
>
> I sympathise none the less. The same set of considerations has kept me relatively inactive, so that I would never even go into Parliament or stand for the Party's Executive. But I have the excuse that I do (or think I do) better work by writing books. Also I *have* to write for a living.[121]

Once the meeting had ended, Brailsford appealed to readers to contribute to the Labour Spain Committee's food ship fund, and by mid-November £2,000 had been raised. A month later another £1,000 had been collected, and a shipment of milk, dried fish, biscuits, and soap was dispatched to Spain.[122] Brailsford, encouraging the efforts of others, sent a personal donation of £50 to Ernst Toller, who, in the months before his suicide, was in America raising money for Spanish relief.[123]

---

[118] Report of the Emergency Conference, 23 Oct. 1938, Labour Spain Committee Collection. See Hugh Thomas, *The Spanish Civil War* (New York, 1961), p. 393.
[119] Letter to Editor, *New Statesman*, 26 Nov. 1938. Also see *Reynolds*, 27 Nov. 1938.
[120] HNB to C. P. Trevelyan, 30 Oct. [1938], Trevelyan Papers, Box 3. Cf. Chap. X n56.
[121] HNB to C. P. Trevelyan, 6 Nov. 1938, Trevelyan Papers, Box 3.
[122] *Reynolds*, 6 and 13 Nov., 18 Dec. 1938.
[123] HNB to Ernst Toller, 11 Nov. 1938, Toller Collection, T578, Box 1.

While in France in April 1937 Brailsford was notified that Jane had died of pneumonia and cirrhosis of the liver. She was sixty-three at the time; they had been married for nearly thirty-nine years, although separated for the previous sixteen. Her death stirred up all his feelings of guilt towards her, self-recriminations for the tragedy of her life. Coming so soon after his profound agitation over Spain, it seems to have precipitated a kind of emotional breakdown. For days he was inconsolable and only his imminent departure for Spain distracted him. But once he returned to England, the psychological scars began to show. For years he had been unable to marry Clare because Jane would not divorce him, and he felt responsible for her. Now that he was free, he seemed to transfer his rancour against Jane to Clare, as though she had been responsible for Jane's death, as though it were a punishment meted out to them for having grasped at illicit happiness while Jane succumbed to alcoholic stupor. The self-laceration, to which Brailsford had grown accustomed, would continue. 'I have to have demons,' he confessed to Clare. 'If I haven't got a demon, I'll make one.' For the next eighteen months he set about destroying the relationship he and Clare had built over the previous decade, not intentionally, yet compulsively, as though driven by a kind of obsession he could not control. Having been almost uxorious in his devotion, he now seized any opportunity to wound her; with deliberate cruelty, he not only rejected the idea of marriage, but tried to arouse her jealousy by flirtations. For years he had tortured himself in a triangular relationship with Jane and Clare; now that Jane was gone, he sought to reconstitute the triangle, with Clare now cast in the role of victim. When her American friend Eleanor Musselman arrived for a visit in the summer of 1937, Brailsford, determined to fall in love with the first woman who came along, became instantly infatuated.[124]

Such bizarre behaviour, a foretaste of what was to follow, was clearly triggered by Jane's death, but his anxiety about the state of the world and his own role in it must have been involved. He had virtually severed his ties with Labour; the Socialist League had been dissolved against his judgement. Increasingly isolated politically and under recurrent attack from the Communists, he felt lonely and vulnerable, much as he had in the early days of the First World War. But now he was conscious of his age, fearful that his work no longer carried the same impact. Jealous of Clare's professional success, he was also frightened by her understandable desire to have a child. Their failure thus far to conceive stirred up, he later admitted, 'unreasonable resentment because you wanted what I feared I could not give you.'[125] When he returned in

[124] Interview, Clare Leighton.
[125] HNB to Clare Leighton, 17 Feb. 1939, CLC.

mid-November from a Le Lavandou holiday, she remained a few weeks longer, working on a projected Mediterranean book. The rift seemed to have healed, at least temporarily, as a letter to her indicated:

... I am hardly alive without you. When you're not here I go on talking to you in my head. My brain's oriented to you & must go on working towards you, even when there's no reply ... [Eleanor's letters] are vaguely affectionate, but otherwise featureless. Happily she doesn't want me for a pseudo-father. It's all fading out quite nicely ....[126]

It was, however, during these weeks and later when Clare returned to the Riviera in February 1938 that his friendship with 'Gwen Blaisty' began to develop. He had met 'Gwen', an intense, highly intelligent woman in her thirties, at political gatherings, and found her stimulating, if infuriatingly argumentative. Although 'Gwen' relished his attention, she rebuffed him sexually, making the flames of his passion burn more intensely. Having refused to marry Clare, he brought 'Gwen' to Four Hedges in order to propose to her. Although she spurned his offer, their relationship continued; the more frustrated he became, the more he turned against Clare. In March Clare became pregnant, but Brailsford now disavowed paternity. Even after he was convinced that he was indeed the father, he resented the fact that, with her prospective loss of income, he would have to write 'potboilers' to make money, postponing further his anthropological study. Still, his moments of cruelty were coupled with outpourings of affection, fluctuations between emotional extremes that played havoc with her nerves.[127] When she miscarried in May, he wrote,

I give you my love again, after this sore blow, strong and whole, to heal you & bring you back to life. We'll keep each other to forget this sore disappointment. I never doubted that I loved you entirely, but the devotion & reverence I have for you rushed over me in a mighty flood when this sore thing happened to you.[128]

Such signs of devotion were only a truce before the conflict was resumed. Fearing for his sanity, she felt a desperate need to escape, to free herself from a relationship that seemed likely to destroy them both.

In the autumn of 1938 Clare finally resolved to leave him, accepting Eleanor's offer of a refuge in Baltimore. Unable to depart for America while Brailsford remained in the flat, she inveigled Martin into sending him to North Africa to report on the Italian penetration of Tunisia and Libya. Martin and his companion Dorothy Woodman, about to embark

---

[126] HNB to Clare Leighton, 23 Nov. [1937], CLC.
[127] Interviews, Clare Leighton, Mabel R. Brailsford, Joe Pole; Clare Leighton to Vera Brittain, 17 May 1938, Brittain Papers.
[128] HNB to Clare Leighton, n.d. [?22 May 1938], CLC.

on a North African vacation, now invited Brailsford to join them. Clare knew that if he was preoccupied, their separation would seem less wrenching. Ostensibly coming to the United States for a visit, she never intimated the finality of her decision. One day in late December she said goodbye to him at Waterloo Station and then, carrying only a suitcase, a typewriter, and a paintbox, caught her own boat-train, the first stage in her voyage to a new life.[129]

[129] Interviews, Clare Leighton, Kingsley Martin.

XIII

'It's a Long Road to Victory'[1] (1939–1946)

When Brailsford returned to London late in January 1939, after his first visit to North Africa in thirty years, an empty flat awaited him. Without Clare he felt 'unendurably lonely'. Deluding himself that she would be gone only for a couple of months, he wrote to her in America, 'I've just one ambition & that's to get mentally well and sane, so that I may be fit to meet you when you return . . . & bury the memory of this dreadful year.'[2] In the mean time he agreed to take in a young Austrian refugee couple, Fritz and Hexl Jahoda, to look after the flat and prepare meals. The Jahodas, the most successful of a series of refugee couples, stayed until August, when they left for New York and an academic appointment at Sarah Lawrence College.[3] He then volunteered to sponsor an Austrian International Brigade veteran, and at the beginning of September Hans Nass arrived from the French internment camp at Gurs. Like Jahoda, he was Jewish and had, before the Spanish war, edited an anti-Nazi weekly in Vienna. Brailsford housed him temporarily and contributed 15s. per week towards his maintenance. 'I had the sense,' he admitted to Clare, 'that I'm a waster who has failed in his personal life. I might as well do some good to another human being in this way.'[4]

In his loneliness he once again sought out 'Gwen Blaisty'. In March he took her to Jahoda's concert, after which they went to a pub where they began to quarrel about politics. It confirmed his view that 'for my own good I must avoid her entirely'. Without wholly blaming 'Gwen', he complained that

> no one, save Kew [their nickname for Jane], has ever harmed me as she has done. She has been a total curse to me, and against that the happy hours I've had with her really fine mind, talking, just don't count.[5]

Her BBC work soon removed her to the West of England, and subsequent encounters were infrequent. The end of any intimacy meant 'a better and happier relationship', based on an 'intellectual friendship' that did not threaten his emotional stability.[6] In fact they soon drifted

---

[1] *Reynolds*, 21 Jan. 1940. [2] HNB to Clare Leighton, 2 and 17 Jan. 1939, CLC.
[3] Interview, Fritz Jahoda. [4] HNB to Clare Leighton, 29 Aug. 1939, CLC.
[5] HNB to Clare Leighton, 28 Mar. 1939, CLC.
[6] HNB to Clare Leighton, 21 Dec. 1939, CLC.

apart, and by the end of 1940 contact between them had virtually ceased.

More than anything else, however, he was consumed with self-recrimination. Ascribing his conduct to the after-effects of Jane's death and his morbid 'tendency to self-torture', he implored Clare to return and save him from himself. On the eve of war he pleaded with her to marry him and permit him to make amends for the pain he had inflicted during the previous year. Once the realization dawned that she would not relent, he became increasingly melancholy. 'I'm facing the fact that I'm wholly alone in the world, and may be so for the rest of my life —which will not, I hope, be too long. I've wrecked it by my own folly.'[7]

It was his deepening sense of futility that prompted his generosity towards those who sought his assistance, especially the refugees from Nazism and the victims of war. Writing letters on their behalf, appealing to the Home Office to reverse negative administrative decisions, addressing exile groups, opening his flat to the homeless, lending money he could ill afford were not merely the responses of a benevolent humanitarian: it was perhaps penance too for the cruelty and destructiveness that had intruded so fatefully into his private life. When his young friend Peter Drucker brought him the manuscript of *The End of Economic Man*, Brailsford was so impressed with its analysis of the breakdown of economic values and the growth of anti-liberal forces that he volunteered to write an introduction, despite their divergent political outlooks.[8] During the next few years he supplied prefaces to books by Continental socialist writers, such as Oscar Pollak, Hilda Monte, and Julius Braunthal. Countless small gestures went unrecorded, but his involvement in the Austrian Centre, his patience in mediating among left-wing factions, his warmth and accessibility were still recalled years later. With so many of the refugees friendless and bewildered, callously treated by hostile officials, the compassion of a figure of Brailsford's eminence seemed all the more remarkable.[9]

So too his political life in the months before the war was governed by loyalty to those risking lives or reputations fighting for the causes in

---

[7] HNB to Clare Leighton, 1 and 8 Sept. 1939, CLC.

[8] HNB to Clare Leighton, 23 Feb. 1939, CLC. Also see the distorted account in Peter F. Drucker, *Adventures of a Bystander* (New York, 1979), pp. 183-5. Brailsford, who neither was, nor was regarded as being, a Communist, had no need to signal his 'defection'. His introduction to Drucker's earlier book merely remarks that the Soviet Union had 'turned opportunist and revised its own operative creed'. Peter F. Drucker, *The End of Economic Man* (London, 1939), pp. vii-xiii.

[9] Interviews, Evelyn Anderson, Julius Braunthal, Heinrich Fraenkel. See Julius Braunthal, *In Search of the Millenium* (London, 1945), pp. 7-11, 323. Oscar Pollak, former editor of the Viennese *Arbeiter Zeitung*, lived in Brailsford's flat briefly in 1940. Nor was it only socialists who sought him out: Count Karolyi approached him with proposals for a Free Hungary movement in 1941. Transcript of broadcast in BBC Overseas Service, 9 May 1941.

which he too believed. In January 1939 Cripps, once an advocate of proletarian unity but now a proponent of a Popular Front, submitted a memorandum to the NEC calling for an alliance with Liberals, Communists, and the ILP. When these proposals were rejected overwhelmingly, Cripps decided to circularize the movement at large. The party leaders, exasperated by his latest antics, would no longer brook such insubordination. Insisting that he reaffirm allegiance or face expulsion, they deliberately goaded him into defiance, and on 25 January he was expelled. Sympathy for Cripps was strong among Socialist League and Unity Campaign veterans, but not in the trade union movement, which disapproved of rebellion against constituted authority. Brailsford, who found the NEC's conduct intolerable, tried to rally the Labour Spain Committee behind Cripps, but few of them would adopt his suggestion to make Cripps their Honorary President as a gesture of solidarity. Disgusted by this timidity, he joined Cripps, Bevan, Gollancz, Strauss, and the Coles at a meeting on 30 January which decided to launch a campaign for a monster petition from electors to the Labour, Liberal, and Co-operative parties urging unity, and was appointed to draft the petition and an explanatory pamphlet.[10] It soon became apparent that the National Petition Campaign was a fiasco. Only a few left-wing MPs joined Cripps, although a number of respected figures expressed outrage at his expulsion.

When a nationwide speaking tour by Cripps and his lieutenants threatened to embarrass Transport House, the Executive retaliated by making support for the campaign a punishable offence. In March Bevan, Strauss, and Trevelyan, refusing to recant, were expelled; others such as Mitchison and Wilkinson returned to the fold rather than risk further retribution. Since he held no official position in the party and was neither an MP nor a candidate, Brailsford's presence among the petitioners was ignored. But, as he told Clare, 'I'm so sick of the Labour Party that I would actually be happier out of it.'[11] He wrote to J. S. Middleton, the Secretary, requesting to be included among the expelled, having 'committed all the offences with which the last batch of criminals is charged'. He reminded the NEC that 'in countries where the art of purging is better understood a confession is held to be sufficient' and warned that he would 'repeat [his] offences'.[12] Although his gesture was widely publicized in the press, the party, refusing to rise to the

[10] HNB to Clare Leighton, 3 Feb. 1939, CLC. The petition campaign is described in Pimlott, pp. 170-82. Sydney Elliott, in an interview with the author, recalled that the pamphlet, which Cripps first approved and then rejected, caused a breach with Brailsford.
[11] HNB to Clare Leighton, 4 Apr. 1939, CLC.
[12] HNB to J. S. Middleton, 3 Apr. 1939, reprinted in *Manchester Guardian*, 5 Apr. 1939. Foot called Brailsford's gesture a 'rare example', most petitioners hastily complying with the party edict. Foot, *Bevan*, p. 291. By the end of April he was informed that the party would not expel him.

bait, ignored his appeal. Once it became clear that the movement was losing ground in the face of official severity, the momentum was quickly dissipated. After the Southport Labour conference in May, most of the rebels, realizing that the Popular Front movement had been routed, applied for readmission. By that time the utter defeat of the Cripps movement was sufficiently dispiriting to make Brailsford 'feel like keeping out of politics for years—perhaps for the rest of [his] life'.[13]

An even deeper source of despair was his realization that the Spanish cause was lost. By the beginning of February Catalonia had fallen to the insurgents, and a few weeks later both England and France granted recognition to the Nationalist government. While Premier Negrin negotiated the surrender to Franco, the Labour Spain Committee continued to demand that the republic be allowed to purchase arms, as though a reversal of non-intervention might still turn the tide in favour of Spanish democracy. Most of the Committee's efforts were focused on raising money for food ships to Spain, a campaign, spearheaded by Brailsford, that managed to amass nearly £5,000.[14] By the beginning of March it was evidently 'all over except the slaughter',[15] and the Committee regretfully began to wind up its affairs, shifting its efforts to soliciting money to resettle Austrian and German veterans of the International Brigade. It collaborated with an Austro-German Committee and tried, apparently without success, to link itself to Eleanor Rathbone's British committee to aid Spanish victims. It also sought sponsorship for those members of the Thaelmann Batallion who might be able to come to England. Brailsford himself offered Four Hedges, but no refugees were sent, and his subsidy for an Austrian brigader was not widely emulated. In June, after a final meeting, the Committee quietly dissolved, its humanitarian accomplishments scarcely compensating for its political failures. Even then, Brailsford did not abandon the struggle: when he discovered that one hundred Brigade veterans were held captive at Burgos, he proposed to enlist the Quakers in an appeal for their release.[16] Before such schemes could be implemented, the war intervened, and in the years that followed Spanish republicans continued to languish in camps in southern France, if not in Franco's prisons.

In contrast to Cripps, Brailsford wanted a Popular Front that would undertake armed resistance to Hitler. While Cripps shunned the anti-appeasers as warmongers, he chastised Labour for failing to demand a national government, including Liberals and Tory rebels, which might

[13] HNB to Clare Leighton, 6 June 1939, CLC.
[14] *New Statesman*, 1 Apr. 1939; miscellaneous letters, Labour Spain Committee Collection.
[15] HNB to Clare Leighton, 7 Mar. 1939, CLC.
[16] HNB to Eleanor Rathbone, 2 Aug. 1939, Rathbone Papers.

'have conscripted wealth, democratised the army, made an alliance with the Soviet Union, and saved what is left of liberty in Europe'. He had come around to support for conscription, but not as long as Chamberlain remained at the helm.[17] Even tacit approval of compulsion aroused many rank and file socialists, and Brailsford's article, however qualified by opposition to Chamberlain, evoked angry correspondence. The labour movement should, he argued, support compulsory service if a new government showed that it meant to resist aggression by basing a grand alliance on Russia and France.[18]

Even his vacillation about conscription ceased as the international situation became more ominous. Compared to the risk of destruction at the hands of Fascist tyrants, the danger that a conscript army might be used for imperialist ends paled. The best safeguard was for workers to join the army 'resolved to keep both their rifles and their Socialist consciences clean'. Unless England prepared itself for resistance, its 'fate may be irreparable defeat'.[19] Nor was there any further point in offering to share economic advantages with the Fascist dictatorships; such 'day-dreams of appeasement' misunderstood the fact that 'they mean to rule and not to share'.[20]

If Brailsford was less shocked than many on the left by the non-aggression pact between Germany and the Soviet Union, he was no less dismayed. Munich had made Stalin question the wisdom of participation in Western collective security, but it could not justify his action. However intelligible his refusal to enter an alliance with half-hearted partners,

> to proceed at the same instant to make with Hitler a pact of neutrality, on the eve of his expected attack on Poland, was a violation of public morality for which nothing in the record of the Soviet Union had prepared us.[21]

Although the pact did not improve the prospects either for peace or for an easy Allied victory, the issue seemed clearer at the end of August than ever before. England's duty was 'to defeat an enemy whose power threatens the survival not merely of democratic liberty, but of any humane civilisation'.[22] Privately he was 'dreading the war more than I dare to admit to myself', but he had become convinced that 'we never shall have peace till that madman is overthrown'.[23] As soon as the war began, he tried to volunteer as a stretcher-bearer or fire-brigader, but

[17] *Reynolds*, 2 Apr. 1939; *New Republic*, 19 Apr. 1939.
[18] *Reynolds*, 30 Apr. 1939.
[19] *Reynolds*, 21 May 1939.
[20] *Reynolds*, 4 June 1939.
[21] *New Republic*, 13 Sept. 1939. See *Reynolds*, 27 Aug. 1939; Bill Jones, *The Russia Complex: The British Labour Party and the Soviet Union* (Manchester, 1977), pp. 40-1.
[22] *Reynolds*, 3 Sept. 1939.   [23] HNB to Clare Leighton, 29 Aug. 1939, CLC.

was, humiliatingly, rejected because of age. 'So I must acquiesce in being useless,' he lamented, 'tho' I watched them accepting men with half my physique.'[24] After the first flight of martial sentiment, he admitted that he could do more to win the war and keep alive 'the permanent values of civilisation' by writing a book and by journalism. Although Gollancz and Unwin both solicited a book on war aims, he was not yet ready. 'I can't see into the future at all,' he remarked, '& until I can, such a book would be beating the air.'[25]

During the early weeks of the war his uncertainty about Soviet aims and fears of wholesale destruction tempered his conviction about the pursuit of victory:

I have hideous moments [he wrote in early October] in which I go shivering, cold & physically sick before writing a war-like article for *Reynolds*. I see all the horror, & yet my reason can find no way out. So when the shivering fit is over I write my bellicose article & no one would guess that I ever hesitated. But at times the thought of the responsibility I'm incurring makes me nearly ill. I envy people who have routine jobs and need incur none of this guilt.[26]

The theme of his early wartime articles is best captured in the headline 'We Must Plan for Peace Now'. Instead of trying to restore the League of Nations, he called for the creation of a Federal Union, which would implement ideas put forward in *A League of Nations* and in *Property or Peace?* Invested with a monopoly of military power, it would assume authority over all dependent colonies and over economic planning. Its constitution would provide protection for cultural minorities, freedom of speech, and a charter of rights for labour.[27] But such a plan presupposed an Allied military victory. While the Communists clamoured for an immediate cessation of fighting, Brailsford warned that such a course would be 'a mere truce between one aggression and the next'. To reassure subject peoples that an Allied victory was in their interest, he thought it essential to articulate a peace plan based on complete disarmament, federal defence, equitable sharing of raw materials (for the vanquished no less than for the victorious powers), and an end to empire, which would 'do more to win this war than all their bombing planes are likely to effect'.[28] Again and again he rejected the Communist allegation that this was an imperialistic war from which workers should dissociate themselves, never perhaps more unequivocally than in an early broadcast:

[24] HNB to Clare Leighton, 8 Sept. 1939, CLC.
[25] HNB to Clare Leighton, 21 Sept. 1939, CLC.
[26] HNB to Clare Leighton, 9 Oct. 1939, CLC.
[27] *Reynolds*, 17 Sept. 1939. Brailsford spelled out his ideas more fully in a pamphlet for a new group called Federal Union. The pamphlet *The Federal Idea* appeared at the beginning of 1940.
[28] *Reynolds*, 8 Oct. 1939.

We must fight because a Nazi victory would rob us of everything that raises man above the beasts—our right to know and to think, our respect for truth, our concern for mercy and humanity, our rights to govern ourselves, our hope of building a society founded on Equality and Law. In short, we are struggling to survive as free men with free minds.[29]

The *Daily Worker*, calling for unity to stop the war, ridiculed this 'burst of heady idealism' from an ostensible critic of imperialism. If the condition for peace was the dissolution of the British Empire, as Brailsford implied in his proposals, then the chief task was to fight Chamberlain, not Hitler.[30] While insisting that the first objective was self-preservation, Brailsford refused to yield to the Communists in repudiating imperialism. The war must be fought on two fronts: against Nazi imperialism, active and expanding, as well as against British imperialism, 'which has lost its impetus and is in retreat'.[31]

Brailsford's ambivalence about the Soviet role sharpened in the early months of the war. Not even the purge trials evoked so indignant a response from him as the unprovoked attack on Finland at the end of November, an assault which

has compelled us to pass the verdict we had hitherto refused to register. His Russia is a totalitarian state like another, as brutal towards the rights of others, as careless of its plighted word. If this man ever understood the international creed of Socialism, he long ago forgot it. In this land the absolute power has wrought its customary effects of corruption.[32]

But as long as Stalin was not the active military ally of Hitler, there was no pretext for diverting resources to a holy war against Communism. By the beginning of 1940 he had a premonition that the Chamberlain government was losing sight of its main objective and that 'a drift into war with Russia [was] inevitable' before the summer ended. If that happened, it would bring about 'military defeat,' he wrote to Hammond, 'but it also means a confusion of the moral and political issues so inextricable that I no longer know where I stand.'[33] In March he signed a letter to newspapers warning against any extension of the war by an attack on the Soviet Union. The letter was swiftly picked up by the Soviet press, which praised its signatories, several of whom, Brailsford among them, did not often receive such laudatory treatment.[34]

---

[29] Transcript of broadcast in BBC Overseas Service, 5 Feb. 1941. Also see *Left*, Nov. 1941.
[30] *Daily Worker*, 9 Oct. 1939.
[31] *Reynolds*, 15 Oct. 1939.
[32] *Reynolds*, 3 Dec. 1939. See Jones, p. 41; *New Republic*, 25 Oct. 1939.
[33] HNB to J. L. Hammond, 19 Feb. 1940, Hammond Papers, Vol. 26, fol. 169.
[34] Letter circulated to press, 2 Mar. 1940, Trevelyan Papers. Signatories included Brailsford, J. B. S. Haldane, Hewlett Johnson, G. B. Shaw, C. P. Trevelyan, and the Webbs. See *The Times*, 25 Mar. 1940.

Since so many journalists were occupied in intelligence or the military, Brailsford became even more useful to the periodicals that employed him. He had spoken to Elliott earlier in 1939 about his future with *Reynolds*: he was then sixty-five and concerned about pension rights. Elliott, who regarded Brailsford as virtually a staff member, agreed in principle, but although his fee was soon raised from six guineas to seven guineas per article, no arrangement had been made concerning pension when Elliott left the weekly in 1941. His successor proved less adept at shielding Brailsford from the hostility of right-wing trade unionists and party officials.[35]

With the *New Statesman* his relations were altogether more congenial. The war removed Richard Crossman and Aylmer Vallance, and until Norman MacKenzie joined the paper as assistant editor in 1943, Martin and Brailsford managed without much additional help. Brailsford, who generally wrote the leading article and at least one other political piece, assisted the editor in putting the paper together every week. No longer able simply to work at home and drop off his articles at the office, he was now obliged to spend Wednesdays and Thursdays copy-editing in addition to the Monday editorial meetings.[36] Although they rarely quarrelled, Martin's indecisiveness could be infuriating. As early as November 1939 Brailsford grumbled that the editor 'wastes endless time discussing his sick conscience',[37] a problem even more besetting during England's lonely struggle in 1940-1. Martin realized that he was exploiting Brailsford, whose health became less dependable as the war continued. Although he continued to be paid by the article, rather than on salary, his rate was increased before the war began, and in March 1940 the *New Statesman* board voted a £100 bonus 'in recognition of his long and very unusual services to the paper'.[38]

As chairman of the *New Statesman* board, Keynes felt responsible for making some restitution to Brailsford, who was about to embark on eye surgery that would require lengthy convalescence. On the other hand, disagreeing sharply with almost everything he wrote, Keynes reproached Martin repeatedly for not curbing Brailsford's emotional outbursts. Complaining in January 1943 about 'an old but ever-increasing grievance', he gave vent to his bias:

He seems to me to have every defect—almost incredibly misinformed and ill-informed, carrying credulity to the point when it is almost certifiable, extraordinarily tendencious [sic] in a frightfully boring sort of way, with bees in

---

[35] HNB to Clare Leighton, 14 Mar., 13 Nov. 1939, CLC; Interview, Sydney Elliott.
[36] Martin, *Editor*, p. 296; C. H. Rolph, *Kingsley* (London, 1973), pp. 289-92; HNB to Clare Leighton, 22 Sept. 1940, CLC.
[37] HNB to Clare Leighton, 13 Nov. 1939, CLC.
[38] Kingsley Martin to W. Whitley, [Mar. 1940], KMP.

bonnets that entirely distort the right balance of attention given in the paper to different subjects without any balanced judgment or wisdom.[39]

Martin, unwaveringly loyal to the friend he regarded as 'the best journalist writing in England',[40] would not be budged. He admitted to occasionally eliminating 'passages of the sort that annoy you and which I cannot stomach', but it was the tone of moral passion, not their accuracy, to which the editor took exception. He assured Keynes that Crossman, their acknowledged expert on Germany, confirmed Brailsford's German articles and that his continual harping on India stemmed from their mutual conviction that it was one of the 'key questions' in the war.[41]

The war also launched Brailsford's career as a broadcaster, an opportunity enjoyed not merely because it supplemented his earnings, but because of the chance to transmit his views abroad. His first talk—actually an interview—on Soviet policy was delivered in the Overseas Service in November 1939. His ten-guinea fee was raised to twelve in 1941, when his broadcasts, beamed to Australia and New Zealand, became more frequent. During the course of the war he delivered several dozen talks on topics ranging from Nazi propaganda and the refugee problem to recollections of Nevinson, Trotsky, the Red Army in 1920, and the Balkans. He was also busier than ever as a lecturer for the Federal Union group, Fabian summer schools, the Fabian International Bureau, and occasionally at Dartington Hall. When he returned from North Africa he was invited to address Chatham House, and in November 1939 he spoke to a PEP meeting of civil servants on plans for peace, but none of this activity could do much to dispel his gloom.

> I'm facing my ruined life [he told Clare in February 1940] and the knowledge that I shall never have a home again nor anyone to love. I don't know how to face it. I'm ill & without courage & I've no hope about public affairs either & no conviction that I have anything of any use to give in that field . . .[42]

If his letters to Clare smack of self-pity, it was certainly true that his health, indifferent at best in recent years, was deteriorating by the end of 1939. By December his cataract had produced blindness in his right eye but, although operable, could not be treated immediately because hospitals had been commandeered for anticipated war casualties. Influenza during the winter aggravated his heart condition, a later exam-

---

[39] J. M. Keynes to Kingsley Martin, 28 Jan. 1943, KMP. See *Encounter*, Feb. 1965, esp. pp. 84-5.
[40] Kingsley Martin to J. M. Keynes, 26 Jan. 1943, KMP.
[41] Kingsley Martin to J. M. Keynes, 8 and 11 Feb. 1943, KMP.
[42] HNB to Clare Leighton, 6 Feb. 1940, CLC.

ination revealing an enlarged aorta and low blood pressure. It became more difficult for him to drown his sorrows in hard work, because he no longer had the stamina for sustained labour. Fortunately, his eye operation, at first postponed indefinitely, could be performed at Moorfields Eye Hospital in March. For several months he was obliged to wear a dark glass over the operated eye, after which his oculist suggested he use the right eye exclusively for reading and plan for a cataract operation in the left eye when it was further developed.

As the *Blitzkrieg* shifted to the Western Front, all doubts about the gravity of England's situation were dispelled. For the first time, Brailsford was obliged to ponder how the war might affect him directly:

I've seen all the possibilities of defeat including a Nazi concentration camp for myself. Against that eventuality I have my precaution handy. Of course, when all struggle was over, but not till then, I'd go if possible to the USA. But the chances are it w'dn't be possible. Those of us who have the cursed Cassandra gift see all these possiblities. Kingsley says he'll disguise himself as a clergyman & vanish into the provinces. I might try to do something of the kind too.

An ironic twist, perhaps, for two rebellious sons of Nonconformist preachers, but not so surprising on the eve of Dunkirk! Still, Brailsford believed that 'under Winston we have at last a fighting chance—years too late'. He filled out an application for the Local Defence Volunteers, but was not called, and offered his services to a Foreign Office acquaintance in some unpaid capacity. 'I'd do anything, even hack translations,' he continued, but this too was met only by a polite acknowledgement. Creative work no longer seemed possible, and he had stopped trying after the situation became acute. 'One has the sense,' he added, 'that everything is only provisional—one's own life, this nation & civilisation itself.'[43]

With the prospect of invasion looming, American indifference seemed all the more galling. He found himself 'hating the *New Republic* rather violently' and, were it not for the fact that they continued to publish his interventionist articles, he might well have resigned. It was difficult for him to believe that American intellectuals were 'as coldly indifferent as [the *New Republic* was] to our European tragedy'.[44] A week after Churchill became Prime Minister, Brailsford, overcoming his inhibitions, penned a long appeal in favour of America's entry. The gist of his argument was that the only hope of victory, and perhaps even of survival, for England was for America to 'fling herself, with her unmatched resources, as a belligerent into the battle for our common

---

[43] HNB to Clare Leighton, 1 June 1940, CLC.
[44] HNB to Clare Leighton, 15 June 1940, CLC.

values'. If England succumbed, the United States would have to combat the same enemy alone; it was preferable to fight Hitler in Europe while the British, still possessing 'an unbroken will', retained reserves of men and material. In a rejoinder to his letter, the editors reaffirmed their belief in neutrality on the grounds that more could be done to save democracy and prepare for 'future world reconstruction' by remaining at peace than by becoming a belligerent.[45] But the communication inspired McGraw-Hill to invite him to expand his argument in a short book. They offered $200 plus fifteen per cent on sales over 5,000 copies, but wanted the manuscript within two weeks for an August publication. Accepting the terms, he claimed that his motive was 'just patriotism. It's the first bit of useful service that's come my way since the war began.'[46]

From England to America, the briefest of his books, hammered away at the theme of common danger. If England was fighting to preserve Western civilization, it was shouldering a burden that rightly belonged to America as well. It was clear that 'a free England could not survive in isolation on the fringe of an expanded German Reich'.[47] If British sea power were crushed, the entire Atlantic coast would lie within the German system, and Latin America would be vulnerable to Nazi penetration. As long as the destiny of the United States was inseparable from that of England, it needed to act with resolute boldness to secure its safety. The book created less of a stir in American circles than anticipated, perhaps because, he convinced himself, it had been 'deliberately boycotted' in the press. On the other hand, Gollancz agreed to publish a slightly revised version as *America Our Ally* in his Victory Books series later in the year.[48]

Much as he lauded Churchill, he was quick to decry the constraints under which wartime journalists had to operate. When he wrote that British forces could only reconquer Europe with the help of the submerged masses behind enemy lines, German workers included, the censors demurred. They objected to his claim that 'our chance of winning the confidence of the masses of Europe depends on our abandonment of all the privileges and monopolies of Empire'. He believed that he was being followed and spied upon by secret service agents. On one occasion he was spotted drawing swastikas on the tablecloth of a restaurant frequented by refugees and was reported to the Home Office. In fact, he had been explaining to his dinner companion that

[45] *New Republic*, 17 June 1940.
[46] HNB to Clare Leighton, 8 July 1940, CLC.
[47] *From England to America*, p. 9.
[48] HNB to Clare Leighton, 1-2 May 1941, CLC. *America Our Ally* was published as Victory Books No. 11 (not under the aegis of the Left Book Club) in November 1940.

the swastika, which Hitler had appropriated, had long historical antecedents, as he knew from his anthropological studies. Vallance subsequently told him that his name had appeared on a confidential Home Office list of suspicious persons. He was, not surprisingly, appalled:

> ... if anyone could have been more patriotic than I've been in this war, I don't know him. The stupidity of our secret service passes belief... The amazing thing is to find this kind of pettiness down below when we've at last got a big man at the top.[49]

It was, however, not so much the personal inconveniences as the humanitarian considerations, so readily disregarded in wartime, that spurred his pen. His concern with the refugees and victims of Fascism also encompassed the enemy population. No more than in the First World War did he believe ordinary people should suffer merely because of the outrages perpetrated by their leaders. He opposed the Continental blockade because the denial of imported food 'might mean starvation for the workers and the stunting of their children'. All he could offer by way of suggestion was a vague notion of co-ordination with the United States to banish famine from occupied lands, while continuing to deny the enemy access to vital resources, such as oil and rubber.[50] Several months later a tour of the East End of London prompted him to protest against the inadequate provision of shelters and to plead for compulsory evacuation of the idle population.[51] The treatment of those aliens interned in England when the war began was reprehensible as well. While avowed Nazis should remain in captivity, there was no excuse for incarcerating 'racial refugees', most of whom approved the Allied cause and might be usefully employed.[52] When it became clear to observers in the West that Jews were being exterminated, he exhorted British and American authorities to attempt the rescue at least of Jewish children, preparing a refuge for them on neutral soil.[53]

His tireless devotion to the interests of others made him less preoccupied with his own lonely struggle for survival. His letters during the Blitz are pugnacious, not morose or maudlin as they had sometimes been before. During the battering of London in mid-September 1940, his Belsize Park flat shook from nearby bombing, but suffered no damage. 'The amazing thing after all this pounding by day and night,' he wrote,

[49] *Reynolds*, 7 July 1940; HNB to Clare Leighton, 8 July 1940, CLC; Interview, Sybil Wingate.
[50] Letter to Editor, *New Statesman*, 6 July 1940. A similar letter was published in *Glasgow Forward*, 13 July 1940.
[51] *Reynolds*, 29 Sept. 1940.
[52] *Reynolds*, 17 Nov. 1940.
[53] *Reynolds*, 20 Dec. 1942; *New Statesman*, 9 Jan. 1943.

is that most of London is normal and unharmed, with tubes and buses running as usual. . . . So far, wisely or unwisely, I've gone quietly to bed. I've even slept fairly well, tho' a heavy bomb in the neighborhood will wake me up. The worst of it is that one is helpless. One can't get one's combative instincts going —the brutes are out of reach. There's nothing to do but sit still—which isn't a militant posture.[54]

Early in November a nearby cinema was destroyed, and a high explosive bomb fell about one hundred yards from his house, cutting off the gas for two days. Although the nightly bombardment began to diminish, the inhabitants of Belsize Park Gardens were organized in squads for fire-fighting. Each group was required to report for duty one night in eight, with every member taking watch, equipped with whistle and pump, for two hours and twenty minutes at a stretch. 'I've had two watches,' he reported in February 1941, 'and nothing whatever happened. I sat up reading in profound calm for 3 hours, & then lay down in my clothes while someone else took his turn.'[55] Somewhat to his own amazement, he was becoming cheerful, although there was little to suggest that a British victory was any closer.

A recurrent theme of his wartime articles, summarized succinctly in the *Reynolds* headline 'Destroy Fascism, Not the Germans', was that Hitler and his cohorts were the enemy, not the mass of the people. In January 1941, while the Blitz still raged, he tried to exonerate the Germans from the charges which Lord Vansittart levied in his notorious broadcasts, later published as *Black Record*. Far from being congenitally barbarous, they had, Brailsford claimed, betrayed their own cultural heritage in succumbing to Hitler's tyranny. Nothing in their past indicated a greater prospensity for aggression or cruelty than other European nations. Nazism was not the fulfilment of the German past; it was, on the contrary,

a conscious revolt against all the values of the rationalist civilisation of the West. Of that civilisation Germany was a member, until this pariah party, aided by the folly of France and Britain, swarmed out of the brothels and slums and trampled on Germany's heritage of moral and intellectual worth.[56]

Convinced that opposition to the regime was mounting and should be encouraged, he pleaded for a sign to the German people that in defeat they would not incur a repetition of the humiliations of Versailles. The first step in changing their outlook would be to show that 'men may be sincere when they profess goodwill, respect and fellowship towards

[54] HNB to Clare Leighton, 19 Sept. 1940, CLC.
[55] HNB to Clare Leighton, 28 Feb. 1941, CLC; transcript of broadcast in BBC Home Service, 5 Mar. 1941.
[56] *New Statesman*, 25 Jan. 1941; *Reynolds*, 26 Jan. 1941.

those of other races'.⁵⁷ If the only prospect offered the enemy was that of political impotence and territorial dismemberment, they would have little incentive to risk their lives by rising up against their rulers.

Ever since Clare's departure, Brailsford had clung to the hope of her return. He was sure that if she did not come back of her own accord, he could overcome her hesitation once they were reunited. When he proposed a visit in May 1939, she prevailed upon him to defer plans indefinitely. A year later he actually booked passage, but when the Germans penetrated the French lines a few days later, he cancelled his reservation. The opportunity once lost, it was difficult for anyone to secure Transatlantic passage unless on official business. But by May 1941, after Martin pulled strings, the Ministry of Information authorized his trip as a *New Statesman* correspondent. Ostensibly, he was coming to New York and Washington to sense the atmosphere, conduct interviews, and lobby informally for American intervention, but in fact his real motive was to bring Clare back. Although permitted to bring only £10 with him, he had guarantees from the *New Republic* and from the *Baltimore Sun*, so that he would earn his keep. Much as he tried to delude himself, he was optimistic neither about reconciliation with Clare nor about his role as emissary.

For the two weeks crossing in a Norwegian freighter he was utterly miserable. The winds were Arctic; the sea rough; and he was sick most of the time. Arriving in New York in June, he visited Johnson, Bruce Bliven, and other *New Republic* associates and discovered that American resistance to entry into the war was deeper than he had anticipated. He stayed with the Jahodas in Bronxville—a happy reunion—before travelling to Baltimore to see Clare. It was clear that she was reluctant to see him, and their meeting did nothing to heal the breach. Anxious to avoid hurting him, she wrote finally to explain her conflict between reason and tenderness:

I cannot come back to live the same old life with you because something happened to that life that has taken from it the joy and peace and security.... My brain may tell me that I need not fear you, but my memory will not be crushed. ... You have suffered and caused me to suffer by reason of deep early bruises and so are able to understand now how I am helpless to remove or even ignore the bruises that were given me. They will always be there to prevent any intimate relationship between us, and our life would be forced and untrue.⁵⁸

There was little during the rest of his visit to restore his spirits. He

---

⁵⁷ *Germans and Nazis: A Reply to 'Black Record'*, Common Wealth Popular Library, No. 2 [1942?].
⁵⁸ Clare Leighton to HNB, 2 July 1941 (Copy), CLC.

found the stifling Baltimore and Washington climate 'unendurable', and his interview with Vice-President Wallace, 'which at least gave me the chance to say what I have to say for England', accomplished little.[59] The Elmhirsts, then in New York, urged him to stay on and lecture on behalf of the British war effort, but he was too dejected for such an undertaking:

> I've seldom felt so depressed or so hopeless in all my life. I don't want to stay and still less do I want to return—which merely means that I have no home on either side of the ocean, and may never hope for a home again.[60]

Personally and professionally, Brailsford was at a loose end much of 1942. His history of socialism, intended for quick completion, was becoming unwieldy; he found himself 're-writing unsatisfactory bits—a new vice for me' and doubted whether he would finish as rapidly as anticipated. Upon returning from America, he had the impression that his *New Statesman* duties had vanished during his absence, but by 1942 he was employed as fully as ever. His role as Martin's confessor was no less exasperating, especially in view of his own pessimism:

> ... I think I keep saner than most because I saw all this in embryo years ago, & never had any bright illusions. But as usual, I'm as useless as Cassandra. The fight has gone out of me. I was militant & spirited enough in 1940 when I wrote my little book. But I'm 'kind of' broken now. Somehow I don't want to write what I feel—either in articles, or even in a letter. It just corrodes me & I keep silent, with a sense of impotence.[61]

Later that spring, faced with the threat of a Japanese invasion of India, the British government sent Cripps with an offer of self-determination intended to placate nationalist leaders. While circumventing previous pitfalls, it did not, in the eyes of Indian leaders, constitute an immediate transfer of power. Brailsford, underlining the fact that the British government had for the first time made 'a dated offer of what amounts to independence', gave qualified support, but he too realized that independence needed to be made more explicit.[62] Two years earlier he had endorsed the concession of dominion status at the earliest opportunity; he now realized that such a gesture would be insufficient to appease nationalist sentiment. With the reluctant admission that Indians 'distrust us and dislike us', he concluded that 'independence is what Indians want and mean to get'.[63] Once the Cripps offer had been rejected, Gandhi launched the Quit India movement, demanding that

---

[59] HNB to Clare Leighton, 4 July 1941, CLC.
[60] HNB to Clare Leighton, 9 Aug. 1941, CLC; Drucker, *Bystander*, pp. 185-6.
[61] HNB to Clare Leighton, 10 and 17 Mar. 1942, CLC.
[62] *New Statesman*, 16 May 1942.
[63] *New Statesman*, 4 May 1940; *Subject India*, pp. 164, 166.

the British authorities withdraw and leave Indians to form their own national government.

With the British government lapsing into what he termed 'majestic inertia', lacking any response to Indian discontent except repression, Brailsford welcomed Allen Lane's suggestion that he write a Penguin on India. It meant postponing his history of socialism, but he was already feeling 'pretty stale over that book & perhaps it was as well to break off for a time & come back to it'.[64] When Lane eventually rejected it, Gollancz was able to arrange its adoption as the Left Book Club monthly selection for April 1943, perhaps in lieu of the history he had never really wanted and would never have the opportunity to publish. *Subject India*, Brailsford's only Left Book Club monthly choice, but his fourth work under the Gollancz imprint, was an old man's work. Pessimistic about the future, weighted down by political weariness, it said more about past mistakes than about future prospects. In place of the reportage that brought immediacy to many of his books, he appended a large segment of his earlier *Rebel India*, now almost twelve years old, but not yet out of date. Although his own views had kept pace with the changing currents of Indian opinion, far more so than did those of British experts, the book had a stale quality, lacking the urgency that direct contact could impart.

By 1942 relations had become sufficiently embittered that Brailsford was convinced that the bond between England and India must be severed. Yet he preferred the Cripps model, with independence evolving out of autonomy, to the abrupt Gandhi approach. Even if the British withdrew and allowed Indians to settle their own affairs, sectarian divisions stood in the way of unity. Always critical of the communal electorates, separating Hindu from Muslim, he dismissed them as 'an audacious irrelevance, foreign to the actual concerns of daily life'.[65] The real divisions were those of class, which separated landlord from tenant. Left to themselves, the Hindu and Muslim peasants would recognize a kindred class spirit. Indeed, he contended that the Muslim League, representing wealthy, conservative landowners, was demanding an independent Pakistan in order to maintain the ascendancy of the existing ruling class.

As far as Brailsford was concerned, the old imperial dependence had ended with the war. With the severing of economic bonds, there was no longer any reason to hesitate in offering India its freedom, however likely its secession from the Commonwealth. With the help of a mediator, Congress and the Muslim League might negotiate an agreement over Pakistan, conceding the right of provinces to self-determina-

[64] HNB to Clare Leighton, 12 Nov. 1942, CLC.   [65] *Subject India*, p. 79.

tion. As long as Bengal and the Sikh territory remained in an Indian federation, the possible separation of Pakistan, undesirable though it was, need not be a mortal blow. He was not so naïve as to believe that the difficulties would evaporate overnight, but only that the obstacles to constitutional accord might be removed when England recognized that she no longer possessed India.

In contemplating the future of Europe, Brailsford saw socialist unity and the re-absorption of Germany into the European community as the central issues. For both these objectives the revival of a Socialist International seemed imperative. He envisaged a European federation, not entirely socialist in composition, but receptive to collectivist economic policies. Such a union could not survive with either Germany or the Soviet Union excluded, any more than the League of Nations had. Although he foresaw 'Himalayan obstacles' to socialist unity, he felt that the key was the consolidation of a single party in each country based on the collaboration of socialists and Communists.[66]

An effective settlement hinged on the resolution of the German problem. Repudiating both unconditional surrender and the 'psychological disarmament' of Germany as tenable goals, he was stirred to affirm before Hitler's victims, in Germany no less than in England, that the war had not wholly extinguished socialist ideals and humanitarian values. He looked to the German underground, to trade unionists and teachers who kept their consciences intact while bowing their heads, to re-educate the next generation. At the suggestion of Woolf, then Chairman of the Fabian International Bureau, he prepared an outline for a meeting of its Germany group. Woolf and others urged him to elaborate his arguments in a pamphlet, but he was at a loss to know what response to make to appeals for a manifesto of the sort he had furnished during the First World War.

I'm besieged by pleas, which move & disturb me [he confided in June 1943] to write something to help my day and generation. But what? I'm so pessimistic about the coming settlement that I'm paralysed. Am I just once again to write, as I did in 1916, a book of amiable day-dreams, which everyone will ignore? And yet, not to fight at all, but just to escape into the past seems too cowardly.[67]

During that summer he decided to expand his Fabian proposals into a book-length manuscript, which Allen Lane, who had rejected *Subject India* several months before, now agreed to publish as a Penguin. The 75,000 copies issued in February 1944 sold out quickly, and an American edition under the John Day imprint appeared later in the year.

[66] *International Socialist Forum*, Mar. 1943. [67] HNB to Clare Leighton, 6 June 1943, CLC.

Our Settlement With Germany was a compassionate and generous declaration, far-sighted in its recognition of the need for European unity, yet strangely oblivious to the depths of anti-German sentiment in Allied countries. To Brailsford, the test of an effective settlement was whether it would enable the German nation to regain self-respect within the European community. So convinced was he that the average German was ignorant of Nazi misdeeds, that he was more concerned to resuscitate Germany than to salve the wounds it had inflicted on others. Arguing that the enemy should be disarmed, not dismembered, he called for a return to those Versailles boundaries he had once denounced so vociferously. If any reparation were exacted, it must not be in territory or forced labour (as the Poles and Russians were demanding), but rather in machinery and equipment, beneficial alike to its recipients and to those Germans who would be restored to useful employment.[68] While conceding that military occupation was inevitable, he urged that it be brief and that any ban on political activity be lifted promptly. Democracy could only take root if there were citizen participation in trade unions, political parties, and interest groups. He insisted that Nazi teachers be identified and purged from the schools, but once this process was completed, Germans themselves should undertake the education of the young.[69]

Its most controversial section dealt with the punishment of Nazi criminals. Without denying their heinous offences, he argued that 'to reverse the moral values of civilised men is not a crime known to international law'.[70] Since it was wrong to create a new code retrospectively, it would be better to exile Hitler and other prominent Nazis to some remote island than to bring them to trial. As far as the party faithful were concerned, they should be debarred from holding political office for the remainder of their lives. Those guilty of actual atrocities in the conduct of the war might legitimately be brought before international courts martial. For SS men he proposed exile in undeveloped regions, where they might start life again as pioneers on the soil. Alternatively, they could be compelled to work, under close scrutiny, to rebuild German towns, while being subjected to moral indoctrination.

One lesson of Versailles was the importance of distinguishing retribution from reconstruction. Whatever penalties were imposed on war criminals, Germany should not itself again be treated as a pariah. The question of devastation was to be dealt with in a European

---

[68] *Our Settlement With Germany*, American ed., pp. 61-3, 81-2, 136-40. Much of this material appeared in a series in *New Republic*, 10-24 July 1944.

[69] *Our Settlement With Germany*, pp. 43-53; 94-100; *Contemporary Review*, Vol. CLXVII, No. 956 (Aug. 1945), pp. 70-5.

[70] *Our Settlement With Gemany*, p. 57.

context, not by extorting punitive reparation from Germany, but by each nation contributing its special skills and resources. Despite his conviction that social revolution in Germany offered the best chance for an enduring peace, Brailsford knew that the British and Americans were disinclined to let it happen. In fact, he was convinced that one motive for an extended Allied military occupation was to forestall the formation of a People's Front of progressive Catholics, socialists, and Communists. But while German heavy industry should be preserved, its productive skills turned to peaceful uses, the power of the Junkers and industrialists must not be permitted to revive. He favoured the internationalization of the Ruhr, with a single multinational consortium controlling its coal and iron, a plan that would relieve Europe of the fear of German predominance while averting dismemberment.[71]

Brailsford concluded with an impassioned appeal to his readers to 'recover for mankind its obliterated instincts and half-forgotten principles of social morality',[72] a plea that fell on deaf ears. Lane had distributed complimentary copies of the book to prominent MPs, but politicians and the press alike accorded it a frosty reception. Its author, who had just turned seventy, lamented that it was

so much ahead of public opinion that (as usual with my books) it might as well not have been written. Ten years hence (when it & I are forgotten) people will begin to think on these lines.[73]

Woolf, who read the work in manuscript, agreed with its basic premises, but felt that to ignore the differences in the German 'communal psychology' was to give the appearance of denying any facts that disparaged pre-Nazi Germany.[74] Dalton, to whom Brailsford sent a copy of the book, complained, 'You seem to think so much about the Germans & how to make them good & happy, that you have little thought left for the Russians or for other victim peoples of these dreadful years'.[75]

The sharpest reaction to *Our Settlement With Germany* came from the Communist camp. In February 1945 *Labour Monthly* reprinted a venomous review by Ilya Ehrenburg accusing Brailsford of defending Himmler and the SS, of seeking to save Hitler, who no doubt would be dispatched to some idyllic island to 'write his memoirs on baby-massacre'. In a work 'that might have appeared just as well in Berlin',

---

[71] Ibid., pp. 38, 57-63, 113-16, 135-6; *New Statesman*, 16 Jan. 1943. The article was reprinted as a pamphlet entitled *Psychological Disarmament* by The Friends Committee for Refugees and Aliens.
[72] *Our Settlement With Germany*, p. 154.
[73] HNB to Clare Leighton, 3 Sept. 1944, CLC.
[74] Leonard Woolf to HNB, 17 Oct. 1943, Woolf Papers.
[75] Hugh Dalton to HNB, 13 Mar. 1944, Dalton Papers, II/8/1.

Brailsford had not concealed 'his tenderness for Fascism' when he conceded that the New Order achieved some positive results or implied that Nazis should be employed in rebuilding German (rather than Russian) cities.[76] Brailsford retorted that it was just this kind of 'mendacity and slander [that] has made cooperation between Socialists and Communists difficult in the past'. Answering Ehrenburg, he insisted that his aim had been to render Nazis harmless in the future while avoiding further bloodshed. Reproving Brailsford for such 'suicidal leniency', Dutt, in the same issue, reminded readers of his shameful record of 'vituperation' in denouncing the Moscow trials and attacks on Stalin during the battle against 'Finnish fascism'.[77]

By 1944 he was fearful that when the war ended, Europe would be divided into rival spheres of interest, one dependent on Moscow, the other on Washington. Yet he tended to ascribe blame for the deterioration of relations to the West, not to Stalinist expansion. Having recognized Russia as 'indisputably the predominant power in the whole of Eastern Europe', it made sense to respect whatever arrangements 'Russia deems necessary for her safety'.[78] But if he condoned an extension of its borders at Poland's expense, he balked at Poland's demand for compensation in East Prussia. The inconsistency in conniving at Soviet ambitions but not Polish ones seemed justified; Poland could not fail to become a Russian satellite, but a healthy Germany was the key to European integration. To cede its territories as a form of reparation would militate against 'a pacific and cooperative habit of mind' and might risk keeping 'the Nazi temper alive and militant'.[79]

Late in 1942 Brailsford chaired a day-long conference on German underground resistance, the speakers including Richard Löwenthal, a prominent New Left theoretician. During the war he had kept in contact with socialist refugees, such as Erich Ollenhauer and Hans Vogel, but also with the left dissidents identified with *Neu Beginnen*. As a leading journalist, untainted by the internecine conflicts within the Marxist camp, he was an inevitable focal figure, one of the few Englishmen universally respected by Europeans of the moderate and far left. He had been among the founders of the *International Socialist Forum*, a monthly supplement of *Left News*, edited by Braunthal in the hope of sustaining an international socialist vision throughout the war.[80]

---

[76] *Labour Monthly*, Vol. 27, No. 2 (Feb. 1945), pp. 58-61.
[77] *Labour Monthly*, Vol. 27, No. 4 (Apr. 1945), pp. 126-8, 104-5.
[78] *New Statesman*, 15 Jan. 1944.
[79] *Left News*, Feb. 1944. His belief that Poland would gravitate towards the Soviet orbit led him to shift support from the London exile regime to the pro-Russian contingent after Yalta. *Reynolds*, 30 Jan. 1944, 18 Feb. 1945.
[80] *Reynolds*, 28 Dec. 1941; Braunthal, *Millenium*, p. 336. See W. Röder, *Die deutschen sozialistischen Exilgruppen in Grossbritannien 1940-1945* (Hannover, 1968), pp. 82, 88, 218.

Among those attending the conference in London was a German refugee in her late twenties named Evamaria Perlmann. Briefly married to an Englishman named Jarvis, she had come to England at the beginning of the war and had been working as a medical aide in St Ives when she met Brailsford. Following his summation at the end of the session, she asked a question; the next day when both were lunching at the Vega restaurant, he recognized her and invited her to supper and to hear his new recording of one of the Rasoumovsky quartets.

That chance encounter started a relationship that lasted for the rest of his life. The next night they attended a concert at the Wigmore Hall, followed by more conversation and recorded music at Belsize Park Gardens. After their third meeting he sent her a note saying that he had fallen in love with her. She remained in London for six weeks and after a brief return to St Ives, where she was long overdue, moved into Brailsford's flat, nursing him through several months in the spring of 1943 when he was seriously ill. Evamaria did more than take care of an elderly man in poor health: she restored his spirits, bringing him out of his loneliness into a new burst of creative energy and interest in the world around him. Despite forty years difference in age, she ministered to his needs and, by rejuvenating him, brought comfort and happiness to his last years. Outspoken and uninhibited, she was a small, vivacious woman, a playful sprite with a fondness for music and slightly exotic clothes. Although his friends found her irrepressible and oversolicitous, he basked in her warmth and cherished her lively company. The only child of a cultured German opthalmologist, Evamaria, whose mother died when she was in her twenties, developed a precocious interest in science and medicine, a keen aesthetic sensibility, and inexhaustible curiosity. Brailsford's busy life, his international contacts, his meetings and conferences, and later his travels, gave a focus to her energies. Involved in his world, sharing his political and humanitarian pursuits, she became his alter ego in a way in which, for very different reasons, neither Jane nor Clare had. Determined to make him live as fully as possible in his remaining years, she concerned herself with his health and diet. Indeed, as Martin put it, she 'made him youthful again'.[81] After several solitary years, the flat in Belsize Park Gardens once again hummed with activity, with visits from Germans and Indians, politicians and scientists, and especially from several young American GIs whom they virtually adopted. They had encountered Luther Allen and Robert Weaver at a concert in 1943 and for the next year opened their home to them. For both men the Brailsfords

---

[81] Interviews, Evamaria Brailsford, Mabel R. Brailsford, Kingsley Martin.

became a substitute family, offering the kind of intimacy few American soldiers could find in England.

In June 1944, much to his astonishment, the University of Glasgow conferred upon him an honorary Doctorate of Laws on the fiftieth anniversary of his degree. He had never regarded himself as a distinguished alumnus, but was grateful to be remembered by his university. In his address on behalf of the honorary degree recipients he acknowledged debts to his professors, especially Murray, Bradley, and Caird. A month later, when her divorce became final, he and Evamaria were married at the Hampstead Town Hall and spent their honeymoon at Dartington Hall. Shortly after their return Brailsford's mother died peacefully at the age of 101. Her mind had become childlike, but she did not suffer and was completely oblivious to the war, her deafness having prevented her from ever hearing a siren or a falling bomb.

As the war came to an end, Brailsford was almost as pessimistic as he had been in 1918 and for much the same reason. He told his young American friends:

I've actually started writing my history book once again—the section of it where I deal with the 'True Levellers' and Winstanley . . . I turn happily to such work, because I'm reasonably sure that it's worthwhile. I don't feel that about my political journalism or even about my political books. In them I may be merely a belated voice from the XIXth century repeating in vain what our age rejects. Or even if my gospel is not out of date, as I fear it is, I cannot reach the decisive minds who make policy. So I'm never sure that these books & articles are worth writing. . . . The policy of unconditional surrender is as wicked as it is stupid. . . . The result is a suicidal resistance which will wholly ruin Germany & half-ruin the rest of Europe, besides rendering any future recovery, moral & physical, impossible.[82]

He certainly anticipated retiring from politics and journalism, as though he too were being demobilized. He was by now writing infrequently for *Reynolds*, which continued his retaining fee of twelve guineas a month and £4 per article until 1947, and tried to negotiate, with Martin's encouragement, a *New Statesman* pension. Nearly seventy-two and no longer robust, he was ready to slacken his pace, and, in any event, Martin now viewed his 'excessively pro-German attitude' as an embarrassment.[83] Arrangements for his retirement progressed slowly, although after 1947 he wrote little aside from an occasional reminiscence or review. The editor continued to authorize £50 a month payment

---

[82] HNB to Luther Allen and Robert Weaver [?1945].
[83] Interview, Kingsley Martin; HNB to Kingsley Martin, 18 July 1945, KMP.

whether or not he contributed, but the *New Statesman* board did not formalize his £600 annual pension until 1952.[84]

There were, to be sure, certain advantages to venerability. Aside from Shaw, there were few other publicists still active who could recall the Boer War, and many of the younger generation of Labour leaders had been raised on such anti-imperialist tracts as *The War of Steel and Gold*. Brailsford was a direct link with Hobson and the pre-1914 critique of empire-building, an important part of Labour's heritage as it looked towards colonial freedom. Thus when the Fabian Colonial Bureau decided to publish a collection of essays, Brailsford was invited to contribute a general assessment of 'Socialists and the Empire'. In it he reiterated the by now familiar Hobson-Brailsford thesis that the 'search [for] colonial markets and fields of investment is a consequence of the wrong distribution of the product of industry'. He envisaged a bold socialist initiative in Africa, where the economic structure could be reshaped to win power for the community. Once in power, Labour should regard these colonies just as it would a depressed area at home: the state had a duty to finance socialized undertakings, furnish machinery, and offer grants for educational and health services. In all of this, benevolent though it was, there is not even a hint about the rapidity of African political advance, much less any anticipation of the economic barriers to British aid in dependent areas. Brailsford's assumptions about imperialism were rooted in the past, and his prescriptions for the future showed little awareness of actual conditions.[85]

Ever since his visit to Palestine in 1930, he had championed Jewish settlement, his advocacy becoming even more fervent after the Holocaust. In denying the absolute Arab claim to ownership, he warned against permitting a backward people to monopolize a territory capable of sustaining a higher civilization. To deny further immigration would be 'more than an injustice to the Jews: it would be a sin against life itself'. The best hope for the region would be a Jordan Valley Authority on the model of the American TVA; within the framework of economic development and a constructive agrarian policy, immigration of both Jews and Arabs could proceed. He felt that Jewish victims of persecution deserved priority and favoured the establishment of a binational state, with each community managing its own education system and social services, while sharing in the benefits of the Jordan scheme.[86]

---

[84] I am grateful to J. A. Morgan for this information.

[85] Rita Hinden, ed., *Fabian Colonial Essays* (London, 1945), pp. 19-35. See Margaret Cole, *The Story of Fabian Socialism* (London, 1961), pp. 282-6; Fischer, pp. 316-17; Kiernan, p. 243. Brailsford also served on the Advisory Committee of the Fabian International Bureau.

[86] Introduction to *Palestine Controversy: A Symposium*, Fabian Research Series No. 101 (1945). Substantially the same analysis appeared in *New Statesman*, 27 Oct. 1945 and in *Commentary*, Feb. 1946.

In November 1945 *Reynolds* proposed that Brailsford go to India to observe the provincial elections scheduled between January and March. The paper would pay his expenses, but he would also be able to write for the *New Statesman* and *New Republic*. It was a perfect opportunity for so redoubtable a friend of Indian freedom to play the role of goodwill ambassador, especially now that Pethick-Lawrence had become Indian Secretary in the Attlee Cabinet. By the time his trip began, he was apprehensive about any solution, as he explained to Clare:

I'm sure to be well received—anyhow by Indians—but it will be painful, for I gather that the bitterness and distrust of us are worse than they have ever been in our day. And the problem of *how* to give this country its freedom is, in detail, so difficult that for the first time I find myself hesitating over what to back or suggest.[87]

During nearly six months in India Brailsford and Evamaria had ample opportunity to meet Indian and British leaders. From Bombay, their port of arrival, they journeyed northward by train to Peshawar to observe elections in the North-west Frontier province. Here, and later in Lahore, they witnessed intimidation by politicians and clerics acting on behalf of Jinnah's Muslim League. A meeting with Jinnah in Lahore did little to revise his estimate of the Muslim leader as an unscrupulous demagogue, inflexible and uncompromising, for whom Pakistan was less a positive goal than a negation of Indian unity. Early in his stay he was granted an interview by the Viceroy, Lord Wavell, who described the meeting with characteristic bluntness:

Then came Brailsford, the aged left-wing journalist, a round-faced benevolent-looking grey-haired old man who brought in his comparatively young wife, dressed in a sort of semi-Tyrolese costume. He had nothing very special to say or ask, while her main contribution was a suggestion that if we built enough small fishing boats we could feed the people . . .[88]

They had a more cordial reception from Sir Claude Auchinleck, the Commander-in-Chief, who invited them to stay at his palace for several weeks, an opportunity to mingle with diplomats, civil servants, and officials.

Just as in his visit sixteen years before, it was chiefly Indians with whom he sought contact. He was struck not merely with the intense desire for nationhood, but the contrasts in the conditions of life compared with his previous visit. New industries had sprung up, offering hope of economic advance, and some of the social barriers had been

[87] HNB to Clare Leighton, 24 Nov. 1945, CLC.
[88] 13 Feb. 1946, Penderel Moon, ed., *Wavell: The Viceroy's Journal* (London, 1973), p. 211.

removed. In 1930 as the guest of a Muslim politician, he had caught only a fleeting glimpse of the veiled women of the household; returning to the son's house in 1946, Brailsford was able to mingle freely with his wife and other female guests.[89] During his first visit he had interviewed Nehru in prison; now at Anand Bhawan he was the house guest of this man destined to become India's first Prime Minister and of Indira, a future one. It was his accessibility that led Brailsford to suggest to Nehru

> that on an early date, as a preface to negotiations, Congress should issue a manifesto addressed to its Muslim fellow countrymen. . . . It might begin by asking the question, must we really separate? It might recall how much there is in common in spite of differences. It might go on to stress the advantages, political and economic, of a United India, and the perils, in this dangerous world, of separation.
>
> It might then face frankly the Muslim fears of Hindu numbers and economic power. It must then show that these fears can be met within an Indian Union. . .[90]

Such a scheme presupposed far more rationality and willingness to compromise than either side evinced, although at Nehru's insistence Congress did offer concessions in the hope of securing a united India.

The Brailsfords enjoyed a memorable interview with Gandhi at Poona in March. As in previous meetings in England, Gandhi poked fun at his guest, first for wearing sandals indoors, instead of leaving them outside as Evamaria had done, and then for his clumsiness at sitting on the ground. Although their conversation ranged widely, Gandhi, enigmatic as ever, claimed that if India were truly non-violent, she would no longer require the protection of the British army or navy. Instead of defensive alliances, he looked to the emergence of 'spontaneous friendship' once both countries possessed the 'moral force' that came from the spirit of non-violence.[91]

The longer Brailsford remained in India, the more convinced he became that a distinct Pakistan was inevitable. He hoped that Muslims might settle for autonomy within an Indian Union, and applauded the scheme to strengthen the provinces at the expense of the central government, a compromise ultimately rejected by Jinnah.[92] Even after it became clear that efforts to prevent schism had failed, he continued to deplore the creation of an independent Pakistan as 'a reactionary step in an age when the need is for economic planning on a continental

---

[89] *New Statesman*, 29 June 1946.
[90] HNB to Jawaharlal Nehru, 26 Feb. 1946, Nehru Papers.
[91] *Reynolds*, 31 Mar. 1946; transcript of broadcast in BBC Home Service, 26 June 1947.
[92] *New Statesman*, 27 Apr., 25 May 1946. The 27 April article also appeared in *New Republic*, 6 May 1946.

scale'.[93] Once the Cabinet Mission left at the end of June, there seemed little likelihood that differences would be resolved quickly, if at all. Since May it had been intolerably hot, the temperature reaching as high as 109 degrees, and he was exhausted as well as discouraged about the future. He enjoyed an excursion to ancient temples in Mysore, but the final weeks in New Delhi seemed an exercise in futility. The return journey took six weeks, since the ship was delayed at Port Said for repairs after a collision. The Brailsfords relished visits to the Sphinx and the Pyramids, but he complained of his 'hearty dislike [for] Modern Egypt & the Egyptians'.[94] He was feeling his age, and his heart had been strained by the exertions of the previous half-year. He informed Evamaria that he was finished with politics and looked forward to resuming the projects he had neglected, his Leveller book and upside down study. But he had left them too long, and time was running out.

[93] *New Statesman*, 10 May 1947.
[94] HNB to Clare Leighton, 27 Aug. 1946, CLC.

XIV
Ripeness is All (1945–1958)

Prospects for peace seemed as bleak in 1945 as they had after Versailles, the expectation of world government and socialist unity receding in the face of mounting East-West tension. From its inception the United Nations, crippled by the same defects Brailsford had decried in the League, proved incapable of delivering the world from the haunting fear of another war. No more than its predecessor did the UN discard the pernicious notion of 'the national sovereign State' whose main function was 'to wield military power'.[1] That autonomy, flaunted by the one superpower, was reflected in President Truman's announcement that the United States intended to retain the secret of the atomic bomb. Instead of offering to disclose it to the Security Council, which Brailsford wanted Americans to do, it aimed to carve out an exclusive sphere in the Western Hemisphere and Far East, but also to intervene where possible in Eastern Europe, Soviet interests notwithstanding. Rather than increase the likelihood of peace, exclusive American control of the bomb precluded disarmament. Britain's response to this 'horrific threat' should be to insist on 'a genuine World Security organisation'.[2] A socialist Britain ought to take the initiative in seeking disarmament, not become subservient to American militarism as it had to French designs in the early 1920s. He looked to England to 'stop the drift towards a third world war' through a direct approach to Stalin for a 'common policy for peace', certain that much of Europe, as well as India and the American left would support the plan.[3]

His Indian trip had proved a welcome respite from anxiety over the future of Europe, even though Muslim intransigence made him pessimistic about independence. England seemed 'dirty and dismal and bitterly cold' after the East, and European tensions showed no sign of having abated during his seven month absence. 'The state of the world,' he complained in August 1946,

> appals me and paralyses me. It feels as if we would go on drifting into war with Russia. I have no magic remedy to propose, and perhaps because I'm getting old and tired, I don't know how to fight any longer. I'm about equally out of sympathy with both sides. . . . I feel like preaching universal disarmament—

[1] *New Statesman*, 14 Apr. 1945.
[2] *New Statesman*, 13 Oct. 1945.
[3] Letter to Editor, *New Statesman*, 5 Oct. 1946.

which England would swallow—but what's the use, when one knows that neither USA nor USSR would look at it?[4]

Freed from regular journalistic obligations he resumed his history, but its focus had changed over the years. He was now contemplating a study of agrarian communism, tracing the tradition from the primitive village community, through peasant revolutionary movements, to the Levellers. After years of desultory reading, he was at last settling down to methodical research in the British Museum, at least when other problems did not encroach on his time.

Unfortunately, they usually did. At the end of 1946 he developed pneumonia, from which recovery was slow. He was commissioned by the Rank organization to write a script for a documentary film series on India. Early in 1947 he received an invitation to deliver the Hobhouse Memorial Lecture at the London School of Economics on the life-work of J. A. Hobson, an opportunity for him to acknowledge a profound intellectual debt. He spent much of the spring rediscovering Hobson's works in preparation for his lecture on 15 May. It was during these months before independence that Sudhir Ghosh, a protégé of Gandhi's with good British contacts, established the Friends of India. Essentially a public relations group, it was devised to attract friendly Englishmen in order to foster closer relations during the transition. Headed by Brailsford, it cast its net widely, sponsoring discussions or lunches at which notable Indians or British politicians spoke. Predictably it soon ran afoul of Krishna Menon's long-established India League, and Brailsford feared the rivalry might undermine Ghosh's effectiveness as an intermediary. In the peronality clash, he sided with Ghosh, having found the conspiratorial Menon too prickly a colleague.[5]

In stressing the need for German integration into post-war Europe, Brailsford hoped to forestall the division of the continent into armed camps. What he had not anticipated was that Germany itself would become the main focus of East-West conflict. Unilateral Soviet actions in its zone prevented unified action by the Control Commission, and the Western powers turned from dismantling Germany's industrial capacity to prepare for its economic build-up as a partner in the Western alliance. When Brailsford was invited to visit universities in the British Zone in 1947, as part of a concerted Anglo-American effort to instil democratic values, conditions were still appalling. Attending a lecture by philosopher Karl Jaspers at Heidelberg, he observed hungry, listless faces of students too debilitated to pay attention. Inadequate food supplies in the first years after the war meant untold suffer-

[4] HNB to Clare Leighton, 27 Aug. 1946, CLC.
[5] HNB to M. K. Gandhi, 24 Oct. 1947, quoted in Sudhir Ghosh, *Gandhi's Emissary* (London, 1967), p. 222.

ing for the civilian population, especially in cities such as Hamburg, where tens of thousands were on the verge of starvation, or Cologne, where an Allied medical mission reported that only twelve per cent of the children were of normal weight. Leaving England on 20 June, the Brailsfords journeyed to Munich to attend a conference of youth organizations held in the burned-out shell of the university. With invited participants from France and Holland, the conference testified to hopes for a united Europe. While reaffirming that Germany could win a tolerable standard of living only through intimate co-operation with its neighbours, it also revealed starkly the confusion of the student generation, its dread of dogmatism and reluctance to become committed to a party or movement, lest affiliation be later deemed a crime.[6]

As they moved north to Hamburg, the situation was a good deal grimmer. Once the most prosperous community in Germany, its warehouses were now 'empty shells', its famous shipyard 'a jungle of tangled briars and creepers of steel'. Aside from the colossal task of rebuilding, its population was struggling to stay alive on daily rations of 1,200 calories.[7] 'Everything in this ruined economy turns on calories,' he noted, 'and these only the Americans can supply'—and did once the Marshall Plan was instituted. Schemes to dismantle industries seemed to confirm the view that the British purpose was 'to prevent the restoration of German industry as a possible competitor with our own', a thesis Brailsford himself had propounded in the twenties.[8] As in the Weimar period, he felt that any attempt to add economic ruin to military defeat would only crush the democratic impulse. Not that Germany in 1947 posed a military threat: 'from this decimated and exhausted population,' he wrote in an underestimation of German recuperative powers reminiscent of *After the Peace*, 'no aggressor can arise in our generation.'[9] But he would not guarantee that the pacific temper would survive continued privation. If the mood of the apolitical masses turned 'to anger when dismantling actually begins, their resistance will bring with it a revival of nationalism'.[10]

Although denied permission to visit the Soviet Zone, Brailsford was invited to a Communist-sponsored Writers' Congress held in East Berlin in October, the first gathering of intellectuals from German-speaking countries in many years. Many of those attending were concentration camp survivors, and the tone, inspired by the Soviets, was vehemently anti-Nazi. Brailsford spoke only once, but Evamaria attracted more attention by appealing, in an unscheduled intervention, on behalf of youth for reconciliation instead of retribution. Even so brief an ex-

[6] *New Statesman*, 19 July 1947.
[7] *New Statesman*, 4 Oct. 1947.
[8] *New Statesman*, 11 and 25 Oct. 1947.
[9] *New Statesman*, 15 Nov. 1947.
[10] *New Statesman*, 29 Nov. 1947.

posure confirmed Brailsford's impression that the Russians felt no hesitation about carrying out 'a social revolution by foreign bayonets'. He applauded the elimination of middle-class privileges in education, but regretted the sacrifice of civil liberty in the ruthless attempt to uproot capitalism.[11]

His LSE lecture had provided an occasion to pay homage to Hobson; Brailsford also offered tribute to another hero in the spring of 1947. Before departing for Germany he had compiled a Nevinson anthology, which Gollancz was to publish, and arranged to share royalties equally with his widow, Evelyn Sharp.[12] Brailsford's laudatory introduction to the collection emphasized those virtues he most admired in his friend, perhaps because he strove to realize them in his own life as well:

If [Nevinson] was often in opposition, that was because he held our English ideals of freedom and humanity with more steadfastness and courage than most of us, just as he spoke our language with a keener sense of its rhythm and its beauty.[13]

He might have been saying what he hoped posterity would say of him. The Nevinson volume had scarcely been completed when he was invited to contribute the central section of a commemorative biography of Gandhi conceived shortly after his assassination. Brailsford was assigned the years from 1915 to 1939 during which Gandhi tried to steer the Indian nationalist movement along a non-violent course. The lawyer and journalist H. S. L. Polak dealt with his early life, while Pethick-Lawrence covered the final decade. Brailsford completed his ten chapters during the summer of 1948, but the book, published by Odhams Press the next year, attracted little notice and did not appear in the United States.[14]

By 1949 Brailsford had concluded that a nationalist resurgence in Germany was no longer a serious danger. The formation of a Communist regime in the East foreshadowed its absorption into the Russian economic and military sphere, while the Western sector, on the verge of remilitarization, seemed destined to become an American satellite. The rigidity of post-war divisions, the continued presence of a large occupation force, had made Germany the crucible of the Cold War. Dismissing a permanent division of Germany as 'intolerable', he

[11] *New Statesman*, 6 Dec. 1947; *Tägliche Rundschau*, 8 Oct. 1947. I am grateful to Norman Naimark for bringing this reference to my attention.

[12] HNB to Victor Gollancz, 8 Mar. 1947, Gollancz Papers; HNB to Evelyn Sharp, 12 Jan. 1948, Evelyn Sharp Papers, d. 279, fol. 156.

[13] *Essays, Poems and Tales of Henry W. Nevinson* (London, 1948), p. 9.

[14] H. S. L. Polak, H. N. Brailsford and Lord Pethick-Lawrence, *Mahatma Gandhi* (London, 1949). Brailsford's contribution appears on pp. 95-224.

believed that as each half became inextricably linked to an ideological and economic system, it would become impossible to reunite the country peacefully. The only alternative was its prompt reconstitution as a neutral and permanently disarmed state under the guarantee of the four Powers, who would evacuate their armies. Dismantling of industry would cease, the entire country would receive an infusion of Marshall aid, and a new constitution would be promulgated to ensure civil liberties and free elections. Democratic elections were calculated to satisfy the West, while neutrality would allay Russian fears that the military potential of the Ruhr might once again be unleashed against them. The proposal hinged on several dubious hypotheses, not least Soviet willingness to sanction elections in which the Communists would probably poll a minority of the total vote. Their failure to comply would reveal their 'insincerity', but it would, he conceded, also mean that 'the whole project falls to the ground'.[15] Decisions had to be taken immediately: should West Germany be admitted to the European Council, the chance for a neutral solution would be lost. 'Once West Germany is armed,' he told Murray, 'I shall expect war promptly.'[16]

Brailsford sent his article to a number of politicians, but those who replied shared Leo Amery's view that 'you are much too optimistic in thinking of your solution of a neutral Germany guaranteed by the four great powers possible'.[17] Dalton doubted whether there was any hope at all of getting the Russians to agree, much less of persuading Germany to accept such status imposed on it.[18] The Western view was that, since Germany would not abdicate from power politics, its energies needed to be oriented towards the West through political and economic co-operation. A Treasury memorandum circulated in response to Brailsford's suggestions expressed the view that the danger of East-West conflict would not be reduced 'by deliberately electing to live in a fool's paradise' in imagining that either the Germans or the Russians would play the part Brailsford wished to assign them.[19]

As the Cold War intensified, he became more vehemently hostile to American policy, especially as manifested in Korea. One of his last articles in *Reynolds* proclaimed 'We will not follow MacArthur into this madness'. Without exonerating the North Koreans for launching an attack, he identified the root of the conflict as the American refusal to

---

[15] *Contemporary Review*, Vol. CLXXV, No. 1005 (Sept. 1949), pp. 133-8. Evamaria collaborated on this article. Brailsford also blanketed the press with letters advocating German neutralization. See *New Statesman*, 7 May 1949; *The Times*, 7 June 1949; *Tribune*, 15 July 1949; *Manchester Guardian*, 25 Oct. 1949; *News-Chronicle*, 26 Oct. 1949.
[16] HNB to Gilbert Murray, 16 Sept. 1949, GMP, 124, fol. 95.
[17] L. S. Amery to HNB, 8 Nov. 1949, HNBP.
[18] Hugh Dalton to HNB, 3 Oct. 1949, HNBP.
[19] Copy of Treasury report on 'Mr. Brailsford's Memorandum' (undated), HNBP.

recognize the Peking government.[20] Like others on the left, he hoped for the emergence of some third force, between the two superpowers, to which a socialist England might affiliate. Bevin's eager espousal of the Western alliance and England's readiness to comply with American demands for rearmament seemed as much a travesty of internationalist ideals as MacDonald's support for France and coolness towards Russia in the 1920s. His suspicion of American motives in seeking to contain the spread of Communism did not make him more indulgent towards Stalin, whose expansion in Eastern Europe, if anticipated, was none the less lamentable. An admirer of Tito, he welcomed his break with the Cominform in 1948 as an indication of the Yugoslav determination to escape Russian domination. During the next few years Tito tried to cultivate Western support by inviting prominent socialist sympathizers to visit Yugoslavia. Zilliacus, one of the first to bask in Tito's hospitality, brought back an invitation to Brailsford, remembered as a stalwart friend of Macedonian liberation and a champion of the partisans during the war.

Accorded VIP treatment by Tito and other officials during his two-month stay in 1950-1, Brailsford responded with an enthusiasm that recalled his visit to Bela Kun's Hungary. His reports in the *New Statesman* and the *Manchester Guardian* spoke glowingly of the creative energy of Yugoslav leaders in transforming a backward country without resorting to bureaucratic tyranny of the Stalinist variety. In the building of universities and technical schools, in the campaign to eradicate malaria, in efforts to mechanize and electrify he saw the fulfilment of his own belief in elevating the standards of the European peasantry. Ever since he had begun to work as a foreign correspondent, he had concerned himself with the abysmal poverty of the Balkan masses. Here in an independent Communist state the long-delayed social revolution had finally begun; what the Turks and their reactionary successors had neglected, Tito was determined to achieve. Having witnessed the problems involved in securing peasant allegiance in Hungary and the Soviet Union, he approved the Yugoslav scheme of voluntary co-operative farms, although he felt some misgivings about the denial of social benefits to those peasants who refused to join. To his credit, Tito had contrived to reverse the tendency toward centralization by instituting a variant of Guild Socialism. Power had been purportedly delegated to six federal republics, not concentrated in Belgrade, while economic planning was henceforth to be generated from below, in the self-governing factories, mines, and farms. Never obsessed with the chimera of workers' control, Brailsford had long

[20] *Reynolds*, 3 Dec. 1950.

favoured more extensive economic democracy, criticizing Labour's programme in 1931 and after for failing to involve workers in decision-making.

The Brailsfords spent half their time in Macedonia, where he renewed his acquaintance with a region he had first visited nearly half a century before. In one village to which he had travelled by mule, carrying food and blankets, an old woman who recognized him declared that everything was fine now since the new regime was giving the people electricity. In Skopje (formerly Uskub) Brailsford attended proceedings in the law court, where the judge told him that there had been only two cases of murder since the victory of the revolution. When he had first visited the area in 1903, murder and assassination were daily occurrences. He could recall peasants ploughing with rifles slung over their shoulders. But the Macedonia which welcomed him in 1951 was the most content of the Yugoslav republics, the scene of a cultural rebirth. During their first evening they attended a performance of Mozart's *Abduction from the Seraglio* in Macedonian.[21]

Tito's revolution had brought peace to the troubled land by introducing three significant changes. First, reform had eliminated the old-world landlord, 'half-brigand, half aristocrat', giving the peasant a stake in the land he farmed. Second, education had reduced illiteracy and begun to train desperately needed technicians and teachers. Finally, the federal structure ended generations of feuding by ensuring equality of opportunity for all races. In fact, time would prove these ethnic hostilities more intractable than even Tito anticipated, but on the basis of his observations in Macedonia, Brailsford had no doubt that the revolution was succeeding.

Yet this rosy picture was not without its shadows. Despite the break with Russia, its 'disastrous influence' was clearly evident in the 'omnipotent police' and party control over the judicial system. As in earlier visits to Hungary and Soviet Russia, the apparatus of dictatorship could not be ignored, however much he admired the economic and educational gains. If Yugoslavs were no longer 'a people stagnant in [their] backwardness and torn by racial feuds', they had as yet achieved neither civil liberty nor the right to discuss major issues of policy. What they did have in the new co-operative farms and engineering workshops was 'a bolder experiment in everyday democracy than you could find anywhere else in Europe'.[22] It was to be his last trip abroad, and if he had not quite discovered utopia on the Adriatic, it left him with the

---

[21] Interview, Evamaria Brailsford; *New Statesman*, 13 Jan. 1951; *Manchester Guardian*, 14, 19 and 21 Mar. 1951.
[22] *Listener*, 1 Mar. 1951; *New Statesman*, 3 Feb. 1951.

happy conviction that his hopes for the socialist future and for a free Macedonia had not been in vain.

Despite his enthusiasm for what he saw, his body could no longer endure the rigours of travel. During his German trip in 1947 he had been confined to bed for a week, and his Yugoslav journey was repeatedly punctuated by illness. His return to England was delayed in Paris, where he was kept in bed for ten days, and when he finally got back to London, his doctor forbade all activity. After several months of rest, he insisted on resuming research at the British Museum, though the stairs in the Underground and at Belsize Park Gardens were becoming an increasing hardship. Even so, his vital interest in people and in the world around him, his enjoyment of music and spirited conversation, never flagged.

By the end of 1949 he could report 'substantial progress' on his book, but months of arduous research still lay ahead.[23] Over the years the project, begun in 1936 as a history of socialism and later narrowed in scope to cover the period from More to Marx, had radically changed. His inquiry into agrarian communism had by 1949 become a study of the Levellers and their social ideas. The deeper he delved the more fascinated he became with men such as Walwyn, Overton, and Lilburne, in whom he discerned his own ideological antecedents. But he wondered whether he was not abdicating his responsibility as a political dissenter, in retreating from an uncongenial world into the revolutionary struggles of a bygone age:

Is it a sympton of old age to take refuge in the past in this way? I confess that hopelessness makes me steadily less inclined to attempt anything in the contemporary world.[24]

At the end of 1951 his angina became so severe that he found it almost impossible to read. Facing the prospect of virtual confinement in the flat, he decided in mid-1952 to move to Greylands, Mabel's bungalow in Amersham. Here there were no stairs to impede him, and he could sit or stroll in the garden. Although intended as a brief, recuperative stay, he was to remain in Amersham for five and a half years, returning to London only in order to enter a hospital in February 1958, several weeks before his death.

The Amersham years were filled with pain and growing infirmity, and Brailsford often despaired of writing anything. At times he felt that the world had passed him by, that he was an old man, helpless and forgotten. He wrote occasional *New Statesman* reviews, and from time to time the BBC came to his bedside to record talks about India or about

[23] HNB to Clare Leighton, 20 Dec. 1949, CLC.
[24] HNB to Gilbert Murray, 23 June 1949, GMP, 124, fols. 90-2.

Martin's editorship. Conscious that his literary facility had diminished, he regretted more than ever leaving the book to which he had become so committed to his waning years. And yet, they brought a certain serenity as well, a deeper attachment to Evamaria, who came down at weekends and filled his days with gaiety, and to Mabel, the devoted sister he had ignored much of his life. They became companions, enjoying birds and flowers together, two elderly people discovering common interests and pleasures. He spent much of his time in bed, where he did his writing and listened to music. After the bustle of public affairs, there was time now for poetry and for Shakespeare, especially *King Lear*. Such friends as Martin, Braunthal, Naomi Mitchison, and the Coles continued to visit him. Margaret Cole found him gentler and less pugnacious than earlier, although he could still greet her bristling with indignation after a morning's reading with the query, 'How could anyone bear Cromwell?' Douglas Cole asked Brailsford to comment on the manuscript of his *History of Socialist Thought* and received a valued critique from the colleague who had once embarked on a very similar project.[25]

Young scholars sought him out partly for the opportunity of meeting so venerable a figure and partly to tap his fund of information about the seventeenth century. Several volunteered to undertake research for him, since he was cut off from books not close at hand. Gerald Aylmer, then a young lecturer, who drove over from Oxford in 1956 in order to meet one of 'the grand old men of early 20th century radicalism', later recalled his impressions:

He was in bed, but surrounded by books and papers. Here was a rather frail old man, physically pretty weak and immobile, but mentally very alert and with a strength and generosity of spirit which were extraordinarily impressive —even after only an hour or so's conversation. He was most interested in whether there was any recent specialist work on the mid-17th century which he might have missed or to which he had not had access . . . I think that he was very conscious of being intellectually isolated as an invalid . . . he was also, quite unnecessarily, self-conscious and modest about trying to write a full-scale historical work when he had no formal academic training as a historian and had been a practising journalist for most of his active life. . . . But he was the kind of older and very distinguished person who made one forget completely the vast difference in age and standing; we were simply two students of the period comparing notes and assessing the value of various recent books and articles. He had no 'side' about him at all; yet one could not fail to be aware that he was a remarkable person.[26]

---

[25] Interviews, Mabel R. Brailsford, Dame Margaret Cole. Margaret Cole, *The Life of G. D. H. Cole* (London, 1971), p. 281n.
[26] G. E. Aylmer to author, 12 Oct. 1968.

Aside from preliminary chapters written at the beginning of the war and later abandoned, most of his work on the Levellers was done between 1947 and the end of 1957. Repeatedly interrupted by illness or journeys abroad, he continued, even while bedridden, to take copious notes in small copy-books, to track down leads suggested by British and American scholars, and to write the thirty-five chapters ultimately published as *The Levellers and the English Revolution*. Although he could barely keep up with post-war scholarship on the Puritan Revolution, his reading, in several languages, showed considerable breadth for someone not trained professionally as a historian. Before his health collapsed, he had done substantial research in the Thomason tracts in the British Museum and even after he was immobilized, he was able to utilize published Leveller documents and transcripts of the Putney debates.

His interest in his subject seemed to grow, refreshed by reading new works or contact with scholars in the field. What he was able finally to achieve was an extraordinary sense of immediacy, as though he were applying his journalist's gift for recounting events he had witnessed. By a remarkable imaginative leap he had transported himself back into the seventeenth century to penetrate the mind of his Leveller heroes as they confronted Cromwell and Ireton. From his bedside he was able to conjure up the scene at Putney church in November 1657, where Colonel Rainsborough challenged the army leaders, or the Guildhall trial of John Lilburne in October 1649, as vividly as he described the Red Army in 1920 or Indian civil disobedience in 1930.

As Brailsford saw it, the Levellers had seized the initiative at a critical juncture in the Civil War, challenging the authority of the Presbyterians in the Long Parliament, and foisting a democratic policy on the reluctant leaders of the New Model Army. The impetus behind the movement came from middling social groups, independent Puritan sects, tradesmen of the cities, and elements among the craftsmen and peasants, thus posing a distinct social challenge to the ascendancy of the gentry. These pioneers anticipated the social and political reforms of the next three hundred years in their demand for unlimited toleration, for the election of all officials, for equality between the sexes, for the abolition of tithes and imprisonment for debt, and for popular sovereignty.

Brailsford was not so naïve as to suggest that the movement represented a spontaneous rising of common men. The book discusses in detail the ideas of Leveller leaders. While paying tribute to the impetuous and humourless Lilburne, whose whole life was 'an unyielding battle for his ideal of liberty',[27] he preferred Walwyn, less flamboyant,

---

[27] *Levellers*, p. 75.

but more consistent in his pursuit of a secular and egalitarian republic. Complementing each other, they provided the sharpest contrast to Cromwell, the book's obvious villain. Instead of fostering the radical spirit, he manipulated it and then sought to extinguish it altogether:

> Throughout a decade he held England in the hollow of his hand, yet he left it no better or happier than he found it. Not a single social reform stands to his credit.[28]

In the short run the Levellers failed: they were unable to ensure that their democratic proposals were implemented, and when they opposed Cromwell's scheme for the reconquest of Ireland, they were suppressed. Although instrumental in bringing about the trial and execution of Charles I and in fostering toleration, it was their failure to move beyond political objectives that explained their limited support, particularly among the poorest groups. Only in the later stages did they advocate the conversion of servile tenure into freehold and the enclosure of wasteland for the benefit of the poor. Their belated recognition of the plight of the peasantry was, he contended, the real cause for their defeat: 'They did enough for the tenants' cause to provoke Cromwell and the gentry to crush them, but not enough to mobilise the villages as their resolute allies.'[29]

In the end it was their legacy rather than their accomplishments that Brailsford sought to celebrate. Their originality lay in the attempt to organize a political party resting on the support of ordinary working people. The first political group to call for complete freedom of conscience, they had the audacity to conclude that the rights they professed could only be secured in a secular republic. At the same time they pointed the direction which later English reformers would take. Brailsford saw direct links between twentieth-century Radicals and his Leveller heroes, defiantly questioning authority, challenging aggressive imperialism, and defending the interests of the socially powerless.

Although some of his judgements have been questioned by scholars less charitable towards the Levellers, none ever attempted so ambitious an undertaking—a full-scale study of the movement, its ideology and revolutionary thrust, its leadership and social composition, designed for the intelligent general reader. Such a project demanded not merely extensive research, but literary gifts that few historians, aside from Trevelyan, possessed. As a writer, Brailsford was ideally suited, but his powers were no longer what they had once been. Too long and lacking in shape, the book suffered from being essentially a first draft, even though he had never needed to revise his prose. What seems remark-

---

[28] *Levellers*, p. 16.   [29] *Levellers*, p. 450.

able in so mammoth a work is its liveliness and humour, the author's evident delight in conveying some dramatic incident or outrageous remark for the reader's pleasure. If it lacks a conclusion that summarized his purpose, it remains a luminous and richly detailed work of scholarship, informed by a passionate commitment, yet scrupulous in probing the weaknesses in the Leveller campaign. Had he written it earlier in life or at least lived to complete it according to plan, it would have been a different and better book, but even as published it is a monument of which he could well have been proud.

Brailsford finished what turned out to be the last chapter, an analysis of British influence on Bordeaux Radicalism in the 1650s, only five months before he died. But four projected chapters were still unwritten, and the unwieldy, handwritten manuscript needed reorganization and editorial revision. 'The sad thing,' Mabel wrote to Luther Allen in April 1958, 'is that after all the Levellers are [sic] not finished—he has worked so hard all through these years, often when we were asleep at night—always in weariness and very often in pain.'[30] With Evamaria's encouragement, Martin took the manuscript in hand, persuading Christopher Hill to prepare it for publication with the Cresset Press. As editor, Hill made minor alterations to avoid repetition, substituted an earlier essay on the Diggers for an unwritten chapter, added needed bibliographical apparatus, but otherwise left the work largely as he found it. Certainly Hill assumed no responsibility for its style or content, although he admired Brailsford and was sympathetic to its ideological temper.[31]

Finally published in June 1961, more than three years after his death, *The Levellers and the English Revolution* achieved a *succès d'estime*. Sixty-three years had passed since his first book appeared, and he was clearly perceived as a figure of the somewhat distant past. Most of the reviews, containing more than a hint of condescension, fastened upon Brailsford's purported exaggeration of the egalitarian spirit of the Levellers. Foot hailed it as 'a glorious book' and praised the 'sweep of his narrative', but conceded that Brailsford probably erred in asserting that the Levellers advocated manhood suffrage.[32] In fact, although Lilburne and Walwyn believed in democracy, Brailsford recognized that the Levellers had been tactically obliged to compromise their principles in the hope of maximizing support—a hope that ultimately proved futile. *The Times Literary Supplement*, severest of critics, admitting that it was 'a book of great power, beautifully organized and written', claimed

---

[30] Mabel R. Brailsford to Luther Allen, 1 Apr. 1958.

[31] Interviews, Kingsley Martin, Christopher Hill. The manuscript of the *Levellers* is on deposit at the International Institute for Social History in Amsterdam.

[32] *New Statesman*, 30 June 1961.

that it was 'already sadly out of date and adds scarcely anything to our knowledge of the period'.[33] If the academic specialists, including Perez Zagorin[34] and W.H. Coates,[35] were respectful, Brailsford's intended audience seemed largely oblivious to the book's existence. What had been designed as a political testament, a parable to inspire the imagination of the younger generation of English socialists, fell on deaf ears. That audience of intelligent general readers (to whom so much of Brailsford's writing had been addressed) had either disappeared or was deterred by the work's inordinate length. Thus the *Levellers*, so laboriously finished, gained a pitifully small following, a worthy curiosity that few bothered to read.

As he entered his eighties, few faces from the distant past were still around. 'No one of my old school and college friends,' he told Murray, with whom he resumed correspondence after the war, 'has survived. My happiest meetings are with comrades and friends like the Coles . . . but they are all twenty years or thereabouts my junior.' At the age of eighty-two his 'eyes and ears [were] nearly as good as ever they were', but his weak heart compelled him to spend most of the day in bed:

I can't complain of this immobility, [he wrote] for I have in the past seen more than most people of the beauty and excitement of this earth. I have a wide pageant of remembered scenes and persons and events.[36]

In July 1957 he tripped on the front steps of the cottage, breaking his arm in the fall, and despite his recovery from the accident, his health began to decline more rapidly by the end of the year. His angina and chronic bronchitis worsened, and he had a mild stroke. Tributes began to pour in: one from suffragist veterans arrived on his eighty-fourth birthday, while another came from India, bearing the signatures of Nehru, Mme Pandit, and other leaders. He was aware that a testimonial written by Foot was being prepared for presentation when signatures of English socialists had been collected. It did not, sadly, arrive in time. At the end of January the chest pains, intermittent for so many years, became constant, and he suffered coronary thrombosis. The cardiologist who examined him at Amersham insisted on admitting him to West London Hospital in Hammersmith for intensive care. Since Brailsford refused to go without Evamaria, his doctor reluctantly consented to her remaining in his hospital room, sleeping on a camp-bed and ministering to his needs. At first he made considerable progress, and his spirit was so vigorous that both he and Evamaria believed he would be discharged from the hospital within a few weeks. In early

---

[33] *The Times Literary Supplement*, 28 July 1961.
[34] *Political Science Quarterly*, Mar. 1962.
[35] *American Historical Review*, Oct. 1962.
[36] HNB to Gilbert Murray, 4 May 1956, GMP, 124, fols. 98-9.

March his condition weakened, but they continued to enjoy gramophone records and lively conversations. On Sunday 23 March they had a heated discussion in the morning, interrupted only by lunch. He took a brief nap in the afternoon, waking to resume the argument where they had left off. In the midst of conversation he had a stroke and was dead within two minutes.[37]

At the funeral five days later at Golders Green Crematorium a small gathering of friends heard Pethick-Lawrence eulogize Brailsford, and a selection from the Brahms *Requiem* was played. The music had special significance for the man whose memory was being honoured. Nothing ever composed, he had once written, 'moves me quite as this *Requiem* does, almost beyond endurance'. In the middle of the Second World War, attending a performance at Southwark Cathedral, he found it appropriate to be listening to a German text, a reminder of a shared sensibility obscured by the bombs. The exalted words, he remarked,

have the same meaning in Southwark and Berlin. . . . The slightly archaic Saxon of Luther's translation affects them as the Tudor English of the authorised version affects us. And the music? Do we not mourn when they mourn and triumph to the same clarion notes? The same subtle sequences of sound bring tears to their eyes as to ours while we listen, and our hearts beat in step with theirs when Brahms sets us marching to Zion.

It was for him the finest expression of common brotherhood, an affirmation of the belief that 'we can work together: we are "neighbours" as the Gospels have it, or comrades and fellow-workers as Socialists put it'. Despite the destruction and hatred engendered by war, the message he drew from the solemn music was that 'our victory will be barren unless we can build our new order on the braver attitude of understanding and cooperation'. For this non-believer the real Communion of Saints included Kant and Tolstoy and Brahms, 'who have served man and God faithfully [and] are still with us, to help and to inspire'.[38] He belonged in their company.

[37] Interview, Evamaria Brailsford; Mabel R. Brailsford to Luther Allen, 14 Mar. 1958; Mabel R. Brailsford to Kathleen Courtney, 29 Mar. [1958], Kathleen Courtney Papers.
[38] *New Statesman*, 14 Nov. 1942. Later reprinted as a pamphlet by the Friends Peace Committee.

XV

The Ideal Republic

Although he lived by his pen, it was not merely his felicitous style and admirable grasp of political affairs that made Brailsford's work compelling. Writing was for him a form of action, a way to impose himself and his ideas on an audience. He was enough the child of Victorian liberalism to believe that the citizens of a democratic society would respond in enlightened fashion if political issues were properly explained. It was this conviction that infused his writing with such urgency and vigour. He really believed that it mattered, that the people, once empowered to act, would take affairs into their own hands. For him the word and the action were inextricable: his writing was an exhortation, no less than the sermons of his childhood that he had found so reprehensible. Too often his expectations were frustrated, his aspirations for a rational world order shattered by jingoism or war. Never in his lifetime did the kind of peace he sought come close to realization, but, however discouraged he became, he never ceased to inveigh against the forces of darkness. Less than two years before his death, he was calling for a 'token general strike' to prevent British involvement in the Suez campaign, 'this craziest of wars', as he called it.[1]

His journalistic career suggests a kind of elective affinity with those regions of the world in which civil strife and international conflict perpetually raged. It was not that they provided grist for his literary mill: Brailsford was ineluctably drawn to those struggling against oppression, whether seeking freedom from native tyrants or imperialist masters. In his belief that the human spirit could only flourish in a society where conscience went untrammelled, he espoused the cause of any group striving for liberty and political autonomy. Never doubting the value of democratic institutions in England, however much he condemned its social élitism, he could not sit idly by while groups under the authority of the British crown were denied basic rights. Thus he became a passionate advocate of women's rights and of self-government for the Irish, the Egyptians, and the Indians. Yet in England during his lifetime he found, even among the governing classes, a spirit of concession; grievances were rectified, albeit belatedly. The full measure of his indignation was reserved for outrages abroad—in the Balkans or in Russia, for example—where the struggle for freedom was often in vain. Like

[1] HNB to Kingsley Martin, 13 Sept. 1956, KMP.

Paine, one of his heroes, he felt himself most committed when the cause seemed more nearly lost than where victory was within reach:

> 'Where liberty is, there is my country.' The sentiment . . . was spoken by Benjamin Franklin, and no saying better expresses the spirit of eighteenth-century humanity. 'Where is not liberty, there is mine.' The answer is Thomas Paine's. It is the watchword of the knight errant, the marching music that sent Lafayette to America, and Byron to Greece, the motto of every man who prizes striving above enjoyment, honours comradeship above patriotism, and follows an idea that no frontier can arrest.[2]

Few statements convey his own outlook more clearly, for he too had begun in heroic fashion, enlisting to fight for Greek freedom in the full bloom of romantic ardour. He too marched to the clarion call of liberal hopes and socialist dreams, committing himself to just causes, however visionary. Despite his modesty and diffidence, he was cast in a romantic mould, a knight on a white charger, as one friend put it, doing battle to succour the defenceless.[3] Although his articles and books were reasoned expositions, there was a quality of the impractical which attached itself to Brailsford's causes that made him so exemplary a figure. His passion expressed itself in a burning hatred of injustice and oppression, a religious zeal secularized into a desire for earthly salvation. Under democratic socialism and international harmony, the meek would truly inherit the earth: economic exploitation and imperialism were the obstacle to the fulfilment of men's hopes.

Those who knew Brailsford found his distinctive characteristic to be an almost total lack of self-regard. 'Never did a man,' Michael Foot wrote, 'so completely subordinate his own personal interests to the cause in which he believed.'[4] His selfless devotion made him seem inflexible to successive editors, obstinacy cloaked in self-righteousness, as some of them believed. In fact he sought nothing for himself and was prepared to sacrifice his career to the pursuit of justice. Much of his work, the Conciliation Committee for example, was not merely unpaid, but earned him considerable opprobrium and damaged his professional prospects. Despite his distaste for organizational politics, he served on innumerable committees and signed petitions or wrote letters to editors. Less publicized than his writings were countless lectures and talks, particularly between the wars, to summer schools, Labour colleges or Fabian conferences, none of which brought remuneration. Whether such activities, distractions from the ambitious books he hoped to write, were more than exercises in futility rarely concerned him. Even at his most pessimistic, he was unable to remain aloof; no matter how

---

[2] *SGC*, p. 42.   [3] Interview, Sybil Wingate.   [4] Foot, *Debts of Honour*, p. 137.

lost the cause, he was ready to volunteer his services. His was a lifetime commission in 'the stage army of the Good'.

In the final volume of his autobiography Leonard Woolf, whose career was in many ways comparable, calculated that he had spent nearly 200,000 hours in 'perfectly useless work' which 'achieved practically nothing'. Had he reflected in similar fashion, Brailsford would probably have come to the same conclusion, doubtlessly adding, as Woolf did, that 'for me personally it was right and important that I should do it'.[5] Once his sympathies were engaged, he committed himself unstintingly, never considering his own advantage. Like the early Radicals he so admired, he had a spark of reforming zeal that could be readily ignited. At the same time he had nothing of the zealot about him. His own gentleness made him recoil from violence, and despite an admiration for revolutionary leaders like Lenin, he never abandoned a belief in the efficacy of rational persuasion. If he yearned for the socialist commonwealth, he did not want it imposed by force. Impatient with patriotic fervour and nationalism, he was none the less willing to wait until public opinion was ready to move. But his reliance on the democratic will made it all the more imperative that the public be instructed. It was this compelling need to reshape popular consciousness that provided the motive for his writing. Like Godwin, one of his intellectual idols, he believed that to make men wise was to make them free.

If Brailsford's journalism was preoccupied with the contemporary scene, his books often reached back to his own intellectual forbears. He had a sense of historical identity, of ideological roots more profound in their impact on his development than family influence. In contrast to the 'mechanical revolutionists'[6] who wanted to achieve socialism by imposing new economic structures, he looked at current problems in a historical context, finding illumination in the legacy of Radical thought. Unlike the Webbs or Cole, he cared more about ideas than institutions, an intellectual preoccupation that bound him to a cultural tradition. His own writing represented a convergence of popular radicalism and romantic idealism onto which the tenets of Marxism were later grafted. His socialism derived chiefly from native sources, from the democratic impulse expressed by Milton and the Levellers and Paine. While Cole is reputed to have had his epiphany after reading William Morris' *News From Nowhere*, Brailsford ascribed his conversion to an exposure to Shelley.[7]

In his last book, *The Levellers and the English Revolution*, he had tried to

[5] Leonard Woolf, *The Journey Not the Arrival Matters* (London, 1969), pp. 158, 172.
[6] Clarke, *Liberals and Social Democrats*, p. 5.
[7] Foot, *Debts of Honour*, p. 137; Cole, *G. D. H. Cole*, pp. 33-4.

probe the origins of democratic ideas in England, but he found that the Leveller experiment, once quashed by Cromwell, produced no immediate offshoots. The true successors to Walwyn and Lilburne were the Radicals of the London Corresponding Society in the 1790s, who figured in his Home University Library volume *Shelley, Godwin and Their Circle* written nearly half a century earlier. This revival of democratic sentiments under the impact of events in France was for Brailsford as momentous as the seizure of the initiative by the Levellers in 1647. Here again, one hundred and fifty years later, propertied forces were massed against those who dared to view history 'from the standpoint of the "swinish multitude"'.[8] Just as he felt closest to Leveller intellectuals such as Walwyn, so too his focus in the earlier work had been on the writers rather than on the organizational politicians. He extolled Paine as one of the 'moral pioneers of his generation', a soldier of liberty who denounced monarchy and aristocracy, expounded the right of revolution, and pleaded on behalf of animals, women, and slaves.[9] In many ways he identified more closely with Paine's notion of government as an instrument of social conscience than with Godwin's philosophical anarchism, while conceding the latter's stature as a thinker. No Enlightenment figure argued more forcefully that human beings were infinitely malleable; once the pernicious influence of religion and government was removed, man might progress towards perfection. Without adopting these presuppositions, Brailsford applauded the assertion that 'the human mind is not necessarily fettered for all time by the prejudices and institutions in which it has clothed itself'.[10]

Godwin had something of the same effect on him that Trotsky subsequently had: the very extremity of such views forced him to question his own position, to search for similar goals by alternative methods. Although he echoed Godwin's defence of equal access to economic resources and unrestricted freedom of opinion, Brailsford insisted that justice was best served by reforming government, not by eliminating it. Never attracted to the anarchist position, he was drawn none the less to the visionary ideals of Shelley, Godwin's protégé. Clothed in poetic lyricism, the doctrines of inevitable progress, universal benevolence, and the efficacy of reason seemed more palatable than the astringent theories of *Political Justice*. Yet if Shelley made him a socialist, it was not for any clear political dogma, but rather for the image of life as a struggle to liberate man from oppressive institutions. Like the atheist Shelley, he regarded himself as belonging to the 'cosmic party of opposition', a rebel against the tyranny of orthodoxy. Too sceptical, too much a disciple of Voltaire, to imbibe the romantic faith in perfectability, he

[8] *SGC*, p. 18.   [9] *SGC*, pp. 44, 47, 51.   [10] *SGC*, p. 118.

never doubted that mankind would become more virtuous once the shackles were removed and that the struggle for freedom was itself life-enhancing. 'Where any mind strives after justice, where any soul suffers and loves and defies, there is the ideal Republic.'[11] His socialism, even where it involved the reorganization of wealth by experts and technicians for the community, always had as its objective the fullest development of individual freedom, never its subordination to the state.

Shelley, Godwin and Their Circle was written during the period of Brailsford's participation in the movement for women's suffrage. While his motives for subordinating his career to the campaign were partly subjective, there was also a transcendent, Shelleyan justification. His own family testified to the subjection of women, and survival of his marriage to Jane seemed to hinge on whether that traditional pattern could be reversed. By committing himself wholeheartedly to the cause, he tried to demonstrate to her that, like Shelley, he too believed that men could not be free if women were enslaved. It was foolish to identify Jane's private anguish so closely with the subjugation of her sex, but his dedication was no less genuine for having been inspired by marital problems. He responded as sincerely to the plight of the women in England as he had to that of the Irish or the Macedonians, and once his sympathy was enlisted, it burned with a flame that prudence could not extinguish. His defence of political rights for women, as a 1912 speech indicated, derived from the revolutionary doctrines Shelley and Mary Wollstonecraft had articulated more than a century earlier: for him it meant

a transformation in the mind and spirit of every human soul which comes into the world a woman. It means a removal from every growing mind and every developing spirit of the shackles which would otherwise have bound her brain, fettered her limbs. It is a mental emancipation and a moral awakening that lie at the root of this great cause of ours.[12]

If Brailsford rejected any socialist system that curtailed the civil liberties of its members, his conception of freedom was to be defined increasingly in social, rather than individual terms. 'The freedom we want,' he wrote in 1944, 'is freedom for the organised community to shape its own life and plan its own development. It can achieve what the individual cannot do for himself.'[13] His conviction about the primacy of freedom of discussion and conscience was unshakable, but he came to realize that these abstractions were inseparable from the

---

[11] *SGC*, pp. 162, 178.
[12] Speech at Connaught Rooms, 12 May 1912, quoted in Foot, *Debts of Honour*, p. 145-6.
[13] *New Statesman*, 19 Aug. 1944.

material basis of society. Under capitalism the promise of political democracy was thwarted; a parliamentary system was no guarantee of liberty if wealth was concentrated in relatively few hands. In these circumstances ordinary people could not order their lives:

> We are the servants of a small directing class, which through its command of machinery, its monopoly of land, its manipulation of prices, its sovereign mastery over credit, and its control of the Press, fixes for us the framework and conditions of our daily existence.[14]

The aim of socialism, then, was to conquer economic power for the whole community, a process which involved the abolition of class.

By the 1920s Brailsford had begun to see the class struggle in Marxist terms, but at the same time he denied their revolutionary implications. If unequal classes were antagonistic, their conflict was not implacable. Violence and coercion were as objectionable in the name of liberty as under a dictatorship. Yet it was not enough to condemn violence; it could only be avoided if peaceful methods were devised to bring about fundamental changes in society. Repudiating the earlier notion of competing private interests, he expounded a 'faith in the power of rational thought, deliberate planning and scientific creation to guide our growth and shape our destiny'.[15] Only after the community gained control over economic life, ensuring a 'transfer of power from "them" to "us" ',[16] would the democratic dream become a reality. His commitment to radical change linked him with the far left, but he remained distinctively undoctrinaire, indifferent to ideological fashions and suspicious of political conformity. Belonging to no camp, he would not sacrifice his integrity in the cause of expediency or to win popularity.

If Brailsford's passion for freedom and democratic faith was inspired by Shelley, his perspective on international affairs was influenced mainly by Hobson. His support for the Boers and the Irish was a reflection of imaginative sympathy for the underdog, the 'knee-jerk' reaction of a nineteenth-century Radical, but the theoretical underpinning for his views was derived from his mentor's critique of imperialism. Brailsford applied Hobson's thesis to the growing tension among the powers before 1914, seeing imperialism less as an English malady than as a concomitant of European capitalism. He was convinced that a small group of financiers determined the foreign policies of these states, their obsession with overseas investment shifting the arena of dispute away from Europe. But if the struggle for a balance of power was being played out in distant lands, its intensity ultimately meant that force governed the relations between rival powers. If Hobson blamed imperialism on

---

[14] *Socialism for Today*, p. 35.   [15] *New Leader*, 24 May 1929.
[16] *New Statesman*, 13 Feb. 1943 and reprinted 21/28 Dec. 1979.

a selfish investing class, Brailsford extended this analysis to explain foreign and military policies:

> ... in every country and across every border there is a powerful group of capitalists, closely allied to the fighting services, firmly entrenched in society, and well served by politicians and journalists, whose business it is to exploit the rivalries and jealousies of nations and to practice the alchemy which transmutes hatred into gold.[17]

Here half a century earlier was clear anticipation of the 'military-industrial complex' so familiar to political analysts of the Cold War.

Although compelled to revise his prediction that a European war would be prevented by the rational calculations of capitalism, Brailsford continued to propound the economic interpretation of imperialism with certain qualifications, which Lenin ignored when he appropriated it. Of course much of the Hobson-Brailsford thesis was subsequently discredited, partly, no doubt, because Lenin gave it a bad name. Later historians demonstrated that there was little correlation between capital investment and territorial annexation, that insecurity and jealousy generated much of the imperialist impulse. It became apparent, even more obviously, that the First World War stemmed from conflicts in Europe, whose borders, which Brailsford believed immutable, proved as fluid in 1919 and 1945 as they had been in the eighteenth century. As late as the 1940s he insisted that the problem of underconsumption and the need for new markets explained Nazi aggression.[18] By 1957, however, he was willing to concede that the driving force behind Nazism had been psychological, not economic: it was 'the emotional satisfaction of their lust for power—power valued for its own sake and not for its economic fruits'. Acknowledging more generally that 'we who were of [Hobson's] school stressed too heavily the economic causation of war',[19] he never recanted completely. That war and imperialism could not be adequately explained by the economic factors did not invalidate this interpretation altogether. Brailsford was correct in seeing that a foreign policy based on the competition of armaments created international anarchy and threatened war. He identified the interpenetration of financial and government circles but failed to give appropriate weight to the susceptibility of the masses to patriotic exhortation. He was also prescient enough to see the dark underside of imperialism: the corollary of high profits and opportunities for younger sons was depressed conditions in certain domestic industries and indifference to the welfare of the subject peoples.

[17] *WSG*, p. 93.
[18] *New Statesman*, 23 Oct. 1943.
[19] *The Life-Work of J. A. Hobson* (1948), p. 26-7; HNB to Kingsley Martin, 28 July 1957, KMP.

When he began to write in the 1890s, Brailsford was a stalwart proponent of national self-determination. Many of the evils in the nineteenth century seemed attributable to the stifling of national impulse. Linking nationhood to freedom, his Shelleyan belief in liberation from tyranny led him to champion the cause of the Balkan peoples. Empathy with their struggle prompted him to enlist in the Philhellenic Legion and later to plead for Macedonian autonomy under Bulgarian sponsorship, since the Bulgarians, not the Serbs or Greeks, had imposed a cultural identity on Macedonia. His prolonged exposure to the Balkans made him doubt whether national independence was either desirable or worth its price in blood, though he appreciated its attraction for oppressed peoples. It was not nationality itself which was the culprit: civilization was, after all, based on the diversity of cultures. Exploited for purposes of power, the nationalist impulse distorted the fraternal instincts of men, producing hatred and bloodshed.

If the natural tendency of an enlightened populace was towards socialism, the same instincts when applied to the world at large led to internationalism. Having rejected national self-determination as a panacea even before 1914, Brailsford consistently advocated world government as a kind of democratic socialism writ large. It was the answer to imperialism, since it would turn those regions not ready to govern themselves over to a supra-national authority. By ensuring an equitable distribution of natural resources and mutual security, it could mitigate the conflicts that generated wars. Yet its attainment required the same popular determination to take matters into their own hands, to act politically in order to gain control over their destinies—at home and in the outside world. He continued to preach against the monopoly of foreign policy-making by a ruling class and against the pursuit of a balance of power that inevitably became a balance of terror. His proposals in the *Nation* in 1912 were refurbished and served up as late as 1949. Even more than in domestic politics, however, it seemed to be a losing battle. The disinterested opinion on which he banked his hopes simply failed to materialize. Just as he had argued that revolutionary violence could be prevented only by promoting necessary changes peacefully, so he argued for concession and conciliation in order to avoid war. He had, in truth, been caught napping in 1914 and was resolved ever after to remain vigilant in the cause of peace. Without a settlement of grievances based on equity, international harmony would continue to elude its advocates. Here too his views could be traced back to the nineteenth century and before. His sympathy for foreign revolutions owed something to Paine, while his abhorrence of national self-aggrandizement linked him with Cobden as well as Hobson. Brailsford remained throughout his life an internationalist

The Ideal Republic

who despised xenophobia, a socialist whose sympathies could never be confined within territorial boundaries. If he was credulous at times, he was never vindictive or mean-spirited, and his commitment to peace and understanding among peoples could not be impugned. His passion for freedom extended far beyond England, whatever its source in native springs of artisan Radicalism. If his hopes for international government were illusory, he had at least, during his tireless struggles for the rights of other people, at home and abroad, transformed himself into a citizen of the world.

In 1935 Brailsford concluded his sketch of Voltaire with the following passage:

He sought above all else to erect for society a new scheme of values among the goods that men desire. He found it in the exaltation of constructive work for the common good. He smashed the barriers of nationality and creed, that in this effort separate mankind. He saw, across wars and schisms, the great cosmopolitan society. He preached, as the one sufficient commandment, the love of one's fellowmen, and made it concrete and vital, by his relentless assaults upon every form of cruelty.[20]

He might have been writing his own epitaph.

[20] *Voltaire*, p. 135.

Sources

UNPUBLISHED MATERIAL

A. Manuscript Collections:

Clifford Allen (Lord Allen of Hurtwood) Papers
  McKissick Library, University of South Carolina
Sir Norman Angell Papers
  Ball State University, Muncie, Indiana
Ernest Bevin Papers
  Modern Records Centre, University of Warwick
Wilfrid Scawen Blunt Papers
  Fitzwilliam Museum, Cambridge
Hermann Bräuning-Oktavio Papers
  Hessische Landes-und Hochschulbibliothek, Darmstadt
Julius Braunthal Papers
  International Institute for Social History, Amsterdam
Vera Brittain Papers
  Mills Memorial Library, McMaster University, Hamilton, Ontario
James (Viscount) Bryce Papers
  Bodleian Library, Oxford
Noel Buxton Papers
  Redpath Library, McGill University, Montreal
Kathleen Courtney Papers
  Fawcett Library, City of London Polytechnic
Leonard (Lord) Courtney Papers
  British Library of Political and Economic Science, LSE
Arthur Creech Jones Papers
  Rhodes House Library, Oxford
Sir Stafford Cripps Papers
  Nuffield College, Oxford
Hugh (Lord) Dalton Papers
  British Library of Political and Economic Science, LSE
Alexander Murray (Lord Murray of Elibank) Papers
  National Library of Scotland
Leonard and Dorothy Elmhirst Papers
  Dartington Hall, Totnes, Devon
Sir Robert Ensor Papers
  Corpus Christi College, Oxford
Millicent Garrett Fawcett Papers
  Manchester Central Library
Joseph Fels Papers
  Historical Society of Pennsylvania, Philadelphia
J. L. Garvin Papers
  Humanities Research Library, University of Texas

Herbert (Viscount) Gladstone Papers
  British Library
J. Bruce Glasier Papers, ILP Collection
  British Library of Political and Economic Science, LSE
Victor Gollancz Papers
  Courtesy of Miss Livia Gollancz
Sir Edward Grey (Viscount Grey of Fallodon) Papers
  Public Record Office
J. L. Hammond Papers
  Bodleian Library, Oxford
Keir Hardie Papers, ILP Collection
  British Library of Political and Economic Science, LSE
Arthur Henderson Papers
  Labour Party Archive, London
Edward M. House Papers
  Sterling Library, Yale University
Francis Johnson Papers, ILP Collection
  British Library of Political and Economic Science, LSE
John Maynard (Lord) Keynes Papers
  Marshall Library, Cambridge
George Lansbury Papers
  British Library of Political and Economic Science, LSE
Clare Leighton Correspondence
  Courtesy of Clare Leighton
Walter Lippmann Papers
  Sterling Library, Yale University
Victor, Second Earl of Lytton Papers
  Courtesy of Lady Hermione Cobbold, Knebworth House, Herts.
Alexander MacCallum Scott Papers
  University of Glasgow Library
James Ramsay MacDonald Papers
  Public Record Office
Manchester Guardian Collection
  John Rylands Library, University of Manchester
Catherine Marshall Papers
  Cumbria Record Office, Carlisle
Kingsley Martin Papers
  University of Sussex Library
David Mitrany Papers
  British Library of Political and Economic Science, LSE
E. D. Morel Papers
  British Library of Political and Economic Science, LSE
Gilbert Murray Papers
  Bodleian Library, Oxford
Jawaharlal Nehru Papers
  Nehru Memorial Library, New Delhi
Henry W. Nevinson Diaries

Bodleian Library, Oxford
George Orwell Archive
   University College Library, London
Arthur Ponsonby (Lord Ponsonby of Shulbrede) Papers
   Bodleian Library, Oxford
Eleanor Rathbone Papers
   University of Liverpool Library
William Rothenstein Papers
   Houghton Library, Harvard University
Walter Runciman (Viscount Runciman of Doxford) Papers
   University of Newcastle Library
Bertrand (Earl) Russell Archives
   Mills Memorial Library, McMaster University, Hamilton, Ontario
C. P. Scott Papers
   British Library
Evelyn Sharp Papers
   Bodleian Library, Oxford
David Soskice Papers
   House of Lords Record Office
Ernst Toller Collection
   Sterling Library, Yale University
Sir Charles Trevelyan Papers
   University of Newcastle Library
W. Van Ravesteyn Papers
   International Institute for Social History, Amsterdam
Oswald Garrison Villard Papers
   Houghton Library, Harvard University
Felix Volkhovsky Papers
   Houghton Library, Harvard University
H.G. Wells Papers
   University of Illinois Library, Urbana-Champaign
Leonard Woolf Papers
   University of Sussex Library

I have also been given access to correspondence in the possession of Luther Allen, Evamaria Brailsford, Michael Foot, Christopher leFleming, Robert Weaver, and Sybil Wingate.

B. *Other Collections:*

Advisory Committee on International Questions: minutes and memoranda
   Labour Party Archive, London
BBC Sound Archives
   Broadcasting House, London
City of London Branch, ILP: records and correspondence (1914-17)
   British Library of Political and Economic Science, LSE
Fabian Society Papers
   Nuffield College, Oxford

Foreign Office: correspondence and minutes (FO 371, 800)
  Public Record Office
ILP National Administrative Council: Executive Committee minutes
  (microfilm), Brynmor Jones Library, University of Hull
Inquiry Papers
  Sterling Library, Yale University
Labour and Socialist International Papers
  International Institute for Social History, Amsterdam
Labour Spain Committee Collection
  Churchill College, Cambridge
Manchester Guardian: contributors' ledgers
  Guardian office, Manchester
Methodist Archives and Research Centre
  Epworth House, London
National Union of Women's Suffrage Societies Collection
  Fawcett Library, City of London Polytechnic
Union of Democratic Control Archive
  Brynmor Jones Library, University of Hull
Women's Freedom League Papers
  Fawcett Library, City of London Polytechnic
Women's Suffrage Collection
  Museum of London

PRINTED SOURCES

A. Books by Brailsford:

The Broom of the War-God
  (London and New York, 1898)
Macedonia: Its Races and Their Future
  (London, 1906)
Adventures in Prose: A Volume of Essays and Sketches
  (London, 1911)
Shelley, Godwin and Their Circle
  Home University Library (London and New York, 1913; 2nd edition, 1951)
The War of Steel and Gold
  (London, 1914; rev. edition, 1915; 10th edition, 1918)
A League of Nations
  (London and New York, 1917; 2nd rev. edition, 1919)
Across the Blockade: A Record of Travels in Enemy Europe
  (London and New York, 1919)
After the Peace
  (London, 1920; rev. American edition, New York, 1922)
The Russian Workers' Republic
  (London and New York, 1921)
Socialism for Today
  (London, 1925)

How the Soviets Work
   Vanguard Studies of Soviet Russia (New York, 1927)
Olives of Endless Age
   (New York and London, 1928)
Rebel India
   (London and New York, 1931)
Property or Peace?
   (London and New York, 1934)
Voltaire
   Home University Library (London and New York, 1935)
Why Capitalism Means War
   New People's Library, Vol. 14 (London, 1938)
From England to America
   (New York, 1940)
America Our Ally
   Victory Books No. 11 (London, 1940)
Subject India
   Left Book Club (London and New York, 1943)
Our Settlement With Germany
   (Harmondsworth and New York, 1944)
The Levellers and the English Revolution
   (London and Stanford, 1961)

B. *Pamphlets by Brailsford:*
Some Irish Problems (1903)
The Conciliation Bill: An Explanation and a Defence (1910)
Treatment of the Women's Deputation by the Police (1911)
Memorandum on the Present Position of the Conciliation Bill (1911)
The Fruits of Our Russian Alliance (1912)
The Origins of the Great War (1914)
   UDC Pamphlet No. 4
Belgium and 'the Scrap of Paper' (1915)
   ILP Labour and War Pamphlet No. 10
Persia, Finland and Our Russian Alliance (1915)
   ILP Labour and War Pamphlet No. 12
Turkey and the Roads of the East (1916)
   UDC Pamphlet No. 18
Poland and the League of Nations (1917)
A Share in Your Motherland and Other Articles (1918)
The Covenant of Peace: An Essay on the League of Nations (1918)
Parliaments or Soviets (1920)
Constructive Relief: The Work of the Friends' Relief Mission in Vienna [1923]
Labour's Road to Power (1926)
Families and Incomes: The Case for Children's Allowances (1926)
Scrap Battleships! (1929)
The City or the Nation (1931)
If We Want Peace (1932)

New Fabian Research Bureau Day to Day Pamphlet No. 11
The Nazi Terror: A Record (1933)
  Socialist League Pamphlet
India in Chains (1935)
  Socialist League Pamphlet
Spain's Challenge to Labour (1936)
  Socialist League Pamphlet
Towards a New League (1936)
  New Statesman Pamphlet
Democracy for India (1939)
  Fabian Society Tract No. 248
The Federal Idea (1940)
Germans and Nazis: A Reply to 'Black Record' [1942]
  Common Wealth Popular Library No. 2
All Souls Day: An Essay in Understanding (1942)
Psychological Disarmament, or The Re-Education of Germany (1943)
Making Germany Pay: The Reparations Problem (1944)
  Peace Aims Pamphlet No. 23
The Life-Work of J. A. Hobson (1948)
  L. T. Hobhouse Memorial Trust Lecture No. 17

C. Books and pamphlets co-authored or containing contributions by Brailsford:

'The Compromise Amendments', in *The Men's League Handbook on Women's Suffrage* (1912), 26-39
'Who Are the Balkan Peoples?', in *The Question of the Balkans: Past, Present and Future* [1912], Balkan Committee Leaflet No. 9
Carnegie Endowment for International Peace, *Report of the International Commission to Inquire into the Causes and Conduct of the Balkan Wars* (1914)
Introduction to Edward J. Trelawny, *Adventures of a Younger Son* (1914)
'The Organization of Peace', in Charles Roden Buxton, ed., *Towards a Lasting Settlement* (1915), 149-76
Postscript to *Russia Free!* (1917)
Family Endowment Committee, *Equal Pay and the Family: A Proposal for the National Endowment of Motherhood* (1918)
'Die psychologischen Voraussetzungen des Völkerbunds', in Alfred H. Fried, ed., *Der Völkerbund: Ein Sammelbuch* (1919)
Preface to Leon Trotsky, *The Defence of Terrorism* (1921)
'A Labour View of Foreign Policy', in R. Palme Dutt, ed., *The Labour International Handbook* (1921), 160-72
Preface to W. P. Coates, *Present Position of Anglo-Russian Relations* (1923)
Preface to *Nailed to the Counter: A Record of Misrepresentation Concerning Soviet Russia* (1923)
'His Political Development', in H. J. Massingham, ed., *H. W. M. A Selection from the Writings of H. W. Massingham* (1925), 93-103
Social Insurance (1925)
Introduction to Leon Trotsky, *Where is Britain Going?* (1926)

The Living Wage (1926)
'The Rise of Nationalism in the East', in *Problems of Peace* (1928), 318-35
Can the League Cope with Imperialism? (1928)
Encyclopedia of the Social Sciences [nine articles] (1932)
'A Socialist Foreign Policy', in *Problems of a Socialist Government* (1933), 252-86
'India's Resurrection', in Samuel D. Schmalhausen, ed., *Recovery Through Revolution* (1933), 90-107
'William Godwin', in A. Barratt Brown, ed., *Great Democrats* (1934), 321-33
Preface to 'Miles', *Socialism's New Start: A Secret German Manifesto* (1934)
Postscript to Otto Bauer, *Die Internationale und der Krieg* (1935)
Henry Brinton, ed., *Does Capitalism Cause War?* (1935), 13-19, 37-41
'La construction économique de la Paix', in *Guerre ou Paix?* (1936), 7-9
Introduction to Voltaire, *Candide and Other Tales* (1937)
Introduction to Peter F. Drucker, *The End of Economic Man* (1939)
Preface to Oscar Paul [Pollak], *Farewell, France!* (1940)
The British Commonwealth and the United States in the Post-War World (1941), Peace Aims Pamphlet No. 19, 44-9
'The Rebel in English Literature', in Anthony Weymouth, ed., *The English Spirit* (1942), 51-6
The Future of Germany (1943), Peace Aims Pamphlet No. 19
Introduction to Julius Braunthal, *Need Germany Survive?* (1943)
Introduction to Hilda Monte, *The Unity of Europe* (1943)
Introduction to Julius Braunthal, *In Search of the Millenium* (1945)
'Socialism and Empire', in Rita Hinden, ed., *Fabian Colonial Essays* (1945), 19-35
Introduction to *Palestine Controversy: A Symposium* (1945)
Introduction to *Essays, Poems and Tales of Henry W. Nevinson* (1948)
'Radical Democracy in the Victorian Era', in *Ideas and Beliefs of the Victorians* (1949), 298-305
Mahatma Gandhi (1949), 95-224
Epilogue to Mosa Anderson, *Noel Buxton* (1952), 174-81

D. *Newspapers and Periodicals (selected list):*

Manchester Guardian (1898-1919)
Morning Leader (1899-1902)
Echo (1902-5)
Speaker (1902-4)
Tribune (1906-7)
Daily News (1907-9)
Nation (1907-22)
New Republic (1914-46)
Herald (later *Daily Herald*) (1917-22)
Baltimore Sun (1921-41)
New Leader (1922-32)
Der deutsche Volkswirt (1927-31)
Radio Times (1930-2)
New Clarion (1932-4)

World Tomorrow (1932-4)
Reynolds's Illustrated News (later *Reynolds News*) (1932-46)
New Statesman (1932-51)

E. *Other Printed Sources:*

BBC, Transcripts of broadcasts (1939-56)
Carnegie Endowment for International Peace, *Yearbook* (1913-15)
Glasgow University Magazine (1893-7)
ILP, *Report of Annual Conference* (1920-7)
Labour Party, *Report of Annual Conference* (1923-7)

Other books and articles used or quoted have been cited where appropriate in footnotes.

Index

Adamson, Robert 22-5, 176
Adler, Friedrich 168, 180, 184
Albu, Austen 252-3
Allen, Clifford 115, 122, 186, 191; regard for HNB's ability 161, 173; and revival of ILP 172; and *New Leader* editorship 173-7; answers HNB's critics 181-2; endorses minimum wage policy 188; loses control of ILP 197-8, 200; withdraws support for *Phoenix* 202; HNB disapproves peerage for 226-7; criticizes *Property or Peace?* 239
Allen, Luther 283-4, 300
Angell, Norman 107-9, 130-1, 177, 216; reviews *War of Steel and Gold* 112-13
Anglo-Russian Committee 97-8
Arnot, Robin Page 142, 247
Asquith, H. H. 71, 75-6, 86-7, 124, 207; opposition to Conciliation Bill 77-9; promises facilities for further debate 81; proposes manhood suffrage bill 83-4
Aylmer, G. E., account of visit to HNB 297

Balkan Committee 49, 55, 98, 105
Baltimore Sun 170, 205, 217
Bauer, Otto 168; quoted 202
Belloc, Hilaire 79
Bevan, Aneurin 148, 251, 258, 265
Bevin, Ernest 189; hostility to living wage programme 193; angered by *New Leader*'s anti-TUC stance 196-7; HNB opposes appointment as Socialist League Chairman 225; and *New Clarion* 226; and post-war foreign policy 294
'Blaisty, Gwen' 261, 263-4
Blatchford, Robert 2, 172-3
Blum, Leon 184
Blunt, Wilfrid Scawen 69, 93, 95, 101-2, 143; and Egyptian nationalism 59-60, 62-3, 164; HNB's admiration for 60 n. 57; impression of HNB 62, 121; charmed by Jane Brailsford 119, 122; HNB's last visit to 179, 215
Bone, James 21, 121
Bone, Muirhead 21, 177
Bradley, A. C. 16, 19, 21, 284
Brailsford, Clara (mother) 6-8, 11, 13, 214-15, 284
Brailsford, Edward J. (father) 3, 5-13, 17, 169; and Methodism 5, 7-8
Brailsford, Evamaria (second wife) 283, 286-8, 291, 297, 300-2
Brailsford, Henry Noel, personal characteristics 3-4, 10, 12-13, 16, 23, 29, 105, 147-8, 156, 160, 173-5, 198, 203, 228, 260, 264, 271, 277, 304-5, 311; education 9-10, 12, 16-21; loss of religious faith 4, 11-12, 19, 213; clash with father 3, 11-13, 17, 169-70; relationship to Mabel 3, 9, 11-13, 297; friendship with Murray 17-18, 27, 32 n. 10, 301; interest in Hegelian philosophy 19-20, 23, 27-8; infatuation with German culture 21, 171; disenchantment with academic life 24-5; as volunteer in Philhellenic Legion 27-32; in love with Jane Malloch 26-8, 33; in Crete for *Guardian* 35-7, 39; first marriage 38-40, 67, 106, 114-22, 125, 128, 161-2, 168-9, 175, 214, 229, 260, 307; covers Dreyfus case 40-1; as leader-writer 43-6, 55-6, 60-1, 64-6; vegetarianism 45; in Macedonia 47-50; and Russian passport case 52-5; and Russian Social Democratic Congress 61-2; in Egypt 62-4; and women's suffrage 67, 73-4, 90, 105, 150; launches Conciliation Committee 72-5; quarrels with Pankhursts 79, 82-7; parliamentary candidacy 71, 79, 148-51; criticism of Grey's foreign policy 93-5, 101-2; joins ILP 95-6, 124, 131, 174; opposition to Russian entente 96-7, 101; and Young Turk movement 98-100; on Carnegie Commission 105-7, 121, 153; and origins of World War I 125-6, 130-2, 134; advocates negotiated peace 135; opposes break-up of Austrian Empire 135, 141-2, 145; and Russian revolution 139-40, 142, 144, 155; as member of Labour Advisory Committee 144, 153, 161, 163-4; travels to Central Europe 154-8, 170-1; and peace settlement 158-60, 179, 223; visits Soviet Russia 164-7, 205-7; as editor of *New Leader* 175-203, 212, 257; dispute with MacDonald 96 n. 19, 173-4, 176-7, 181-7, 191, 194, 197-8; conflict with CPGB 142, 152, 180, 247-8, 269, 281-2; and living wage programme 188-95; lectures in US 205, 210-11, 214, 230, 240; relationship with Clare Leighton 211-15, 228-30, 253, 260-3, 276; love of music 116, 213-14; interest in anthropology 213, 236, 288; in India 218-21, 286-9; and Palestine 221, 285; opposes ILP disaffiliation 224-6; and Socialist League 225-6, 228, 231, 235, 244, 254, 260; and rise of Nazism 231-5, 242, 309; and Abyssinian crisis 241-2; and Spanish Civil War 231, 249-55, 258, 266;

322   Index

and Unity Campaign 244, 251; and Russian purges 245-8, 255; and Munich 258; and Popular Front 240-1, 243-4, 247, 256, 266; and Indian nationalism 217, 220-1, 277-9, 287; and World War II 267-9, 272-5; attitude towards Germany 273, 275-6, 279-82, 284, 290-3; health of 229-30, 271-2, 296, 301-2; marriage to Evamaria 284, 297, 301-2; in Germany 290-2; in Yugoslavia 294-6

Books by HNB: *Broom of the War-God* 29-34; *Macedonia* 50-1, 56-9, 208; *Shelley, Godwin and Their Circle* 67, 91, 228, 306-7; *Adventures in Prose* 91; *War of Steel and Gold* 96, 102, 107-13, 123, 127, 132, 134, 136, 138, 163. 208-10, 236, 245, 285; *A League of Nations* 136-9, 143, 163, 208, 268; *Across the Blockade* 161; *After the Peace* 162-3, 171, 208, 210, 291; *Russian Worker's Republic* 164-8, 208; *Socialism for Today* 190-2; *How the Soviets Work* 205-8; *Olives of Endless Age* 208-10, 216, 237; *Rebel India* 222, 278; *Property or Peace?* 228, 231, 236-9, 245, 268; *Voltaire* 228, 239-40, 311; *Why Capitalism Means War* 248-9; *From England to America* 273; *Subject India* 278-9; *Our Settlement with Germany* 280-1; *Mahatma Gandhi* 292; *Levellers and the English Revolution* 296, 298-301, 305-6.

Pamphlets by HNB: *Origins of the Great War* 130, 160; *Belgium and 'The Scrap of Paper'* 131; *Covenant of Peace* 145-6; *Eqaul Pay and the Family* 148; *Socialism in Our Time* 191-2; *The Living Wage* 193, 225, 237; *If We Want Peace* 216; *The Nazi Terror* 231; *Towards a New League* 243, 245; *Life-Work of J. A. Hobson* 290, 292, 309

HNB and *Scots Pictorial* 25-6, 28; and *Morning Leader* 42; and *Echo* 45-6; and *Speaker* 44, 213; and *Tribune* 56-7, 60, 94; and *Manchester Guardian* 1, 25, 34-6, 38, 40-3, 45, 47-9, 51, 55-6, 117, 147, 217, 294; and *Daily News* 43, 60-2, 64-6, 68, 92, 174; and *Nation* 1, 61, 66, 70-1, 91, 95-6, 102, 124-7, 129, 140, 147, 164, 168, 174, 178, 204, 217, 310; and *Herald* 43, 131, 139-40, 142, 147, 152, 154, 161, 174, 178, 204; and *New Leader* 1, 147, 175-204, 211, 217, 224, 226, 257; and *New Statesman* 1, 147, 205, 213, 226, 228, 246, 249, 254-5, 270, 277, 294, 296; and *Reynolds* 1, 147, 205, 226, 228, 232, 240, 258, 268, 270, 293; and *New Republic* 1, 129, 131, 140, 145, 168, 170, 204-5, 222, 247; and *Baltimore Sun* 170, 205, 217; and *New Clarion* 226

Brailsford, Jane Malloch (first wife) 24, 34, 49-51, 56, 100, 151, 164, 283; description of 26-7; HNB's courtship of 26-8, 33-4; marriage 3, 38-40, 114-22, 125, 128, 161-2, 168-9, 214, 307; and Macedonian relief 50; as a suffragette 67-70, 79, 84-5, 89-90; and alcoholism 120-1, 128, 162, 168, 229, 260

Brailsford, Mabel R. (sister) 3, 7, 9-13, 21-2, 115, 214, 296-7, 300

Bräuning-Oktavio, Hermann 127-9, 171, 232-3

Braunthal, Julius 3, 168, 180, 264, 282

Brockway, Fenner 172-3, 199-201, 224, 251

Bryce, James 49, 133, 139-40

Buchan, John 21, 34, 149

Buckler, William H. 135 n. 34

Buxton, Charles Roden 134, 140-1, 144

Buxton, Noel 49, 55, 140-1

Cadbury, George 64-5

Caird, Edward 15-16, 19-23, 284

Carnegie Commission on Balkan Wars 91, 105-7, 121, 153

Central Labour College 148

Chermside, Sir Herbert 35-7

Chesterton, G. K. 45

Christian, Bertram 49, 54, 100

Churchill, Winston 71, 82, 86, 90, 149; as Home Secretary 75-7; quarrel over Conciliation Bill 78; and Black Friday 79-80; wartime leadership of 272-4

Clemenceau, Georges 41, 61

Cole, G. D. H. 144, 225, 265, 297, 301, 305

Cole, Margaret 225, 265, 297, 301

Conciliation Committee: proposes compromise measure 75; first bill 76-8; second bill 81; Lloyd George's efforts to discredit 82-5; defeat of third bill 86-7; Election Fighting Fund 87-9, 304

Courtney, Kathleen 79, 83, 85, 147, 168-9

Courtney, Leonard 44, 54, 76, 98

Creech Jones, Arthur 189, 196

Crete 35-40, 114, 116

Cripps, Sir Stafford 238, 243-4, 251, 253-4, 256-8, 265-6, 277

Crossman, Richard 270-1

Daily Chronicle 27, 41, 43, 57

Daily News 41, 43, 45, 52, 55, 57, 60-2, 64-6, 68, 92, 94-5, 97, 127, 174

Daily Worker 247, 254, 269

Dalton, Hugh 177, 202, 258, 281, 293

Dartington Hall 212, 218, 271, 284

Denshawai incident 59, 95

Der deutsche Volkswirt 204, 217

Dickinson, G. Lowes 133-4, 136, 215

Dollan, P. J. 198-200

Dreyfus affair 40-1

Drucker, Peter 264

Dundee High School 10, 12

Index

Durbin, Evan 4, 225
Dutt, R. Palme 142, 238-9, 247, 251, 282

Echo 45-6, 49-50, 55-6
Eden, Anthony 2, 256
Egypt 59-60, 62-4, 92, 95, 133, 150, 164, 185, 217, 288
Ehrenburg, Ilya 281
Elliott, Sydney 226, 255, 270
Elmhirst, Dorothy Whitney 129, 198 n. 89, 202, 210, 212, 252, 277
Elmhirst, Leonard 210, 212, 218, 277
Ensor, R. C. K. 61, 95-6

Fabian Society 35, 95, 133, 271, 304; at Glasgow University 24, 26; New Fabian Research Bureau 216, 225; Fabian Colonial Bureau 285; Fabian International Bureau 271, 279, 285 n. 85
Family Endowment Committee 147-8, 169, 192
Fawcett, Millicent Garrett 72-4, 76-7, 86-7
Fels, Joseph 61-2
Foot, Michael 1, 246-7, 257, 300, 304
Forster, E. M. 177
Friends of India 290

Gandhi, M. K. 3, 156, 217-20; interviews with 222, 287; biography of 292
Gardiner, A. G. 60, 64-5, 94, 97, 124
Garvin, J. L. 168
George Watson's College 10
Ghosh, Sudhir 290
Gladstone, Herbert 66, 71
Glasgow University: curriculum 14-20, 22; student life at 15, 20, 23; awards honorary degree to HNB 284
Glasgow University Magazine 15, 19-20, 22, 25, 27
Glasier, J. Bruce 172
Glasier, Katherine Bruce 172
Gollancz, Victor, suggests book linking capitalism and war 236; proposes history of socialism to HNB 245; objects to HNB's anti-Stalinist views 248-9; influence on Cripps 257, 265; solicits war aims book 268; publishes *America Our Ally* 273; publishes *Subject India* 278; publishes Nevinson anthology 292
Grey, Sir Edward 64, 75, 81, 97, 100; HNB's criticism of 2, 93-5, 101-2, 131-2
Griffiths, James 148
Grosvenor House Committee 36-7
Guild socialism 152, 294

Hamilton, Mary Agnes 161, 176, 182, 200
Hammond, Barbara 54, 60

Hammond, J. L. 44-5, 57, 60-1, 70, 94, 124, 127, 269
Hardie, James Keir, and 1895 election 24; 96; HNB ghost-writes Russian speech for 97; invites HNB to produce anti-war pamphlets 131, 156; and *Labour Leader* 172-3; 250
Henderson, Arthur 75, 88-9, 161
Herald 43, 131, 139-40, 142, 152, 154, 161, 172, 174, 178, 186, 204
Hill, Christopher 300
Hilmi Pasha 48, 58
Hirst, F. W. 44-5, 54, 70, 95, 105, 107
Hobhouse, L. T. 57, 60, 70, 94, 124, 127; Memorial Lecture 290
Hobson, J. A. as reporter in South Africa 42; on *Tribune* staff 57; analysis of imperialism 95, 109, 111-12, 285; and *Nation* 127; as advocate of international federation 133; 139, 177; and underconsumption 188; involvement in living wage commission 189, 191, 193-4, 202, 216; influence on HNB 95, 124, 185, 190-1, 194 n. 75, 290, 308-10
Home University Library 228, 239, 245, 306
House, Colonel E. M. 135, 143

Independent Labour Party 24, 91, 95-6, 130-1, 148, 172-5, 179-82, 184, 187-9, 191-202, 207, 217, 224-6, 235, 244, 250, 254, 265; National Administrative Council of 172-6, 181, 197-201
India 96, 188, 217-22, 277-9, 286-8
India League 221, 290
Internal Macedonian Revolutionary Organization 47-8
International Brigade 252, 254, 258, 263, 266

Jahoda, Fritz 263, 276
Jaurès, Jean 3, 41, 96, 156
Jinnah, Muhammed Ali 286-7
Johnson, Alvin 205, 276
Jones, Thomas 23-4

Karolyi, Michael 155-6, 264-n. 9
Keynes, John Maynard, HNB reviews *Economic Consequences of the Peace* 160; *After the Peace* compared to 163; invited to write for *New Leader* 177; influence on HNB's economic ideas 188-9; criticizes living wage report 194, 195, 243; disapproves of HNB's articles 255, 270-1
Kirkwood, David 185, 199-200
Kropotkin, Peter 52, 98
Kun, Bela 155-6, 161, 294

Labour Leader 131, 165, 170, 172-3, 175, 197
Labour Monthly 251, 281

Labour Party 148, 151-2, 161, 163-4, 172, 187-9, 194-6, 201-2, 223-5, 235, 250-1, 256, 259-60, 265; Advisory Committee on International Questions 144-5, 153, 161, 163-4
Labour Spain Committee 253-6, 258-9, 265-6
Lansbury, George 62, 142, 198, 225
Laski, Harold 165, 215, 238, 248, 251, 253, 258
League of Nations 111, 136, 145, 150, 152-3, 159, 185, 209, 216, 241-3
League of Nations Society 133, 136, 147
Left Book Club 236, 244-5, 249, 257, 278
Leighton, Clare 177, 211-15, 228-30, 253, 260-3, 265, 276, 283, 286
Lenin, V. I. 61-2, 111, 142, 167, 305, 309
Leys, Norman 24, 200
Lippmann, Walter 129, 199, 204-5, 217; HNB compared to 2
Litvinov, Maxim 61, 165, 207
Lloyd, E. M. H. 188, 190
Lloyd George, David 3, 45, 65, 158, 195, 207; HNB confers with 68-9, 82-6; opposes Conciliation Bill 77, 81, 90; insists on guarantees before peace negotiations 136
Lukács, Georg 156, 171
Lytton, Lady Constance 69-70, 73
Lytton, Victor, Earl of 73-6, 78-9, 81, 84-5, 218, 226

MacCallum Scott, Alexander 22-9, 47; view of HNB 22-3, 27, 33-4
MacDonald, J. Ramsay 47, 82, 96-7, 130, 139, 151, 207, 224, 227, 246; and Election Fighting Fund 87-9; conflict with HNB 96 n. 19, 176, 183-7, 194, 197-8; opposes HNB's appointment as editor 173-4, 177, 182; hostile to living wage programme 189, 191; HNB dismisses as a charlatan 223; and 1931 betrayal 235; and support for French foreign policy 294
Macedonia 47-50, 56-9, 67, 92-3, 98-100, 102-7, 116, 118, 122, 140, 155, 239, 310
Macedonian Relief Committee 49, 53, 100, 105, 118
MacKenzie, Norman 4, 270
Maisky, Ivan 52, 245-7, 252
Malloch, Jane: *see* Brailsford, Jane Malloch
Manchester Guardian 1, 25, 34-6, 38, 40-3, 45, 49, 51, 55-6, 116, 161, 178, 217, 231, 233, 294
Marshall, Catherine 136, 169
Martin, Kingsley 4, 169, 272, 283, 300; admiration for HNB 1, 3-4; and *New Statesman* 178, 226, 249, 270, 297; advises HNB against fighting in Spain 252; sends HNB to N. Africa 261; indecisiveness of 270, 277; defends HNB against Keynes's allegations 271; secures permission for HNB to visit US 276, regards HNB as 'excessively pro-German' 284
Marxism: influence on HNB 2, 95, 111, 177, 232, 236, 238-40, 242, 308
Massingham, H. W. 1, 61, 91, 139; leaves *Daily Chronicle* editorship 43-4; refuses to disavow forcible feeding 65; disagrees with HNB over treatment of women prisoners 70-1; admonishes Conciliation Committee 80; HNB's regard for 94; as *Nation* editor 95, 124, 147, 164, 175; quarrels with HNB during First World War 125-7, 145; opposes conscription 135
Masterman, C. F. G. 70
Maxton, James 197, 200-1, 224, 251
Mellor, William 4, 225, 244, 256-7
Menon, Krishna 221, 290
Men's League for Women's Suffrage 71-2, 78, 91
Menzies, Joseph 28-9, 34
Methodism 5-6; Edward Brailsford as minister 7-8, 10; HNB's attitude towards 2, 4, 11
Miliukov, Paul 105-6
Mitchison, G. R. 265
Mitchison, Naomi 206, 297
Mitrany, David 215-16
Morel, E. D. 94, 130, 142, 186
Morning Leader 42-4, 52
Mosley, Sir Oswald 177, 188, 192, 195
Murray, Gilbert 15, 21, 24, 26, 28, 32-4, 42-3, 293, 301; as teacher 16-18; influence on HNB 17-18, 27, 56, 284; reconciles politics and social conscience 23; recommends HNB for lectureship 24-5; gives HNB revolver 32 n. 10; Jane Brailsford's infatuation with 39, 115-16, 122; provides Balkan introductions 47; lends HNB money for legal defence 53, 61; supports British entry into war 124; condemns HNB's 'pro-Germanism' 132
Murray, Jessie 80
Murray, Lady Mary 17, 37

Nation 1, 61, 66, 70-1, 91, 94-6, 102-3, 112, 124-7, 129, 135, 140, 161, 164, 168, 174-6, 178, 204, 217, 310
Nation (US) 161, 204, 210-11
National Union of Women's Suffrage Societies 68, 76-9, 83, 86, 88
Nehru, Jawaharlal 3, 217; HNB praises 220; HNB advises on Muslim problem 287; and tribute to HNB 301
Neu Beginnen 233-4, 282
Nevinson, Henry W. 26, 54, 74, 104, 114, 127,

182, 198, 218, 231, 251, 271; meets HNB in Greece 32; as journalist 44, 61, 64-6, 94, 177, 202; in Macedonia for Balkan Committee 50; loyalty to HNB 55; resigns from *Daily News* with HNB 66; support of women's suffrage 70, 120; opposes Russian *entente* 95; collaborates with HNB on Kropotkin pamphlet 98; attachment to Jane Brailsford 115, 117-22, 169; HNB pays tribute to 292
New Clarion 226
New Leader 1, 176-9, 181-2, 184-91, 196-204, 211-12, 217, 224, 226, 257
New Republic 1, 129, 131, 140, 145, 161, 164, 168, 170, 204-5, 211, 217, 222, 247, 272, 286
New School for Social Research 205, 211
New Statesman 1, 178, 198, 205, 213, 226, 228, 246-7, 249, 254-6, 270, 277, 284-6, 294, 296
Nicolson, Arthur 100, 143-4
Nicolson, Harold 184
No-Conscription Fellowship 136

Orwell, George 156, 248, 252-5

Pankhurst, Christabel 72-4, 76, 79-80, 82-4, 89, 120
Pankhurst, Emmeline 73-4, 76, 79-80, 85-6, 89, 120
Peace Research Group 215-16
Perlmann, Evamaria: *see* Brailsford, Evamaria
Perris, G. H. 57
Pethick-Lawrence, Frederick, and *Echo* 45-7; and WSPU 83, 89, 120; as Indian Secretary 286; and Gandhi biography 292; delivers eulogy at HNB's funeral 302
Philhellenic Legion 27, 29-32, 106, 310
Pilsudski, Josef 3, 155
Plummer, Leslie 176, 178, 198-9
Polak, H. S. L. 292
Pole, Joe 253
Pollak, Oscar 180, 264
Ponsonby, Arthur 129, 133, 151, 177, 184, 197, 202
Pooley, Clara: *see* Brailsford, Clara
Pooley, Henry (grandfather) 6
Postgate, Raymond 154, 225
Price, M. Philips 159
Pryor, S. J. 60-1

Queen Margaret's College 22, 26

Radek, Karl 207, 246
Rakovsky, Christian 183-4, 246-7
Rathbone, Eleanor 147, 266
Reid, Sir Robert 54

Reynolds 1, 147, 205, 226, 228, 232, 240, 246, 255, 258, 268, 270, 284, 286, 293
Rodocanachi, C. P. 30-1
Rothenstein, William 218, 222
Rothstein, Fedor 52, 61-2, 127, 207
Royden, Maude 147, 151
Runciman, Walter 63 n. 71, 69, 75
Russell, Bertrand 115, 130, 132, 137, 167, 177, 197, 201-2

Scots Pictorial 25-6, 28
Scott, C. P. 1, 44, 49, 55, 60, 70, 80-1, 84, 91, 178, 187; inquires about *Guardian* prospects 25; recruits HNB for *Guardian* staff 34-5, 40, 45, 47, 51, 56; sends HNB money for Cretan relief 36; offers loan for legal defence 53, 61; acts as intermediary with Lloyd George 82, 85
Sharp, Evelyn 292
Shaw, George Bernard 32 n. 10, 54 n. 35, 177, 209, 269 n. 34, 285
Shelley, Percy Bysshe 2, 10, 12, 305-8
Simon, Sir John 54, 128-9
Snowden, Philip 137, 224
Socialist League; HNB helps to launch 225-6, 228; 231; seen as disruptive force 235; sponsors *Problems of a Socialist Government* 237; influence of Cripps on 238; favours socialist unity 243-4; dissolved 254, 259-60, 265
Society of Friends of Russian Freedom 52, 97, 105
Soskice, David 52, 55, 57, 97-8
South Africa Conciliation Committee 44
Spanish Civil War 247, 249-55, 258, 266
Speaker 44-5, 50, 61, 213
Stalin, Joseph 61, 166, 207, 246-8, 267, 269, 282, 289
Stolper, Toni 204
Strachey, John 193, 197, 199, 235-6, 238, 245
Strauss, George R. 256, 265
Swanwick, Helena M. 82, 151
Sturrock, J. Leng 149-51

Tagore, Rabindranath 218, 222
Tawney, R. H. 201
Taylor, A. J. P. 2, 104, 112
Taylor, J. E. 40-1, 45, 56
Thomasson, Franklin 56-7, 60
Toller, Ernst 259
Trevelyan, C. P. 130, 151, 197, 259, 265, 269 n. 34
Tribune (daily) 56-7, 59-61, 94
Tribune (weekly) 244, 247, 256-7
Trotsky, Leon 3, 61-2, 142, 166-8, 180-1, 207, 238, 246, 271
Tukhachevsky, General M. 166, 246

Union of Democratic Control 125, 129-30, 132-3, 144, 147, 151, 215
Unity Campaign 244, 251, 254, 256, 265

Vallance, Aylmer 270, 274
Vandervelde, Emile 96, 184
Veitch, John 17, 22
Venizelos, Eleutherios 3, 39
Vienna International 168, 174, 179-80, 185, 212
Villard, Oswald Garrison 204-5, 210-11
Volkhovsky, Felix 52

Wallas, Graham 168
Wavell, Lord 286
Weaver, Robert 283-4
Webb, Beatrice 194, 269 n. 34, 305
Wells, H. G. 164, 177, 252 n. 97
Wheatley, John 181, 185, 192, 197

Wilkinson, Ellen 225, 265
Wilson, Woodrow 135-7, 139, 143, 152-3, 158-9
Wingate, Sybil 253, 261, 273, 304
Wise, E. F. 177, 189-90, 202, 225
Women's Social and Political Union 68, 71-85, 87, 89, 119-20
Woolf, Leonard 133, 144, 215, 305; and War Aims Memorandum 142; temporarily replaces HNB on *Nation* 164; publishes *If We Want Peace* 216; and Fabian International Bureau 279; disagrees with HNB's analysis of German question 281
World Tomorrow 205

Young Turks 98-100, 103-4

Zilliacus, Konni 294